THE 15 GENIUSES BEHIND THE LENS

THE 15 GENIUSES BEHIND THE LENS

HOW THE GREATEST FILM DIRECTORS SHAPED THE MOVIES WE SEE TODAY

By Gary Olsen

TABLE OF CONTENTS

This book is dedicated to my late mother, Doris Smith Olsen, who inspired me to the imaginary world of cinema.

ABOUT THE AUTHOR

Gary Olsen is a retired director/producer/cameraman/editor for the United States government who oversaw production of films and documentaries. An Emerson University Advanced Degree graduate, Mr. Olsen worked in every phase of movie production and has an intimate knowledge of the film-making process. His study in cinema produced a series of lectures on the *History of the Academy Awards' Best Pictures* and *The Best Film Directors of All-Time*, which plays to overwhelming audiences nationwide. He currently lives in Fredericksburg, Virginia.

Introduction

"Each film is interlocked with so many other films. Whatever you do now that you think is new was already done by 1913" — Martin Scorsese.

Film director Martin Scorsese's observed by the year 1913 everything in cinema had been practically invented. A director/scholar in film history, Mr. Scorsese is partly accurate in claiming moving pictures had reached the height of innovation by 1913. Quick research on the year reveals feature films were first introduced to the viewing public and a handful of large entertainment venues were being built to project the lengthened movies. Biograph Company's primary director D.W. Griffith was transforming the look of movies by 1913, leading the way with advanced sophisticated plots with new camera angles, lighting and editing effects.

And the first custard-pie-thrown-in-the-face sequence was released in 1913 by director Mack Sennett and his Keystone Cops' movie, *A Noise From The Deep.*

As we celebrate over 100 years of the existence of cinema, film directors have continually invented new techniques and improvements upon the aesthetics of moving pictures from that 1913 date. In the pantheon of movie innovators, 15 film directors stand apart for their enormous contributions in shaping the movies we see today. Their influence can be seen in a majority of current films, decades after the release of some of these directors' last movies.

Alfred Hitchcock said aspiring directors and producers should learn how to make films by studying the best known movies and directors of the past.

Besides actually viewing these directors' works, there is no better way of studying the best that cinema offers than reading this book. These 15 mavericks absorbed the language of film from their predecessors and were able to forge a unique style that was a departure from their contemporaries. To adopt the French term "auteur," these directors, despite working in an art form that requires a collective team effort, were able to craft their distinct vision by their individual talents and unmatched creativeness. These 15 directors weren't imitators, they were inventors.

Most worked within a monopolist film studio system which was designed to create uniformity in all its movies. Such sameness almost guaranteed the studios' bottom line in economics as well as catered to the public's known tastes in pictures. The last thing these studios were willing to do was to experiment on new art compositions and ideas with their bank rolls at stake. Through sheer will and personality, these talented and unconventional directors ultimately proved their vision was refreshing to the standard movie fare and warmly accepted by the paying public. Once their prescience became accepted, these directors were able to command the freedom to select their own stories, film in their own styles, and largely dictate the final edits for their movies' releases.

For the most part, these directors became intimately involved from the beginning of their productions in the scripting process. Many wrote or co-wrote their own scripts, such as Billy Wilder and Woody Allen. And many achieved the power from their studios to shape their projects all the way through the final releases.

There were exceptions: Orson Welles fought the system from the beginning of his second movie and was constantly frustrated by the studios' intransigence. John Ford regularly fought off studios' tight controls by manipulating on the film stage what the editors could later work with his limited footage.

What these 15 directors brought to the screen during their long careers is today dissected and studied by students in film schools and universities. Their long-lasting influences have been absorbed and imitated by current working directors, professionals and amateurs alike.

It is my intention to tell the story of these 15 directors, not necessarily through their biographies, even though understanding how they arrived at their positions is important, but by their methodical workmanship and idiosyncratic personalities. They all possessed a strong personal drive that percolated their creative juices on and off the set. Many of their traits are considered quirky by normal standards, but they all exhibited a free-wheeling force which gave them the luxury to create something new and profound in cinema.

There are fascinating personal behind the scenes and on-the-job stories concerning each director portrayed here. I have scribed their habits either chronologically from their childhood upbringing to their last breath, or I have broken down each profile by the three broad phases of movie-making. The first phase is pre-production, how they received their story ideas, the shaping of their scripts and the selection of the actors and crew. Next is the production or filming phase, detailing the directors' work-habits on the movie set and the successes and problems facing them while filming. Lastly is post-production or the editing phase, describing their work in the edit room and the reception of their movies once they were released.

This book emerged from a series of lectures I presented on each of these 15 directors. I took up Hitchcock's philosophy of studying the great movies from the past and presented the directors' work in this lecture series. I showed to my many viewers how these influential directors shaped their films, what techniques they used, and how they related to the actors to achieve their vision. My audiences' responses were overwhelmingly positive to this series.

The decision to tell the story of each director was further encouraged during my research in creating my power-point presentations. I failed to find the one definitive publication that described the methods of each director in producing the classics of theirs we admire today. Snippets of information on their direction were found in expansive biographies for each director. But for the aspiring student learning the art of movie-making there was not one book addressing what Hitchcock's advice clearly referenced to by studying the past masters' techniques in creating their films.

This book can also be read as pure entertainment. Each of the 15 directors has had an engaging life on and off the movie set. Episodes of their behind-the-scenes lives, some beneficial, some not so complementary, reflect what their strong personalities brought to the screen.

Lastly, this book also came about from my newspaper articles on each director published in the Fredericksburg Virginia Free-Lance Star. I have expanded my features to include many sources of information that I was unable to include because of the newspaper's space limitations.

I would like to thank the news editor for the Free-Lance Star, Andi Russell, who accepted and presented each article I had submitted on these 15 film geniuses. I also want to thank my untiring wife, Janice, who copy-edited this book and who displayed unwavering grace at the many hours I devoted to this project. Kudos go to Kevin Hunt, who volunteered to double-check Janice's and my work to make sure each "t" was crossed and every "i" dotted. Also thanks go to novelist Brian Kelliher, who gave me invaluable advice on the avenues to take to get this book out to as many hands as possible.

One final observation I made while writing this book. I was fascinated that all 15 directors had a passion for directing films. They never surrendered that fire to direct right up to the days before they died. Their desire to continue making movies, even in old age, never left them. Because of their long careers, cinema drew away from some of them during their later years. Younger audiences looked for more modern themes and new ways of projecting these contemporary stories. Societal changes left the studios no choice but to seek other creative forces and leave these giants rocking in their chairs viewing the sunsets.

But their stamp on today's films is undeniable. As long as movies are being produced, these titans of cinema will never be forgotten. Their place in movie history is too great to be erased. An appreciation and understanding of today's movies cannot be fully experienced without the knowledge of these 15 film directors.

As Scorsese recognized: "Young people perceive the world and information in a completely different way to when I was growing up. So what I did in the past, I don't know how they'll see that in the future and if it will mean anything to them. I hope the scripts for *Taxi Driver,* or *Mean Streets,* or *Raging Bull,* or any of these things, will have some resonance in the future for other people, if they see them at all. Things fall out of favor, out of fashion. I have no idea."

One thing Mr. Scorsese and the other 14 directors in this book can be reassured is their work will be studied and imitated as long as movies are part of our culture.

To see an active list of presentations and offerings by this author, please refer to www.filmlectures.com. And check out my Facebook page.

D.W. Griffith

There is a stirring scene in a famous old Civil War movie where a Confederate officer spots a wounded Union soldier injured nearby in no man's land. This officer grabs a canteen of water, jumps over the protective trench and runs to the prone man administering much needed assistance.

Clearly, the screenplay writer had in mind Richard Kirkland, the Confederate sergeant who was willing to sacrifice his life during a lull in the Battle of Fredericksburg to comfort numerous Union wounded by giving life-saving water and aid.

The scene is a pivotal one in the 1915 silent movie that changed the course of cinema. Although *Birth of a Nation,* because of its extremely controversial subject matter, is today basically restricted to being shown only in film schools and on YouTube, over a hundred years ago the film overnight altered the way theater audiences would view movies.

Its director, David Wark Griffith (D.W. for short), got the idea to have his audiences spend an entire evening watching one film. It would be a radical departure from cinema's early days when a series of short 15-minute films were shown in dusty nickelodeons. Griffith, a film director of over 400 short films for the Biograph Company, wanted to produce deeper, more sophisticated movies. Ultimately, because of this three-hour picture, cinema would take the form of what we see today.

"He was the father of film," said Lillian Gish, star of many of Griffith's early movies. "He didn't do everything the first time, like the close-up, but he gave us the grammar of filmmaking. The cutting, the handling of humanity before the camera. He understood the psyche, the strength of the lens."

Charlie Chaplin, who emerged as a comedy silent movie star during the height of Griffith's career, labeled him "the teacher of us all."

Griffith had a special fondness for Civil War themes. He would return time and again to a period predating his birth by 10 years. Films like his 1930 talkie *Abraham Lincoln* and short silent movies such as 1910's *In The Border States* and 1911's *The Battle* reflect the human drama amidst war's carnage.

"I used to get under the table as a child and listen to my father and his friends talk about the battles they've been through and their struggles," remembers Griffith about his father, Jacob "Roaring Jake" Griffith. "Those impress you deeply."

"Roaring Jake" was a Confederate lieutenant colonel in the 1st Kentucky Calvary. The elder Griffith's most memorable war moment was when General Joseph Wheeler asked the wounded Jake to lead a desperate charge. Jake, unable to ride his horse, commandeered a horse and buggy and rode in front of his troops to win the day.

Jake also escorted Jefferson Davis to Irwinville, Georgia, after Robert Lee's surrender, only to be captured with the former Confederate president on May 10, 1865.

THE PIONEER OF HOLLYWOOD

As a stage actor, Jake's son D.W. earned extra cash by working in front of the camera as an actor for Biograph Company, one of many film production film studios located at Fort Lee, New Jersey, the "Hollywood" of cinema's early days. Griffith was pressed into the director's chair when the studio's main director became incapacitated. His 1908 directorial debut, *The Adventures of Dolly,* was a standard one-reeler. But during his next five remarkable years, Griffith would introduce or incorporate previous film techniques into new formats, revolutionizing the look of movies with a special emphasis on enhancing film narratives.

For instance, in only his second month of directing, Griffith decided to move his camera closer to the pair of actors dominating a scene in *Greaser's Gauntlet* from a wide shot to a medium shot. The film, shot in August, 1908, was made in the days before the invention of the zoom lens. Griffith instructed his cameraman, Billy Bitzer, to pick up his camera and get closer to film the actors reenact their scene. After the sequence was shot in two different angles, Griffith spliced the two shots together in the editing room to give his movie audiences a unique view of stepping in closer for a more intimate look at the two actors.

He anticipated Sergei Eisenstein, the Russian film-editing theorist who greatly admired Griffith, with the director's October, 1908, *After Many Year.* In the early Griffith movie, the director introduced a series of shots filmed in different settings linked solely to a purely emotional common theme. Griffith's "montage of attractions" predated Eisenstein's tonal montage editing explanations by several years.

Griffith felt his writing and directing two to three one-reelers a week during his Biograph Studio days was akin to making sausages. He felt all his efforts would be neglected long afterwards because these short films were relegated to small nickelodeons. "Movies are written in sand: applauded today, forgotten tomorrow," he would say.

In the winter of 1910, Griffith took his production crew and actors to a small village in Southern California where he previously acted in a couple of stage plays during his theater days. He detested the New Jersey winters and decided to head toward a warmer climate during the chilly months. The sparsely-settled suburb of Los Angeles, named Hollywood, welcomed Griffith's troupe, although the village barely had enough beds to accommodate the Northeasterners. The movie produced was *Old California,* and the motion picture would prove to be the first in countless of films to emerge from soon-to-be nicknamed "Tinseltown."

Back in New Jersey, Griffith directed what emerged as cinema's first gangster movie, 1912's *The Musketeers of Pig Alley.* The film is acknowledged as influencing Martin Scorsese and his 1990 movie *Goodfellas,* as well as Scorsese's historic gangster period piece, 2002's *The Gangs of New York.*

GRIFFITH, CINEMA'S INNOVATOR

Previous to Griffith, acting in silent movies was completely different. Griffith's films stand apart from his early silent movie contemporaries by the understated mannerisms of his actors. He was the first director to fully realize the difference between the eye of a camera filming up close to his actors versus the eye of viewers sitting in theater seats far away from the stage actors. He single-handedly transformed his actors' movements from the exaggerated ones so familiar to silent movie fans and on the Victorian stage to more subtle, nuanced acting adopted in his post-1910 films.

As a stage actor himself, Griffith appreciated the preparations that went into a play before premier night. He would carry such detailed acting performances into his films. Conducting hours of rehearsals with his actors, Griffith made sure they were well prepared before he turned them loose before the camera. He and his actors would often deviate from the scripts by improvising and reshaping the plots' structures during those lengthy rehearsals.

Griffith very rarely referred to his script while filming. Each scene and every movement was contained in Griffith's memory. He was so familiar with the narrative he would bark instructions for the next scene while the crew was still in the middle of setting up for the next shot.

Griffith is credited with popularizing the flashback, which, widely used in literature, was surprisingly rarely used in cinema until Griffith began applying the technique. What is even more interesting is in his later *Birth of a Nation,* the "switchback" narrative method was adopted where the story goes back some months from the present and then hurdles forward toward the future.

As a theatre actor, Griffith knew the focal point on the stage at certain parts of a play was a confined area where the audiences' main attention primarily took place. He knew the viewers concentrated on those actors and subconsciously blurred out the other area of the stage. Griffith used his theatre knowledge to create a mask within the iris of the camera, darkening the unimportant areas of the frame and illuminating just the part of the scene he intended to emphasize. The masking of the frame was either static or, in one of the first cases of fade-ins and fade-outs, Griffith manipulated the mask effect to open and close the iris. Such a device cued the audience a beginning or an ending of a particular scene was taking place.

Another trick up Griffith's sleeve was popularizing the use of the split screen. Even though double exposures in movies were used back in the late 1800's, Griffith filmed two separate scenes and optically split the frame in half, showing the two scenes together. He first used the split-screen effect in *Birth of a Nation* inside and outside Atlanta, reflecting the chaos taking place during the Battle of Atlanta.

Griffith also pioneered in-focus panorama shots, first seen in *Birth,* where the foreground is in-focus while the background is equally sharp. This complicated shot is observed in the scene where Sherman's Union Army is marching to the sea in the distance while the camera, situated on a hill, pans left to capture a comforting mother huddling her two children. The totally in-focus shot underscored the complexity Griffith and his cameraman Bitzer faced working with their primitive movie lens during those early days of motion pictures. To get the shot, Griffith asked his reliable cinematographer to keep in focus both the foreground of the family and the background of the Union Army in the far distance. Bitzer, puzzled at such a request, answered such a shot would be impossible to achieve. "That's why I asked for it," retorted Griffith. Bitzer was able to place the camera at such a distance from both groups that the unique shot became a template for future directors.

In *Birth,* Griffith also filmed the first night scene using phosphorus flares during the burning of Atlanta sequence to show the mass destruction the South experienced during the closing days of the Confederacy. He also initiated the first musical score written specially for a film, and had, for the larger venues in big cities projecting *Birth,* hired a full orchestra to play the score.

IMPORTANCE OF *BIRTH OF A NATION*

These techniques Griffith invented were largely new to the vast movie audiences: the subtle acting, the numerous camera placements, the varying shot selections, and the special effects. These innovations were all compressed into Griffith's epic *Birth of a Nation.*

Birth was also an eye-opener to future actors and film directors. Griffith hired soon-to-be directors Raoul Walsh and Donald Crisp (who directed 72 films himself and was also an actor) among others who had lesser roles in cinematic history to assist him in the picture's filming. Walsh appeared before the camera as an actor playing Lincoln's assassin, John Wilkes Booth. Another future director, John Ford, asserted he was one of the Klansman on a horse riding to the rescue. In one of the more unusual claims for being in the film was Milton Berle, who said he was one of the babies in the movie.

Birth served as a predecessor to the first sequel in cinema history, 1916's now-lost silent film *Death of a Nation,* directed by *The Clansman* book author Thomas Dixon, picking up the narrative where *Birth* ends.

Birth of a Nation, as repugnant as it appears today, was truly the first widespread feature film in America. There had been previously released films over 60 minutes, defined as "feature films," shown in the United States, including several Italian epics, but Griffith's highly controversial film's popularity opened up an entirely new age on the silver screen, spurring a surge in larger movie house construction and shifting the focus of movie studios to produce more full-length movies instead of their short one and two reelers.

The film single-handedly elevated what was considered a medium for the lower classes to a high art form which attracted many more people to the cinema. The movie industry we recognize today was for all intents and purposes born on the day *Birth of a Nation* premiered at Clune's Auditorium in Los Angeles on February 8, 1915.

CONTROVERSIES SURROUND *BIRTH OF A NATION*

Fierce protests surrounded the showing of *Birth* in several cities once the movie was released. Riots broke out in Boston and Philadelphia where the film was screened. Chicago, Denver, Kansas City, Minneapolis, Pittsburgh, and St. Louis simply refused to allow the film to be shown. The recently formed NAACP tried to impose an outright ban of the film throughout the country. When the effort failed, the group tried to get Griffith to excise the more objectionable scenes out of the picture.

Birth did spawn a new industry for African-Americans, that of creating black-only movie businesses addressing the bigotry and repulsive viewpoint Griffith's film showcased. Movies with black-positive themes were produced in Jacksonville, Florida, which became the Hollywood of the East for the African-American film industry. These studios released films by the dozens during those silent-movie days, reflecting the goodness of the people.

Ironically, because of the controversies surrounding *Birth,* including being banned in several states and large cities, and evoking the U.S. Supreme Court in Mutual vs. Ohio to rule films did not have 1st amendment protections, *Birth* became an immediate financial success. Despite an astronomical $2.00 ($20 in today's prices) per ticket in New York City, the film made enormous profits for Griffith and those associated with the movie. Louis B. Mayer (later the last "M" in MGM Studios) began his fortune as the sole New England distributor for the film. Over one million people bought tickets to see *Birth* in its first year of release, and by the end of World War Two over 200 million people globally viewed it. *Birth* had the highest financially grossing movie receipts until 1939's *Gone With The Wind.* In terms of production cost ratio to box office receipts, *Birth* is still one of the most profitable films ever released.

President Woodrow Wilson, who purportedly described *Birth* as "History written in lightning," viewed the movie at the White House, the first film to be shown at the executive mansion. Later, when the film's controversies mounted, Wilson denounced the movie.

Griffith, raised amidst a Land-of-Dixie sentiment setting as a child, was mystified by the fierce reaction of the movie. He recognized the importance of *Birth* and the way it changed cinema. "Remember how small the world was before I came along?" Griffith later asked. "I brought it all to life: I moved the whole world onto a twenty-foot screen."

INTOLERANCE--SILENT FILM'S BEST MOVIE

Griffith was stung by the controversies of *Birth,* and he poured all his efforts into what some film historians regard as the best silent film ever produced, 1916's *Intolerance.*

Making *The Mother and the Law* while editing *Birth,* Griffith was advised by a close associate such a non-epic film was not in keeping with the great director's elevated status. Griffith decided to embark on a project concerning a subject percolating in his mind ever since the release of *Birth* where he personally felt the wrath of the "moral righteousness" of a select group of people. His new movie would add to the film he was in the middle of directing, *Mother,* by introducing three new narratives to his theme of intolerance.

The four stories interweave throughout *Intolerance*, all converging in several breathless "ride-to-rescue" endings. What proved to be the most popular segment is the *Babylonian Story*, taking place in 500 BC, where the Persians threaten peace-loving Babylonians. Griffith's partially-filmed second plot, *The Modern Story*, which was the original *The Mother and The Law*, details an exploited worker framed for murder, and only a governor's pardon can save him from the gallows. *The French Story*, set during St. Bartholomew's Day Massacre in the late 1500's, pits France's Catholic royalty against the Huguenots. *The Judaean Story* reflects on Christ's final days and his struggles with the Pharisees.

The lavish production is light years in every way ahead of *Birth*. The film played a huge influence on European cinema: the movie's innovative cross-cutting inspired Soviet Sergei Eisenstein to formulate his ground-breaking editing theories. German Impressionism, so popular in the early 1920's, replicated many Griffith's scenes of contrasting light and shadow set lighting. Future directors Erich von Stroheim, Tod Browning, and Woody van Dyke worked as assistant directors on *Intolerance*. The movie also pioneered the Biblical epic genre, motivating Cecil B. DeMille later to produce his classics on ancient civilizations.

The film's influence is seen today by the architecture at Los Angeles' Hollywood & Highland Center, home to The Dolby Theatre, where the Academy Awards' ceremonies take place every year. The elephant statues, so prominent in the courtyard, weigh 33,500 pounds apiece, while the massive archway seen in the complex is a replica of the designs drawn up for *Intolerance's* Babylonian set.

As one movie historian wrote, "This film sparked one of the most exciting and concentrated creative eras in the history of art."

Griffith poured more than $2 million of his own money to fund *Intolerance*. The Babylonian orgy scene, much of it cut in the final release, cost over $200,000 alone. Tabulating at $8.4 million, *Intolerance's* budget was the most expensive film produced until 1954's *20,000 Leagues Under The Sea* at $9 million.

Intolerance was filmed well before the advent of computer special effects, so Griffith was forced to employ tens of thousands of extras for his big scenes. According to assistant director Josef von Sternberg, Griffith, while high up on a platform, barked an order to "Move these 10,000 horses a trifle to the right, and that mob out there three feet forward."

The movie wasn't the money-maker Griffith had hoped it would be. The reason wasn't so much a lack of ticket sales but Griffith's insistence that full orchestras accompany the film through 12 regions in its theatrical projections.

Griffith's pockets were so empty after *Intolerance's* run he couldn't afford to tear down the huge Babylon set on Sunset Blvd., where the Vista Theater sits today in Hollywood. The gates, made up of lath and plaster framed with wood, were 100 feet high and supported by steel cables. Four years of decay diminished the weight size of the structures and finally made it affordable for Griffith to remove the Gates of Babylon.

Griffith partially recovered his money when he re-released *The Fall of Babylon* and *The Mother and the Law* in 1919 in separate movies, giving him the funding to tear down and cart off the tons of material that made up the Gates of Babylon.

GRIFFITH'S LATER FILMS

The film director eventually made other highly-acclaimed films, such as *Broken Blossoms* (1919), *Way Down East* (1920), and *Orphans of the Storm* (1921), but his cutting-edge cinematic innovations would never be eclipsed by *Birth* and *Intolerance*.

These three later films should not be ignored, however.

1919's *Broken Blossoms* tackled themes considered taboo on the big screen when the movie was first released. Child-abuse, inter-racial love relationships (most likely the first in cinema), and revenge killing were among the repulsive subjects Griffith chose to portray in this very moving film. *Blossoms* also humanized the Chinese-Americans at a time when xenophobia was running rampant against anything and anyone from the eastern part of Asia.

The influential film also set precedence with the stylized lighting by cinematographer Henrik Sartov, who introduced to the screen an ethereal quality never seen before. Using two indoor sets, the production captures the poor neighborhood of East London, the Limehouse district, showing both the exteriors and interiors of the fabricated area in a realistic yet dreamy atmosphere.

Long-time Griffith-associate Lillian Gish was hesitant to take the role of a 15-year-old daughter to an abusive professional boxer father, played by Donald Crisp. The actress finally relented when she found out her favorite director, Griffith, was going to direct the film. Gish claimed to have been indebted to Griffith in teaching her so much about movie-making. Living to be 100 years old, Gish was able to sustain a long acting career in Hollywood. During the filming of Robert Altman's 1978 *The Wedding,* Gish criticized how a cameraman was positioning his lens to photograph her. "Get up from there!" she barked. "Get up! If God had wanted you to shoot me from that angle, he would have given you a camera in your belly button. Mr. Griffith always said, `Shoot from above for an angel, shoot from below for a devil.' "

While filming 1987's *The Whales of August,* director Lindsay Anderson said after one particular scene, "Miss Gish, you have just given me the most marvelous close-up!" Co-star Bette Davis, herself a veteran of cinema, chimed in, "She should. She invented them."

Broken Blossoms is drenched in pathos as Crisp's unrelenting brutality inflicts both physical and emotional pain on the young Gish. One enduring image is of Gish using her two fingers to hold up the edges of her lips to force a smile after some particular savage beatings. During rehearsals, Gish remembers instinctively using her fingers for the cheerful smile. Griffith came over to her and asked how she thought of doing that. She didn't know, Gish told him, she just did it. The gesture proved to be one of cinema's most poignant movements.

One particular scene especially stands out in *Blossoms* when Crisp, finding out Gish had been sheltered by a Chinese flower shop owner after she had run away from one of his particularly brutal floggings, drags her home and proceeds to roll up his sleeves. The daughter escapes into a closet. The filming of the famous closet scene, which influenced Stanley Kubrick's *The Shining,* where Jack Nicholson uses an axe to knock down the door to get after Shelley Duvall, was intense as Griffith barked orders to her on the set as she was yelling in hysterics. A passerby outside the studio happened to hear the commotion and tried to break into the building to stop what he thought was a brutal situation. The concerned citizen had to be restrained by members of the studio's crew.

The movie does have a happy ending, that is for Griffith anyways. The film director had just signed a contract with Charlie Chaplin, Mary Pickford, and Douglas Fairbanks to form an independent film company called United Artists. *Broken Blossoms* was produced by Adolph Zukor's subsidiary business Paramount Pictures. When Zukor saw the ending, he was mortified and yelled at Griffith, "How dare you deliver such a terrible film." Griffith, knowing he had produced a great movie, left Zukor's office, only to return the following day with $250,000, whereby he threw the money on Zukor's desk. "Here," said Griffith, "If you don't want the picture, I'll buy it from you." Zukor gladly accepted the offer. *Broken Blossoms* became United Artists' first film, and the movie subsequently earned enormous financial riches for the newly-formed company.

Italian film director Federico Fellini was such a big fan of "Broken Blossoms" he based his highly-acclaimed 1954 film *La Strada* on its plot.

BACK IN THE EAST COAST

The next year, Griffith embarked on a film which became the fourth biggest box office hit in the silent movie era, 1920's *Way Down East*. The melodramatic film, a genre Griffith embraced throughout his career, shows how a slow-moving Victorian-era narrative can be saved by one of the most exciting heart-stopping endings ever filmed.

The Soviet filmmakers, who loved Griffith's previous work, embraced *Way Down East* and its stirring ending. The movie's concluding sequences illustrate the Russian film theorist Lev Kulesov, innovator of the Kulesov Principle, description of separate filmed images spliced together to create an entirely new emotion to the viewer. In *Way Down East,* Kulesov labeled the climatic effect as "Creative Geography," where Griffith had filmed the ending on three different rivers: Niagara Falls, the Farmington River falls in Connecticut, and White River Junction in Vermont, where most of the ice-flow rescue scenes were shot during the winter. Splicing together the footage on those three rivers creates in the viewers' mind the image our heroine, Lillian Gish, is on the verge of plummeting hundreds of feet over the falls to her death.

Immediately before the river ice flow scenes in *East,* Gish is kicked out of a warm house to face what in reality was an actual howling blizzard during the shoot. Gish stumbles about trying to see through the thick falling snow and icicles are seen forming on her eyelashes and hair. Griffith asked the cameraman to get a close-up of Gish's face, which by the look of her on the film she appears in utter agony.

Soon afterwards Gish faints as she walks on the frozen river where the break-up of the sheets of ice occurs. Passed out, Gish rides on an ice flow down the river towards the cascading falls. Down for the count, Gish's right arm dangles in the cold water. Submerged in the icy cold Vermont water for the length of time the actress took to film her scenes, Gish's right hand was impaired throughout the rest of her life because of nerve damage she incurred filming the winter scene. Meanwhile, Griffith had one side of his face nearly frost-bitten during the filming at the constant below-freezing temperatures. So frigid was the anticipated weather, Bitzer devised a special heater encased around the camera he was operating to keep the film flexible and the gears working.

Despite all the hardships and stunning photography filmed in Vermont that winter, Griffith was not satisfied with the ice-flow rescue footage. He had his crew construct wooden-hollowed fake ice flows in late spring, and had them hauled to the Farmington River with its small waterfall near the Riverside

Cemetery in Farmington, Connecticut. He filmed the scenes showing just the top edge of those falls which, when spliced together with the wide shots of Niagara Falls, appear to movie audiences having Gish about to go over the immense high falls.

Way Down East was the first film shot in Griffith's newly-purchased Mamaroneck, New Jersey, studio, which was the former home to millionaire Henry Flagler. Those living in St. Augustine, Florida, know Flagler as the main catalyst in developing the entire Florida Atlantic Seaboard. Griffith had not felt fully at home in the city he had made popular, Hollywood, and was more comfortable back East, despite his aversion to the cold winters in New Jersey.

He next embarked on what many consider his last great film, 1921's *Orphans of the Storm*. Griffith returned to the historic epic and transformed the sets at Mamaroneck into a sprawling late-1700 Paris.

One notable scene among many in *Orphans* is where the separated Gish sisters, Lillian and Dorothy, who played the blind sister, discover each other. Lillian, living on the second floor in a city tenement, hears, then spots, long-lost Dorothy begging in the street. The scene is a classic example of the auditory effect viewers believe they are hearing the two sisters shouting at each other from the screen despite *Orphans* being a silent film. Only Lillian's untimely arrest does the sequence—and the yelling--end.

After *Orphans*, the Gish sisters signed more lucrative contracts with MGM Studios than Griffith and United Artists could offer. For the first time in a decade, Griffith looked at a future without Lilian's presence.

"Everything went downhill after Lillian left me," reflected Griffith.

The remainder of the Griffith cannon produced no comparable films as those described above. But the "Father of Film" did not predict during his peak years the possibilities of silent movies giving way to pictures with sound.

"There will never be talking pictures," Griffith predicted at a time when his silent movies were thriving. "We do not want now and we never shall want the human voice with our films. Music -- fine music -- will always be the voice of the silent drama."

Ironically, Griffith would end his film directing career producing two talking pictures. *Abraham Lincoln,* with Walter Huston, was cinema's first epic with sound. But the picture proved to be a box office failure. Griffith's next and last film, his self-funded 1931 *The Struggle,* was critically acclaimed, but was equally a bust at the cash register.

Griffith's body of work was recognized during the 1935 Academy Awards when the aging director was honored with the Academy's golden statuette. He said during the ceremony, "We had many worries in those days, small worries. Now you people have your worries and they are big ones. They have grown with the business - and no matter what its problems, it's the greatest business in the world."

Despite Lillian Gish's claim Griffith died in poverty, in actuality he had wisely invested in an annuity while he was raking in cartloads of money. Because of his foresight, Griffith in his later years lived reasonably well. Ultimately, the cinematic world had long passed Griffith, and he would die in relative obscurity in 1948 in a Los Angeles hotel. But his legacy in elevating cinema from simple entertainment into true art remains. Griffith's passing prompted Orson Welles to say: "No town, no industry, no profession, no art form owes so much to a single man."

TOP TEN BEST D.W. GRIFFITH FILMS

#1. INTOLERANCE (1916)

Griffith's 1916 film is considered by most as the best silent film of all-time. The massive sets, the interweaving four stories, and the innovative camera and editing techniques place *Intolerance* as one of the most, if not the most, influential movie of all time. It was not, as Griffith himself said, an apology for his previous controversial movie, *Birth of a Nation*. The film, according to Griffith, was designed as a retort for all those who expected him to say he was apologetic for producing such a racially-tinged picture. Some of the public's reaction to *Birth*, he claimed, was similar to the four stories presented in *Intolerance* where the righteous get battered by those who think they are solely responsible to uphold the morals of contemporary society. The San Franciscan Bulletin at the time of the picture's release stated "Griffith's film comes powerfully to strengthen the hand of the believers in love."

#2. BROKEN BLOSSOMS (1919)

Blossoms inspired early German film directors such as G. W. Pabst and Josef von Sternberg and their set and lighting techniques. To think when viewing every scene that *Blossoms* was shot indoors on an enormous studio set. Film critic Richard Schickel said of the memorable closet scene, "It is heartbreaking – yet for the most part quite delicately controlled by the actress. Barthelmess reports that her hysteria was induced by Griffith's taunting of her. Gish, on her part, claims that she improvised the child's tortured movements on the spot and that when she finished the scene there was a hush on stage, broken finally by Griffith's exclamation, 'My God, why didn't you warn me you were going to do that?' "

3. BIRTH OF A NATION (1915)

History of the evolution of cinema contrasts *Birth's* repugnant theme to Griffith's refinement and introduction to new camera and editing techniques still used today. Actress Mary Pickford noted the importance of this film. *"Birth of a Nation* was the first picture that really made people take the motion picture industry seriously." Nearly every film historian has denounced *"Birth's"* overall message, but as Richard Brody wrote, "The worst thing about *The Birth of a Nation* is how good it is. The merits of its grand and enduring aesthetic make it impossible to ignore and, despite its disgusting content, also make it hard not to love."

4. WAY DOWN EAST (1920)

Having the fourth biggest box office ticket sales in silent movie history as well as showing the most gripping ending in silent films, *Way Down East* is based on a late 1890's Victorian stage play. *East* was purchased by Griffith for an enormous sum in order to bring this melodrama onto the screen. Movie expert Mark Adamo said of this film, "What's amazing is that so much of Gish's tough, funny, intuitive performance, particularly in the film's middle section as she bears her illegitimate child, transcends time, place and technology. Equally amazing is Griffith's mighty striving, with his arty location shots, quirky close-ups and riskily staged set pieces, to forge a new and expressly cinematic style."

5. ORPHANS OF THE STORM (1921)

Considered Griffith's last classic film which elevated the director's vision of a spectacular epic showcasing pageantry and drama on a heightened scale. The French Revolution of the late 1700's swallows up two sisters caught in the maelstrom of brutal political fighting. The New York Times said, "As the vivid scenes of the historically colored melodrama flashed one after another on the screen everyone surely felt that Griffith was himself again."

6. THE MUSKETEERS OF PIG ALLEY (1912)

Many regard this as the first film in cinema to deal with organized crime. *Musketeers* starred Elmer Booth, whose mannerisms as a swaggering, confident gangster, is acknowledged as playing a huge influence in later underworld characters portrayed by Jimmy Cagney, Humphrey Bogart, Edward G. Robinson, and George Raft among others. Booth tragically died at the young age of 33 in a car crash right when Griffith was planning to give him a major role in *Intolerance*. *Musketeers* is also one of the first instances in cinema where a rack focus was used to follow the main characters in the foreground while the background remains slightly out-of-focus.

7. JUDITH OF BETHULIA (1914)

Griffith's first feature film, clocking in just over an hour, shows the potential of his showcasing a Biblical epic. Based on the *Book of Judith, Bethulia* would be the final picture Griffith made for Biograph Company, and preceded his wildly-popular *Birth* and *Intolerance*. The Moving Picture World publication in 1914 said of the production, "A fascinating work of high artistry, *Judith of Bethulia* will not only rank as an achievement in this country, but will make foreign producers sit up and take notice."

8. IN OLD CALIFORNIA (1910)

The first film ever shot and produced in Hollywood, California. Credit had long gone to Cecil B. DeMille, in his directorial debut, when he shot in its entirely his 1914 *The Squaw Man,* acknowledged as the first "feature-length" movie filmed in Hollywood. But the real credit belongs to Griffith in introducing to the movie community the benefits of filming in the suburban township of Los Angeles, despite the existence of several small movie studios already in the nearby big city of L.A. at the time he produced *In Old California.*

9. A DRUNKARD'S REFORMATION (1909)

Griffith's first film to have a social impact. *Drunkard's* contains an early sophisticated example of parallel editing Griffith later refined in his career. One noteworthy influence of the film had an Iowa city showing *Reformation* during a temperance meeting, and immediately afterwards the city government voted to make the community a "dry town."

10. THE MOTHERING HEART (1913)

Lilian Gish's subtle performance is illustrative of Griffith's realization the camera lens can capture the subtle emotions of an actress without resorting to the exaggerated movements so popular on the Victorian stage. The director's acting philosophy before the camera became widely accepted and proved to be a departure from the standard over-embellishments of performers in previous cinematic pictures.

Charlie Chaplin

THE GENIUS WHO CHANGED COMEDY

A young, aspiring comedian, Charlie Chaplin, had been a film actor less than a year. Yet in December 1914 he inked what was at the time a very lucrative contract with Essanay Studios for $1,200 per week. Never had anyone in the nascent movie picture industry risen so fast in such a short period of time. His next contract, signed in 1916, with Mutual Film Corporation, would make Chaplin the highest paid "employee" in the United States.

Chaplin is remembered today in many different ways: he's the dexterous comedian who raised comedy from simple slapstick to a new sophisticated level; he's the aging actor who married late-teenage girls; he's the iconoclast who frequented with socialists and became self-exiled from the states in the 1950's.

Everyone, however, knows Chaplin as The Tramp. He entertained millions with blockbuster productions such as 1921's *The Kid,* 1925's *The Gold Rush,* 1931's *City Lights,* 1936's *Modern Times* and 1940's *The Great Dictator* among others. Chaplin, whose career was launched in the beginning twenty years of motion pictures' existence, was one of the first shining lights of cinema, doing it all: writing, directing, editing, and in his later sound films, composing music, all which contributed to a unique style repeatedly imitated, but never equaled.

Chaplin films are still popular over one hundred years later. Remarkably, when many silent pictures have been lost, every picture Chaplin released can be viewed either on YouTube or DVD. Today's interested viewer can see how Chaplin's vision evolved over the decades. Chaplin's legendary perfectionism on and off the screen has resulted in breathtaking celluloid moments which still amaze sophisticated audiences today.

EARLY CAREER MOVES

So American in appearance were Chaplin's movies, people little realize the comedian was born and raised in England. His upbringing was unhappy and cloaked in the seamy side of poor central London's life. His father, a vaudeville actor who drank too much, died at an early age of 37, while his mother was eventually admitted to the insane asylum.

"My childhood was sad," recalled Chaplin, "but now I remember it with nostalgia, like a dream."

To escape such poverty and bitterness, he turned to the stage. Among his acting colleagues was Stan Laurel, later of Laurel and Hardy. He and Laurel, members of an English troupe, journeyed to the United States where Chaplin was hired by Keystone Studios after its movie producers saw him on a Philadelphia stage in 1913.

"The first time I looked at myself on the screen, I was ready to resign from the movie contract I had just signed," said Chaplin. "That can't be me, I thought. Then when I realized it was, I said, 'Good night.' Strange enough, I was told that the picture was a scream. I had always been ambitious to work in drama, and it certainly was the surprise of my life when I got away with the comedy stuff."

Soon after his debut at Keystone, he fell into The Tramp character for the film *Mabel's Strange Predicament* accidentally. Looking for some clothes for his role as a drunken man down on his luck, he spotted studio actor Roscoe "Fatty" Arbuckle's pants hanging on the wall. He asked if he could use his pants as well as Arbuckle's father-in-law's derby hat. Encouraged by his findings, Chaplin continued to rummage through the studio's dressing room and found a jacket belonging to the undersized actor/director Charles Avery. To round out his new look, he cut some black crepe paper for a mustache to make him appear older. Chaplin took his personal cane for an added prop to twirl.

"I had no idea of the character," Chaplin remembered. "But the moment I was dressed, the clothes and the make-up made me feel the person he was. I began to know him, and by the time I walked onto the set he was fully born."

Once Chaplin appeared before the lens, he became itchy after four months and convinced studio executives to give him directorial reigns. When Keystone's veteran directors gathered in the screening room to view Chaplin's first finished film, they expected this new upstart to fail. But when the closing scene of *Caught in the Rain* concluded, they were applauding. His physical comedy was brilliant, and the directors quickly realized what they just witnessed was a revolution in cinematic comedy.

Some of those early films at Keystone involved just a bench in the park and the predicaments The Tramp would get into with a parade of characters, most notably law enforcement officers, passing by.

"All I need to make a comedy is a park, a policeman and a pretty girl," said Chaplin on those spare outdoor sets and equally spare storylines.

Remarkably, Chaplin didn't receive any screen credit for the many films he made at Keystone since the studio's policy was to not acknowledge any of its actors, no matter how popular. His name finally appeared in Essanay's first film when he signed a more lucrative contract with the movie studio, 1915's *His New Job*.

In the following year, he would ink an even richer contract with Mutual Pictures, who played up his Tramp image. Chaplin would look fondly back at those days with Mutual. Critics agree some of Chaplin's finest comedy was produced during those Mutual years.

Chaplin remembered The Tramp's early-screen involvement with the bottle, which provided him with many hilarious scenarios.

"Even funnier than a man who has been made ridiculous is the man who, having had something funny happen to him, refuses to admit that anything out of the way has happened, and attempts to maintain his dignity," detailed Chaplin. "Perhaps the best example is the intoxicated man who, though his tongue and walk will give him away, attempts in a dignified manner to convince you that he is quite sober. He is much funnier than the man who, wildly hilarious, is frankly drunk and doesn't care a whoop who knows it. Intoxicated characters in the movies are almost always 'slightly tipsy' with an attempt at dignity because theater owners have learned that this attempt at dignity is funny."

By taking the role of The Tramp, who was always down-on-his-luck and lived in abject poverty, Chaplin realized his character provided him with the opportunity to poke fun at those who were supremely wealthy.

"One of the things most quickly learned in theatrical work is that people as a whole get satisfaction from seeing the rich get the worst of things." Chaplin said. "The reason for this, of course, lies in the fact that nine tenths of the people in the world are poor, and secretly resent the wealth of the other tenth."

Reflecting on his portrayal of a poverty-stricken character who constantly got slapped around, he felt his example would be an inspiration to those who found themselves in similar positions, especially during the Great Depression.

"Failure is unimportant," said Chaplin on his acting career. "It takes courage to make a fool of yourself."

CHAPLIN'S DIRECTING STYLE

Chaplin the director was unique in so many ways. First, he concentrated on the actors in front of the camera and gave the camera operator responsibility for all the other filming assignments, including camera placement and framing. Chaplin acted out each movement of every performer during rehearsals, similar to Griffith's pre-production work before arriving on the film set.

As Robert Parish, who played a bit part as a newsboy in *City Lights,* remembers seeing "Chaplin blowing a pea from the peashooter, playing both my part and the part of Austen Jewell, the other newsboy. He then would run over and react as The Tramp being hit by it, then back to the newsboys and blow another pea. He would then play Virginia Cherrill's part of the Blind Girl. Then he was The Tramp. Then he would instruct what the background people should be doing. Everyone watched as he acted out all the parts for us. When he felt he had it all worked out, he reluctantly gave us back our parts...I believe he would have much rather played them all himself if he could."

Even in his later years, Chaplin didn't deviate from his directing style. When producing his final film, 1967's *The Countess of Hong Kong,* Chaplin, recalled Tippi Hedren, one of Alfred Hitchcock's favorite blond actresses who had a small role in the film, recalls, "The way Chaplin directed was unlike anyone I ever saw. He acted out all the parts himself. None of us believed it. Marlon (Brando, a method actor) hated it."

CHAPLIN THE PERFECTIONIST

As Chaplin's popularity soared, his excessive attention to detail caused him to miss tight deadlines. At the height of his career, he founded his very own film studio in October 1917, allowing Chaplin the luxury to become the ultimate perfectionist in his craft. He spent over $1,500,000 of his personal money to finance *City Lights.* In another production the script required him to film a river scene, so he constructed one at his studios, digging up five acres and spending $15,000 to build. He also needed two downtown streets for scenes set in a city's business district. For an expense of $100,000 in 1930 money, his studio constructed a look-alike urban setting.

The *City Lights'* production took three years to complete, even though just 180 days were devoted to the actual filming. Chaplin had hired non-actress Virginia Cherrill for the lead role of a blind flower seller solely based on how her near-sighted unfocused gaze looked. For Virginia's first on-screen appearance, Chaplin took six weeks to shoot her introductory simple scene, yet he was still not satisfied with any of the takes filmed. He then shot other portions of the script before returning to the opening scene a year later. Six days and 342 takes in total, Chaplin finally gave his nod of approval.

The prestigious amount of film Chaplin used to make his movies is legendary. In *The Gold Rush,* his cameraman shot 27 times more film than appeared in the final cut. Chaplin was just as particular about his own performance as with others: in the famous shoe-eating scene in *The Gold Rush,* the shoe he and Big Jim ate was made of licorice. The scene required 63 takes, and Chaplin digested so much licorice he had to be rushed to the hospital for insulin shock.

He took seven days to shoot the sequence of him being an experimental guinea pig for an automated food machine in *Modern Times.* Chaplin would perform his own stunts into his later years, reprising an earlier roller skating sequence (1916's *The Rink)* with the one in *Modern Times,* which required eight days of filming--with Chaplin blindfolded.

The director was such a perfectionist that as a producer for his Chaplin Film Company he hired up-and-coming film director Josef von Sternberg (*The Blue Angel* and *Shanghai Express* fame) to direct a previous flame of his, Edna Purviance, in an effort to boost her sagging career. The 1926 film, *A Woman of the Sea,* was an uninspired work in Chaplin's eyes. Rather than see the movie in public, Chaplin ended up burning the only negative of the film and deducting the picture as a tax loss.

THE COMEDIAN'S IMPROVISING

Until *Modern Times,* Chaplin never followed a completed script while in production. Short descriptions written into a script such as "The Tramp hired at a bakery" allowed Chaplin and his actors to improvise the constantly fluid story-lines while in the progress of filming each scene. In the evenings, Chaplin viewed the dailies (footage shot during each day) and offered his criticisms to his assistant directors. If he felt the stories should go in a different direction, which he often determined they would, he laboriously reshot earlier scenes to agree with the revised plot. He spent months, if not years, on one movie, resulting in inflated budgets associated with the lengthened productions. Occasionally, Chaplin would take a hiatus from the studios and keep everyone, cast and crew, on standby for days until he had an inspiration that resolved his dilemma. Until Chaplin was one-hundred percent satisfied, he wouldn't release any of his films.

All the perfection was worth his extreme work habits at the box office for those studios funding his movies. For *The Gold Rush,* a film that was the one movie Chaplin had said he would have liked to be remembered, the 1925 comedy became the fifth biggest box office hit in silent film era.

THE MICROMANAGER ON THE MOVIE SET

As stated, Chaplin was personally involved in almost every aspect of his movies' productions. In *Modern Times,* he composed most of the musical soundtrack, with assistance from David Raskin. The score included the song *Smile,* popularized in 1954 by Nat 'King' Cole. Music composer Raskin praised Chaplin's innate ability to comprehend melody and the instrumental qualities of certain pieces. The comic's violin playing in his youth contributed to his musical understanding.

Micromanaging a production was exhausting for Chaplin. Making *Modern Times* became a taxing marathon for the director/producer/actor, taking up to 18 hours a day for Chaplin. He was so engaged in the movie, to create the sounds of an upset stomach, he personally blew bubbles into a pail of water. Standing high up on a tower commanding hundreds of extras for the opening scene of *Modern Times,* Chaplin coordinated the large number of extras on the location, something an assistant director normally does.

During the famous "chicken-stalking" scene in *The Gold Rush,* a stagehand was wearing the costume of the fake foul. Chaplin had instructed the man how to strut The Tramp's signature walk. After several takes, Chaplin got totally flustered on the poor man's inability to perform up to the director's high standards. Chaplin put on the chicken costume and more than adequately acted the stunts himself.

So caught up in the moment of making sure everything was perfectly presented in his film *Monsieur Verdoux*, Chaplin, directing on the set, spotted some old gum on the floor and proceeded to get on his hands and knees to scrape the stuff off with a knife.

LOVE RELATIONSHIPS

Having romantic relationships with his leading ladies caused some added tension for Chaplin. Girlfriend Paulette Goddard recalls while making *Modern Times,* her role as an orphaned homeless woman required her to avoid make-up and to wear shabby clothes. One morning after Goddard had spent some time styling her hair, Chaplin, furious, dumped a bucket of water over her head to wash out all the curls.

Chaplin had a penchant for young women. Lita Grey, who worked with Chaplin in *The Kid* as a 12-year-old angel, auditioned three years later in *The Gold Rush* for a role as the dance-hall worker with whom The Tramp falls in love. Chaplin, at 35, had a fling with the 15-year-older soon after she won the role, got her pregnant, and married her the next year. Things soured fast between the couple. Chaplin decided to replace Grey and resumed the auditions for *The Gold Rush*, seeing a line-up of inspiring actresses, including a young Carole Lombard, before settling on actress Georgia Hale. Chaplin, still married to Grey, developed a crush with Hale during the film's production. The original 1925 print shows a long, lingering kiss between Chaplin and Hale at the picture's conclusion. When *The Gold Rush* was re-released several years later with a new musical score, Chaplin's affair with Hale was long over and he excised the kiss at the end.

One actress playing opposite him in *City Lights* held little attraction for Chaplin. Virginia Cherrill, later Cary Grant's wife who played the blind girl The Tramp falls in love with on-screen, never produced any sparks on or off the movie set.

"I was 20," rationalized Cherrill. "Charlie liked them younger."

MIX OF COMDEY AND PATHOS

With the release of 1921's *The Kid,* Chaplin began the unusual combination of comedy and pathos rolled into one film.

Chaplin said of his feature films after the release of *The Kid*, "All my pictures are built around the idea of getting in trouble and so giving me the chance to be desperately serious in my attempt to appear as a normal little gentleman."

What Chaplin took away from these trials and tribulations of the fictional Tramp wasn't so much as fate affecting the life of this poor, unfortunate character but the people who came in his contact that made his life burdensome.

"It isn't the ups and downs that make life difficult," he philosophized, "It's the jerks."

Chaplin saw comedy as a way to address all facets of life, not just the slapstick or the hilarious situations comedy is known for.

"Naturalness is the greatest requisite of comedy," explained Chaplin. "It must be real and true to life. I believe in realism absolutely. Real things appeal to the people far quicker than the grotesque. My comedy is actual life, with the slightest twist or exaggeration, you might say, to bring out what it might be under certain circumstances. Through humor, we see in what seems rational, the irrational; in what seems important, the unimportant. It also heightens our sense of survival and preserves our sanity."

Comedy and pathos were never more expertly combined than in Chaplin's *City Lights*. Critics have hailed the film's ending as one of the greatest sequences in cinematic history. Italian director Federico Fellini, perfectionist director Stanley Kubrick and film pioneer Orson Welles all have claimed the ending was on their top list of favorite conclusions. People who attended the premier of *City Lights* in Los Angeles claimed to have seen tears falling down the face of the usually stoic scientist Albert Einstein when the lights in the theater turned up following the emotional ending.

LOVE OF TENNIS

A viewer of Chaplin's films today notices how fit and trim the actor was while performing his hair-raising stunts. Throughout his life, Chaplin was in great physical and mental shape. His passionate sport was tennis, playing regularly well into his 70's.

While residing in Beverly Hills, California, Chaplin regularly invited numerous guests to his estate, nicknamed the "Breakaway Home." Designed by Chaplin and constructed with the help of his studio's carpenters, the complex's nickname derived from the fact the home was a scene of giddy entertainment and upbeat relaxation for his many guests. Contained inside was a pipe organ Chaplin played to the amusement of his visitors. He also hosted screenings of his films. With a backyard tennis court on Summit Drive in the Pickfair neighborhood, his grounds' witnessed a steady line of players hitting the ball with Chaplin, including the reclusive Greta Garbo, a frequent player testing the homeowner's strokes.

"I like friends as I like music, when I am in the mood," reminisced Chaplin. "To help a friend in need is easy, but to give him your time is not always opportune."

Only after directing 1967's *A Countess From Hong Kong* did Chaplin, living in Switzerland, began experiencing health issues which plagued him for the remainder of his life.

CHAPLIN FILMS WITH SOCIAL COMMENTARY

As early as *Modern Times,* Chaplin addressed many issues of what he felt was industry's and society's failings to the common man. Chaplin illustrated through his comedy how dehumanizing the factories' assembly work was to their workers. Also, the film predicted the age of electronic surveillance by featuring TV sets and cameras to monitor the laborers' production every moment of their work day. Public institutions were also criticized in the movie for their handling of the economic situation of millions during the Great Depression.

With war storm clouds gathering in Europe, Chaplin's satire on German leader Adolph Hitler and his Nazi Party in *The Great Dictator* struck a chord with the American public after Germany's invasion of Poland in 1939. There were many similarities between him and Hitler, noted Chaplin to his son.

"Their destinies were poles apart," said Charlie, Jr. "One was to make millions weep, while the other was to set the whole world laughing. Dad could never think of Hitler without a shudder, half of horror, half of fascination. 'Just think,' he would say uneasily, 'he's the madman, I'm the comic. But it could have been the other way around.'"

Chaplin was born four days before Hitler. The German Chancellor, upon seeing Chaplin's great popularity during the early 1920's, where the comic was the first actor to appear on a 1925 Time Magazine cover, grew a similar mustache, thinking such facial hair would make him equally popular.

When *The Great Dictator* was released, rumors had Hitler sitting through two viewings of the film. "I'd give anything to know what he thought of it," mused Chaplin.

Chaplin regarded 1947's *Monsieur Verdoux* as his most brilliant and cleverest film of his career. Orson Welles sold the idea to Chaplin back in 1941 for $5,000. The movie's plot was based on French serial killer Henri Désiré Landru, who, during World War 1, killed 11 widows and embezzled their money before he was caught, convicted and executed in 1922. Not a very uplifting message for a director/actor who was legendary in making people laugh.

Chaplin's press agent, Russell Birdwell contacted newspaper columnist Hedda Hopper right before the film's premier, writing "I contend that Charlie Chaplin's *Monsieur Verdoux* is the greatest and most controversial picture that has ever come from the Hollywood mills. If I lose I will publicly eat the negative of the film in front of the Chaplin studios. Sincerely, Bird." Hopper, after seeing the film, wired back: "DEAR BIRD: START EATING. HOPPER."

Monsieur Verdoux is Chaplin's political statement on the late 1940's events occurring in the United States, which included the dawning of the nuclear age as a delivery of mass destruction as well as the Communist paranoia sweeping throughout the United States.

Chaplin's quote, taken from 18th-century abolitionist Bishop Bailey Porteus, sums up the picture: "One murder makes a villain; millions a hero."

The movie proved to be a box office bust for Chaplin, but the French loved it, with over 2,500,000 customers paying to see the film.

Monsieur Verdoux, especially Verdoux's fiery speech at the end, provided a truckload of material for anti-Communist politicians to go after the

Englishman, who never earned his American citizenship after all his years living in the country.

At first Chaplin let such accusations slide off his skin. "Words are cheap," Chaplin said. "The biggest thing you can say is 'elephant.'"

Once he was caught up in the Communist Red Scare of Hollywood in the early 1950's, Chaplin left the shores of the United States.

"I remain just one thing, and one thing only, and that is a clown," Chaplin said of his situation. "It places me on a far higher plane than any politician."

Chaplin continued to direct movies overseas, none of them high on the list of his great classics. He bowed out of the movie business after his 1967 film *A Countess From Hong Kong* with Sophia Loren and Marlon Brando (whom Chaplin clashed with on the set) received critical reviews.

"If they don't like it, they are bloody idiots," reacted Chaplin to the bad critiques. "A diplomat falls in love with a prostitute - what better story can they get than that?"

Not that Chaplin, whose mind was ever-churning like the cogs in the factory machine portrayed in *Modern Times,* ever stopped working on other projects. But toward the later part of his life he realized "my only enemy is time."

Reflecting on his life in the later years, he was still in a state of optimistic bliss.

Chaplin summed up living as "Life is a beautiful magnificent thing, even to a jellyfish."

CHAPLIN'S LASTING INFLUENCE

After leaving cinema's limelight, Chaplin feared people would forget his body of work after he died. Before his death, he allowed The Tramp's trademark character to appear on commercials pitching a number of companies' products during the 1970's.

He shouldn't have worried about his comedy fading into the misty past. His influence is apparent in all phases of media today.

Cartoons and comedies, such as Adam Sandler's 1995 *Billy Madison*, have widely imitated his hallucination sequence in *The Gold Rush,* where The Tramp's starving cabin mate thinks Chaplin is a live chicken.

In the same film, a widely parodied situation is where the shifting of the cabin on the precipice of a cliff caused by Chaplin and his roommate scampering from one end of the room to the other. Numerous movies show people transferring themselves from one end of a boat, car, swimming pool, truck and other self-contained areas, producing hilarious situations.

The scene where Chaplin creates an entertaining dance with dinner rolls pierced by forks is constantly seen in light-hearted comedies, as seen in Johnny Depp's 1993 *Benny & Joon.* When *The Gold Rush* was first released, the audience howled for the projectionist to play the scene back, whereby the reel was reversed and the scene was repeated.

One of comedian Lucy Ball's most famous skits on her *I Love Lucy* show was her and Ethel trying to keep up boxing pieces of chocolates streaming on a conveyer belt. The scene plays a direct homage to *Modern Times* with the Tramp frantically working to keep up tightening the widgets while they are carried in ever increasing speed on an assembly belt.

There exist numerous scenes in movies of the analogy between workers and herds of animals being corralled into pens, reflecting the opening montage in *Modern Times* of sheep walking down a gangway while factory employees are clocking in for a day of labor.

Also, as a precursor to George Orwell's *1984* and other so-called "Big Brother" themed films, the barking head of a supervisor yelling at his employees to get back to work via a TV monitor in the bathroom in *Modern Times* is revolutionary in its delivery.

The *Modern Times* scene where Chaplin gets caught in the gears of the huge machine which keeps the factory operating has been imitated by its symbolic imagery in countless movies. On the actual movie set, the positioning of Chaplin's body through the machine's cogs was so uncomfortable the actor dictated this scene had to be shot in only one take, an unusual practice for a director who demanded multiple takes. The finished movie shows Chaplin going backwards inside the cogs after a working colleague discovers his predicament. Chaplin, while editing *Modern Times,* simply reversed the film showing him going backwards through the gears. That way he didn't have to subject himself to the agony of bending his poor body any further.

Chaplin's style in his films, never artsy, was meant to showcase Charlie the performer. And what is eternally preserved has everyone who has ever seen a Chaplin film agree with French film director Rene Clair's assessment: "Chaplin was the most beautiful gift that cinema has made to us."

TOP TEN CHARLIE CHAPLIN FILMS

#1--CITY LIGHTS (1931)

Numerous famous film directors have called this their favorite Chaplin film, while Orson Wells went further and labeled this his all-time favorite movie. After the release of *City Lights,* playwright George Bernard Shaw said

Chaplin was "the only genius to come out of the movie industry." A reviewer for the Los Angeles Examiner wrote, "Not since I reviewed the first Chaplin comedies way back in the two-reel days has Charlie given us such an orgy of laughs." The ending is considered one of the most tear-jerking finishes in all of cinema.

#2--MODERN TIMES (1936)

Chaplin's final "silent movie," this film struck a chord during the Great Depression with its finale "chin up" and the *Smile* theme song, written by Chaplin. Frank Nugget of the New York Times said, "*Modern Times* has still the same old Charlie, the lovable little fellow whose hands and feet and prankish eyebrows can beat an irresistible tattoo upon an audience's funny bone or hold it still, taut beneath the spell of human tragedy. Time has not changed his genius." *Modern Times* probably has more imitated scenes in later films and cartoons than any other movie ever produced.

#3--THE CIRCUS (1928)

Chaplin's most underrated movie, *The Circus* showcases Chaplin's most athletic performances witnessed on film with death-defying stunts that will leave viewers aghast. Variety described *The Circus* as "For the picture patrons, all of them, and for broad, laughable fun - Chaplin's best. It's Charlie Chaplin's best fun maker for other reasons: because it is the best straightaway story he has employed for broad film making, and because here his fun stuff is nearly all entirely creative or original in the major point." Some of Chaplin's funniest situations are contained in this film and also reflects Chaplin's most creative, original gags and storylines in his career.

#4--THE GOLD RUSH (1925)

This is the film Chaplin wanted to be remembered by, and one can see why. Chaplin mixes pathos and comedy perfectly to reflect The Tramp's quest for both gold and love in the Klondike. Variety, the movie trade magazine, was effusive of Chaplin's work at the time of *The Gold Rush's* release. "The greatest and most elaborate comedy ever filmed, and will stand for years as the biggest hit in its field, just as *Birth of a Nation* still withstands the many competitors in the dramatic class."

#5--THE KID (1921)

The first Chaplin film that introduced sentimentality to his hilarious comedy, unfolding a complete story of adopting an abandoned baby who grew up to become practically a son, played by Jackie Coogan (Uncle Fester in TV's "The Adams Family") to The Tramp. Mary Pickford said, "*The Kid* is one of the finest examples of the screen language, depending upon its actions rather than upon subtitles." Jeffrey Vance, who wrote a biography on Chaplin, said of the film," *The Kid* remains an important contribution to the art of film, not only because of Chaplin's innovative use of dramatic sequences within a feature-length comedy, but also because of the revelations *The Kid* provides about its creator. Undoubtedly, when Chaplin penned the film's opening subtitle, 'A picture with a smile--and perhaps, a tear,' he had his own artistic credo—and life—in mind."

#6--THE GREAT DICTATOR (1940)

Chaplin's first talking picture, *The Great Dictator* was his only nomination for the Academy Awards' Best Picture as well as nominations for Best Actor and Best Screenplay. Considered one of cinema's great satires of all-time, this parody on Adolf Hitler and his Nazi Party was regretted by Chaplin upon the discovery of the Holocaust after World War Two because of the brutality of the German regime to Europeans. Chaplin biographer Jeffrey Vance said of *Dictator,* "Chaplin's *The Great Dictator*' survives as a masterful integration of comedy, politics and satire. It stands as Chaplin's most self-consciously political work and the cinema's first important satire."

#7--MONSIEUR VERDOUX (1947)

Bombing at the box office in the United States because of its dark themes but highly successful in Europe, *Verdoux* was made when Chaplin's personal life was embroiled in a public paternity suit as well as a recent marriage to playwright Eugene O'Neill's 18-year-old daughter, Oona. It didn't help when the movie's lasting image of the Chaplin character expressed justification of his killing rich widows with the parallel to the slaughter of millions in war, stated shortly after World War Two was won by the Allies. Funniest sequence: when Verdoux attempts to drown Martha Raye on a boat while fishing on a lake.

#8--SHOULDER ARMS (1918)

Clocking in at 46 minutes, *Shoulder Arms* is considered Chaplin's shortest feature film and one that has more combat pratfalls than any war comedy movie ever made. Released two weeks before the end of World War One, *Shoulder* was the funnier to the American viewers since the euphoria concluding the "War to End All Wars" heightened the laughter. The New York Times published, "The fool's funny. *Shoulder Arms* at the Strand yesterday—and, apparently, that's the way everybody felt. There have been learned discussions as to whether Chaplin's comedy is low or high, artistic or crude, but no one can deny that when he impersonates a screen fool he is funny. Most of those who go to find fault with him remain to laugh. They may still find fault, but they will keep on laughing."

#9--THE RINK (1916)

One of Chaplin's funniest films during his glorious Mutual Studio days, *The Rink* shows the comedian's dedication in learning a sport (in this case, roller skating) and applying it with as much dexterity and gusto as a pro.

#10--THE TRAMP (1915)

Chaplin's signature character gets a film all his own for the first time in Chaplin's body of work as The Tramp receives employment on his assumed-lover's father's farm in hopes of getting an "in" with the farmer's daughter. The ending shows the pathos Chaplin would use later more extensively as he gives an added dimension to the Tramp's personality.

John Ford

"My name is John Ford. And I am a director of Westerns," proclaimed one of Hollywood's most influential film directors during a 1950 Screen Directors Guild ceremony.

The irony of Ford's famous statement is that, though he is recognized as the person most responsible for elevating American Western movies and catapulting John Wayne's acting career, the film industry has bequeathed him with a mantle of awards apart from Westerns. Ford holds the Academy Awards Best Director Oscar record with four, all non-westerns: 1936's *The Enforcers*, 1940's *The Grapes of Wrath*, 1941's *How Green Was My Valley*, and 1952's *The Quiet Man*.

Astonishingly, Ford never attended any Academy Awards ceremonies, saying, "I didn't show up at the ceremony to collect any of my first three Oscars. Once I went fishing, another time there was a war on, and on another occasion, I remember, I was suddenly taken drunk."

The general public identifies the director with Western movies, but even Ford recognized "None of my so called better pictures are westerns." His work has defined what American cinema is all about. Today's big-name directors consistently attribute their cinematic appreciation to this man.

"I try to watch a John Ford film before I start work on any movie simply because he inspires me," says film director Steven Spielberg, "and I'm very sensitive to the way he paints his pictures, and the way he blocks people, and frames the action while giving the illusion that there's things happening outside of the camera when there's not. He celebrates the frame, not just what happens inside of it. He's like a classic painter. So I have to watch *The Searchers*. Almost every time. I never tire of it. It has so many superlatives."

To prep Robert De Niro and Harvey Keitel for an early Martin Scorsese movie, *Mean Streets,* the director made them see 1956's Ford western "The Searchers."

When the young Orson Welles, a radio personality hired by RKO Pictures to direct his first Hollywood film, wanted to learn all about framing, camera placement, lighting and all the other facets of movie-making, he screened Ford's 1939 film *Stagecoach* over and over again forty times, absorbing everything contained in the picture.

"John Ford was my teacher," Welles recalled. "And *Stagecoach* was my movie textbook. I wanted to learn how to make movies, and that's such a classically perfect one."

Years later, Welles was asked to name his top three favorite film directors. He responded, "John Ford, John Ford, and John Ford."

FORD'S EARLY DAYS

Ford's directing career spanned from motion picture's infancy through the 1960's. He became one of cinema's most prolific directors—creating over 140 movies. Named by his parents John Martin "Jack" Feeney at birth, Ford followed the footsteps of his older brother Frances to Hollywood in 1914. Frances was a silent film actor who became a minor director. The younger Ford changed his name to Jack Ford once he went to Hollywood and appeared in fifteen of his brother's films. As notated in the Griffith section, he is seen as a member of the Ku Klux Klan riding to the rescue in *Birth of a Nation.*

His short, caustic wit got the best of interviewers. When Jean-Luc Godard, the legendary French New Wave film director whose earlier career was as a working journalist when he interviewed Ford, asked the American director what brought him to Hollywood. Ford replied, "A train."

In another interview, a reporter, after seeing *Stagecoach,* and sensing a major hole in the story, drew attention to Ford about the climactic scene where the Indians are chasing the stagecoach in the middle of Indian territory. The reporter asked why the Indians didn't simply shoot the horses hauling the stagecoach. Director John Ford fired back, "Because that would have been the end of the movie."

Ford was given the director's chair three years after arriving in Hollywood because, as one story goes, Universal Studio head Carl Laemmle, so impressed with Ford's booming voice as a director's assistant when he was positioning the extras for a scene, elevated the young man to head director.

Ford perfected his craft early on as film director, churning out dozens of silent movies, most lost in a Universal Studio fire. Those surviving movies clearly show he had absorbed lessons from Griffith to German Impressionistic directors to actor Harry Carey, one of silent Western movies' superstars who played the lead in numerous early Ford films.

He worked with a small crew in those early days, producing low-budget westerns at a remarkably fast pace. Ford said his visual style was instinctive: "Walk on the set, look at the set, at the locations. You tell the cameraman to place the camera here, and so forth."

Ford's visual style is not artsy in the avant-garde sense. "It's no use talking to me about art," he said honesty, "I make pictures to pay the rent."

Ford was one of those rare persons who "directed in his head," visualizing the entire script and uncannily knowing exactly where to place the camera, how to light the scene and what was required of his actors the second he sat down on the set. Ford's productions were mostly on schedule and within budget.

FORD'S DIRECTING STYLE

Ford never trusted the "editing-by-committee" process, where less than talented studio people would have input during the editing process once the filming was finished. Ford shot his movies in sequence, from the beginning of the script to the conclusion, provided the studio sets allowed for this chronological method of filming. He consciously performed "in-camera" editing, filming individual scenes which required few alternate camera angles. He rarely shot more than three takes of a particular scene. Such a practice gave editors little footage to work with after the filming was completed. Ford would sit underneath the camera in his director's chair, and when he yelled "cut," he immediately placed his fist in front of the lens.

Through the years, Ford gathered an assembly of performers who were familiar with his directing style. Actors such as Carey, John Carradine and Henry Fonda consistently were used by Ford to star in his films. They knew how to work with Ford and they knew his directing style.

"I tell the actors what I want and they give it to me, usually on the first take," said Ford

One of the earliest actors he loved to direct was satirist Will Rogers. In 1935's *Judge Priest,* Rogers claimed this was his finest role. Ford worked the comedic angle of Rogers' dry wit. Soon after *Judge Priest,* the director hired Rogers again for his 1935 movie *Steamboat Around The Bend.*

After filming was completed on *Steamboat,* Ford, an avid sailor, invited Rogers to sail to Hawaii on his yacht. Rogers declined, electing to fly to Alaska with veteran pilot Wiley Post. Rogers told Ford he needed some material for his newspaper column and decided an Alaskan adventure would make good copy. The actor thanked him, saying "You keep your duck and go on the water. I'll take my eagle and fly."

Wiley's plane crashed 20 miles outside of Point Barrow, killing both Rogers and Post. Ford took Roger's death hard.

WESTERNS' GROUND BREAKING FILM

Stagecoach is considered Ford's most influential picture. This pivotal film marked the beginning of serious, big-budgeted Western-themed movies. Prior to 1939, for nearly 10 years, Western-themed movies were cheaply produced, Saturday afternoon Grade B matinee pictures--so-called Poverty Row Pictures since only minor Hollywood film studios would make them. Westerns in the 1930's were geared towards kids; they were simple and void of any moral complexities. Raul Walsh's expensive and expansive 1930 *The Big Trail*, starring John Wayne, absolutely bombed at the box office. The film basically killed the genre as well as buried Wayne's career for a number of years.

Ford loved a short western story he had read in Colliers Magazine and hired Dudley Nichols, screenwriter for *The Informer,* the film that earned Ford his first Oscar for directing, to write the script for *Stagecoach.* Ford also could see the movie as a strong possibility to relaunch Wayne's career. Years earlier, the director hired Wayne, a drop-out from the University of Southern California in the late 1920's, to play bit-parts in his pictures and was purposely holding him back for just the perfect vehicle. Ford had been friends with Wayne over those years and felt *Stagecoach* could be a good fit for the Grade B actor. The script was a tough sell to major movie studios, however. Ford hadn't directed a Western since his highly-successful 1924 *The Silent Horse* and the studios were a bit wary of the story's treatment. Ford eventually got the film financed—and the rest is history.

There is an argument *Stagecoach* was a natural progression of more intellectually-layered Westerns making their way through the Hollywood major studios' pipeline during the 1938-1939 years which erased the cowboy Property Row stigmatism. *Dodge City*, *Destry Rides Again*, and *Union Pacific* were among those elevating Westerns to premier feature film status. However, *Stagecoach,* with its numerous awards, including two Oscars (Thomas Mitchell for Best Supporting Actor and Best Musical Scoring) and five Academy Award nominations (one of them for Best Picture and another for Best Director), opened critics' eyes to the sophistication developing in the newly-released Western films.

Some of Ford's ideas during the making of *Stagecoach* were revolutionary in cinema at the time of the picture's release. Interior shots in the years prior to *Stagecoach* were largely filmed in studios where the lighting grid hanging from the ceilings provided the movie sets' illumination. Consequently, cameras never framed above the top of the rooms' walls. In *Stagecoach,* however, Ford read the passages from the script placing the story's characters trapped in the middle of dramatic tensions, especially when the traveling passengers were inside a deserted stage station bickering amongst themselves while hostile Indians were lurking outside. To literally illustrate the "roof collapsing on them," Ford felt it was important to break tradition and film the low ceilings within the frame to emphasize the claustrophobic human drama, trailblazing a new way of filming interiors (see Orson Welles' *Citizen Kane).*

In *Stagecoach,* the secret to John Wayne's on-screen presence is the camera lens' particular focus on the actor's eyes.

"Anybody can direct a picture once they know the fundamentals," said Ford. "Directing is not a mystery, it's not an art. The main thing about directing is: photograph the people's eyes. "

During the Indian chase sequence with the stagecoach, the script called for a number of Indians to be shot by the drivers and passengers on the stagecoach, sending their horses cascading to the ground. To achieve such an effect, the technique labeled the "Running W" had a strong, invisible thin wire attached to a metal post anchored to the terrain just out of frame. At the other end, the wire was attached to one of the horse's legs. As the horse with the stuntman riding on top galloped at full speed, the wire became taunt, sending the horse to the ground at the moment the Indian pretended he was shot. Many horses were killed as a result of this stunt, and the practice was eventually banned.

Stagecoach was the first of several Ford films to use Monument Valley located on the Arizona/Utah border, for its distinctive landscape as a backdrop for his Westerns. One reason for the shooting location was Ford loved the area's stunning visuals to compliment his unfolding narratives. Another reason was the monuments were near a Navajos reservation, giving employment to impoverished Indians by paying them to construct sets and to assist on his productions.

In 1946's *My Darling Clementine,* Ford, taking advantage of the valley's breathtaking setting (in contrast to the bland landscape where the original Tombstone, Arizona, town was situated) and knowing how appreciative the Navajos were for the income earned while employed on *Stagecoach,* scheduled his studio to spend $250,000 toward a replica of Tombstone next to the large rock formations.

Ford was fully aware of the devastating effects Western civilization had on the Native American population through the years.

"We've treated them badly, it's a blot on our shield," said Ford. "We've robbed, cheated, murdered and massacred them, but they kill one white man and God, out come the troops."

ENJOYING THE FRUITS OF *THE GRAPES OF WRATH*

Ford was awarded his second Best Director Oscar for *The Grapes of Wrath,* based John Steinbeck's Pulitzer Prize-winning novel. The year 1940 resulted in one of those unique career periods no other director has ever experienced before or since. His *The Long Voyage Home* alongside *Grapes* were both nominated for the 1940 Academy Awards' Best Picture. Alfred Hitchcock's *Rebecca* received the Academy's top prize, Best Picture, the only one in that category Hitch ever won. Greg Tolland, Hollywood's most creative cameraman during the time, assisted Ford on *Voyage.* The cinematographer is forever remembered for his work in Orson Welles' directorial debut the following year, filming the landmark movie *Citizen Kane.*

Soon after Nazi Germany invaded Poland in September, 1939, Adolf Hitler viewed *Grapes* several times. Drawing on the impression America was filled with downtrodden migrants as portrayed in the film and who, Hitler thought, would become the backbone of the United States fighting forces in case the United States went to war, the German dictator felt his army would simply walk over such gaunt, malnourished men and easily win the war.

Joseph Stalin, dictator of the Soviet Union, permitted the film to be viewed in his country in 1948, one of the very few American movies to be shown by the Communist regime. Stalin thought the movie dealing with capitalist owned mega-farming estates taking advantage of the mass of poor crop pickers living in Hooverville shacks would show the inequality between greedy rich kingpins and the poor proletariat. When the movie was screened in Russia, Stalin failed to realize the Soviet audiences viewing *Grapes* became envious of the Joads and their downtrodden friends. They saw these poor American proletariats driving a car, a luxury most Soviets couldn't afford or even obtain since automobiles were so scarce in the Soviet Union at the time.

FORD'S CAREER IN WARTIME

Ford won his second consecutive Oscar for Best Director for *How Green Was My Valley,* his personal favorite of all the movies he had directed. *Green* also won Best Picture against two of Hollywood's most celebrated films, *Citizen Kane* and *Maltese Falcon.* The win is considered one of the most improbable upsets in the history of the Academy. Ford called the Phillip Dunne screenplay as "nearly perfect a script as could be possible."

World War II was already blazing overseas in Europe before the United States became involved in the war with the Japanese attack on Pearl Harbor. Because of the German bombing campaign in England, the setting for *Green* about mining in Wales had to be filmed at a reconstructed Welsh village requiring 150 workers six months to build in the foothills of Malibu, California. The film, with the color green contained in the title, was planned to be shot in color, but the Southern California landscape was anything but green, so the movie was filmed in black and white.

Released in October, 1941, the picture became a huge audience grabber. *Green's* narrative detailing life and death in the coal mines, the separation of sons to the parents, and the changes of the Welsh town through economic stresses, coincided with the crisis *Green's* American viewers knew was about to face them personally soon after the Japanese dropped their bombs on Hawaii.

Green became Ford's last film he directed before heading into World War II in the Navy Reserves as head of the Office of Strategic Services photographic unit. The World War II assignment was not without its dangers. Ford was wounded in the arm from Japanese shrapnel during the Battle of Midway in 1942 while filming the aerial attack on the island of Midway. He later photographed the landing of American troops at Normandy during D-Day.

After witnessing the bloody savagery of the war in both theaters, Ford was able to make a statement on his combat experiences in allegorical fashion in 1946's *My Darling Clementine.*

Through a cathartic gunfight at the OK Corral, the wild town of Tombstone is transformed from anarchy to domestic tranquility, serving as a metaphor for Ford's return to a peaceful United States from the worn-torn Pacific and Europe.

Wyatt Earp, one of the town marshals in Tombstone during that fateful historic day, described to Ford when the young director was starting out in Hollywood how the events unfolded. But *Clementine* showed a different version than the one Ford had documented to a reporter years earlier. A film researcher noticed the difference between Earp's account (according to Ford) and the movie's. He questioned the director about the discrepancy. "Did you like the film?" asked Ford. It was one of his favorite pictures, replied the researcher. "Then what more do you want?" Ford responded.

AMBITION TO FILM HIS FAVORITE PROJECT

Ford always wanted to direct one of his most favorite scripts he had ever read, the Ireland-based *The Quiet Man.* Ford was contracted to Republic Pictures at the time and the studio green-lighted the project with the stipulation he would direct one additional Western movie before embarking to Ireland. Republic head Herbert Yates thought *The Quiet Man* was going to be a financial bust with the expensive Irish location and the projected lavish color filming. Ford had produced two other Westerns during the previous two years dealing with the U.S. Calvary, 1948's *Ft. Apache* and 1949's *She Wore A Yellow Ribbon*, both starring John Wayne. With 1950's *Rio Grande,* the movie Republic Pictures wanted him to direct, film historians claim these pictures are Ford's finest Westerns. The three films combined were soon packaged after *Rio Grande's* release as Ford's "Calvary Trilogy."

Ford considered *Rio Grande* a "vacation project," consisting of a relaxed cast and crew enjoying themselves throughout the shoot. *Rio Grande* was given only half the budget *Ft. Apache* received. The director's feelings toward the film was this was a "can't lose project," and the pressure was off him to produce a financially viable film. He did still feel resentment at the studio executives forcing him to direct the Western and he let his feelings known when Republic Studio head Yates and other studio executives happened to drop in unannounced on his Moab, Utah, set. As they arrived at 10 in the morning one day during the shoot, Yates asked Ford when he would begin to film. "Just as soon as you get off my set," Ford replied.

Rio Grande became one of Republic's most financially-successful films the studio ever released and is one of the highest regarded movies in the Ford canon. Once the director finished *Rio Grande,* he concentrated on his personal pet project, 1952's *The Quiet Man.*

Anyone who has been to Ireland knows the weather is not the country's main attraction. The lack of sun was especially challenging for cinematographer Winton Hoch and his crew. During the entire shoot, there were only six days of partial sunshine. Otherwise, clouds and rain ruled the day.

"Most of the time the clouds were moving across the sky, and the light was constantly changing," Hoch remembered. "I had to light each scene three different ways: for sunshine, for clouds, for rain. I worked out a set of signals with the gaffer, and we were ready no matter what the light was."

Viewing *The Quiet Man,* the film's admirers should give Hoch and company a pat on the back. But studio president Yates was not impressed. "It looks all green," observed Yates when seeing the daily rushes. The Irish greenery dominating the landscape probably had something to do with the color saturation.

The climatic fight in *The Quiet Man* between John Wayne and Victor McLaglen is one of the most thrilling and comical brawls in movie history. Republic executives insisted Ford trim the proposed two hours and nine minute length down to two hours to suit theater owners' tight scheduling. Ford said there was no way he could trim another minute of footage from the nearly completed film. A couple of days later, during the roll-out preview of the final print of the movie for the studio heads, everyone was enjoying the picture. Suddenly, during the middle of the fight sequence the screen went white and the lights in the theater went up, followed by a deathly silence. Ford informed the studio decision-makers he had stopped the film exactly at the two-hour mark. The executives were stunned. Ford followed up by questioning those responsible for shortening the movie what the viewers' opinion will be when the movie ends in the middle of the fight. Needless to say, Republic Studios changed its mind and let Ford continue the picture with the nine minutes left in the film reel. The additional length must have proven to be effective since *The Quiet Man* gave Ford his fourth and final Best Director Oscar.

As the end credits are ready to roll in *Quiet Man,* O'Hara whispers something in Wayne's ear. His reaction shows a wide-eyed startled look. Ford gave O'Hara an unscripted line to say to the Duke before shooting the concluding scene. The blushing actress told the director she could never repeat that line to Wayne. Ford figuratively twisted O'Hara's arm and she relented. The reaction on Wayne's face is priceless. Neither parties ever revealed what was said, and O'Hara, who died in 2015 at the age of 95, was the last one to take the comment secretly to her grave.

As stated earlier, Steven Spielberg is a huge Ford fan. He is known to watch two Ford movies before he directs his own films. Showing homage toward Ford, Spielberg borrowed a scene in *The Quiet Man* for his 1982 *E.T.: The Extraterrestrial,* where Wayne meets O'Hara inside his farmhouse early in the film and embraces her with a kiss. The sequence was one of the first scenes scheduled to be shot for *The Quiet Man.* On the set O'Hara broke her hand while she was slapping Wayne, who blocked her swinging arm. She suffered enormous pain throughout the remainder of the shoot since she couldn't be filmed wearing a cast.

THE BEST WESTERN EVER

With 1956's *The Searchers,* Ford produced what is universally regarded as one of the best, if not the best, Western of all time. Despite John Wayne winning a "sentimental" Best Actor's Oscar for his role in 1968's "True Grit," his portrayal in *The Searchers* of Ethan, a former Confederate soldier who journeys to his brother's ranch out West, only to see the family butchered and their two daughters kidnapped by Indians, is much more dramatic and riveting. Ethan is shaken by what he sees; an additional layer of Ethan's hatred toward the Indians is the tombstone one of the daughters, Debbie, hides behind during the initial raid. The inscription reads "Here lies Mary Jane Edwards killed by Commanches May 12, 1852. A good wife and mother in her 41st year." Mary is Ethan's mother.

Spielberg, Martin Scorsese and George Lucas all claim to have been heavily influenced by *The Searchers*. Spielberg watched the movie twice before filming his *Close Encounters of the Third Kind*. Notice the similarities between the UFO abduction of little Barry to the initial Comanche attack on the Edwards. Scorsese's *Taxi Driver* follows the similar guilt and paranoia seen in Ethan as Robert De Niro attempts to rescue a teenager from the clutches of an evil pimp. And Lucas's *Star Wars* has Luke discovering his parents' brutal death as Ethan does.

David Lean, assigned to direct 1962's *Lawrence of Arabia,* viewed *The Searchers* several times to gain a grasp of filming landscape scenes.

And singer Buddy Holly so loved the phrase repeatedly said by John Wayne, "That'll be the day," that he composed the song of the same title, now a classic.

DIRECTING ADVENTURES WITH HIS ACTORS

First-time actors for Ford were sometimes confused with his manner of directing. Constantly chewing on either his pipe or a handkerchief, Ford's verbal directions were confusingly scant.

"You never knew what he said," said actress Jean Arthur, who appeared in Ford's 1923 *Cameo Kirby* and his 1935 *The Whole Town's Talking,* referring to the director's mouthful of handkerchiefs. "I don't think he gave much direction, but everybody seemed to understand what they were supposed to do."

Yet Edward O'Brien, the newspaper editor in 1962's *The Man Who Shot Liberty Valence*, said Ford would spend an entire morning with him to hash out his lines. "In all the years, I have never enjoyed an acting experience so much."

O'Brien was one of the lucky ones to receive Ford's warm attention. The director's harsh treatment on some of his actors on the set is legendary: it has been claimed he was the only one to ever make John Wayne cry. His caustic remarks delivered in full earshot of film crews shrank Hollywood's mightiest. Whether such behavior was to draw the best out of his actors (his pictures are full of numerous Academy Award acting performances) or his apparent rudeness derived from his sarcastic Maine-Irish demeanor, Ford upset so many of the screen's superstars they refused to work with him again.

While filming Wayne's breakout role in *Stagecoach,* Ford was merciless to the Duke. Though Ford loved the first take for its spontaneity, in one scene where Wayne washes his face, Ford called for repeated takes. The director verbally abused him until Wayne's face turned raw from the repeated rubbings. "Can't you wash your face?" Ford barked, lacing each sentence with four letter profanities. "Wash your face! Don't you ever do that at home? You're dabbing your face!" Wayne admitted he wanted to kill Ford--but "Ford knew what he was doing," the actor said.

Claire Trevor remembers: "Ford put him through agonies on that picture. Duke was his whipping boy. Ford was only cruel when he had to be. He was trying to take away Duke's bad habits. I felt embarrassed for him, it was very upsetting, but he was improving every day. Ford gave him a style which he kept."

When *Stagecoach* came out, Wayne's performance elevated him out of the Grade B movie pits he had wallowed in for close to a decade and into stardom. Wayne could thank Ford with erasing his poor acting style developed during his Poverty-Row film studio years.

Wayne eventually turned out to be Ford's favorite actor to direct; Ford went so far as labeling the actor as the best in Hollywood.

But more than a few experienced actors refused to be subjected to Ford's sharp tongue. Andy Devine, the driver of the coach in *Stagecoach,* was lambasted by Ford. Devine was selected to be in the driver's seat because Ward Bond, who Ford wanted for hold the reins, couldn't handle the horses.

"You big tub of lard. I don't know why the hell I'm using you in this picture," yelled Ford at one point during the filming. Devine raspy retorted, "Because Ward Bond can't drive six horses."

Ford also ripped into Thomas Mitchell, whose role as a drunken former physician later earned him the Oscar for Best Supporting Actor in *Stagecoach*. Mitchell responded after receiving one of Ford's tirades, "Just remember: I saw *Mary of Scotland*." Mitchell was referring to Ford's 1936's *Mary of Scotland,* which starred Ford's fling Katherine Hepburn, and was considered not one of the director's better pictures.

Actress Doris Bowdon, Rosasharn in *The Grapes of Wrath,* found working for Ford difficult in the extreme. Not quite knowing why he was picking on her, Bowdon found herself on the receiving end of his barbs, always nick-picking on everything she did, which included Ford harping on her hairdo. The relationship came to a head when Bowdon approvingly applauded after co-star Jane Darwell nailed a difficult talk-while-you're-dancing number. Ford openly yelled at Bowdon for her spontaneous moment, sending the actress off the set in tears. Ford, never in the habit of apologizing, used some off-color joking the next day when Bowdon was scheduled to appear in her scene. Ford eased up on the actress thereafter, and the rest of the filming went smoothly. But Bowdon never forgot Ford's treatment.

"I was glad I never had to work with him again," said Bowdon.

But, as most performers who had been verbally beaten down by Ford, she recalls one emotional scene Bowdon was particularly apprehensive about where the director spent a considerable amount of his time to go over. Because of Ford's coaching, she credited him of giving her the ability to perform the scene in only one take.

"He was a superb director," she said. "I never saw another director work in a way that was as skilled."

Sara Allgood, an Irish actress who played the matriarch for the Morgan family in *How Green Was My Valley* and who was nominated for Best Supporting Actress for her role, was one of the few females who stood her ground to Ford. During one scene where she was unhappy about the script, Allgood had to say certain lines and move a certain way which made her uncomfortable. Screenwriter Philip Dunne happened to be nearby on the set. Ford told the writer Allgood's concerns. Dunne, who could read Ford like a book, ripped the pages the actress was criticizing from the script folio and said, "Now, this settles that."

Allgood was impressed, until Ford countered, "The sonofabitching writer won't do anything to help us, so we'll have to shoot it the way he wrote it."

Ford did not like to be corrected on set, even from a leading actress. Maureen O'Hara, in the same movie, noticed the basket where the women were dropping their earrings into was not a period piece belonging to the era when *Green* takes place. The actress saw the container was a modern Kraft basket. She interrupted filming to say the basket was wrong. Ford became furious, told O'Hara to leave the set and wait on top of a nearby hill and to remain there until summoned. O'Hara waited, waited and waited until an assistant to Ford called her back to the set. Nothing was said between the two when she returned, but she noticed the basket had been changed to an older version while she was gone.

Despite O'Hara appearing in three Ford films, the director wasn't exactly enamored with the actress.

"Maureen O'Hara is one of the actresses I most dislike," recalled Ford. "Everybody thought I was her lover. Actually, I hated her and she hated me, but she was right for the parts."

Toward the end of *The Quiet Man*, the script called for Wayne to literally drag O'Hara across the field from the railway station to her brother, played by Victor McLaglen, conducting business in the distance. Ford and Wayne kicked several clogs of sheep dung on the path so O'Hara could be dragged through the muck. She witnessed what two were doing, and asked some friends to kick the clogs out of the pathway. Wayne and Ford saw O'Hara and company were ruining their plans and kicked the piles back on the path. This went back and forth until it was time to shoot the scene, with the piles remaining on the pathway. The movie shows O'Hara being dragged through the field over the excrement.

"Duke had the time of his life dragging me through it," said O'Hara. "It was bloody awful. After the scene was over, Mr. Ford had given instructions that I was not to be brought a bucket of water or a towel. He made me keep it on for the rest of the day. I was mad as hell, but I had to laugh, too. Isn't showbiz glamorous?"

Ford's acerbic personality didn't wane as he got older. Walter Brennan disliked John Ford so much from his experience on *Clementine* the actor vowed never to work with him again. One time when Brennan was having a little trouble getting into the saddle, Ford yelled, "Can't you even mount a horse?" Brennan shot back, "No, but I got three Oscars for acting!"

The one actor who seemed to have the luxury of not irritating Ford on the set was Lee Marvin, who appeared in *The Man Who Shot Liberty Valence*. Some speculate Marvin's acting was perfect in the eyes of Ford as well as the director appreciating his service in the Marine Corps during World War II. The actor's honesty also helped Marvin in his relationship with the director, especially during one occasion when the actor saw Ford arriving on the set and began loudly whistling through his teeth as the director settled into his chair. Everyone braced for what surely would be a long tirade of Ford confronting Marvin about disturbing the cast and crew. But Ford simply smiled. Later he revealed Marvin was whistling the Navy admiral's notes signaling the director was "on board" his vessel.

FORD'S ADMIRERS

Ford's smooth and distinct style is evident in all the film productions he directed over the years. Even though the stringent studio system hamstrung even the best of the film directors during that constricting era, Ford's unique handicraft always came through on the large screen.

"For a director there are commercial rules that it is necessary to obey," he related. "In our profession, an artistic failure is nothing; a commercial failure is just a verbal sentence. The secret is to make films that please the public and also allow the director to reveal his personality."

Ford advised young aspiring directors throughout his later years. One movie-obsessed young man working at Universal Studios came into his office one day seeking his sagacious cinematic wisdom. Ford pointed at two pictures on the wall showing landscape scenes, one with the horizon favoring the upper half of the print, the other favoring the bottom half. Ford cut the interview short by saying "When you know why the horizon goes at the top of the frame or the bottom of a frame, then you're a director." The young man left his office, absorbing what Ford had just said. That twenty-something year old was none other than Steven Spielberg.

Ford famously said, "I love making pictures but I don't like talking about them."

Akira Kurosawa revealed, "I have respected John Ford from the beginning. Needless to say, I pay close attention to his productions, and I think I am influenced by them." Alfred Hitchcock, meanwhile, loved the look of a Ford film. "A John Ford film was a visual gratification."

And Swedish director Ingmar Bergman labeled Ford simply "the best director in the world."

Pat O'Brian, who starred in several Ford movies, aptly described the master's directing style.

"John Ford is the orderly type. Working for him is like being part of a ballet. He hardly ever moves the camera, but composes his shots like a master painter, a Rembrandt or Degas. The actor becomes part of the scene. Ford lets the action swirl past his lens. But the reality of his sailors, miners, dust-bowlers, horse soldiers, or western heroes, when he is at his best, is a literature that the screen rarely gets. Working for him one feels a special pride. Lewis Milestone is a bouncing camera mover. For him the seeing eye is all. He stands the camera on its head, rolls it, rushes it, brings it in on the run. The actors are part of the scenery, and they must fight to survive, come alive while he catches them on the run. Neither men are static directors. They don't care for too much talk in their script, or stage business over meaningless chatter."

Once Hollywood's busiest director, Ford would be eased out of the industry late in life. As time wore on, he found himself afflicted with cancer. It was reported that on Ford's deathbed, the priest was performing the last rites on the seemingly comatose patient, going on and on. Suddenly, the old man opened his eyes and said "Cut!" before passing away.

TOP TEN BEST JOHN FORD MOVIES

#1--THE SEARCHERS (1956)

Considered the greatest Western ever. Scott McGee in Turner Classics noted: "More than just making a social statement like other Westerns of the period were apt to do, Ford instills in *The Searchers* a visual poetry and a sense of melancholy that is rare in American films and rarer still to Westerns." This is the movie where high schooler Natalie Wood, playing the older Debbie, would be picked up at school by John Wayne or Jeffrey Hunter among others when she was required to be on the set. Also, a memorable anecdote occurred when Ford was reportedly stung by a scorpion while he was in his trailer waiting for the crew to set up the next scene. Financial backer C.V. Whitney tugged at John Wayne and nervously asked, "What if we lose him? What are we going to do?" A concerned Wayne said he would go into Ford's trailer to check on his condition. Whitney waited several minutes before Wayne emerged. The actor said, "It's O.K. John's fine, it's the scorpion that died."

#2--THE QUIET MAN (1952)

With the exteriors filmed in County Mayo and County Galway, *The Quiet Man* is Ford homage to his Irish roots. Wayne and O'Hara have never been better as this romantic comedy-drama is frothy with each sequence. Watch the final fight where McLaglen's first punch flinches Wayne, causing The Duke's toupee to adjust a bit and showing his receding hairline. Empire Magazine said of *The Searchers,* "John Wayne at his best, striking cinematography and character ambiguity makes this a powerful and thought-provoking Wild West Odyssey."

#3--STAGECOACH (1939)

Rejuvenated the American Western genre that reintroduced John Wayne back to the Grade A circuit. A journey through Arizona to New Mexico via a stagecoach by a group of diverse people, each with a clouded past, achieves high melodrama surrounded by deadly adventures. Variety stated, "Directorially, production is John Ford in peak form, sustaining interest and suspense throughout, and presenting exceptional characterizations. Picture is a display of photographic grandeur."

#4--GRAPES OF WRATH (1940)

Ford directed what is considered one of the great "Great Depression" films of all-time. In Variety, this reviewer said "Here is outstanding entertainment, projected against a heart-rending sector of the American scene...It possesses an adult viewpoint and its success may lead other producers to explore the rich field of contemporary life which films long have neglected and ignored."

#6--MY DARLING CLEMENTINE (1945)

Henry Fonda stars as Wyatt Earp in Ford's version of the gunfight at OK Corral. The movie is concerned with more than a simple gun battle. *Clementine* shows the progression from a lawless town into a civilizing one. Said film critic Bosley Crowther: "The eminent director, John Ford, is a man who has a way with a Western like nobody in the picture trade...Every scene, every shot is the product of a keen and sensitive eye—an eye which has deep comprehension of the beauty of rugged people and a rugged world."

#7--HOW GREEN WAS MY VALLEY (1941)

An economic downdraft affecting a Welch mine hits the town dependent on prosperity as well as the mining families in this gripping remembrance of the youngest Morgan boy, played by Roddy McDowall. Reportedly Clint Eastwood's favorite movie, *Green* is also known for receiving the Best Picture Oscar over two of cinema's most highly regarded films of all-time, *Citizen Kane* and *Maltese Falcon*. Film reviewer Whitney Seibold said of *Green*, "There are a lot of rich characters and good instances of moral outrage. It may not be better than *Citizen Kane*, but it's still a pretty darn good movie."

#8—THE MAN WHO SHOT LIBERTY VALENCE (1962)

Ford's last classic. The director clashed with Wayne on the set during the filming of *Liberty*, partly because Ford was resentful of Wayne, who had hired Ford to direct a few scenes in Wayne's 1960 *The Alamo*, but had barely used any of them in the final release. Also, Paramount Pictures insisted Wayne had to be in the movie after Ford was hesitant to use the actor for the role of Doniphon. Ford's pent up anger at the studio's strong arming spilled over onto Wayne, with the director needling him for not being a four-year college football player to his lack of military service during World War II, while actors war veterans Lee Marvin and James Stewart were praised in front of Wayne. In the end, Ford saw the power of Wayne's acting, saying "Wayne was the central character, the motivation for the whole thing."

#9—RIO GRANDE (1950)

Known as the final film of Ford's *Calvary Trilogy* produced within a three-year period. *Grande's* premise is reflected in the contemporary time the film was produced, when the Korean War was raging. The US Calvary was obligated to honor a Mexican treaty prohibiting its northern neighbor from crossing the border to attack marauding Indians, similar to the US Army's restriction of crossing over from Korea to China to hunt down members of the Communist Army. *Grande* marks the first of five movies Wayne and O'Hara appeared in together, and the first of three directed by Ford.

#10—JUDGE PRIEST (1934)

Seeing satirist writer and actor Will Rogers perform as a Southern judge is reason enough to view this early Ford film. The performance of African-American actor Stepin Fetchit, who was criticized for playing in stereotyped slow-witted roles, is priceless as Roger's assistant. Fetchit shows how he was actually one of the most successful 1930's actors possessing an extreme intelligence throughout his career. Rising star Hattie McDaniels, who became the first African-American to win an Oscar for her performance in 1939's *Gone With The Wind,* displays her grace as Aunt Dilsey. McDaniels' singing duet with Rogers is one of the many highlights in *Judge*.

FRANK CAPRA

THE GENIUS WHO LOVED PEOPLE

Admirers tag film director Frank Capra's sentimental movies as "Capraesque." Detractors bemoan his pictures as "Capra-corn."

But there is no disputing Capra left his indelible trademark on today's top tier directors such as Steven Spielberg, Ron Howard, David Lynch, Oliver Stone and Martin Scorsese. His spotlight on the individual, his fast-paced dialogue and editing, and his movies' memorable characters all prevail on the modern screen. As such, Capra's stature in cinema, with a record three Best Director Oscars in one decade during the 1930's, is unparalleled.

Capra's trailblazing achievements include: originator of screwball comedies, elevating "feel-good" entertainment, and showcasing the "common man," the American individual as seen in Mr. Deeds, Mr. Smith, and John Doe, with their heroic ideals battling against the collective evil. Each of Capra's films also contains moral implications emphasizing the values and ethical principles of his characters contained within his storylines. After producing several films with those themes in mind, he was asked if there was still a way to make films with such a message. "Well if there isn't, we might as well give up," Capra responded.

THE EASY-GOING FILM DIRECTOR

As a director, Capra was easily approachable. Gregarious and friendly, Capra has been labeled the "actors' director." When the cameras rolled, Capra made it known to members of his technical crew they couldn't make any mistakes. "You guys are working for the actors," he would tell them. "They're not working for you."

Such loyalty to those in front of the camera drew out memorable performances from Jimmy Stewart, Jean Arthur, and Barbara Stanwyck among others.

"It was inspirational to work with Capra," recalled assistant cameraman Al Keller. "We felt that working with him, we were the elite."

Capra's magic with his performers translated onto the awards stage. He directed eight actors in Academy Award-nominated performances: May Robson for Best Actress in 1933's *Lady For A Day,* Gary Cooper for Best Actor in 1937's *Mr. Deeds Goes To Town,* H.B. Warner for Best Supporting Actor in 1938's *Lost Horizon,* Spring Byington for Best Supporting Actress in 1938's *You Can't Take It With You,* James Stewart (twice) in 1939's *Mr. Smith Goes To Washington* and in 1946's *It's A Wonderful Life,* Claude Rains and Harry Carey, both getting Best Supporting Actor nominations in *Mr. Smith,* and Peter Falk, Best Supporting Actor in 1962's *Pocketful of Miracles.* Clarke Gable and Claudette Colbert won Oscars for Best Actor and Actress for their roles in 1934's *It Happened One Night.*

Capra loved working with certain actors, especially Gable. The director would listen to his actors and adopt some of their better suggestions. When filming Gable undressing in the same motel room as Claudette Colbert in *It Happened One Night,* once he unbuttoned and took off his outer shirt the actor had trouble removing his undershirt while still keeping up his constant humorous banter. The scene also took too much time to unfold. Gable suggested he discard the undershirt, a piece of clothing men always wore in those days, even in the hottest weather. Capra agreed and on screen Gable is seen bare chested after taking off his buttoned shirt. Men thought the look was cool and undershirt sales plummeted.

Capra saw Gable's performance in *Night* as a departure from the macho screen persona Hollywood studios developed for the actor soon after his Oscar-winning performance.

"He was never able to play that kind of character except in that one film," said Capra on Gable and his role as an unemployed newspaper reporter in *Night.* "They had him playing these big, huff-and-puff he-man lovers, but he was not that kind of guy. He was a down-to-earth guy, he loved everything, he got down with the common people. He didn't want to play those big lover parts; he just wanted to play Clark Gable, the way he was in *It Happened One Night,* and it's too bad they didn't let him keep up with that."

Another actor Capra felt didn't live up to his acting potential was singer/actor Frank Sinatra, whom he directed in 1959's *A Hole in The Head.* Late in his directing career, Capra thought Sinatra had the potential of being the greatest actor in cinematic history. Capra recalled a time when he advised Sinatra to give up his singing career and focus on his acting since the director was convinced he would be right up there with the greats. In fact, Capra wanted to produce a film on Saint Paul, which was never realized, with Sinatra in the starring role.

CAPRA: GENERATOR OF IDEAS

Despite having an open ear to his actors' suggestions during the filming process, Capra came up with ideas of his own which improved the movies he was working on as well as revolutionized some aspects of the motion picture industry as a whole.

The idea of the "Walls of Jericho" where a bedsheet was draped across the room in *Night* was the director's when Colbert said she didn't want to undress in front of the camera. Capra had to think fast on a solution to the scene to address the actress' qualms. Hiding Colbert behind the sheet while Gable was bantering away on the other side solved the problem.

During his days working with comedian Harry Langdon, Capra remembered how the silent movie star would wear certain clothes to make himself appear younger. He took Langdon's dressing practices and applied them to Gary Cooper during the opening scene of *Mr. Deeds Goes To Town* to make him look innocent and not as old as he actually was in real life. Capra made Cooper wear a bow tie with a jacket that was too short and tight for him to achieve the innocence of his the script called for.

Capra recognized others who contributed to his films' successes. Joe Walker, his primary cinematographer, produced a Capra look which goes straight from the eye to the heart. His screenwriter, Richard Riskin, was so crucial in producing award-winning Capra scripts. Riskin's screenplays had audiences cheering at the end while wiping away the tears at the same time.

Early in his Columbia Pictures days, Capra was asked by studio head Harry Cohn to audition an up-and-coming actress, Barbara Stanwyck, for Capra's 1930 film *Lady of Leisure.* Stanwyck, a stage actress, had been in three film failures and wanted to return to the stage. During the interview with Stanwyck, Capra sensed her hesitation and turned her down for the role.

The popular actor Frank Fay, Stanwyck's husband, dialed up Capra and said his wife came home crying. Capra told him it seemed she didn't want the part.

"Frank, she's young, and shy, and she's been kicked around out here." explained Fay. "Let me show you a test she made at Warner's."

Fay brought over the film. Capra saw the clip of Stanwyck, was impressed, and hired her for the lead. *Ladies of Leisure* was a hit and catapulted Stanwyck's career to stardom.

Capra knew how to calm down the very nervous actress Jean Arthur right before the cameras cranked. Ms. Arthur would get violently sick before stepping on the set, but remarkably, once Capra yelled "Action!" Arthur would appear like nothing was wrong and stepped right into her role.

"Never have I seen a performer with such a chronic case of stage jitters," recalled Capra on Arthur's fears. "They weren't butterflies in her stomach. They were wasps."

CAPRA'S FAST DIRECTING STYLE

Capra saw *Night* as something magical that agreed with his fast paced filming philosophy.

"We made the picture really quickly--four weeks," Capra said during an interview. "We stumbled through it, we laughed our way through it. And this goes to show you how much luck and timing and being in the right place at the right time means in show business; how sometimes no preparation at all is better than all the preparation in the world, and sometimes you need great preparation, but you can never out-guess this thing called creativity. It happens in the strangest places and under the strangest of circumstances. But I didn't care much for the picture (*Night*)."

Neither did Claudette Colbert, who constantly complained nearly every day on and off the set. On the last day of the shoot she told a friend, "I just finished making the worst picture I've ever made."

Colbert's negative attitude bled onto the sound stage, making Capra's life somewhat difficult. "Colbert fretted, pouted, and argued about her part," Capra said. "She constantly challenged my slap happy way of shooting scenes. Fussed constantly. She was a tartar, but a cute one."

Colbert didn't think she had a snowball chance in Hades to win an Oscar for her performance in *Night* despite her nomination for Best Actress. She was waiting for a train at the Los Angeles station dressed in traveling clothes waiting to go to Arizona when an Academy representative hailed her on the train's platform and told her she had just won the Oscar. Colbert was asked to go to the ceremonies still in progress and give her acceptance speech. There is existing film footage of the actress dressed in very informal attire being handed her Best Actress Oscar.

Night ended up receiving "The Big Five" at the 7th Academy Awards: Best Picture, Best Actor, Best Actress, Best Director and Best Screenplay, the first of only three pictures to do so in Academy history. (The other two are 1975's *One Flew Over The Cuckoos' Nest* and 1992's *The Silence of the Lambs*.)

Capra's directing style was unique. He believed the first take, without any flubs, was the best. Stanwyck reinforced his impression on the first take being the best during her on-screen debut for Capra. Sparks shot out of her like lightning bolts on the first go-around, according to the director, but Capra witnessed subsequent takes wilted her energy and performance.

Capra's life-long insistence on minimal rehearsals on the set drove perfectionist Edward G. Robinson crazy in 1959's *A Hole In The Head*. The actor was used to conducting multiple rehearsals and felt totally uncomfortable with the director's quick work.

Capra's fast directing habits were derived partially as a result of being under the frugal thumb of Columbia Pictures president Harry Cohn. The studio head countermanded all his directors' more expensive decisions because of projected high costs (in his estimation). Cohn's policy was to limit his directors to print just one take from the numerous shots they may have filmed for a scene. Cohn figured the restriction would keep down film printing costs. Capra, always thinking, found a way around Cohn's print rule. At the end of each take, instead of shouting "Cut," he would command "Do it again." As the cameras continued to roll, the actors would redo their scenes until Capra was satisfied.

Like most directors who hated to work in front of studio executives' observing eyes, Capra found a way to keep control of his set when the occasion arose. Whenever Cohn arrived while filming was in progress, Capra would call a 30-minute coffee break. The practice cost Columbia Pictures time, so Cohn rarely paid a visit to a Capra movie set after seeing coffee recesses breaking out whenever his presence was made. After Capra won the Best Director Oscar for *Night*, he had his contract reworked with Columbia Studios. One of the stipulations was banning Cohn from visiting the set altogether while Capra was working. Never would Capra have to worry again about his studio boss looking over his shoulder.

Compounding his "one-take" philosophy was Capra's desire to film multiple angles of the same scene at the same time. Several cameras were used to achieve this during particular scenes, making his lighting directors' jobs more difficult. Getting the uniformed atmospheric lighting true to all cameras was complicated in the extreme. Consequently, Capra had to keep his cameras stationary.

"He didn't move the cameras all over so that you were conscious of them," said Stewart. "The long filibuster scene in *Mr. Smith*--you know I talked forever--I only found out later that he had six cameras recording." Because the cameras weren't moving, Stewart said he soon forgot about them.

The usage of multiple cameras shooting simultaneously in one scene is highly unusual in Hollywood practices. While editing the filibuster sequence in *Mr. Smith* Capra inserted numerous reaction shots of the chamber's spectators while Stewart was speaking. He wanted their reactions to coordinate with the emphasis Stewart put on particular portions of his speech. For Capra the only way to get a natural flow of such facial reactions was to set up and film the scene using a multi-camera operation.

"We might still be there," Capra said reacting to the hypothetical if the studio forced him to use the standard one-camera shoot. He noted his technical team "devised a multiple-camera, multiple-sound method of shooting which enabled us, in one big equipment move, to film as many as a half-dozen separate scenes before we made another big move."

The Senate chamber used in *Mr. Smith* was a recreated set of the United States Capitol Senate chambers built on the Columbia lot. The set contained four sides seating hundreds of people. Those cameras had to record the action on three levels: the Senate floor, the rostrum where the Vice President (actor Harry Carey) sat, and the galleries holding the press, the pages, and the public.

"How to light, photograph, and record hundreds of scenes on three levels of a deep well, open only at the top, were the logistic nightmares that faced electricians, cameramen, and soundmen," remembers Capra.

All that footage, consisting of hundreds of reaction shots, helped Capra enormously in post-production, where his rapid cross-cutting produced a frenetic pace described in the script.

QUICKENS THE RHYTHM OF CINEMA

Capra learned early on the difference between what he witnessed in the director's chair versus what he was watching on the big screen. He noticed the pace of the finished picture wasn't the same as what he observed live on the studio sound stage as well as what he saw while viewing the raw footage and the dailies on a small screen. Capra's early movies appeared to him to be much slower on the big screen than what he had experienced in shooting. Capra surmised the projection on the screen increased the size of his camera frame, slowing down the movements between the actors when they appeared on the screen in movie theaters.

Capra decided to take directorial steps to increase the pace of his movies on the large screen. He eliminated his actors' long entrances and exits in and out of a wide-shot frame, a standard practice directors did in the early 1930's films to sustain a wide-shot throughout. Instead, he had his actors walk a couple of steps toward the primary focal point in the frame as well as walk away, all done in medium shots rather than expansive wide shots. In addition, instead of using a gradual dissolve in editing, Capra would cut into the next scene by notating the changes in time or location.

He was one of the first directors to deliberately overlap dialogue between two or more people. This was a radical departure from the early talkies when actors were told to let the other actors finish their lines completely and pause before speaking. The pause-and-talk practice gave editors the ability to cut between camera shots and not have to worry about picking up dialogue in mid-sentence, something that slowed the rhythm of movies.

When Capra first implemented his newfound ideas into his 1932 film *American Madness*, he was scared, especially with the movie containing numerous scenes of crowds. He was worried the accelerated pace was too frenetic when he was filming the hordes of people. But it worked for Capra as well as the other viewers who saw the movie in the theaters. The quickened pace was especially appropriate by giving the film a sense of urgency, showing desperate bank depositors attempting to take their money out of the bank in the midst of a financial panic. More importantly, the quicker pace throughout the film kept his audience's attention riveted to the screen.

Capra, with the exception of filming scenes calling for slower measures, such as love scenes, continued to use the techniques he adopted in *American Madness* for all his future film.

CAPRA'S EARLY BEGINNINGS

Capra's rise to fame wasn't an easy climb for this influential film director. He experienced fierce highs and lows by working for small movie studios as well as employed as a gag writer for film producer Mack Sennett, Keystone Cops fame, early in his career. Capra left Sennett in 1927 to direct a First National Studio film set in New York City, *For the Love of Mike*. The movie was Claudette Colbert's debut in front of the camera, and the actress and Capra fought like tigers. Besides problems on the set, Capra went over budget. National refused to pay him, the picture was a flop, and Capra, with empty pockets, had to hitchhike cross-country back to his home in Los Angeles.

He returned to Sennett as a writer. Harry Cohn, the head of Columbia Pictures saw the potential of Capra's by viewing his early movies and hired the hungry director along with his small salary. Cohn thought he made a mistake when he saw the initial dailies of Capra's first film for Columbia, 1928's *That Certain Thing*.

Cohn was astonished to see every shot the first day from Capra were long shots, something the studio head had never seen before. The second day's shooting consisted of medium shots, further infuriating Cohn. The third day, just close-ups.

Cohn called Capra into his office, furious and ready to fire his new film director. He asked Capra for a convincing explanation.

"I did it that way for time," Capra explained to Cohn. "Other directors shoot a long shot, then they would have to change the setup to shoot a medium shot, then they would take their close-ups. Then they would come back and start over again. See?" Cohn nodded his head. Yes, that's the way it should be done, the studio president said. Capra continued, "You lose time, you see, moving the cameras and the big, heavy lights. I told my crew, 'I'll get all the long shots on that first set first, then all the medium shots, and then the close-ups.' I wouldn't shoot the whole scene each way unless it was necessary. If I knew that part of it was going to play in long shot, I wouldn't shoot that part in close-up. But the trick is not to move nine times, just to move three times. This saves a day, maybe two days."

Cohn was sold.

That Certain Thing was a hit, and Capra was on his way to becoming the front-line film director for Columbia.

Columbia felt they had a bonafide hit on its hands in Capra's 1933 film, *Lady For A Day*. In fact, the movie was up for the Academy Awards' Best Picture nomination as well as Capra for Best Director.

At the Ambassador Hotel in Los Angeles, on March 16, 1934, Capra was fixated by the great odds of his winning the Best Director Oscar. When ceremony host Will Rogers opened the envelope for Best Director, he said, "Well, well, well. What do you know? I've watched this young man for a long time. Saw him come up from the bottom, and I mean the bottom. It couldn't have happened to a nicer guy. Come on up and get it, Frank!"

Capra was overwhelmed. Here he won the award he was dreaming about for weeks. Getting up out of his chair, Capra squeezed past several tables (the ceremonies were held in a dinner-table setting back then) and walked to the open dance floor to accept his Oscar.

Capra remembers in agonizing detail: "The spotlight searched around trying to find me. 'Over here!' I waved. Then it suddenly swept away from me -- and picked up a flustered man standing on the other side of the dance floor - Frank Lloyd!"

The director of *Cavalcade*, which later garnered the Best Picture award, went up to the dais to accept the Oscar while a voice in back of Capra yelled, "Down in front!"

Capra said the walk back to his table amidst shouts of "Sit down!" turned into the "Longest, saddest, most shattering walk in my life. I wished I could have crawled under the rug like a miserable worm. When I slumped in my chair I felt like one."

"Big 'stupido,'" Capra thought to himself, "running up to get an Oscar dying with excitement, only to crawl back dying with shame. Those crummy Academy voters; to hell with their lousy awards. If ever they did vote me one, I would never, never, NEVER show up to accept it."

Capra would ultimately win three Oscars for directing as well as being voted the president for the Academy of Motion Picture Arts and Sciences four times. He was also a founding member of the Directors Guild of America where he became president three times.

His first Oscar was for 1934's mega-hit *It Happened One Night*. The Oscar evening was also a big one for actor Clark Gable, the Best Actor award winner that year. He spontaneously gave the Oscar to a child who told the actor he thought the golden statuette was pretty. Gable told the boy the gratification for him was winning the statue, not owning it. Following Gable's death in 1960, the boy, now an adult, gave the Oscar to Gable's widow.

THE "SCIENTIFIC" FILM DIRECTOR

As a chemical engineering student in college, Capra later in life was always intrigued about searching for technological ways to create certain effects in his movies. There are numerous scenes in *It's A Wonderful Life* showing falling snow, something which never happens in Hollywood where the picture was filmed. Because of Southern California high temperatures and the hot lights, movie studios' normal practice was to use cornflakes painted white for falling snow. When *Life* was being filmed the temperatures soared into the 90s. As Capra was shooting the bridge sequences near the river, Steward is visibly sweating because of the scorching heat. Also, Stewart's run through fictional Bedford Falls streets in the middle of a snowstorm near the end of the movie was filmed on a summer-like evening.

The trouble with cornflakes falling is they are loud when hitting the ground and make a crunching sound when actors walk over them. In the past, the loud noise didn't pose any problems since the actors' dialogue was dubbed later in sound-proof booths. However, Capra wanted to record the sound live. He had his technicians experiment with the chemical foam that comes out of fire extinguishers and blend the substance with soap and water. This mixture was then pumped through a wind machine using very high pressure, thus creating silent, falling snow.

Six thousand gallons of the mixture were required throughout the filming to create the illusion of a snowstorm on the steamy Los Angeles movie sound stage. An Oscar for Scientific or Technical Award was given to the technical team for its development of the new method for making snow for movies.

It's A Wonderful Life isn't just remembered for its technical advances. If there is one film today's audiences know of Capra's, *Life* is the one. This James Stewart/Donna Reed feel-good vehicle is shown a number of times annually on television leading up to the Christmas holiday.

Based on Philip Van Doren Stern's 1939 short story, *The Greatest Gift,* Capra was immediately hooked on producing the tale for a movie.

"My goodness, this thing hit me like a ton of bricks," remembered Capra. "It was the story I had been looking for all my life. The kind of an idea that when I get old and sick and scared and ready to die - they'd say 'He made *The Greatest Gift.*"

The short story and the resultant script hit a personal note in Capra's life. "*It's a Wonderful Life* sums up my philosophy of filmmaking," Capra said. "First, to exalt the worth of the individual. Second, to champion man - plead his causes, protest any degradation of his dignity, spirit or divinity. And third, to dramatize the viability of the individual - as in the theme of the film itself. There is a radiance and glory in the darkness, could we but see, and to see we only have to look. I beseech you to look."

Even though he loved the story, Capra didn't necessarily think the plot would fly in the movie capital. "There is one word that aptly describes Hollywood: 'nervous,'" Capra famously said.

RKO Studios eventually sold the project to Capra's independent film company, Liberty Films, and after several rough drafts, with the assistance of Capra's touch to the final script, the film director went on to produce today's annual ritual. The director said of its growing popularity on the TV screen after its initial box office failure when first released: "It's the damnedest thing I've ever seen! The film has a life of its own now, and I can look at it like I had nothing to do with it. I'm like a parent whose kid grows up to be president. I'm proud, but it's the kid who did the work. I didn't even think of it as a Christmas story when I first ran across it. I just liked the idea."

Capra pointed to one of the reasons why the movie has such an endearing quality was lead actor, James Stewart, and his popularity on the screen: "His appeal lay in being so unusually usual."

Life became Stewart's favorite film the actor ever appeared.

Donna Reed, who played the squeaky-clean librarian/wife to Stewart in *Life*, would say later in her career the sexism in Hollywood, with the exception of Capra, was so overwhelming. "Forty pictures I was in, and all I remember is 'What kind of bra will you be wearing today, honey?' That was always the area of big decision - from the neck to the navel." Reed went on after *Life* to win an acting Oscar for playing a prostitute in 1953's *From Here To Eternity.*

Capra later commented on his leading ladies showing their subtle sexuality, comparing them to Marilyn Monroe. "Breasts she (Monroe) had," Capra said. "And a wiggly figure. But to me sex is class, something more than a wiggly behind. If it weren't, I know 200 whores who would be stars."

At the conclusion of almost every Capra film, especially *Life,* weepy viewers emerge from the dark theaters emotionally overcome by Capra's sentimental magic displayed on the screen. He originally thought early in his career that "drama was when the actors cried. But drama is when the audience cries."

As Angel Second Class Clarence demonstrates to George Bailey one person's enormous influence in *Life,* Capra's affirmation of the significance of a human being's life was the perfect anecdote to America's challenges during the confusing post-World War II years.

"Compassion is a two-way street," said Capra.

Happily married to Lucille Warner since 1928, Capra noted "Behind every successful man there stands an astonished woman."

Like most film directors in this book, Capra couldn't bear giving up his director's chair. But like most veteran film directors, cinematic changes in themes, appearances and attitude leave those aging directors behind.

"Film is a disease," Capra explained in his reluctance to abandon his film career. "When it infects your bloodstream, it takes over as the number one hormone; it bosses the enzymes; directs the pineal gland; plays Iago to your psyche. As with heroin, the antidote to film is more film."

He was able, however, to impart several pieces of wisdom to up-and-coming film directors late in his life.

"My advice to young filmmakers is this: Don't follow trends. Start them!" Capra would tell them. "There are no rules in filmmaking. Only sins. And the cardinal sin is dullness."

When Capra accepted his Lifetime Achievement Award from the American Film Institute in 1982, he boiled down his career's philosophy in a succinct few words, "The art of Frank Capra is very, very simple: It's the love of people. Add two simple ideals: the freedom of each individual, and the dual importance of each individual, and you have the principle upon which I based all my films."

TOP TEN FRANK CAPRA FILMS

#1--IT'S A WONDERFUL LIFE (1946)

A main staple on television during the Christmas holiday season, Capra's endearing classic affirms each individual's importance and mark in life. The finale is about as stirring a finish as ever produced in Hollywood. Australia's David Stratton, film critic, noted "I love it, corny as it may be, because it reminds every one of us that we all make contributions to the people around us, contributions we ourselves don't even realize."

#2--MR. SMITH GOES TO WASHINGTON (1939)

Anytime politicians walk out of a movie theater showing the exposure of corruption in the nation's capital, as they did during this movie's October, 1939, premier in Constitution Hall, Washington, D.C., the film is considered a success in getting its message across. Jimmy Stewart's climatic filibuster speech is one of the emotional highlights in cinematic history. Eric Mellon said of *Mr. Smith,* "It isn't a political film at all. In fact, it draws its power from its simple underdog story and its modern resonance from the fact that little has changed since then."

#3--IT HAPPENED ONE NIGHT (1935)

The first movie to ever win all five major Academy Awards (Best Picture, Best Director, Best Actor, Best Actress and Best Screenplay), Capra's comedy is still entertainingly funny today. So many highlights are in this film, such as the hitchhiking scene, the "Walls of Jericho" sequence, the singing in the bus are all classics of the big screen. As film critic Christopher Machell wrote, "*It Happened One Night* is as lively, witty and romantic as ever. Buoyed up by dual performances from two of the era's greats, Capra's film maintains its status as a classic."

#4--MR. DEEDS GOES TO TOWN (1936)

Capra takes on the greedy business establishment in this Gary Cooper vehicle. Cooper inherits a fortune from a distant relative and the sharks hover around trying to suck the last penny out of the idealist figure. Brad Laidman described *Mr. Deeds,* "It's tough enough to film a credible morality play without being laughed out of town. It's altogether mind boggling to do so and provide a grade A romantic comedy to boot."

#5--YOU CAN'T TAKE IT WITH YOU (1938)

Best Picture winner of the 11th Academy Awards, this film portrays an eccentric family standing up to a banker's proposed building development in its neighborhood. Lionel Barrymore, suffering from crippling arthritis and later Mr. Potter in *Life*, gives a bravado performance as the sage patriarch of this nontraditional clan. Kate Cameron of the New York Daily News wrote, "The comedy moves smoothly and briskly under Capra's canny method of direction."

#6--ARSENIC AND OLD LACE (1944)

One of Capra's darker comedy films is somewhat tainted by Cary Grant's "over the top" performance. The film director encouraged the excessive exuberance of the actors' actions which he was planning to return to reshoot later, but was unable because of the war. Grant, seeing his performance on the screen, was embarrassed by his over-acting, but eventually attributed Capra with sharpening his overall comedic skills. Variety said of *Arsenic* at the time of its release, "Capra's production, not elaborate, captures the color and spirit of the play, while the able writing team of Julius J. and Philip G. Epstein has turned in a very workable, tightly-compressed script. Capra's own intelligent direction rounds out the movie."

#7--LOST HORIZON (1937)

Capra's massive expenditures with little financial gains caused a fissure between the director and Columbia Pictures. The idealistic film adapted from James Hilton was writer J.D. Salinger's favorite film. Fred Nuget of the New York Times wrote enthusiastically about this picture. "There is no denying the opulence of the production, the impressiveness of the sets, the richness of the costuming, the satisfying attention to large and small detail which makes Hollywood at its best such a generous entertainer. We can deride the screen in its lesser moods, but when the West Coast impresarios decide to shoot the works the resulting pyrotechnics bathe us in a warm and cheerful glow. The penultimate scenes are as vivid, swift, and brilliantly achieved as the first. Mr. Capra was guilty of a few directorial clichés, but otherwise it was a perfect job. Unquestionably the picture has the best photography and sets of the year. By all means it is worth seeing."

#8--MEET JOHN DOE (1941)

Gary Cooper loved working with Capra so much he agreed to be in this film before reading the script. The final scene where Barbara Stanwyck tries to convince Cooper not to jump off a roof in the dead of winter was shot inside a

Los Angeles ice house. After the shoot, Stanwyck had to go to "the hospital for a defrost." Bosley Crowther loved the picture, saying, "Mr. Capra has produced a film which is eloquent with affection for gentle people, for the plain, unimpressive little people who want reassurance and faith. Many of his camera devices are magnificent in the scope of their suggestion, and always he tells his story well, with his customary expert spacing of comedy and serious drama. Only space prevents us from enthusing loudly about individual touches."

#9--A HOLE IN THE HEAD (1959)

Presidential-candidate John F. Kennedy used the Oscar winning song *High Hopes* from this Capra film as his campaign tune. This was the film when Capra recognized Sinatra's acting talent, stating the singer could be Hollywood's greatest actor if he would only give up being a crooner. Film critic Emmanuel Levy described the film, "Capra's next to last film, a tale of a widower and his young son, is not up to his level but the film is entertaining due to the star turn of Frank Sinatra, and of course the popular Oscar-winning tune *High Hopes,* which he sings."

#10--A LADY FOR A DAY (1933)

Capra's first film to be nominated for Best Director and Best Movie, remade in 1961 as Capra's last film, *Pocket Full of Miracles.* The New York Times wrote *Lady* was "a merry tale with touches of sentiment, a picture which evoked laughter and tears from an audience at the first showing."

Orson Welles

THE GENIUS WHO MADE CINEMA'S BEST MOVIE

When the name Orson Welles is brought up, people have varying images of the late actor, film, and stage director.

Some remember him as the commercial huckster peddling Paul Mason wine. Others recall numerous television appearances on Merv Griffin, Johnny Carson, and Dean Martin shows. In fact, Welles' repeated presence on TV discouraged George Lucas from selecting him as his first choice for Darth Vader's voice in his new *Star Wars* movie, fearing his voice would be too recognizable. And some have heard about his 1938 radio show that scared the dickens out of millions by his vivid description of a Martian invasion in New Jersey.

But the remarkable imprint Welles created in the public's eye is mostly remembered for his motion pictures.

THE YOUNG DIRECTOR'S STUNNING DEBUT

The 1941 premier of *Citizen Kane,* a movie Welles produced, directed, acted, and co-wrote, changed the way cinema's aesthetics look today. So advanced was *Citizen Kane* from those preceding it that some have drawn parallels to movies before and after talking pictures.

Numerous polls throughout the decades have consistently placed *Citizen Kane* as the most influential film of all-time. Narrative plots, filming techniques, lighting accents, and audio bridging were all presented in a fresh new way in *Citizen Kane,* the one movie future generations of directors have said affected them the greatest.

The irony of Welles' career was his first movie, *Citizen Kane,* in which RKO Pictures gave him carte blanch in everything he wanted to do except determine the budget, was the only time in his career a film studio would grant him the total freedom allowing his creative juices to flow unchecked. "I started at the top and worked my way down," Welles would famously say.

After *Citizen Kane,* Welles went on to direct twelve more movies with a handful labeled as "masterpieces." But it was *Citizen Kane* that defined

Welles throughout his long career. The director continually attempted to imitate in subsequent films the unique stylization he largely engineered in his debut film. The powers in the film industry, however, always stood in his way.

The French director Francois Truffaut said of *Citizen Kane:* "It is the only 'first' film directed by a famous man."

Welles' background on the Broadway stage established the young man's genius at innovation. At age 21, Welles directed the New York City Shakespearean play *Julius Caesar.* His novel staging of the play opened the eyes of several Hollywood producers to his celluloid possibilities. Two years later when his radio broadcast *War of the Worlds* caused a national hysteria, the red carpet to Tinseltown was all but rolled out for him.

Welles knew practically next to nothing about making films. The ink on the RKO contract was hardly dry on August 21, 1939, when Welles embarked on a year-long learning lesson on film production. RKO employee Mariam Geiger created a textbook by pasting actual film strips of other movies onto paper describing what long, medium, and close-up shots looked liked. Welles also sat down with each production unit, from filming to editing, sound, and graphics, absorbing every specialty existing in a movie production.

Welles closely studied his contemporary directors, most notably John Ford, viewing over forty times 1939's *Stagecoach.* One, among many observations he noted was the way the camera angle was positioned on certain characters. He assimilated Ford's technique by adopting the camera positioned low and looking up at the rising Charles Foster Kane conversing with his best friend Jedediah Leland. Welles would place the camera high and aim down on weaker characters like wife Susan Alexander Kane.

Welles was also fortunate to come across two of Hollywood's top film practitioners. One was writer Herman Mankiewicz, who largely, with Welles' input, wrote *Citizen Kane's* brilliant script which eventually won him and Welles the Academy Award for Best Screenplay.

Mankiewicz had a nasty habit of loving the bottle, and it wasn't grape juice he chugged down. His imbibing was so well known Welles and RKO Pictures drew up a contract forbidding him from drinking during the film's scripting phase. To make sure he wouldn't be tempted, Welles arranged Mankiewicz to ensconce himself in the small desert town of Victorville, California, where the supply of liquor was scarce. Just to make sure Mankiewicz wasn't hitting the hard stuff, Welles sent producer John Houseman to babysit the screenwriter.

RKO Studio executives were naturally leery of seeing the company's funds being spent on a novice directing *Citizen Kane.* Welles possessed enough foresight to have in place in his initial RKO contract a non-interference clause restricting the studio's executives from observing and giving forceful suggestions. To get around the restrictive clauses set by Welles, the executives assigned non-descript employees to dress as janitors to clean around the sound stage and report back to them what they saw and heard.

Uncomfortable about some of the reports they were receiving, the executives dropped by the film set unannounced. Welles, anticipating such unwanted visits, instructed his cast and crew to pick up baseballs and bats sitting nearby just for the occasion and begin playing until the prying pests left.

Gregg Toland, Hollywood's most innovative cinematographer who had just finished filming John Ford's 1940 *The Long Voyage Home,* approached Welles to join forces on the radio personality's movie debut. "I want to work with somebody who never made a movie," said Toland.

On the first days of filming, Welles, as he did during his theatre days, would get up on a ladder and position the set's lights. Toland followed Welles, silently signaling his lighting crew to make adjustments to Welles' work. Actor William Allard remembered the Toland/Welles relationship: "They got along beautifully. No matter what Orson wanted, Gregg would try to get it for him."

The two constantly discussed how each camera shot would give them something new and compelling. Camera movements, panning, and dollying eliminated cuts that normally interrupted visual interpretations. Virtually every indoor shot contains a full ceiling, an unusual practice patterned after director John Ford and his movie *Stagecoach,* adding to *Citizen Kane's* realism.

WELLES, THE WORKAHOLIC ON "CITIZEN KANE"

Because of the enormous time it took to prepare filming *Citizen Kane,* Welles ate poorly and didn't exercise. He especially suffered from the effects of drinking thirty to forty cups of coffee a day while working long hours. He decided once filming began he would switch to tea since brewing the beverage would take much more time. By the third week, Welles was consuming as much tea as he previously did with coffee. Because of so much tea poured down his gullet the young director's skin turned an orangish brown color, much to the amusement of the crew.

Once in production, Welles would go long stretches without eating. More than once during breaks in filming he found he had the time to sit down and eat. Making up for lost calories, Welles would promptly put down two to three huge steaks with vegetables and potatoes on side.

Welles usually spent 16 to 18 hours a day in production on *Citizen Kane.* His workday normally started at four in the morning with four-hours of make-up applied on him. Sitting in the chair for those long stretches allowed Welles time to map out the day's filming with Toland and the other crew members.

Citizen Kane shows Welles' character aging from his youthful beginnings in the newspaper business to the movie's conclusion when he's seen as an elderly man who dies lonely and heartbroken. People watching the film thought the "old" Kane required hours of putting on make-up, while they felt the "young" Kane was Welles' natural appearance at the time he made the film. According to Welles, nothing could be further from the truth. He noted the make-up artists used more putty and cream during the young Kane phase than as the aging, sagging newspaper tycoon. Playing the young man, Welles, at 27, had his facial skin tightened and lifted and his hair styled. He even had lighting and the camera positioned at strategic angles to make him appear years younger than he actually was.

Soon after the premier of the film, people remarked to him what an immense ordeal it must have been to make the picture since he looked years older in person than he did in the movie. Viewers assumed the youthful image of Kane was how Welles really looked on the set. Welles said he spent years making excuses for his real life appearance despite never really looking that good naturally.

As well as mental challenges cropping up while making *Citizen Kane* there were physical ones as well. In one scene, Kane discovers his wife Susan had left him. Welles, as Kane, is seen whipping his arms around in anger, knocking Susan's objects over as well as picking up items and throwing them around her room. Unfortunately for Welles, he was wearing special eye contacts to make him look old. Looking through the contacts, Welles saw everything as a blur. Thrashing his arms about, Welles' caught a sharp edge, badly cutting his wrist. When finished with the take, Welles examined his hands and saw they were bleeding.

"I really felt it," Welles said, looking for bandages to staunch the flow of blood.

Another painful episode was filming the scene where Welles was chasing actor Ray Collins, playing Kane's political rival, down the stairs. Welles tripped and chipped a bone in one of his ankles during one take. He was forced to sit in a wheelchair for two weeks to recover. Following the injury were scenes scheduled calling for Kane to stand, so Welles had to wear metal braces to support his injured ankle.

For those young filmmakers who have a skimpy budget yet require crowd shots, a good way of showing an audience sitting in a theater is to do what Welles' technical crew did in *Citizen Kane*. As Kane delivers a campaign speech on the stage's podium, the camera starts wide and pushes in before cutting to the candidate. That initial shot is a still photograph. To make it appear people in the audience were shifting around in their seats, numerous holes were pricked through the photograph using a pin. As the camera pushes in, lights flicker underneath the photo, creating the illusion Kane's enthusiastic supporters in the auditorium are moving.

Later in his career Welles would fondly look back at the production of *Citizen Kane,* admitting it was the best film he ever worked on.

ROCKY FOLLOW-UP FILM

Welles discovered his association with Toland was a unique filming experience, spoiling him in his subsequent movies. For 1942's *The Magnificent Ambersons,* Welles' next picture after *Kane,* he hired veteran cinematographer Stanley Cortez since Toland was under contract with Samuel Goldwyn working on another project. Even though Welles was able to employ some of Toland's understudies, Cortez, responsible for the overall photographic aesthetics of the production, didn't see eye-to-eye with his director. One example reflecting the adversarial relationship between Welles and Cortez was the portion of the script calling for the shot where actor Tim Holt walks into the deserted Amberson mansion. The house had been seen earlier in a lively setting for Holt's family. Welles wanted a long shot where the camera would be the point-of-view of Holt, a reasonably difficult shot requiring four days of organizing. When it came time to review Cortez's shot, Welles was so disappointed with the results he ended up not using it. Subsequently, he replaced Cortez, whom he demoted to second-unit director, and promoted Cortez's assistant, Harry Wild, to handle the camera responsibilities.

After his incredible successes in theater and radio, Welles saw his new profession as a film director a step down.

"Movie directing is the perfect refuge for the mediocre," Welles reflected late in his career.

But he saw the unique qualities of filmmaking overriding all the other media as long as a director possessed an artistic aesthetic.

"A film is never really good unless the camera is an eye in the head of a poet," philosophized Welles.

WELLES THE MICROMANAGER

Welles was a micromanager when it came to details in his movies. Such a practice could be attributed to the fact he either wrote his own screenplays or contributed heavily to his movies' scripts, a practice where directors are much closer to their films' production values.

"I know that in theory the word is secondary in cinema, but the secret of my work is that everything is based on the word," explained Welles on his scripting. "I always begin with the dialogue. And I do not understand how one dares to write action before dialogue. I must begin with what the characters say. I must know what they say before seeing them do what they do."

In one *Citizen Kane* sequence early in the movie the director was bothered by the scene of a young Kane sledding down a hill in back of his parent's house during the winter. Welles noticed while editing that not a breath could be detected emitting from the warm exhalation of the actors' mouths in this winter setting, filmed on a soundstage inside the RKO Studios. He made note of the unreality of the scene and promised himself never to repeat it if the occasion arose for directing another winter scene in a future film.

That winter scene appeared in his next film, *Ambersons,* whose script called for a snow sleigh drawn by a horse being contrasted by an early automobile struggling with the same elements (in fact the car used in the movie is one of the earliest American-built cars, the 1892 Philion Road Carriage. The Philion can be seen in the National Automobile Museum, Reno, Nevada, and was the only one made by Achille Philion. The same automobile also appeared in the 1951 Red Skelton movie *Excuse My Dust.).* Welles decided to shoot inside an icehouse in Los Angeles instead of the warm RKO set. Filming this sequence was laborious: perfectionist Welles wasn't satisfied with neither the footage shot of the snow nor the exhalation of the actors' breaths, despite temperatures dropping well below freezing in the ice house, until the twelfth day after watching the rushes. Welles and company failed to learn the lessons of D.W. Griffith and his experiences with the cold in 1920's *Way Down East,* where the film pioneer took steps to install a heater wrapped around the camera. The *Ambersons'* camera crew was constantly frustrated by the camera lens fogging up, its film jamming because of the condensation built up inside the camera mechanisms, and other technical malfunctions. The entire cast in the icehouse came down with terrible head colds from the daily frozen exposure, especially actor Ray Collins, who was sick with pneumonia. Miraculously, Welles was about the only one who emerged healthy from the frigid ordeal.

DIRECTING HIS ESTRANGED WIFE, RITA HAYWORTH

On the opposite side of the temperature spectrum, Orson Welles spent 35 days filming near tropical Acapulco, Mexico, for his 1947 *The Lady From*

Shanghai, a setting one would think would be paradise. The production was anything but. Shooting during the day had its challenges: the temperatures were brutally high, causing Welles' estranged wife, Rita Hayworth, to faint from the heat. At night the filming posed additional problems. Millions of insects were attracted to the film crew's outside arc lights. The swarm of insects was so thick the light from the lamps was dimmed considerably. Welles, while directing, was bit near his eye socket by one of the hovering insects. The area around the eye swelled to nearly three times its normal size, shutting the vision in his eye.

At least Hayworth didn't have her signature long red locks weighing her down in the heat during the *Shanghai* shoot. Welles made the actress cut off her luxurious, lengthy hair before the production began and dye it a platinum blonde. When studio executives first saw the rushes of the Mexican footage, they were horrified their starlet's trademark look had been sheared. Welles explained he wanted to create a new femme fatale persona for his wife. But rumors swirled the scissors came out as a revenge for the constant bickering the two engaged in towards the end of their marriage before beginning *Shanghai's* filming.

Hayworth also was suffering from sinus problems and a nervous condition throughout the production. She was so sick Welles was forced to close down the shooting for a month, much to the chagrin of the bean counters back at Columbia Studios who saw the film's budget escalate because of the delays.

Hayworth's ordeal was nothing compared to Donald Ray Corey, an assistant cameraman working outside in the Mexican heat on *Shanghai.*

Welles had hired his buddy Errol Flynn and his big yacht for some boat scenes in Mexico. Cameraman Corey, working without a hat in the scorching sun on Flynn's boat, suddenly dropped dead of a heart attack. Flynn, who liked his drink at any time of the day, scuttled down in the boat's berth and emerged with a duffel bag. He began to stuff the dead Corey into the bag for a "dignified" burial at sea. Welles wasn't quite comfortable with the traditional rite of sailors disposing human remains while on the water, so he sent an assistant to inform Mexican authorities on Cory's condition. Flynn was somewhat mortified his command on his own yacht was overruled by a landlubber.

CROSSOVER FROM STAGE TO SCREEN

Welles and his "Mercury Theatre" radio and stage performers were brought to Hollywood from New York City for the casting of *Citizen Kane*. They were all novices in film, but they would eventually learn the difference between acting on the stage and appearing before the camera. Subtle movements like whispering and slight glances, so crucial on film but non-existent on stage, had to be studied by this talented troupe.

Similar to D.W. Griffith, who came from a theatre stage background, Welles prepared for his production with extensive rehearsals. To plan for the *Ambersons,* Welles spent five weeks with his cast before filming began. For a dramatic kitchen sequence, Welles had his three actors rehearse for five days showing Tim Holt and Ray Collins (Uncle Jack) teasing Agnes Morehead (Fanny). There was not one word in the Welles script for this sequence. The scene would rely on the improvisation of the actors based on the characterization of each person. Because the actors worked on their ad-libbing during rehearsals, they knew exactly what to do once the camera rolled. Today's viewers can see the four-plus minutes scene play out as a single take.

One of the highlights in the *Ambersons* which many attribute for her being nominated for the Academy Award's Best Supporting Actress, was Agnes Morehead's breakdown scene with Holt in the deserted mansion near the end of the movie. Welles rehearsed the scene with Morehead, which required a highly charged and very dramatic piece of acting on her part. Working with his technical crew, he mapped out an intricate, uninterrupted dolly shot. They spent hours on the scene; Welles called for multiple takes, beginning with the Morehead soliloquy, but was not quite satisfied with the camera movement beginning three-quarters into her dramatics.

People would ask her how she sustained such a high level of energy throughout the day. At first she said performing the scene was exhilarating. But later Morehead admitted she was so jacked up by the intensity of acting the breakdown scene she couldn't sleep for a week.

If Morehead's scene was exhausting for the actress, picture how Welles' schedule was while making *Ambersons.* He was filming *Ambersons* while at the same time acting in another movie. After spending all day directing on the set, he would then journey over to another RKO sound stage early in the evening where he had a role playing a Turkish police official in *Journey Into Fear.* Many claim Welles had directed several scenes in the movie, but Welles denied the accusation, stating director Norman Foster controlled the entire production.

Later in his career, Welles loved to play psychological mind games with his cast, with some actors labeling his habit manipulative. Welles claimed he wanted to achieve a certain collective personality within his cast. The script in *The Lady From Shanghai* painted its characters pretty much suspicious of everyone--including the lovers. To get that edginess bathed in his actors' performances, he would unnerve his cast on purpose to get them to snipe at one another.

Tipping his actors off-balance during the shoot, Welles was constantly penning amendments to the dialogue of the *Shanghai* script. When the actors thought they had nailed down their lines in rehearsals before the next day's shoot, Welles greeted them the morning with his alterations, changing how the actors would deliver their lines to one another, a frustrating ordeal for all.

At other times he would purposely get the actors so flustered by clamoring contradictory orders they would forget their lines and attempt to cover up with improvised lines, something Welles encouraged. This practice is evident in the scene where actor Erskine Sanford as a judge, in total bewilderment, shouts out, "This isn't a football game!"

One actor particularly upset at Welles during the *Shanghai* production was Glenn Anders. Not knowing what kind of movie his agent scheduled him to be in or what role he had, Anders arrived on the set without a contract the first day of shooting. Welles barked at him to play dead by lying on a nearby stretcher and pull a sheet over himself. He did as Welles ordered. Meanwhile, a studio representative with Anders' contract already printed up walked over to the stretcher. He gave Anders a pen and told the actor to sign the paper he was holding. Confused, Anders listened to the order and without see the papers signed his contract. That's how Anders became George Grisby in *Shanghai*. Despite the duplicity, Welles still bullied him during the production. The actor was so visibly shaken by the ordeal the crew nicknamed him "Glenn Anguish."

WELLES' ADVENTURES IN "TOUCH OF EVIL"

Welles wasn't as intense dealing with his actors later in his career. His ego wasn't so big by then: his resume was filled with large gaps, indicating his Hollywood track record was uneven at best. By the time he directed 1958's *Touch of Evil,* Welles' approach toward his cast was entirely different. Janet Leigh recalled how Welles would seek his actors' advice in shaping the characters and dialogue.

"It started with rehearsals," said Leigh. "We rehearsed two weeks prior to shooting, which was unusual. We rewrote most of the dialogue, all of us, which was also unusual, and Mr. Welles always wanted our input. It was a collective effort, and there was such a surge of participation, of creativity, of energy. You could feel the pulse growing as we rehearsed. You felt you were inventing something as you went along. Mr. Welles wanted to seize every moment. He didn't want one bland moment. He made you feel you were involved in a wonderful event that was happening before your eyes."

In one of the most famous opening sequences in cinematic history, *Touch's* first scene is a single long crane tracking shot involving one of the most complex shots ever mapped out. The evening sequence took the entire night to nail down, in part because the actor playing the customs officer kept stumbling and forgetting his lines, which, in his earlier years, Welles would have ripped the man's head off.

An astute viewer will be able to see the sunrise in the distance dawning as the opening filmed over several city blocks unfolds. Welles, as night slowly became dawn, had one more chance to nail the sequence.

"All right, let's try it one more time." Welles said, eyeing the actor who was the customs officer. "If you forget your line this time, just move your lips and we'll dub it in later, but please God do NOT say, 'I'm sorry, Mr. Welles!'"

Fortunately, the actor said his lines correctly and the clip shown on the screen is that final take before the sun overtook the dark sky.

Actor Dennis Weaver was recruited to play a manager at a remote motel because Welles was such a huge fan of the TV series *Gunsmoke.* When he first sat down with Weaver, Welles asked him what his character Chester in *Gunsmoke* was all about. Weaver detailed Chester was always trailing behind people and treating others deferentially. Welles told Weaver he wanted him to play *Touch's* night motel manager just the opposite of Chester. He saw Weaver's film personality in *Touch* as being very pushy, an in-your-face type of guy. Welles labeled Weaver's character as a "Shakespearean loony."

Weaver remembers, "We went into his whole background--about his mother and how he was a mamma's boy. He had this terrible guilt about sex and yet he had a large sex drive. There were no words to indicate such a thing in the script at all, but it gave him an interesting behavior pattern when we put it all together. The main thing was his attraction to women and his fear of them at the same time. That was the thing that was basic to his character."

One is struck upon seeing the Janet Leigh sequence with Weaver while she was overnighting at the remote motel. There are strong psychological similarities between the traits of Dennis Weaver the night manager and Norman Bates in 1962's Alfred Hitchcock's *Psycho,* based on the Robert Block's 1959 novel *Psycho.*

While Weaver was approached to play in a Welles production, Ms. Leigh and Charleston Heston were dying to be in an Orson-directed film.

Welles offered Leigh a low salary, given the constraints of the budget for *Touch.* Without even telling Leigh, her agent rejected the offer out of hand because the offer was so low. Welles knew his bid was going to be rejected, so he sent the actress a letter saying tenderly how much he was looking forward to working with her. Once Leigh read the letter, she called her agent and told him in no uncertain terms having the opportunity of being directed by Welles was far more important than the amount in her paycheck.

Charlton Heston, already a big star and would one year later appear in his greatest film, *Ben Hur,* had similar feelings as Leigh about having the honor of being directed by Welles. *Touch* producer Albert Zugsmith originally intended for Welles to be only an actor in the film and not the movie's director. But the producer knew Heston wouldn't act in this low budget film noir unless Welles was at the director's helm. Zugsmith gulped and bravely told the studio Welles, who hadn't made a mainstream movie since *Shanghai,* would be directing *Touch.*

Welles stepped into the project by making major alterations to the existing approved script: Heston's role was changed from being a white district attorney residing in the United States to a Mexican drug enforcement agent. Leigh's nationality was swapped from Mexican to American. And the town the movie was set in was relocated from a small southern California village to a Mexican-American border town.

Heston later had regrets on certain aspects of his character. Acting in a hispanic role, Heston spoke clear English with not a hint of a Spanish accent. He said his non-accented dialogue was one of the biggest mistakes he ever made as an actor.

Veteran actress Marlene Dietrich described playing Tanya, a last-minute insertion in the script, was one of the most rewarding acting performances she had ever experienced. Welles, while in production, called Ms. Dietrich up one afternoon out of the blue and asked her as a personal favor to play a small part in *Touch.* She reportedly jumped out of bed, went over to Paramount Studios, consulted with a wardrobe expert, rounded up some outfits with a hat and a wig and sped to the border where filming was taking place. She agreed as a favor to her friend Orson to be in the picture for a minimum wage.

Her performance was shot in one evening. She later reflected that her performance with the line "What does it matter what you say about people?" was the most "dramatic acting she had ever done."

A secret can't be kept hidden from studio executives when an actress' face is projected on the big screen. Welles failed to inform the studio about Dietrich's appearance in *Touch.* When they saw her in the rushes the executives realized they couldn't give her mere salted peanuts for her night's work. They ended up putting Dietrich on the credits, which by virtue of the on-screen recognition her pay shot up considerably for her brief evening's performance.

WELLES' GIRTH

Welles' weight gain throughout his public career was always the subject of tabloid headlines.

Arriving in Hollywood for the first time for the *Citizen Kane* production, Welles chunked down 18 hot dogs in one sitting. This eating frenzy happened at Los Angeles' hot dog stand Pink's, established in 1939 and is still serving dogs at 709 North La Brea Avenue.

The director became obese in his later years. His standard daily dinner consisted of two rare stakes washed down by a pint of scotch whiskey. One day during an office examination, his doctor noticed his weight gain. "My doctor told me to stop having intimate dinners for four," Welles said. "Unless there are three other people."

Making *Touch,* everyone in the studio took for granted Welles was as big as a whale. His character, the rotund Police Captain Hank Quinlan, was described as being 20 years older than Welles, possessing a pork chop face and an equally round-ball figure. Welles did not carry as large a girth as portrayed in the movie; make-up artists spent hours inserting extra poundage inside his suit as well as applying prosthetics on his face, including a fake nose, to fill him out.

He remembered attending a late-night dinner party during the production, conveniently leaving his make-up on. A famous actress was so taken by his appearance she said in all earnestness, "Orson! You look wonderful!"

TRICKS OF THE TRADE

Welles wasn't, unlike the shortcuts taken in *Citizen Kane,* all for austerity when it came to his later movies. Toward the end of shooting the black and white film *Shanghai,* Welles wanted the entire set repainted over the weekend for his filming on Monday to get the "right" look. Fearing the outrageous overtime bill the unionized studio painters would charge, the studio executives felt there was no way they could call in the crew for a Saturday and Sunday work schedule. Studio head Jack Fier did agree to Welles' wish to have the set repainted, but told the director he would have to wait until the painters came into work on Monday.

Not to be stymied, Welles enlisted several of his friends to break into the studio's paint room and grab several gallons of paint and brushes. The team set out to work and painted the entire set themselves. When they finished

Sunday evening they made a banner reading "The Only Thing We Have to Fear is Fier Himself" and hung the sign for all to see

On Monday, when the studio painters were rolling up their sleeves to begin with the set, they saw the buildings were already sheening with new paint. The painters were mortified, so much so they immediately set out to picket the studio. Their union boss informed the studio the painters would remain on strike until they were paid triple overtime for the work they didn't do but were willing to do if the studio had called on them to paint the set that weekend.

Fier, fearing the union, agreed to pay the painters the triple overtime charge even though they didn't do the work. Incensed, he put the costs the studio had to pay out onto Welles' personal bill. Rubbing salt in Welles' wound, Fier also had the painters compose a banner and hang it up, proclaiming "All's Well That Ends Welles."

Welles considered black and white film stock used in *Shanghai* as well as his other B&W films to be "the actor's best friend." His reasoning was the audience paid more attention to the actors' and actresses' emotions and expressions rather than the vibrant clothes, their colorful hair styles and eye make-up.

EDITING CONTROVERSIES

Welles teamed up with editor Robert Wise, future director of 1961's *West Side Story*, to produce innovations in rhythmic editing and audio bridges for *Citizen Kane*. Welles attached special importance to editing throughout his career, saying "The whole eloquence of cinema is created in the cutting room. It's there that the director is in full measure of his artistry."

In post-production, Wise noticed the fake newsreel filmed front ending *Citizen Kane* was too clean. Old newsreels, as replicated in *Citizen Kane's* opening, were always grainy since they had been run through projectors repeatedly for multiple showings. Wise had one of those light-bulb moments. He physically dragged the film strips over a stone floor and rubbed the film with cheesecloth filled with sand, producing the desired worn look Welles and Wise felt was befitting a normal newsreel.

Some theater owners, stopping the movie right after the beginning newsreel, called up RKO and complained the film stock was horrible. The owners demanded a replacement print or they would refuse to show *Citizen Kane*. Fortunately, those at RKO were aware of the technique used and informed those complainers to continue watching the movie past the newsreel footage to get a sense of the condition of the films' prints.

As harmonious as Wise's relationship with Welles was during the post-production of *Citizen Kane*, working on the *Ambersons* was a tale of legendary discord.

During the editing process of *Ambersons*, Welles received an assignment from the United States government in the early stages of World War II to produce a Latin American good-will film in South America. Welles immediately left the remainder of the editing chores to Wise with detailed instructions of what scenes to assemble where.

RKO was one of many studios at the time conducting surprise previews in certain nearby Los Angeles movie houses of its rough-cut versions of work-in-progress pictures in conjunction to their regularly scheduled films. The audiences would be asked after the preview to fill out survey cards rating the film and for their opinions.

Ambersons had its first preview on March 17, 1942, in Pomona, California, a few months after Pearl Harbor. Moviegoers in the theater, a large proportion consisting of teen-agers paying to see *The Fleet's In*, a light-hearted musical with Dorothy Lamour, and came prepared to laugh. However, the *Ambersons* was a dark film, spiced with mental breakdowns and savage, cutting adult dialogue. The audience howled at the scene of Morehead coming to grips with reality. Other serious scenes in the picture were greeted with chuckles. One comment card read, "People like to laff [sic], not be bored to death." The positive opinions, however few in number, very much acknowledged Welles' effort. "Too bad audience was so unappreciative," one reviewer wrote.

RKO president George Schaefer attended the preview. "Never in all my experience in the industry have I taken so much punishment or suffered as I did at the Pomona preview," remembered Schaefer.

RKO panicked. Among those who felt the problem with the film with its downbeat ending was its producer Bryan Foy. He agreed with the RKO consensus that over half-an-hour should be excised from the film. Foy told the editors "Just throw all the footage up in the air and grab everything but 40 minutes."

Welles, on hearing the problems, wanted Wise to come down to Brazil to see what they could do together, but war restrictions prevented the trip. So RKO assigned Wise, actor Joseph Cotton and studio representative Jake Moss to shorten the film.

Moss had a phone installed in his office feeding directly to Welles' hotel room in Rio de Janeiro. Welles was obsessed by the changes to his movie and repeatedly called Moss to get the latest editing updates. The director's constant phone calls became increasingly irritating to Moss and he began letting the phone ring without answering it. The frustrated Welles then sent lengthy telegrams to Moss writing out more suggestions. Moss chucked the telegrams into his circular file.

Wise fell into his first directing role by shooting additional scenes the studio demanded to tighten the film.

Besides Wise's footage, Welles' assistant director for *Ambersons,* Freddie Fleck, directed the movie's new ending, which was much more upbeat than Orson's original. The conclusion bears no resemblance to the camera placements and lighting atmospherics to the earlier footage Welles shot.

Welles' was especially upset about the alterations to the ending. He considered the original to be one of the best scenes in the picture. The director had filmed for the stunning conclusion showing Holt visiting Morehead in her new home some months after her mental breakdown. Residing in the same boarding home is a group of very excitable eccentrics. Like the ending in *Citizen Kane* with the burning of the sled, Welles' *Amberson* ended just as memorable. As Holt leaves the bleak boarding house where Morehead is being treated, the camera pulls back to a wide shot, revealing the insane asylum was the former Amberson mansion.

Welles carried a lifelong grudge for all those responsible for participating in the re-editing job. He said the final version was like having the movie "being edited by a lawnmower".

RKO destroyed all the footage Welles filmed for the original movie. The studio claimed it did so because of limited storage space. People suspicious of RKO's move claim the footage's destruction was really to spite Welles and to prevent him from ever re-editing the film to his original intent.

OTHER WELLES' TRIALS IN POST-PRODUCTION

The editing experience of the *Ambersons* was repeated in his future projects, such as *Shanghai.* Welles' first rough cut ran 155 minutes. Columbia Studios Harry Cohn, who saw the preliminary version, wanted faster pacing rather than the long takes Welles had chosen. For the next year, without any advice from Welles, Cohn and his team re-edited *Shanghai* with newly filmed sequences. What especially disturbed Welles was the climatic funhouse scene highlighted by the layers of mirrors on the walls surrounding the main characters. Whittled down from twenty to just three minutes, the thrilling final sequence is still considered a classic in cinematic history. But whatever lengthened suspense was filmed to make the ending even more impactful will never be known, since, like the *Ambersons,* the footage was destroyed by Columbia Studio.

In *Touch of Evil,* Welles submitted to the studio what he considered to be a tightly-wound picture. He was scheduled to be in Mexico immediately after he was finished with the filming to begin another project. Welles, with his track record, wasn't surprised the studio had completely re-edited *Touch*. The studio was so concerned about the viability of the picture in commercial theaters it altered many of Welles' scenes.

A mature Welles took his Hollywood struggles in stride. Constant conflicts with studios' bean counters and their executives, as well as Welles experiencing personal financial difficulties, created a vast library of projects and partially completed films he was never able to see to full fruition. Laurence Harvey's sudden death stopped the director's 1970's *The Deep* production, while 1969's *The Merchant of Venice* and 1992's *Don Quixote*, movies which Welles spent a considerable amount of his time and resources, never made it to the screen.

"I'm not bitter about Hollywood's treatment of me, but over its treatment of D.W. Griffith, Josef von Sternberg, Erich von Stroheim, Buster Keaton and a hundred others," noted Welles on how the film industry has dealt with its once-considered brilliant film directors. "We live in a snake pit here. I hate it but I just don't allow myself to face the fact that I hold it in contempt because it keeps on turning out to be the only place to go."

"I'm not rich," Welles added later. "Never have been. When you see me in a bad movie as an actor (I hope not as a director), it is because a good movie has not been offered to me. I often make bad films in order to live. I think I made essentially a mistake staying in movies. I can't regret because it's like saying, 'I shouldn't have stayed married to that woman, but I did because I love her.' I would have been more successful if I'd left movies immediately. Stayed in the theater, gone into politics, written--anything. I've wasted the greater part of my life looking for money, and trying to get along, trying to make my work from this terribly expensive paint box which is a movie. And I've spent too much energy on things that have nothing to do with a movie. It's about 2% movie making and 98% hustling. It's no way to spend a life."

"Living in the lap of luxury isn't bad, except you never know when luxury is going to stand up," laughed Welles.

For Welles, even his most highly-regarded movie, *Citizen Kane*, was not a money maker for RKO. In subsequent films, only one, 1946's *The Stranger*, did a Welles film show profitability. It was for this reason Welles mostly lost control of final editing decisions after *Citizen Kane*. Today's fans of Welles' work lament what the possibilities would have been if he had full control of all his movies as he did in *Citizen Kane*. Welles' optimism never waned despite experiencing constant frustrations that failed to damper his enthusiasm towards the human condition. He noted, "Even if the good old days never existed, the fact that we can conceive such a world is, in fact, an affirmation of the human spirit."

Welles would die the night shortly after appearing on October 9, 1985's *The Merv Griffin Show*. Merv remembers previous interviews with Welles he did not want to speak about his past. On this October day, however, Welles told Griffin before the cameras rolled "for this interview, there are no subjects about which I won't speak"

Somehow, the brilliant stage actor/director turned film actor/director knew his time was up. All those visions Welles had in his head for unrealized feature films would be carried to his grave. The genius of "Rosebud" can be cherished for what we have today in his body of work, even if it is just in studio-edited form.

TOP TEN ORSON WELLES FILMS

#1--CITIZEN KANE (1941)

The movie that jump-started Welles' film directing career and introduced numerous innovations to the film arts. Acknowledged for decades as the best movie of all-time, *Citizen Kane* is a quasi-biographical film thinly veiled to newspaper publisher William Randolph Hearst. So striking were the similarities, Hearst refused to have any of his papers run ads or give reviews on the film. As New York Times Bosley Cothers wrote at the time of *Citizen Kane's* release, "It comes close to being the most sensational film ever made in Hollywood. Count on Mr. Welles: he doesn't do things by halves. Upon the screen he discovered an area large enough for his expansive whims to have free play. And the consequence is that he has made a picture of tremendous and overpowering scope, not in physical extent so much as in its rapid and graphic rotation of thoughts. Mr. Welles has put upon the screen a motion picture that really moves."

#2--THE LADY FROM SHANGHAI (1947)

Welles' classic film noir movie, starring his wife Rita Hayworth, is so innovative in its set design and camerawork this film has to be seen to be believed. The final shootout in the hall of mirrors is one of the unique and famous endings in all of Hollywood movie history. London's Tom Huddleston said of the film, "The plot is a magnificent mess of switchbacks and revelations, climaxing with one of cinema's most outrageously inventive sequences: a shootout in a funfair hall of mirrors. The result may not have the crystalline perfection of *Citizen Kane*, but that's a flaw it shares with every other film in history."

#3--THE MAGNIFICENT AMBERSONS (1942)

The tragedy is Welles' second film was butchered from the director's original intent. He was in Brazil shooting a movie for the United States Government and was unable to oversee the final editing process. *Ambersons* is still an incredible picture to see despite over a half hour of crucial scenes thrown in the incinerator. During the 1970's Welles had intended to shoot the ending he originally had in mind and replace the one the studio had reshot, but financing for the production was unavailable. Pauline Kael wrote, "The film wasn't completed in the form that Welles originally intended, and there are pictorial effects that seem scaled for a much fuller work, but even in this truncated form it's amazing and memorable."

#4--TOUCH OF EVIL (1958)

Considered the last of Hollywood's popular, low-budgeted film noirs, this picture is a cult favorite for its brilliant performances within a very convoluted plot. Welles plays a corrupt police captain matching wits with a Mexican drug enforcement officer, Charleston Heston, whose lack of a hispanic accent was the actor's main regret in his career. Shades of Hitchcock's *Pyscho* emerge in the sequences where Janet Leigh ensconces herself in a remote motel. Film critic Tony Sloman said of *Touch*, "Welles made the film that virtually capped a style he had helped create: you could say that the span of film noir started with *Citizen Kane* and ended with this movie."

#5--THE STRANGER (1946)

Edward G. Robinson plays a commissioner for the UN War Crimes Division hunting down ex-Nazi Welles, married to the innocent and lovely Loretta Young. Embedded in this movie is the first time the harrowing footage of the German concentration camps liberated on the final days of World War II was shown in a Hollywood feature film. This fast paced movie was Welles' testimony he could direct a traditional studio film on time and under budget. Variety praised the film, saying *Stranger* is "a socko melodrama, spinning an intriguing web of thrills and chills. Director Orson Welles gives the production a fast, suspenseful development, drawing every advantage from the hard-hitting script from the Victor Trivas story. A uniformly excellent cast gives reality to events that transpire. The three stars, Robinson, Young and Welles, turn in some of their best work, the actress being particularly effective as the misled bride."

#6--MACBETH (1947)

In typical Welles fashion, the studio forced the director to cut two reels from his proposed final edit. Audiences who saw the shortened version were less than complementary. However, in 1980 when the UCLA Film and Television Archive and the Folger Shakespeare Library restored the cuts and placed back Welles' original soundtrack, viewers and critical opinion agreed this was one of Welles' finest films he ever produced. James Kendrick says the movie is "a film that had an unfortunately deleterious effect on Welles's career, but can now be seen and appreciated as a unique, daring take on a familiar text that rendered it new and strange."

#7--THE TRIAL (1962)

When Welles first released this film, he proclaimed it the best movie he had ever made. Critics at the time were of the opposite opinion, but over the years *The Trial* has gained a fair share of positive reflections, including Roger Ebert, who gave the movie four stars. Welles biographer David Thomson said the film was "an astonishing work, and a revelation of the man ... a stunning film."

#8--OTHELLO (1952)

Welles condensed Shakespeare's play to only 91 minutes, earning the Cannes Film Festival's highest award for that year. This movie was three years in the making, which reflects Welles' laborious attempts to raise money to complete the project. In post-production, Welles emerged with two different versions, one European and one American, adhering to the tastes of each region. TV Guide wrote at the time, "The text of the original play has been slashed to its bare bones, with bravura cinematography and editing also helping make this a taut, visceral experience."

#9--CHIMES AT MIDNIGHT (1965)

Like most of Welles' later works, this movie was under-appreciated by the public until years later when critics realized the film's greatness and labelled *Chimes* as one of the director's highest achievements. The rotund Welles plays Shakespeare's Sir John Falstaff (of course), and he nails the role with the swagger and braggadocio personality Shakespeare must have intended his Falstaff to be portrayed. Film critic Bill Goodykoontz wrote, "Welles' vision and imagination is unmatched in film. His use of light in a forbidding, dark castle is a wonder."

#10--F FOR FAKE (1974)

Fake is Welles' final film, and the film is patterned as a documentary concerning an art forger. The fast-paced but meandering film is regarded as the fore-runner of the MTV "attention deficit" style of presentation. Welles appears to have amped up the French New Wave method of delivery. Emma Simmonds, writing her review of the film, reflected the more appreciative assessment of the movie to today's appreciative audience by stating, "If *Citizen Kane* is testament to a young man's genius then *F For Fake* is testament to a veteran's rebellious spirit and wicked sense of humour."

Alfred Hitchcock

The "Master of Suspense," Alfred Hitchcock, couldn't quite figure out why people loved to have the dickens scared out of them by going on roller coasters rides, into haunted houses, or viewing horrifying films.

"Why do people pay money to be scared?" questioned Hitchcock late in his career. Asked if he knew the answer, he replied "Of course not. But I earn my living doing it."

That basically sums up Hitchcock's film career of almost 60 years in placing millions of paying customers on the edge of their seats. He was, after all, the practitioner of thrillers.

"I am typecast as a director," Hitchcock once said. "If I made Cinderella, the audience would immediately be looking for a body in the coach."

His cinematic style and story lines are still very visible in today's movies. Pick any listings of current films screening in theaters, and there is at least one picture owing its direct lineage to this British-turned-American director.

Hitchcock perfected film murder mysteries and spy thrillers during celluloid's early years. The James Bond film series adopted his unique narrative development. For better or worse, Hitchcock practically invented the psycho-thriller in today's teenage slasher films.

The late film critic Roger Ebert called Hitchcock "the dominant figure of the first century of film."

Film director Martin Scorsese says "You can watch Hitchcock's films over and over and find something new every time. As you get older, the films change with you."

HITCHCOCK'S EARLY CAREER

Hitchcock started in film as a title card artist during the 1920's silent film era in England's nascent movie industry. From there, he rose to become Britain's top film director, specializing in murder who-done-its, producing such classics as 1927's *The Lodger,* 1929's *Blackmail* and 1935's *The 39 Steps.*

In fact, Hitchcock's stock in England was so high his studio, British

International Pictures (BIP), bankrolled him to produce the first talking picture produced in the United Kingdom.

In 1929, a mere one year after *The Jazz Singer* introduced to mass audiences the viability of sound in movies, BIP had Hitchcock re-shoot certain scenes of his already completed silent film *Blackmail* to record sound coinciding with the visuals. There was one complication, however. The leading actress, Anny Ondra, who was filmed throughout the completed silent movie, was Czechoslovakian and spoke English with a very heavy accent. The accent did not go with the character she was portraying, England-bred Alice White.

As technology improved, an English-speaking female would normally be whisked into a narration booth and her voice recorded while she was viewing the already-shot footage. However, since this was the first talking picture ever to be made in the United Kingdom, the post-production audio technology hadn't existed yet. The solution was to have Joan Barry, selected to be the voice of Alice White, stand just out of frame to the side and read Ondra's lines into a microphone while Ondra was mouthing the words in front of the camera.

There is an existing sound test film taken right before re-shooting the scenes between Hitchcock and Ondra. The test film goes like this:

"Now Miss Ondra," said the youngish-looking Hitchcock. "You asked me to let you hear your voice on the talking picture."

"But Hitch," said Anny, "You mustn't do that."

"Why not."

"Well, because I can speak well."

"Do you realize a squad van will be here at any moment."

"No, really," giggles Anny, "I'm terribly frightened."

"Well, have you been a bad woman or something."

"Well, not just bad, but..."

"But you've slept with men," Hitchcock asks teasingly.

Anny giggles some more and begins to move away.

"You have not?" queries Hitchcock. "Come here, stand in your place, otherwise it will not come out right as the girl said to the soldier."

A decade later Hitchcock's international fame was so widespread Hollywood and producer David O. Selznick in particular bid for his services to direct in America. The British film director was enticed by the American studios offers with bigger production budgets, better weather and a wider audience than he experienced in England. Arriving in the United States, he proceeded to direct top suspense thrillers including 1940's *Rebecca*, 1943's *Shadow of A Doubt*, 1945's *Spellbound,* and 1946's *Notorious*, huge hits which today are considered Hollywood classics.

EARLY FASCINATION WITH CRIME

Hitchcock was fascinated by crime and murders at an early age. He grew up in the London suburb of Essex where Jack the Ripper had been running rampant killing local women. Once in the film business, Hitchcock concentrated mostly on cloak-and-dagger thrillers early in his career. His English films made in the 1930s mainly featured overseas European secret agents bent on causing destruction on the local populace, as in 1936's *Sabotage*.

Unusual for suspense films of his time, however, Hitchcock created a certain empathy for his villains. This was especially seen when the criminals were in danger of being caught.

"Man does not live by murder alone." Hitchcock said, explaining the humanizing touch of his bad hombres. "He needs affection, approval, encouragement and, occasionally, a hearty meal."

Hitchcock especially felt sympathetic towards the Raymond Burr character, Lars Thorwald, in 1954's *Rear Window*. Hitchcock says Thorwald was minding his own business (besides secretly killing his wife), and James Stewart (Jeff Jefferies) had to butt into his personal life by spying on him through his window. During their confrontation, Thorwald asks why Jeff is he making his life miserable. Jeff remains silent. Hitchcock said it was "during that moment it makes one think, 'you know, he (Jeff) is really kind of a bastard.'"

SHADOWY IMAGERY

In his early films, Hitchcock used shadows, most of them cast upon a wall, to create an added element of suspense. In 1941's *Suspicion*, Cary Grant, whose wife Joan Fountain thinks is trying to kill her, walks up the stairs to administer a glass of "glowing water." A sinister shadow is cast on the wall, adding to the audience's feelings Grant's palliative concoction actually contains poison. The opening credits in 1942's *Saboteur* contains a shadow on the wall where the titles are shown, reflecting the ominous mood of the film's theme.

Filming his last silent movie re-shot using sound, Hitchcock noticed in an important scene in *Blackmail* where criminal Cyril Ritchard is filmed with a thick shadow running across his upper lip, which made him resemble a heavily mustached villain seen in so many silent flicks. The shadow, caused by a light casting the shadow from an arm of a chandelier hanging overhead, was seen sentimentally by Hitchcock as "my farewell to silent pictures."

In one instance, instead of a shadow, Hitchcock used dense, black smoke to symbolize the character of Uncle Charlie, played by actor Joseph Cotten in 1951's *Shadow of A Doubt*. Cotton arrives in bucolic Santa Rosa, California via a train, belching black smoke from its stack, symbolic of the impending evil arriving into town and descending upon the unsuspecting Newton family. In his interview with François Truffaut on *Shadow* (first published in 1967), Hitchcock said the dense smoke gushing from the train bringing Charles Oakley to Santa Rosa was a deliberate symbol of imminent evil. Hitchcock listed *Shadow* his favorite film he had directed, partly because he loved the idea of bringing criminality into such an innocent town.

HITCHCOCK'S FOCUS WAS ON THE VISUALS

From the onset of his directing career in the United States, Hitchcock made sure his films featured major, well-known movie stars. He felt the plot was the most important part in his films, and with the personalities of his stars already known to the public, he could dispense with character development and focus on the crucial points of his narratives.

The minimizing of character development with an emphasis on the visuals and the narrative created a huge gulf between the scriptwriter of 1951's *Strangers On A Train* and its director. Raymond Chandler, the hard-boiled detective writer of novels such as *The Big Sleep* and who previously composed several screenplays including one he co-wrote with director Billy Wilder, *Double Indemnity,* was hired to work alongside Hitchcock. However, the sessions between the two turned acrimonious, with Chandler reportedly calling Hitchcock behind his back "that fat bastard." In a letter to a studio executive after submitting his first draft, Chandler complained he would have preferred working with a director "who realizes that what is said and how it is said is more important than shooting it upside down through a glass of champagne."

One aspect Hitchcock learned when producing a movie was to avoid making a picture a long, drawn out affair on the screen. His axiom was "the length of a film should be directly related to the endurance of the human bladder."

Adhering to that doctrine, there are no superfluous scenes in a Hitchcock film: every shot is crucial to the movies' denouement at the conclusion. His philosophy on plots was "Drama is life with the dull bits left out. Some films are slices of life, mine are slices of cake."

PRE-PRODUCTION

PREPARATION BEFORE FILMING

Going into each film, Hitchcock meticulously visualized each planned sequence and notated in great detail on paper camera placements, types of lighting, and acting commentary before shooting. Such preparation made the staged film set-ups almost automatic, leaving nothing to chance. Actor Farley Granger, who worked on a couple of Hitchcock films, remembers the director looking somewhat unhappy on the set during the lighting and equipment changes. When Granger asked him if there was anything wrong, Hitchcock complained, "Oh, I'm so bored!"

Cinematographer Robert Burks categorized Hitchcock as a perfectionist. Burks began working with the director on *Strangers On A Train* and would continue his association with Hitchcock for the next 13 years.

"You never have any trouble with him as long as you know your job and do it," Burks said. "Hitchcock insists on perfection. He has no patience with mediocrity on the set or at a dinner table. There can be no compromise in his work, his food, or his wines."

Hitchcock discussed his visualizing a scene well before going on the studio set:

"I don't understand why we have to experiment with film," he felt. "I think everything should be done on paper. A musician has to do it, a composer. He puts a lot of dots down and beautiful music comes out. And I think that students should be taught to visualize. That's the one thing missing in all this. The one thing that the student has got to do is to learn that there is a rectangle up there - a white rectangle in a theater - and it has to be filled."

Hitchcock explained key elements a director had to keep in mind when making a film: "when the price of the dinner, the theatre admission and the babysitter were worth it."

Hitchcock attached great importance to the script. He said, "To make that great film you need three things - the script, the script, and the script."

There were times when Hitchcock realized what seemed like a great idea on paper just wasn't good enough to get past the pre-production stage.

"I wanted once to do a scene, for '*North by Northwest,*' and I couldn't get it in there," Hitchcock recalled. "I wanted it to be in Detroit, and two men are walking along in front of an assembly line. And behind them you see the automobile being put together. It starts with a frame, and you just take the camera along, the two men are talking. And you know all those cars are eventually driven off the line, they load them with gas and everything. And one of the men goes forward, mind you you've seen a car from nothing, just a frame, opens the door and a dead body falls out."

SECRET TO HITCHCOCK'S THRILLERS

Hitchcock knew through his many years as a director how to create suspenseful, hair-raising sequences, guaranteeing his audiences they would squirm on the edge of their seats while viewing his movies. These sequences, essentially highlights of his films, were purposely lengthened to achieve their fullest white-knuckled effect. Hitchcock alternated between varying shots to extend the cinematic suspenseful length of time.

Hitchcock early on used the practice of "point of view" to stretch out a pivotal scene, such as in 1936's *Sabotage*, showing a boy, unbeknownst to the innocent child, carrying a bomb on a bus. The sequence is alluded to in Quentin Taratino's 2009 *Inglorious Basterds*, which serves as an explanatory example of describing the flammable volatility of nitrate film. *Sabotage* shows the boy taking a package containing several reels of film to an unknown person at a designated delivery place and time. Delayed by traffic congestion and an intersecting parade, the bus the boy is riding is late to its destination. Through several close-ups of the package, the boy looking at the clock, the advancing clock, and the clogged streets, Hitchcock lengthens the timeline of the delivery, working up an anxious audience viewing the sequence. The director's only regret, Hitchcock admitted on The Dick Cavett Show, was he had the bomb explode inside the bus, killing the boy, running counter to what a "suspense scene" is all about.

Hitchcock recalled after a review of the film, a critic approached him and said how disappointed she was about the conclusion of that scene. Her comment made him realize the audience needed to be relieved after a series of suspenseful shots. The deadly result in *Sabotage* didn't allow his viewers to get a breathtaking resolution without the tragedy. He noted on the Caveat Show he would have written the scene differently, such as someone grabbing the package and tossing it out of the window with the bomb exploding in a park. Hitchcock equated the tension in a movie similar to thrill seekers on a roller coaster who are relieved when the ride is finished--without the cars going tragically off the rails. Viewers need a series of ups and downs before the final resolution of a suspenseful scene ends.

"There is no terror in the bang," Hitchcock said, "only in the anticipation of it. Always make the audience suffer as much as possible, however."

Another extended dramatic sequence is the concluding staircase scene in *Notorious,* where Cary Grant and a woozy Ingrid Bergman are descending the steps in front of the movie's villains. The peculiar aspect of this nail biting finale is just minutes earlier Grant bounded up those same stairs in a flash to enter Bergman's second floor bedroom. As they walk down those stairs several minutes later with Grant clutching the drugged-up Bergman, Claude Rains and his Nazi guests confront Grant. A continuing dialogue between the parties lengthens the sequence so much it appears the number of stairs have almost triple in number to what Grant pranced up earlier. For the sake of heightening the suspense Hitchcock increased the tension by also lengthening the time it took for the pair to descend the flight of stairs to make their escape. The director intercut close-up, medium, wide, and point-of-view shots, moving the camera down the steps in concert with the pair as the villains looked on dumbfounded.

"I enjoy playing the audience like a piano," Hitchcock said of such techniques.

The carousel scene in *Strangers On A Train* was a meticulously drawn and complex sequence to film since it combined live action with rear screen projection. Hitchcock's technical crew spent at least half a day to arrange each shot so the actors and the projected image would match. The director claimed he was bored by the laborious detailed set-ups required to make this scene realistic and did not rely on trick photography when the script called for a carnival worker to crawl under the fast-circulating merry-go-round to reach the brakes in its center. Hitchcock was hesitant to film such a dangerous shot using a human since the stuntman underneath could be easily clipped and instantaneously killed with one wrong move. The stuntman assured the director he could safely perform the tight crawl under the actual, spinning merry-go-round. When the stunt was successfully filmed, Hitchcock let out a huge sigh of relief and said the shoot was the most dangerous he had ever directed. Hitchcock promised himself he would never do another one like that again.

While watching the stuntman under the carousel perform his death-defying maneuver, Hitchcock experienced a deep, emotional panic attack inside him.

"Fear isn't so difficult to understand," Hitchcock said. "After all, weren't we all frightened as children? Nothing has changed since Little Red Riding Hood faced the big bad wolf. What frightens us today is exactly the same sort of thing that frightened us yesterday. It's just a different wolf. This fright complex is rooted in every individual."

In the suspenseful concert scene at London's Royal Albert Hall in 1956's *The Man Who Knew Too Much,* the sequence consists of twelve minutes without dialogue and is composed of 124 separate shots. To carry out the suspense, Hitchcock felt the less conversation the better. The movie's final script contained a page-long monologue delivered by James Stewart on the reasons why the concert had to be stopped (an assassin was about to shoot and kill a foreign ambassador in the audience).

Hitchcock didn't like the idea of so much yapping. "You're talking so much, I'm unable to enjoy the London Symphony," Hitchcock said, going over the script with Stewart. "Just wave your arms a lot and run up the stairs."

SUSPENSEFUL CAR SCENES

Hitchcock was especially adept in creating tension in several driving sequences in his films. In 1959's *Northwest By Northwest*, Cary Grant is forced under gunpoint to drink massive amounts of hard liquor by the henchmen who had kidnapped him. They place Grant behind the steering wheel of a car with the intention of him driving off the high curvy road and over a cliff. Hitchcock alternated between Grant's fuzzy viewpoint of being unable to control his car weaving from side to side of the road crosscutting with several varying shots viewed from outside the car, including the point of view from the henchmen's perspective as they look on, to others driving opposite of Grant's car veering toward them. These numerous cuts made the movie's anxious audience participate in Grant's ordeal as he struggled to keep his car on the road.

Another hair-raising automobile scene occurred at the ending of 1941's *Suspicion*. Joan Fontaine thinks her hubby Grant is planning to intentionally kill her as they drive on a windy road above the Pacific Ocean. Fountaine feels by Grant pushing her out of the speeding car he is driving, he can easily do away with her. Her paranoid point of view is augmented by her eyeing the excessive miles-per-hour on the speedometer, close-ups of the crazed look on Grant's face, her looking down over the edge of the passing cliffs, intercut with shots of her anguished wide-eyed expression. We especially experience her horror when the door on her side accidentally opens up showing the long drop to the water and back to Grant's mad reaction of him lunging toward her.

Hitchcock could relate to being frightened and said he had some personal elements that sent shivers up and down his spine.

"I am scared easily," he related. Then he offered his list of things which intensely frightened him: "1: small children, 2: policemen, 3: high places and 4: that my next movie will not be as good as the last one."

Hitchcock saw the universality of scaring the bejesus out of people throughout the world. "If you've designed a picture correctly, the Japanese audience should scream at the same time as the Indian audience."

PRODUCTION

AVOIDED OUTSIDE LOCATION AT ALL COSTS

Hitchcock hated to film outside. This was likely because during the first half of his career while directing in England, the notorious British weather was habitually wet and unpredictable. Filming inside the studio, he had total control of lighting, sound and other factors, whereas outside anything could go amiss in the middle of unforeseen and unmanageable elements. Hitchcock used a number of special effects on the studio set, including composite and rear screen shots, to duplicate the outside environment. This was Hitchcock's standard practice he would use until the end of his directing days.

One early example of foregoing exterior location shooting and opting for filming comfortably inside the studio was when Hitchcock created his first signature trademark of using famous buildings and memorials to serve as backdrops to the action.

The final chase scene in *Blackmail* was mapped out to take place inside the British Museum. But the light levels in the spacious museum's rooms and hallways were too low to produce any reasonably looking shot, no matter how much light was poured into the cavernous areas. Hitchcock, aware of German cinematographer Eugen Schufftan's special effects trick he used in Fritz Lang's 1927 *Metropolis,* took a photograph of the interior of the museum and burned the photo's plate onto a mirror. The reflective surface of the special mirror where the live action shot in the studio would be filmed was scraped off, leaving a transparent glass so the camera could see through. The mirror was then placed in front of the camera lens. The final result is the viewer thinks the sequence was filmed inside the museum, a seemingly realistic shot that worked for Hitchcock.

The preference for shooting inside the studio did create some hardships for Hitchcock's crew. In *The 39 Steps*, a scene called for the actors being chased by some villains to blend in with a herd of sheep. Sixty two sheep were brought in from the local farms. The set designers had meticulously created an interior field inside the studio with handmade ferns and bushes. However, the sheep, thinking the plants were the real deal, munched on them voraciously, creating mass confusion between the animals, their handlers and the hard-working film crew. Hitchcock's team had to hurriedly travel to a local nursery and purchase all the plants they could buy. With the handlers maintaining a tight control over their sheep this time, the film crew replanted the sound stage with the real flora.

Because of the strict scenario requirements in some of his films, Hitchcock was forced to film outside on location. One situation occurred in *Shadow of A Doubt*, whose main draw for the director in using the town of Santa Rosa, California, for his movie's backdrop was the village looked as an ideal setting for an innocent community. Hitchcock, through the diligent work of his location scouts who scoured for days in the Santa Rosa area for the perfect locale, found what they felt was a fitting house for the Newtons, the family the evil Uncle Charlie would stay with. The house fit the script's description to a tee, consisting of a weathered look with faded exterior paint, bordered by an overgrown lawn, supplemented by an adjacent shopworn garage, and possessing other rough edges. In short, this was a home your average American family in an average American town would be living.

Hitchcock loved the property's appearance he saw in the photographs and agreed to rent out the property. When he arrived at the property to begin filming, however, Hitchcock was horrified in what he saw. The owners, excited by the prospect of a major motion picture studio using their house for a feature film, hired painters on their own and without informing the studio to apply a new coat of fresh paint to their house. They also employed landscapers to mow and manicure their lawn and fix whatever rough spots were on their lot. Hitchcock had to tell the studio set designers to laboriously mess up and age the house to reflect exactly what was he saw in the scouts' photos.

In the 1956 flick *The Wrong Man*, Hitchcock took a chance to film the scene where innocent Henry Fonda gets locked up in the real Queens City New York Prison with actual prisoners in their cellblocks. As the camera follows Fonda into his prison cell, one inmate can be heard in the background yelling, "What'd they get ya for, Henry?" followed by the other inmates laughing, all of which was left in the final release.

In the same movie, the film crew arrived at a country hotel. Hitchcock remained in his limo with the engine running, refusing to get out into the cold. It was at that point in the production he decided to move the remainder of the filming to Hollywood to finish *The Wrong Man*.

The outside locations Hitchcock needed to film for 1959's *North By Northwest* where he couldn't duplicate inside a studio without an enormous expense were New York City's exterior buildings and street scenes. During the *North* production, partially set in the city, the director was perturbed by the amount the studio was paying for the city police to serve as security for him and his crew. He also noted how lackadaisical they were in guarding the production's perimeter line. In a newspaper interview while in New York, Hitchcock labeled the city police as "New York's worst" instead of the normal "finest" nomenclature the men in blue were normally called. Immediately after the interview was published, the production crew arrived at its next location, The Plaza Hotel. Unsurprisingly, there was not a policeman to be found to offer guard protection.

The United Nations refused Hitchcock permission to shoot inside or outside the building's grounds for *North*. The director decided to go the "guerrilla filmmaking" route, where he would use a skeleton crew to quickly set up the scene where Cary Grant scampers up the steps of the UN before going inside. From a van, the crew set up the movie camera on the other side of the street and quickly filmed the actor leaving a cab to climb the stairs. The clip in the final version shows Grant bounding up the steps with at least one passerby distinctively noticing the actor.

Hitchcock had a change of heart when it came time to film 1963's *The Birds*. He couldn't resist shooting on location for this movie, particularly at the schoolhouse, in Bodega, California. The building had long been known as haunted. When the director heard about the house, he knew he had to film inside and around the house's exteriors. When the cast was inside the schoolhouse before and during the shoot, everyone claimed they got a strange feeling about the place, like "the building was immensely populated, but there was nobody there," described Hitchcock. The large house is now a private residence.

Fake gas station pumps were constructed on an empty Bodega lot next to the "The Tides" restaurant. The scene called for a man who lights a cigarette while pumping gas, seemingly unaware a stream of petroleum is flowing under him. Business people must have been inspired by the scene in the movie since several years later a service station was built in that exact same spot.

FILMING ON THE SET

It was on the studio sound stage Hitchcock showed he was always the steady director. In discussion one day on the set with cinematographer Ted Tetzlaff talking about a scene about to be filmed in *Notorious*, Hitchcock noticed a fire had broken out nearby. The fire had the potential of engulfing the entire studio with its massive amount of expensive equipment. The director turned to some of his stagehands nearby and coolly pointed out, "Will someone please put that fire out?" Without missing a beat, he went back to Tetzlaff to resume their conversation.

For 1954's *Rear Window*, the interior set depicting a New York City apartment complex and its courtyard was massive, the largest Paramount Studios had ever built up to that time. The enormous stage required every light Paramount possessed in the studio's inventory. Roughly 1,000 huge arc lamps and 2,000 smaller ones were installed, and four separate extensive lighting set-ups were required for the production to simulate daylight, nighttime, and the sunrises and sunsets. When the lights were switched to the daylight mode, the upper level of the studio set became oppressively hot.

One day the sprinkler system was triggered by the excessive heat, sending water everywhere and shutting down the entire studio's electricity. In the dark, Hitchcock calmly asked for an umbrella and told an assistant to let him know when the "rain" had stopped.

Hitchcock's main camera in *Rear Window* was placed in James Stewart's (Jeff's) apartment overlooking the apartment complex and its courtyard with facing windowed rooms and staircases. The director was stationed in Stewart's apartment throughout the entire shoot. He communicated with each actor separately in the other apartments via a radio, transmitting his directions into their flesh-colored earpieces.

In one scene, Hitchcock played a practical joke on a couple of actors by directing on separate audio lines for one actor to pull the mattress the two were carrying one way, while telling the actress listening on another separate audio line to pull the other way. The two were unaware of Hitchcock's conflicting instructions, resulting in a slapstick comedy. A fight between them broke out, causing one of the actors to stumble into the apartment with the mattress. Hitchcock so loved the spontaneity of the take he told his crew the footage was a "wrap and print."

The ultimate interior studio production was 1948's *Rope*. Here, Hitchcock would devise the most complex film set-ups on a sound stage ever created in cinematic history. With movable walls and furniture, the film would be shot in ten long takes, with each take ranging from four and a half minutes to ten minutes, the maximum amount of time a camera's film magazine could hold. Those ten takes were joined in post by meticulously planned "invisible" edits. Any mistake would necessitate long periods of resetting the entire stage. Everyone was highly aware of the extreme perfection such a production required.

During one take which had the camera dolly between two rooms, the heavy movable tripod on wheels supporting the camera ran over an assistant cameraman's foot. The great weight broke his foot, but because the scene was still playing out, someone next to him gagged his mouth. In pain the assistant was dragged off the set while the actors continued with the scene uninterrupted.

At another point during the filming of *Rope*, an actress had put her glass down and stepped forward. However, the glass was placed on the edge of the table and began to tilt over. A stagehand, out of camera frame, dived to catch the glass in midair before it hit the ground. Both sequences were used in the final cut.

In Hitchcock's most personal film, 1958's *Vertigo*, James Stewart plays a retired detective who wants to remake a woman resembling his late girlfriend, both played by Kim Novak. Stewart selects her clothes, make-up, and hairstyle to duplicate the looks of his dead amour. Once Ms. Novak emerges from her hotel bedroom, voila, Stewart's deceased girlfriend comes back to life.

The camera dollies around the couple as they kiss. The background of the hotel room where all this kissing is going on turns black. Then a picture emerges showing the livery horse stables at San Juan Bautista, recalling an earlier highly-charged scene between Stewart and his former girlfriend. The scene was shot using rear projection on background plates. While the camera revolves around the couple kissing on a circular platform, the background is also moving. The complex scene was difficult to coordinate in the extreme, and during one take Stewart became dizzy and fell, slightly injuring himself. But the apparatus in the studio made possible the scene envisioned by Hitchcock, something an outside location would never be able to accommodate.

There is a sequence in *North* where Eva Marie Saint and Cary Grant are running through the woods atop Mt. Rushmore to escape the villains toward the end of the film. Hitchcock didn't want to journey to South Dakota to shoot the scene and instead had 100 ponderosa pine trees planted on the MGM soundstage.

While the conclusion in *North* is considered one of the most thrilling endings in motion picture history, the United States Park Service refused to grant permission for Hitchcock to film on Mt. Rushmore. A replica of Mt. Rushmore presidents' stone faces was constructed inside the studio. And deferring to the government's sensitivities, the camera avoids the chiseled out faces when violence breaks out on the cliff.

And yes, the house where the evil spies are staying in at the foot of Mt. Rushmore was also studio bound. MGM, the studio which Hitchcock produced his only film for in *North*, meticulously designed the house in the Frank Lloyd Wright style, the premier architect during the 1950's. All materials, furniture, and layout of the rooms conformed to Wright's unique designs. The shot of the exterior of the same house was filmed using matte paintings.

Even the corn stalks Grant seeks shelter from a low-flying crop-dusting plane trying to clip him was constructed in the studio. Whenever Grant is filmed amongst the dry corn stalks, he's in the actual MGM studio. But the wide shots and other clips showing Grant standing in the scripted Indiana hot sun waiting for a meeting with a George Kaplan was actually filmed on Garces Highway, Route 155, near the towns of Wasco and Delano, north of Bakersfield in Kern County, California.

North opens with the interior of New York City's famed Oak Room. Viewers watching the scene swore Hitchcock filmed inside the restaurant, but MGM reconstructed the dining area so realistically people to this day are confused by the realism.

Hitchcock compromised in 1960's *Psycho* when he was convinced by the movie studio to shoot the wide shots of the Bates Mansion's facade constructed on the back lot of its studio. The exterior front porch and interior of the mansion were built inside on a sound stage to allow for a dolly shot between the porch and inside the house. The astute viewer can see the two different locations when Vera Miles approaches the mansion from the outside. The lighting changes when the scene cuts from her back as she is walking outside the studio to when she gets close to the front door, located inside the studio.

The director even devised a way to shoot actress Tippi Hedren on a runaway horse in 1964's *Marnie* without taking the entire crew out into the sun. To avoid being outside, Hitchcock came up with the idea of having the horse run on a huge treadmill inside the studio. The objections were numerous, including the treadmill would be unsafe for both the horse and the human (Tippi) riding on its back. Hitchcock wasn't totally convinced the system would be a dismal failure and insisted on at least giving the treadmill a try. The set-up, complete with rear projection to show the landscape racing by, was created. The entire operation worked without a hitch. To insure Hedren's safety, a harness was originally attached to her. The harness, after several takes, was removed from the actress because the camera could see it dangling from the top of the screen.

HITCHCOCK'S DIRECTING STYLE WITH HIS ACTORS

Hitchcock, unlike the dark themes and characters he was directing, was anything but demonic on the studio set. There is an urban legend Hitchcock once labeled his actors as cattle.

"There is a dreadful story that I hate actors." Hitchcock said, trying to correct the record. "Imagine anyone hating James Stewart. I can't imagine how such a rumor began. Of course it may possibly be because I was once quoted as saying that actors are cattle. My actor friends know I would never be capable of such a thoughtless, rude, and unfeeling remark, that I would never call them cattle. What I probably said was that actors should be treated like cattle."

He would use his self-taught psychological knowledge to get the best performances out of his actors. His lead actors in *The 39 Steps*, Madeleine Carroll and Robert Donat, were total strangers to each other before embarking in making their first picture together. Hitchcock planned to create a close chemistry between the two by not introducing them to each other until the first day of filming. He chose a scene to film first where they are handcuffed together. After recording a few takes, Hitchcock told them he lost the cuff keys and had to leave the set to look for them. First the two were annoyed at him and with each other. They grew increasingly flustered as the director hadn't return for quite some time. After a long stretch of waiting they strategized how to go to the bathroom. Eventually the actors warmed up to each other and got along swimmingly when Hitchcock returned, saying he "found" the key.

He loved directing certain actors throughout his career. Hitchcock worked with Cary Grant on several of his movies. The director's innate understanding of the complex British-born Grant smoothed out the actor's prickly behavior which drove other directors crazy. In one instance, in *Notorious*, Grant complained he was having trouble opening the door with his right hand because that hand was occupied holding his hat.

"Have you considered the possibility of transferring the hat to the other hand?" Hitchcock asked.

In the same film, the script called for Grant and actress Ingrid Bergman to passionately kiss one another in the initial stages of the film. The Film Board of Censors in those days forbade any kiss lasting longer than three seconds. To get around the onerous rule, Hitchcock came up with the idea that Grant and Bergman would kiss, then neck, then nibble, then get back kissing, before repeating the sequence several times while they moved around the apartment talking about food and speaking on the telephone.

Hitchcock remarked on shooting such scenes: "Film your murders like love scenes, and film your love scenes like murders."

Ben Hecht, the screenwriter for *Notorious*, referred to his script when he first viewed that particular kissing scene and couldn't find any of the couple's dialogue he had written. Confused, he said to Hitchcock, "I don't get all this talk about chicken!"

Hitchcock did trust Grant's opinions in a number of films while in production. In *North*, Grant looked at the set which had his character hiding in an upper berth of a studio-constructed interior train. Grant was unhappy with the look of the berth and complained to Hitchcock, saying the construction was sloppy and wasn't up to the film's high standards. Instead of looking at the set himself, he accepted Grant's assessment and ordered the studio carpenters to rebuild the berth to Grant's satisfaction.

Hitchcock, however, capitalized on circumstances when the opportunity was right to get perfect acting performances. In *Rebecca*, the only Best Picture Oscar awarded to a Hitchcock-directed film (he would never be handed an earned Oscar for his direction), star Laurence Olivier was highly upset when his then-girlfriend Vivien Leigh (Scarlett O'Hara in *Gone With The Wind*) failed to get the lead role as his wife in the movie, the second Mrs. de Winter. Olivier treated the actress who received the role, Joan Fontaine, with visible disdain throughout the production. Fontaine, not used to such behavior, was shaken by the actor's attitude and comments. Hitchcock witnessed Olivier's lack of civility was upsetting her. Instead of calming the situation, Hitchcock told Fontaine not only did Olivier hate her, but everyone on the set, the other actors, the technical crew, even the janitors hated her. Fontaine's lack of confidence, which her frail character in *Rebecca* was intended to possess, is clearly seen on the screen. Her performance earned the actress high critical acclaim from newspaper critics and an Academy Award nomination for Best Actress.

ACTORS' SUGGESTIONS TO HITCHCOCK

Hitchcock didn't particularly care for certain actors who felt they could direct the film themselves. When Ingrid Bergman wanted to deliver a line a certain way, counter to Hitch's vision of the scene, Hitchcock advised her to "Fake it!" to achieve the results he expected.

He also wasn't fond of hiring so-called "method actors," those performers who live deep within the soul of the characters they are portraying both on and off the screen.

"When an actor comes to me and wants to discuss his character, I say, 'It's in the script'," Hitchcock explained. "If he says, 'But what's my motivation?' I say, 'Your salary.'"

Hitchcock had a preconceived image of what his actors' expressions would look like at certain key moments of the film. Gregory Peck in *Spellbound* said Hitchcock expressed dismay his facial expressions were so limited.

"I couldn't produce the facial expressions that Hitch wanted turned on," recalled Peck. "I didn't have that facility. He already had a preconception of what the expression ought to be on your face; he planned that as carefully as the camera angles. Hitchcock was an outside fellow, and I had the Stanislavski training from the Neighborhood Playhouse, which means you work from the inside."

Casting for *North*, MGM Studio lobbied Hitchcock for Peck to play the lead role of Roger Thornhill. The director cringed, remembering Peck's role in *Spellbound*. He cast aside the studio's selection, claiming the actor was too stone-faced. Cary Grant eventually got the lead.

To see how Peck would have played the Thornhill role, one only has to look at Stanley Donen's 1966 *Arabesque*, a movie similar to *North*'s plot and character development. Coincidentally, during the production of *Arabesque*, director Donen advised Peck to lighten up when reciting a humorous line. Peck smiled and said "Remember, I'm no Cary Grant."

When Mary Anderson asked Hitchcock during 1944's filming of *Lifeboat* what side was her best so she could situate herself toward the camera while in the boat, the director replied, "You're sitting on it."

Hitchcock for the most part met his deadlines, but sometimes he would be involved in longer unanticipated production schedules. Normally a director would rehearse with his actors for the next scene while the crew was changing the lighting on the sets. However, Hitchcock found the noise distracting and wouldn't rehearse with his actors until the set-ups were completed.

James Stewart remembers Hitchcock uninterested in the dramatics of acting, but the director expected the actors to know what was expected of them. The most Hitchcock would say to Stewart about his acting was on the lines of "This scene is tired," which meant to the actor the timing of his lines were off.

Thelma Ritter recalled Hitchcock had never informed his actors whether he approved of their performances after each scene. But what the actors did know is that if he didn't like their acting, "he looked like he was going to throw up," said Ritter.

That lack of feedback from a director was a startling revelation to actor Martin Landau, who played the villain in *North*. After one scene was filmed, he noticed Hitchcock conversing with Cary Grant, James Mason and Eva Marie Saint, seemingly giving them instructions. Landau was puzzled because Hitchcock rarely, if ever, said anything of note to him about his lines during the production. He eventually approached Hitchcock and asked if he was doing okay with his performance. Hitchcock emphasized if he ignored Landau, that's because he was doing fine. Referring to Hitchcock's conversation with the trio, Landau was told by the director there was something not right about their acting in the scene and he wanted to correct it.

HITCHCOCK AND BLONDES

Throughout Hitchcock's movie career, especially in his later films, his leading actress is almost always a blonde. Grace Kelly, Doris Day, Kim Novak, Susan Marie Saint, Janet Leigh, and Tippi Hedren come instantly to mind. Film critics point to these actresses' body of work and claim their working relationship with Hitchcock produced their finest moments on the screen.

Several books have been written about Hitchcock's relationship with his leading ladies, some complementary, like John Taylor's *The Life And Times of Alfred Hitchcock*, and some not so complementary, such as Donald Spoto's *Alfred Hitchcock: The Dark Side of Genius.*

A common thread tracing throughout Hitchcock's professional relationship with his favorite blondes was that his most successful period of creativity, beginning in 1954 with *Rear Window* and lasting through 1963's *The Birds,* coincided with the emergence of stellar performances from his leading actresses. Hitchcock consciously selected actresses with blond hair, reasoning, "Blondes make the best victims. They're like virgin snow that shows up the bloody footprints."

In his mind he knew exactly what was required from them, and through his advice and input to apparel and hairstyle details, these actresses stole the spotlight in his films.

Edith Head, the multi-Academy Award costume design winner, spent a large amount of time with Hitchcock going over Grace Kelly's attire in *Rear Window.* One concern the director had was the negligee Kelly wears to spend the night at Stewart's apartment. He quietly told Edith he wanted Kelly to have a fuller look up top and suggested the costume designer slip in some falsies. Edith knew with a few changes in the negligee and Kelly's posture, the falsies wouldn't be needed. She didn't tell Hitchcock about the alterations, and once seeing Kelly, the director happily approved her revised appearance, thinking the falsies really made the difference.

In another Hitchcock film Edith worked on, *Vertigo,* the director wanted to give Kim Novak's clothing an eerie appearance in the scene when she agrees to dress as Stewart's old flame. A grey suit was selected since both Edith and Hitchcock felt all-grey on a blonde woman would look seemingly odd. They both agreed a black scarf draped over her white coat Novak wore later would also appear an odd contrast, fitting for the bizarre character she was playing.

Filming *North,* Hitchcock didn't like the dresses MGM Studios had tailor-made for his leading actress, Eva Marie Saint. He took the actress to the clothing store Bergdorf Goodman and personally selected the clothes he felt would suit her character better.

Janet Leigh had a similar experience with Hitchcock and her wardrobe choice in *Psycho*. Playing Marion Crane, who made a living as an office secretary, Leigh was told she wouldn't get the tailor-made dresses she was accustomed to wearing in her other films. Hitchcock wanted her to look like an ordinary secretary, and to add realism to her character, Leigh had to purchase her clothes off the rack in a local clothing store.

DIRECTING WOMEN

Hitchcock instinctively knew how his leading actress's off-screen magnetic personalities could transfer onto the screen, and there were occasions when he didn't want to dampen their spark. Doris Day, in 1956's *The Man Who Knew Too Much*, felt she was floundering in front of the camera because Hitchcock didn't say anything about her acting. She eventually had a sit-down talk with the director, telling him "You're not telling me what to do, and not what to do." Hitchcock's reply: "You have been doing what I felt was right for the film and that's why I haven't told you anything." Ultimately, critics agreed her role as a mother of a kidnapped son was the top dramatic performance in her career.

Novak was equally perplexed in her difficult dual role in *Vertigo*. Offering a suggestion to Hitchcock on revealing her character's inner motivation, Novak was told by the director, "Kim, this is only a movie. Let's not go deeply into these things." Surprisingly to her, even though she was not too happy about her delivery, all agree Novak's performance in *Vertigo* is her best ever.

Hitchcock, the master of psychology, saw levity as a release valve right before filming his actresses' highly-charged emotional scenes. Such attempts on his part, though, were met with mixed results. Novak was greeted by a plucked chicken hanging from the ceiling of her dressing room on the day of filming a crucial scene in *Vertigo*, and she made it known she was disgusted by the practical joke. However, Janet Leigh in *Psycho*, found Hitchcock's humor especially funny. To gauge which mummified skeleton of Mrs. Bates would be the scariest, Hitchcock propped up the corpse in her dressing room chair before she would return from lunch. The level of Leigh's yells determined which one to use in the movie.

Janet Leigh, whose character dies by an intruder knifing her in the shower in *Psycho*, said initially she wasn't in the least bothered filming the shower scene. But when she saw the scene on the big screen, Leigh was deeply disturbed by the violence. She realized how vulnerable people are when they take a shower, with the curtain obstructing an assailant and the noise of the shower obscuring any sound to the attacker's approach. Since that viewing, she had forsaken showers and took only baths for the remainder of her life.

Leigh wasn't the only one who was jarred by the shower scene. A father mailed a letter to Hitchcock soon after *Psycho* was released describing the effect his movie had on his daughter. The father detailed how his daughter after viewing the 1955 French movie *Diabolique,* where a victim is killed in a bathtub, refused to take a bath. Now her daughter doesn't want to take a shower after seeing *Psycho.* Hitchcock said he sent back a note to the father which read "Send her to the dry cleaners."

Hitchcock viewed *Psycho* differently than Leigh or the reviewers who critiqued the film. "To me, *Psycho* was a big comedy. Had to be."

Leigh received acting advice from the director which greatly enhanced her effectiveness in her difficult conflicted role. Likewise, Eva Saint-Marie, playing opposite Cary Grant in *North,* thought highly of Hitchcock's skills. "One of his greatest gifts as a director was that he made you feel you were the only perfect person for the role and this gave you incredible confidence," praised Saint-Marie.

Rookie actress Tippi Hedren was at first appreciative of Hitchcock's tutelage. The former TV commercial and magazine ad model had little acting experience, and her preparation for *The Birds*, besides serving as a pincushion to hundreds of pecking birds, required a natural acting personality during her physical ordeal.

"I probably learned in three years what it would have taken me fifteen years to learn otherwise," said Hedren of her association with Hitchcock.

One particular sequence was especially dangerous to Hedren when she goes upstairs into a bedroom, only to be confronted by hundreds of birds who had broken in through the roof. This climatic scene took several days to film and exacted both a physical and emotional toll on Hedren. "It was the worst week of my life," Hedren remembers.

Before shooting the scene she asked Hitchcock, "Hitch, why would I do this?" Hitchcock's response was, "Because I tell you to."

After the filming in the upstairs bedroom, Hedren had to go to the hospital to recover from exhaustion. The scene at the end of the movie shows Rod Taylor carrying Melanie down the stairs. The woman Rod is cradling is really a body-double filling in for the hospitalized Hedren.

"You know, I've often wondered what the Audubon Society's attitude might be to this picture," Hitchcock said of *The Birds*.

During the filming of Hitchcock's next film, *Marnie*, things got a bit dicey between the director and Hedren. A series of complications and uncomfortable proposals drew the relationship to an acrimonious close. Despite claiming Hitchcock ruined her acting career--even though she appeared in over 80 films and television shows after *Marnie*--Hedren appreciated his working talents.

"He was brilliant," Hedren says. "He will always be remembered as one of the major motion picture giants. There are so many things I would have to thank him for and I would certainly never take that away."

One helpful piece of advice Hitchcock relayed to Hedren was early on during the filming of *Marnie*. Her co-star was the debonair Sean Connery and her role was to play a cold, insecure women Connery is attracted to.

"Marnie is supposed to be frigid - have you seen him?" Hedren said, pointing to the handsome, young Connery. "Yes, my dear," replied Hitchcock. "It's called acting."

HITCHCOCK'S MACGUFFINS

Hitchcock films are known for their plot devices known as MacGuffins. These are mostly objects his film characters are aware of and are on a number of occasions the basis for their actions introduced early in his movies. Yet, as the films progress, these MacGuffins lose their importance as other motivations arising from such objectives propel forward. Examples abound in Hitchcock's works, such as the bottled uranium in *Notorious*, the wedding ring in *Rear Window*, the microfilm in *North*, and the $40,000 in cash contained in the envelope in *Psycho*.

The idea of MacGuffins predated Hitchcock's usage in his films, such as King Arthur's search for the Holy Grail during the Middle Ages as well as Dashiell Hammett's use of a black bird statuette in his 1929 novel *The Maltese Falcon*. Hitchcock did, however, popularized the term "MacGuffin," although he downplayed its importance as he described the term during a 1939 lecture.

"It might be a Scottish name, taken from a story about two men on a train," said Hitchcock. "One man says, 'What's that package up there in the baggage rack?' And the other answers, 'Oh, that's a MacGuffin.' The first one asks, 'What's a MacGuffin?' 'Well,' the other man says, 'it's an apparatus for trapping lions in the Scottish Highlands.' The first man says, 'But there are no lions in the Scottish Highlands,' and the other one answers, 'Well then, that's no MacGuffin!' So you see that a MacGuffin is actually nothing at all."

During the 1979 American Film Institute Achievement Award, when he received the group's Lifetime honor, Hitchcock made note of his one and only wife and working companion, Alma Reville.

"Had the beautiful Ms. Reville not accepted a lifetime contract without options as Mrs. Alfred Hitchcock some 53 years ago, Mr. Alfred Hitchcock might be in this room tonight, not at this table but as one of the slower waiters on the floor."

Hitchcock was the type that even though he had occasional bouts of sickness, nothing was too serious to lay him up for long periods of time while he was producing his movies. But the director did dread the eventuality of a long, lasting period of being ill right before death.

"It is terribly embarrassing to be sick, and one's own death is so undignified," Hitchcock lamented. He and his wife always wanted to have their ashes scattered in the ocean.

"There is nothing quite so good as a burial at sea," he envisioned. "It is simple, tidy, and not very incriminating."

Hitchcock received his wish at the age of 80 when he died just a few months after being knighted (en absentia) by Queen Elizabeth II while he was lingering from a prolonged illness. His body was cremated and his ashes were scattered in the Pacific Ocean, just as he wanted.

TOP TEN ALFRED HITCHCOCK FILMS

#1-- VERTIGO (1958)

Acknowledged as the number one thriller of all-time, *Vertigo* was produced during Hitchcock's peak directing years. The only slightly uneasy criticism of the film is the age difference between Jimmy Stewart and Kim Novak, but that's the beauty of Hitchcock: he can make a romance between the two believable while delivering a socko punch as the twists and turns unfold. Richard Brody of the New Yorker took a modern, sophisticated view of the movie, "It's as much a wonder of suspense as it is a catalogue of the director's themes and an allegory for his own art of enticement-and for the erotic pitfalls of his métier."

#2--PSYCHO (1960)

Hitchcock labeled the movie a comedy, but millions can't take a shower without locking the bathroom door because of the famous Janet Leigh knifing scene. This psychological thriller paved the way for the modern slasher thriller genre while the movie has spawned several books and documentaries explaining everything from homoerotic tendencies of Norman Bates to the purgation washing of Janet Leigh's embezzlement guilt during the shower scene. David Jenkins, film reviewer, says of *Psycho*, "It blazed a bloody trail for the much-loved slasher cycle, but it also assured us that a B-movie could be A-grade in quality and innovation."

#3--THE BIRDS (1963)

Combining pioneering special effects with real live birds, this horror-thriller introduces the public to actress Tippi Hedrin, who gets plucked more times making this movie than a Thanksgiving turkey. Hitchcock's film also explores the oedipal relationship between son Rod Taylor and mother Jessica Tandy and the frustration of school teacher Suzanne Pleschette to break that strong connection. "In the thick of an impeccable narrative that pays deep attention to all those involved, the great filmmaker manages to reach far inside the psychological chasm and find a rich inspiration," David Keyes wrote.

#4--NORTH BY NORTHWEST (1959)

One of Cary Grant's better roles as he plays the stereotyped mistaken victim who ends up going on the lam, a plot device Hitchcock frequently used. The classic crop duster sequence as well as the climatic Mt. Rushmore chase scene are more than enough to witness one of cinema's most thrilling films without the heavy psychology of certain Hitchcock personalities. *North* was a template for the producers of James Bond's early films. Time Out's review, fifty years after *North's* release, said, "Fifty years on, you could say that Hitchcock's sleek, wry, paranoid thriller caught the zeitgeist perfectly: Cold War shadiness, secret agents of power, urbane modernism, the ant-like bustle of city life, and a hint of dread behind the sharp suits of affluence. Cary Grant's Roger Thornhill, the film's sharply dressed ad exec who is sucked into a vortex of mistaken identity, certainly wouldn't be out of place in *Mad Men*. But there's nothing dated about this perfect storm of talent, from Hitchcock and Grant to writer Ernest Lehman (*Sweet Smell of Success*), co-stars James Mason and Eva Marie Saint, composer Bernard Herrmann and even designer Saul Bass, whose opening-credits sequence still manages to send a shiver down the spine."

#5--REAR WINDOW (1954)

Hitchcock explores voyeurism like no other film had done before--or since-- as Jimmy Stewart, laid up in his apartment recovering from a broken leg, suspects a neighbor of killing his wife. But skeptical friends find his story hard to believe. This movie features Grace Kelly in her most glamorous role and showcases why, in her brief career, she was one of the most highly-regarded actress in her time. Roger Ebert, 30 years after the *Rear Window's* release, wrote the movie "develops such a clean, uncluttered line from beginning to end that we're drawn through it (and into it) effortlessly. The experience is not so much like watching a movie, as like ... well, like spying on your neighbors. Hitchcock traps us right from the first. And because Hitchcock makes us accomplices in Stewart's voyeurism, we're along for the ride. When an enraged man comes bursting through the door to kill Stewart, we can't detach ourselves, because we looked too, and so we share the guilt and in a way we deserve what's coming to him."

#6--SHADOW OF A DOUBT (1943)

Hitchcock said this was his favorite film he had personally directed, and it's easy to see why. Friendly Uncle Charlie (Joseph Cotton) reunites with his family, but Teresa Wright discovers Uncle Charlie isn't as innocent as he makes himself to be. Film critic Bosley Crowther wrote, "You've got to hand it to Alfred Hitchcock: when he sows the fearful seeds of mistrust in one of his motion pictures he can raise more goose pimples to the square inch of a customer's flesh than any other director of thrillers in Hollywood."

#7--FRENZY (1972)

Hitchcock returns to his British roots to produce this late-career thriller, creating one of the director's most violent, erotic films. Hitchcock's only R-rated film. His daughter Patricia Hitchcock found this film so disturbing she would not allow her children to see it for many years. "This is the kind of thriller Hitchcock was making in the 1940s, filled with macabre details, incongruous humor, and the desperation of a man convicted of a crime he didn't commit," wrote Roger Ebert.

#8--NOTORIOUS (1946)

Yes, this is the film containing the famously long kissing scene between Cary Grant and Ingrid Bergman which baffled film censors. Also, Hitchcock's most recognized complex crane long shot of the key to the wine cellar held in Bergman's hand is seen during a party sequence. Film critic Roger Ebert called the film "the most elegant expression of the master's visual style." Wally Hammond of Time Out added, "It's the accuracy, efficiency and control of Hitchcock's direction that most impress. They enable him to dovetail the film's thriller format and romantic story to dizzying, expressive and unique effect."

#9--ROPE (1948)

Rope is Hitchcock's most unusual movie in that it unfolds as one long continuous take (although there were at least two discernible cuts). *Rope* is about two friends who think they just committed the perfect murder no one would ever figure out, that is until their college professor Jimmy Stewart arrives at the party they're hosting. Film reviewer Kevin McCarthy said of the movie, "*Rope* is Hitchcock's underrated classic that contains some of the most unique filmmaking of its time. Hitchcock was so far ahead of filmmakers back then and so far ahead of a lot of the filmmakers today."

#10--THE MAN WHO KNEW TOO MUCH (1955)

The Oscar winning song, *Que Sera Sera,* sung by Doris Day is reason enough to see this international thriller. But Hitchcock, who remade his 1934 picture of the same name ("Let's say the first version is the work of a talented amateur and the second was made by a professional," said Hitchcock) adds a panache of color and heightened lively action to present a thriller putting the viewer on the edge of the seat through the finale. Film critic Emanuel Levy said of the updated movie, "Far superior to the 1934 version, *The Man Who Knew Too Much*, underestimated at its 1956 release, should be considered as one of Hitchcock's masterpieces."

Billy Wilder

THE GENUIS WHO WROTE AND DIRECTED BRILLIANT FILMS

Film director Billy Wilder was tearing out what little hair he had on his head after multiple takes of Marilyn Monroe botching her line during the scene where she's looking for a bottle of bourbon in a bureau drawer while filming 1959's *Some Like It Hot.*

The director decided to write her line on a piece of paper and tape it inside one of the drawers she was supposed to open. On the next take, she opened the wrong drawer. Exasperated, he taped the line inside every drawer in the cabinet so there wouldn't be any chance she failed to see it. Eighty-three takes later, she nailed her line "Where's that bourbon."

Wilder's adventures with Monroe's work habits during the *Some Like It Hot's* shooting are legendary. Filming a kissing scene on a couch with Monroe would be nirvana to most American males, but for Tony Curtis it was pure agony. Wilder told the actor he would have to nail his lines repeatedly in the hopes one of the multiple takes Monroe required would be good. "It was like kissing Hitler," Curtis remembered as take after take of love making with the starlet was wearing him down.

Both he and co-star Jack Lemmon were required to wear high heels when filming the sequences where they are disguised as women. In the scenes where Monroe wasn't on the set, the two would rip off their shoes and soak their feet in agony during a break. But in scenes with Monroe the actors suffered excruciating pain standing in frame wearing the torturous high heels while multiple takes were needed.

Visibly seen in the final release is an example of where she clearly couldn't remember her lines when saying goodbye to Tony Curtis on the phone. The actress' eyes are moving back and forth as if she were reading off a blackboard. And she was. Wilder had to set up an off-screen blackboard with the portion of her lines written in chalk. Lemmon claimed the only scene Monroe correctly performed in one take was when she got into bed with him in the sleeper on the train.

During the production of *Hot,* Monroe was constantly two to three hours late arriving to the studio. A number of times she simply refused to leave her dressing room to go on the set.

The strain Monroe created on Wilder while making *Hot* caused him to lose sleep as well as his appetite. At the same time jolts of pain ran up and down the director's spine, causing him immense discomfort.

"It takes a real artist to come on the set and not know her lines and give the performance she did," Wilder said sarcastically.

But he knew Monroe's drawing power to film audiences was the reason Wilder hired her for *Hot*. He reminded himself "There was an actress named Marilyn Monroe. She was always late. She never remembered her lines. She was a pain in the butt. My Aunt Millie is a nice lady. If she were in pictures she would always be on time. She would know her lines. She would be nice. Why does everyone in Hollywood want to work with Marilyn Monroe and no one wants to work with my Aunt Millie? Because no one will go to the movies to watch my Aunt Millie."

Once filming is finished for every movie, the cast and crew get together for what is called the "wrap" party to say goodbye to one another. Wilder, who was physically sick during *Hot,* didn't invite Monroe to the gathering, a real slap in the actress' face. Wilder described the experience working with her akin to flying cross-country: "We were in mid-flight, and there was a nut on the plane."

When *Hot* was released, critics cited Monroe's role in the movie as her best performance in her career. Wilder was astonished at what he saw in the movie theater versus what he witnessed in the studio. "It (Monroe's performance) looks like nothing on the set," said Wilder, "and then when it goes on the screen, it all comes out in neon light. It's fantastic how celluloid loves Monroe. Just incredible."

Despite all the hardships Wilder experienced with her making *Hot,* the director considered her for the lead in 1963's *Irma la Douce,* so impressed was he by her performance on the screen.

After discussing with his doctors the possibility of working with Monroe again, he realized the impossibility.

"I have discussed this with my doctor and my psychiatrist and they tell me I'm too old and too rich to go through this again," recalled Wilder.

The director knew mentally Monroe was going through some problems. He described her as having "breasts like granite and a brain like Swiss cheese. She was an endless puzzle without any solution."

Wilder was genuinely saddened by Monroe's premature death in August 1962, at 36 years old. But familiar with a litany of other troubled actresses, Wilder noted, "Hollywood didn't kill Marilyn Monroe. It's the Marilyn Monroes who are killing Hollywood."

PRE-PRODUCTION

WILDER THE SCRIPTWRITER

Wilder is recognized as both a genius at scriptwriting as well as having a sharp eye while directing. He won a combined six Academy Awards for both directing and writing, an achievement never equaled. His talent for producing topnotch scripts separated himself from his contemporary directors. When asked whether the ability to write was a prerequisite to being a successful director, Wilder responded, "No, but it helps if he knows how to read."

Wilder's career is unique in the roster of influential film directors in that he was a product of Austria-Hungary before gaining employment in Berlin, Germany, as a journalist and as a part-time movie scriptwriter. He escaped the oppression of Adolf Hitler in 1933 by immigrating to the United States, but lost his grandmother, mother, and stepfather in the Holocaust following the Nazi takeover of the region. He gave praise to his native Austria by noting, "The Austrians are brilliant people. They made the world believe that Adolf Hitler was a German and Ludwig van Beethoven an Austrian."

Speaking little English, Wilder arrived in America in the hopes of continuing his writing career. To become familiar with the English language, Wilder took night classes. Sharpening those skills he learned in the classroom, Wilder made it a point to date women who spoke only English.

His meteoric rise in Hollywood once he mastered the language is out of a fairytale storybook: screenplay Oscar for Greta Garbo's 1939 *Ninotcka,* assuming directorial reigns in 1942 after studying veteran director Howard Hawks' on-set directing skills, Best Director and Screenwriter Academy Awards winner three years later for 1945's *The Lost Weekend.* And that was just the beginning of his stellar Hollywood career.

Wilder's witty scripts served the basis for his films and are noteworthy because they are uniquely different from other studio-produced movies made in that era. Wilder advised aspiring moviemakers, "Trust your own instinct. Your mistakes might as well be your own, instead of someone else's."

Wilder hated to work alone on his typewriter. He wrote his scripts with the assistance of several fellow screenwriters. Early in his Hollywood days, beginning with 1942's *Major and the Minor,* he corroborated with writer Charles Brackett. The older Brackett was the more experienced of the two when it came to writing movie scripts. He consistently offered an alternative to the plot Wilder outlined as well as provided deeper developed characterizations of the main protagonists than initially drawn by the director. With the exception of 1944's *Double Indemnity,* a film where Wilder brought in detective novelist Raymond Chandler to help him, the duo cranked out brilliant screenplays until after 1950's *Sunset Boulevard.*

For *Double Indemnity,* a film based on James Cain's hard-boiled novella of the same name, Wilder decided to work with Chandler to produce the edgy, street-wise dialogue the movie's characters portrayed. Hitchcock would later have his own troubles with Chandler during their corroboration on 1951's *Strangers On A Train.*

The four months it took to write the screenplay was an ordeal for both while they labored in Wilder's film studio office. It didn't take long for the two to begin yelling at each other. The admittedly sexually-repressed Chandler was tormented by Wilder, who flaunted his ability to get a carload of women at any time. Wilder's taunting became so outrageous Chandler refused to work with the director and stayed home. A studio representative drove to Chandler's house to find out the reasons he wouldn't report to work. The writer said he could no longer be with the director.

"Mr. Wilder frequently interrupts our work to take phone calls from women," Chandler complained. Then he rattled off a list of other complaints percolating in his psyche for quite some time: "Mr. Wilder ordered me to open up the window. He did not say please" ... "He sticks his baton in my eyes" ... "I can't work with a man who wears a hat in the office. I feel he is about to leave at any minute."

Chandler told the representative unless Wilder apologizes, he was going to quit. The studio eventually persuaded Wilder to approach the novelist and admit some of his shortcomings.

Wilder, who did recognize Chandler's gift for the dialogue the screenplay needed, said, "It was the first, and probably only time on record in which a producer and director ate humble pie, in which the screenwriter humiliated the big shots."

In retrospect, Wilder admitted he was hard on Chandler, a recovering alcoholic who was attending Alcoholics Anonymous sessions at the time. "He had a tough time with me," Wilder said, "I think I drove him back into drinking."

As an admirer of the film, novelist James Cain said the solutions to the plot Wilder and Chandler came up with would have been incorporated into his original book since they were superior to what he wrote for the novel's denouement.

WILDER AND HIS SCRIPTWRITERS

Returning from New York to Los Angeles on a train after the release of

Indemnity, Wilder picked up some reading material at a stopover in Chicago. He perused one of the books he bought, Charles Jackson's *The Lost Weekend.* The director realized, with Chandler in mind, the book's subject matter about an alcoholic spending a weekend alone and his adventures during those couple of days in a big city would make a fascinating movie on the disease afflicting the detective novelist.

The Lost Weekend garnered seven Academy Award nominations and won four Oscars, including Best Picture, Wilder for Best Director, and Wilder and Brackett for Best Screenplay, a stunning collection of awards at the time.

Wilder continued to partner with Brackett until, much to Brackett's surprise, Wilder informed him their partnership was over after completing 1950's *Sunset Boulevard.* The two had written 17 highly-regarded screenplays, but Brackett had failed to remember one heated debate that ultimately caused the permanent rift. During *Sunset's* story development, the writers fought over the sequence involving actress Gloria Swanson's character (Norma Desmond) as she prepared for her grand comeback into pictures after so many years away from Hollywood. Brackett felt showing how old the once glamorous actress had grown since her heyday in silent pictures would be too unbearable to watch. Wilder thought the sequence was crucial in understanding the aging actress' insane obsession to turn back the clock and revert to her youth. Wilder got his way, but the argument was so fierce and emotional for the director he told friends privately the partnership with Brackett was coming to an end.

The break-up would serve as a convenient excuse for Wilder later on. He didn't particularly harbor any desire to remake his movies during the later years of his career. Wilder received constant phone calls from producers who wanted him to remake *Sunset* in color. He cut the conversations to the quick, saying he didn't own the rights to the script and hung up.

Wilder worked with other writers following *Sunset,* some without much success. The ones who had difficulty with the director complained about his work habits. The most critical noted if they came up with an idea and Wilder hated it, he would turn cruel and insulting toward them.

Wilder eventually found a soulmate in scripting when he partnered with I. A. Diamond in 1957's *Love In The Afternoon.* Diamond, whose view of the world was more in line with Wilder's than any previous writer, produced alongside Wilder classics such as *Some Like It Hot* and 1960's *The Apartment.* Diamond, like Wilder, was cynical, yet he saw the humor in almost every circumstance.

STORY IDEAS POP UP IN WILDER'S HEAD

Some of Wilder's story ideas were adopted from real events.

For his controversial 1951's *Ace In The Hole,* Wilder recalled a 1925 incident where cave explorer Floyd Collins was stuck in a Kentucky Crystal Cave crawlway. William Miller, a reporter for the Louisville Courier-Journal newspaper, was assigned to cover the incident. The stories dispatched from Miller on the site gained national attention, and while rescue efforts proved to be unsuccessful, Miller's reporting earned him a Pulitzer Prize for his coverage as well as a job for the *New York City Morning World.*

Kirk Douglas plays a similar role as a reporter whose sole coverage of a man trapped in a New Mexican cave captured the imagination of the country. The dark underbelly of the premise was that Douglas elongated the trapped man's ordeal unnecessarily in order to get a bigger payout with the public interest increasing every day. Upon seeing the film, critics scoffed at such an idea.

"I was attacked by every paper because of that movie," said Wilder, whose portrayal of the press in *Ace* was critical. "They loathed it. It was cynical, they said. Cynical, my butt. I tell you, you read about a plane crash somewhere nearby and you want to check out the scene, you can't get to it because 10,000 people are already there: they're picking up little scraps, ghoulish souvenir hunters. After I read those horrifying reviews about *Ace in the Hole,* I remember I was going down Wilshire Boulevard and there was an automobile accident. Somebody was run over. I stopped my car. I wanted to help that guy who was run over. Then another guy jumps out of his car and photographs the thing. 'You'd better call an ambulance,' I said. 'Call a doctor, my ass. I've got to get to the 'L.A. Times'. I've got a picture. I've got to move. I just took a picture here. I've got to deliver it.' But you say that in a movie, and the critics think you're exaggerating."

Wilder gave *Ace* as an example in his ability to deliver a societal message while still entertaining his viewers.

"In certain pictures I do hope they will leave the cinema a little enriched," Wilder said. "But I don't make them pay a buck and a half and then ram a lecture down their throats." And his philosophy of delivering a deep message was, "If you're going to tell people the truth, be funny or they'll kill you."

"I was not a guy writing deep-dish revelations," Wilder said about his own themes. "If people see a picture of mine and then sit down and talk about it for 15 minutes, that is a very fine reward, I think."

Wilder was a big fan of British film director David Lean, especially his early pictures. He got the idea of *The Apartment* from Lean's 1945 classic *Brief Encounter,* where a husband and wife from separate marriages, portrayed by

Trevor Howard and Celia Johnson, borrow a friend of Howard's city apartment for a tryst. Wilder always wondered about the guy who owned the apartment and where the owner went while Howard and Johnson were performing their deeds in his flat.

Wilder believed there are certain scenes viewers remember long after the movie is over, even though most of the picture is forgotten by them. He called these memorable scenes "hooks." One so-called "hook" in *The Apartment* is the sequence where Jack Lemmon lends his apartment keys to one of his working colleagues where he tangos with his girlfriend. Fans of Lemmon recalled the scene years after the movie was released and asked him when they saw the actor, "Hey, Jack, can I have the key?"

Wilder believed a film's main selling point was its plot and its characters rather than any aesthetic maneuver a director would make to create an artsy shot. "The best director is the one you don't see," was Wilder's motto.

He always wanted to make "pictures I would've liked to see. The Wilder message is don't bore--don't bore people."

Knowing Hollywood film directors have huge egos, Wilder never deluded himself as far as his own reputation. "You're only as good as the best thing you've ever done," he told people. Wilder was always fearful of the clunker he was capable of producing, no matter how great his body of work.

"A bad play folds and is forgotten, but in pictures we don't bury our dead," Wilder said. "When you think it's out of your system, your daughter sees it on television and says, 'My father is an idiot.'"

PREVIEW AUDIENCES

The standard practice for Hollywood studios was to "preview" their films in front of select audiences in nearby Los Angeles suburban theaters before the movies' general releases in order to solicit the public's responses, mostly through survey cards (see Orson Welles). Reading those opinion cards, the directors and editors then fine-tuned their movies with either additional filmed scenes or excised certain sequences to make them more acceptable. Wilder was a big proponent of the practice.

"An audience is never wrong," Wilder observed. "An individual member of it may be an imbecile, but 1000 imbeciles together in the dark--that is critical genius."

The Lost Weekend's preview in Santa Barbara, California, was anything but a rousing success for Wilder. *Weekend* is an intense, dark film whose reaction from one preview audience appeared its viewers were more amused than somber when the movie flickered onto the screen.

"The people laughed from the beginning," remembered Wilder. "They laughed when Birnam's brother found the bottle outside the window, they laughed when he emptied the whiskey into the sink."

When it was time to hand out the survey cards to get the viewers' opinions, those who had remained in their seats (many had walked out during the screening) wrote comments ranging from "disgusting" to "boring." One survey taker wrote he thought the film was great, but felt all the "stuff about drinking and alcoholism" should be left out.

Attending the preview, Wilding was walking out of the theater and overheard a couple's conversation. "I've sworn off. Never again." "You'll never drink again?" he was asked. "No, I'll never see another picture again."

Some Like It Hot played horribly to a sneak preview audience with similar walk-outs and negative comments as *Lost*. Studio executives and others associated with the production gave Wilder a long list of scenes he should reshoot, add, or simply cut. Actor Jack Lemmon asked Wilder what he planned to do, hearing all the advice cascading upon the director.

"Why, nothing," responded Wilder. "This is a very funny movie and I believe in it just as it is. Maybe this is the wrong neighborhood in which to have shown it. At any rate, I don't panic over one preview. It's a hell of a movie."

Wilder and his studio scheduled another preview in Westwood, a section of Los Angeles. The audience reaction was completely opposite than the first preview. No one walked out and after the movie ended the picture received a standing ovation.

Wilder said of such experiences, "I have ten commandments. The first nine are, thou shalt not bore. The tenth is, thou shalt have right of final cut."

He did fear certain film critics critiquing his movies, most notably Judith Crist. "Inviting her to review one of your pictures is like inviting the Boston Strangler to massage your neck."

PRODUCTION

DIRECTING CHALLENGES

Directing films offers daily challenges. One element Wilder consciously avoided was scripting children into his movies. "I could direct a dog. Kids, I don't know," he said.

The swimming pool scene opening *Sunset Boulevard* shows a dead William Holden floating on top of a swimming pool with police investigating the murder. The sequence appearing in the final release wasn't intended to be the original opening. The intended scene Wilder filmed to begin *Sunset* was one the director labeled the best he had ever shot. The planned opening begins with Holden's body wheeled on a gurney into the Los Angeles County Morgue with about thirty other corpses lying in wait. Some of the dead conversed in voice-overs such as "Where did you drown? The ocean?" Holden: "No, the swimming pool." Dead Man: "A husky fellow like you?" Holden: "Well I had a few extra holes in me, two in the chest and one in the stomach." Dead Man: "You were murdered?" Holden: "Yes I was murdered."

The reason why this scene didn't make the final release is the studio conducted three previews before *Sunset's* release and viewers in all three theaters laughed uproariously. For a morgue setting, audiences felt the scene was not appropriate; hence, Wilder had to reshoot the opening and closing at Norma Desmond's outside swimming pool.

Shooting the opening posed several challenges. In the finished picture, viewers see a dead William Holden on the surface of the swimming pool with detectives and a photographer looking down at him from the pool's edge. Wilder wanted to capture both Holden's front facing downward as well as the investigators standing above him. The trouble was when the film crew placed a waterproof camera on the pool's bottom, the people above the waterline appeared murky and indistinguishable. To solve the problem, art director John Meehan experimented with several methods of filming before he found one which produced the opening we see today. He placed a mirror on the bottom of the pool. He then had the camera, stationed above the pool and out of the water, filming the image of the mirror, which produced a clear picture of Holden and the detectives.

Hot posed several challenges for Jack Lemmon and his side-kick Tony Curtis. The pair wanted to look convincing in their female disguises since the script called for the two escaping the mob by impersonating as a couple of women. To see if they could fool unsuspecting people, the actors stepped into their dresses, wore high-heel shoes, applied heavy makeup to their faces, put on their wigs, and walked around Goldwyn Studios all day to see if anyone would notice their real gender. Not one person caught on. With their confidence rising, they decided to walk into the public ladies' rest room to freshen up. The bathroom was full of women, but everyone thought they were one of them. The actors recreated the scene in *Hot* as they affix their makeup in the women's room.

WILDER'S DIRECTING STYLE

Working on the set usually poses problems for the best of film directors.

Describing the varying roles a director has to assume while on the set, Wilder said, "A director must be a policeman, a midwife, a psychoanalyst, a sycophant, and a bastard."

There's an early sequence in *Sunset Boulevard* where Norma Desmond experiences the loss of her pet monkey. The crew was perplexed on how to set up the viewing for Norma's dead monkey. Wilder simply described the scene in the script as "You know, the usual monkey-funeral sequence."

Wilder was with former First Lady Nancy Reagan during a mid-1990's party when a woman came up to the director and asked him what the chimp scene was all about. His answer, probably wanting to shock Mrs. Reagan, said, "Don't you understand? Before Joe Gillis (William Holden) came along, Norma Desmond was screwing the monkey."

One of the easiest scenes Wilder ever filmed was the Christmas party in *The Apartment*. Wilder purposely scheduled the sequence for December 23, 1959, so the cast would be in a holiday mood. Almost every scene shot that day was completed on the first take.

"I wish it were always this easy," Wilder said at the time. "I just shouted 'action' and stood back."

Wilder loved to play card games, particularly bridge and poker. His films are replete with his characters playing cards. Holden and Swanson in *Sunset Boulevard,* Holden and company in *Stalag 17*, and the ending of Lemmon and McClain in *The Apartment* are among a few Wilder films showing the interaction of his leads while dealing cards. In fact, he used card games as a metaphor to his style of directing.

"The close-up is such a valuable thing--like a trump at bridge," Wilder said, noting he only filmed close-ups to emphasize an important emotional action and re-action of his actors.

So adverse was Wilder in using numerous close-ups in his movies, the director and the cinematographer for *The Apartment,* Joseph LaShelle, butted heads because of the dearth of requested close-ups. LaShelle had shot mainly for television directors who had called for multiple close-ups before he worked with Wilder. LaShelle was quizzical about Wilder's avoidance of the close-up and let the director know.

Sometimes Wilder joked to his cameramen on several productions, "Shoot a few scenes out of focus. I want to win the foreign film award."

For a director, Wilder had a unique arrangement with his primary film editor. Doane Harrison, Paramount Studio's veteran editor, was constantly on the set since *The Major and the Minor,* consulting with Wilder on the type of shots he needed to complete each day's filming. The director never shot more than he had to. "I just shoot the way I think it's going to look," Wilder said.

"And when I'm finished with a picture, there's very little celluloid left on the cutting-room floor."

WORKING WITH ACTORS

As a director relying on his personally-written scripts, Wilder was insistent his actors recite almost verbatim what he wrote on paper. Sometimes his demands caused frequent clashes with his actors, most notably Bing Crosby in 1948's *The Emperor Waltz,* and Peter Sellers in 1964's *Kiss Me, Stupid.*

Crosby, in the habit of ad libbing with Bob Hope in their happy-go-lucky *Road* films, battled with Wilder during the making of *Emperor.* Wilder asserted the actor's dialogue should not divert for any reason from his written script. *Sunset Boulevard* contains a mild jab at Bing in the scene where Norma Desmond was called to Paramount Studios to see director Cecil B. DeMille because the studio wanted to rent her luxurious car seen (fictitiously) in "the Crosby picture."

Peter Sellers was in films where his directors such as Stanley Kubrick allowed the actor to set aside the scripts and let his imagination go wild. Wilder reined in the actor during the filming of *Kiss Me, Stupid*, causing some friction between the two. "I realized that there was no way for me to work within Wilder's system," Sellers related. The relationship lasted only one month before Sellers experienced a series of heart attacks, forcing Wilder to replace him.

Shirley MacLaine, as an elevator operator, was kept on a short leash by the director in reciting her dialogue. MacLaine had the habit of improvising her lines, driving Wilder crazy. In one elevator sequence, Wilder demanded MacLaine retake the scene five times because she kept leaving one word out. MacLaine, who would go on to act in another Wilder film, said of the director in a complementary fashion, "Once in thirteen lifetimes do you come across someone like this."

Because of sentiments expressed by MacLaine, there were a number of actors who would give their right arm to appear in a Wilder movie, including Jack Lemmon, Walter Matthau, and William Holden

Working with Wilder on *Hot* was such a delightful experience for Lemmon that when the director began to relate the plot for his next film, *The Apartment,* the actor said he was ready to ink a contract for any role in the movie. "I'd have signed even if he said he was going to do the phone book," Lemmon admitted. The eventual role he received and acted in was so perfectly performed by Lemmon he received an Academy Award nomination for Best Actor.

The working relationship also went the other way. Wilder loved directing Lemmon.

"I'm terribly fond of Jack," Wilder said at the time of making *The Apartment.* "We understand each other very well and it's a pleasure to work with him. He is a thinking actor, but not an argumentative one. By that way I mean if we start shooting at nine o'clock, he would be there at 8:15 and would come to my office and say, 'Hey, I've got a great idea! Look, why don't we do this? Blah, blah, blah, blah.' And I just look at him, and he says, 'I don't like it either.' And he walks out."

Wilder had such confidence in Lemmon that, in a departure to the director's strict adherence to his script, he gave the actor the reins to further develop on his own his character Bud Baxter in *The Apartment.* Wilder compared Lemmon to Charlie Chaplin and put him on par with the comedic genius.

Two particular scenes in the film are especially evident that shows Wilder giving Lemmon unusual acting latitude to ad lib. One was the scene where Lemmon has a cold after spending a frigid night on a Central Park bench while lending out his pad. In MacMurray's office, Lemmon was feeding his nose with a cold solution when he accidentally sprays the liquid across the room, landing on his boss. The other is when Lemmon is in his apartment with a sick Shirley MacLaine. Lemmon is singing away in the kitchen cooking some spaghetti and spontaneously uses his tennis racket as a strainer.

The role as Baxter was an ordeal for Lemmon in some scenes. *The Apartment's* exteriors were filmed during the early winter in New York City. In one scene the script called for Lemmon to spend part of the evening in Central Park. There was a cold rain on the night of the shoot with sub-freezing temperatures. As Lemmon was lying on a park bench being filmed, Wilder had to spray the actor between takes with anti-freeze to prevent him from turning into one big icicle.

WILDER'S CLASSIC DECISIONS

Barbara Stanwyck, Wilder's first choice to play Phyllis Dietrichson, read the *Double Indemnity* script and said she was rattled by portraying such a ruthless killer without a conscience. "Are you a mouse or an actress," said Wilder. Stanwyck replied, "Well, I hope I'm an actress." Wilder's comeback: 'Then do the part.' Stanwyck later remembers, "And I did and I'm very grateful to him."

To cheapen Stanwyck's look to fit her character's personality, Wilder decided to cut the actress' long brown hair and place her in a blonde wig. As the movie was a month into production, Wilder realized his mistake. He gradually saw how really awful she looked with the wig. With the great amount of footage she already appeared in, Wilder couldn't afford to reshoot Stanwyck's earlier scenes and the wig stayed on her. Upon reflection after seeing the finished movie, Wilder took back how he felt about the wig and said the blond look rounded out Stanwyck's character perfectly.

But Buddy DeSylva, production head of Paramount Pictures, was none too pleased with his studio's highly-paid actress' appearance when he saw the rushes of the film. "We hired Barbara Stanwyck, and here we get George Washington," lamented DeSylva.

Actor Fred MacMurray was a cheapskate in real life, according to Wilder. In *The Apartment*, MacMurray, who had just signed a multi-picture deal with Disney Studios, was worried about playing a cheating husband in the Wilder film, but was obligated to fulfill his contract. The director was filming a scene where MacMurray flips a quarter to a shoeshine man after his shoes were polished. The quarter was causing problems for MacMurray because the coin was so small. Wilder came up with an idea to use a larger 50-cent piece to serve as a tip. No way, said MacMurray. "I would never give him fifty cents - I couldn't play the scene if I did!"

William Holden's career was resurrected by *Sunset Boulevard*. After several actors turned down the male lead role as a gigolo, Wilder was told by the studio he should audition Holden. In Wilder's opinion the actor played several mediocre roles since his 1939 film debut *Golden Boy* and wasn't impressed by his style. But Holden auditioned well for the role, and once on the set, the actor excelled. Wilder and Holden went on further to work on several films after *Sunset* and were close friends throughout their lives.

Wilder played a practical joke on Holden while filming *Sunset Boulevard*. The script called for a scene where Holden and actress Nancy Olson, whose characters fall in love, kiss for the first time. Wilder had filmed the take he was satisfied with, but without telling the two, the director asked the couple to continue the scene with several more takes. As instructed, the two kept kissing repeatedly while Wilder let the camera roll before someone yelled "Cut!" The order didn't come out of Wilder's mouth; it was Holden's wife, Brenda Marshall, who just happened to be in the studio the day the kissing scene was being shot.

Because of *Sunset* followed by 1953's *Stalag 17,* the World War II POW film which Holden received the Best Actor Oscar, the actor's career catapulted during the 1950s and 1960s.

Wilder remembered how he felt about Holden after the actor died alone in his apartment in a fall with a bottle of booze sitting on a table. The director lamented, "If someone had said to me, 'Holden's dead,' I would have assumed that he had been gored by a water buffalo in Kenya, that he had died in a plane crash approaching Hong Kong, that a crazed, jealous woman had shot him, and he drowned in a swimming pool. But to be killed by a bottle of vodka and a night table--what a lousy fade-out of a great guy!"

WILDER'S LATER CAREER

Wilder's later films are considered somewhat inferior compared to the ones he created during his peak years. But like most top-tier film directors, retirement wasn't in his vocabulary.

"You have to have a dream so you can get up in the morning," Wilder said during the twilight of his career.

He saw as time went on studios weren't offering him the big budgets for his movies as they once did, something he eventually had to confront.

"Today we spend 80% of the time making deals and 20% making pictures," Wilder tabulated.

As he aged, Wilder wasn't pleased by the direction Hollywood was headed.

"People copy, people steal," Wilder observed. "Most of the pictures they make nowadays are loaded down with special effects. I couldn't do that. I quit smoking because I couldn't reload my Zippo."

Someone told him as the studio offers were drying up that maybe it was time to go in a different direction.

"Well, number one, it's too late for me now to change and to become a gardener," Wilder said of his persistence in remaining as a director. "Number two is to get away from the house and the vacuum cleaner. I want to be in my office and think. And number three, it's very exciting. I like to tell stories. Ultimately it's interesting. You meet nice people, it's glamorous, and, if you get lucky, very profitable. You suffer a great deal, but to paraphrase President Harry Truman, if you can't take all that crap, get out of the studio. Believe me, this is not a profession for a dignified human being. I can see the interest in pictures when I talk to students, especially now that almost every university has something connected with movies. But if I had a son I would beat him with a very large whip trying to make a gardener, a dentist or something else out of him. Don't do it. It's just too tough. It hurts, and the moments of glory are very far between. Well, it's too late for me to turn back, too late for me to become a gardener. I can't bend over the azaleas. Not anymore."

TOP TEN BILLY WILDER MOVIES

#1--SOME LIKE IT HOT (1959)

Regarded as the best comedy of all-time, *Hot* showcases one of Marilyn Monroe's best screen performances. She's supplemented by side-splitting comedic acting Jack Lemmon and Tony Curtis. Film reviewer Roger Ebert called the picture "one of the enduring treasures of the movies, a film of inspiration and meticulous craft." The tagline at the end by actor Joe E. Brown is priceless.

#2--SUNSET BOULEVARD (1950)

A blazing satire on Hollywood, *Sunset* has more classic lines than most films. Dialogue such as "I am big, it's the pictures that got small!" and "All right, Mr. DeMille, I'm ready for my close-up," reflect the genius of writers Wilder and Brackett. Gloria Swanson got robbed for the Oscar for Best Actress (It's said veterans Swanson and Bette Davis in *All About Eve* split the vote for the best acting Academy Award, allowing relatively unknown Judy Holliday in *Born Yesterday* to snare the statuette.)

#3--THE APARTMENT (1960)

Wilder was catapulted into rarefied air when the Academy awarded five Oscars to Wilder and company, including Best Picture, Best Director and Best Screenplay. The mix of melodrama and comedy worked for this film and Lemmon's acting ranks as one of his top performances in an illustrious career. MacMurray wouldn't make another serious movie after *The Apartment,* preferring television's *My Three Sons* type of roles upon receiving so much criticism playing a philandering husband.

#4--DOUBLE INDEMNITY (1944)

Who says insurance salesmen don't lead exciting lives, especially if they have Barbara Stanwyck as a customer. Regarded as a top film noir with Stanwyck playing the prototype femme fatale, *Indemnity* never gets old. Complementing the superb acting is a solid performance by Edward G. Robinson, who could smell a rat in a perfume factory. Wrote film critic Louella Parsons, "*Double Indemnity* is the finest picture of its kind ever made, and I make that flat statement without any fear of getting indigestion later from eating my words."

#5--WITNESS FOR THE PROSECUTION (1957)

Wilder injects some zest in this Agatha Christie play where audiences were warned not to reveal the surprise ending. This was actor Tyrone Powers' last completed film--he would die of a heart attack the following year at 44 while starring in *Solomon and Sheba*. Wilder was able to get sensational acting from Charles Laughton and Marlene Dietrich in this courtroom drama.

#6--ACE IN THE HOLE (1952)

Kirk Douglas plays a shady newspaper reporter who will do anything to advance his career. A reviewer of TV Guide called this "An uncompromising portrait of human nature at its worst, the film . . . stands as one of the great American films of the 1950s." Wilder was sued by a screen writer who claimed to have given the director the story idea, but Wilder went to court to argue the tale of the man-trapped-in-a cave situation was a highly publicized event. The director won the first go-around, but the California Supreme Court ruled an oral submission by the accuser to Wilder's secretary constituted plagiarism. Wilder settled out of court.

#7--THE SEVEN YEAR ITCH (1955)

Marilyn Monroe's famous skirt-lifting over a city subway vent scene is one of the highlights in Wilder's theme of fidelity in marriage. Many domestic arguments have taken place over the years as some husbands have admitted they would love to be in Tom Ewell's shoes, whose family is away for the weekend while the luscious blonde neighbor comes knocking on his door.

#8--THE LOST WEEKEND (1945)

Hard to watch and depressing, this Wilder film, which won Oscars for Best Picture, Best Directing, Best Screenplay and Ray Milland for Best Actor, packs an enormous punch to the gut. The destruction of alcohol to the human body is something to behold and Wilder doesn't let up as he strings scene after dark scene showing the secret world of an alcoholic.

#9--STALAG 17 (1953)

The popular TV show *Hogan's Heroes* was based on this film's premise of American POW's doing time and plotting their escape in a German prison camp during World War II. William Holden received his only Best Actor Oscar for his role as a potential turncoat. The actor is on record as giving one of the shortest acceptance speeches in all of the Academy ceremonies--a simple "Thank you" (The producers of the show said time was running out and he was told to make it short.). Wilder was nominated for Best Director.

#10--THE SPIRIT OF ST. LOUIS (1957)

Although Jimmy Stewart was miscast as Charles Lindbergh, the first person to fly across the Atlantic Ocean, the story of aviation's milestone is still riveting. A reviewer for Time Magazine said it best: "Stewart, for all his professional, 48-year-old boyishness, succeeds almost continuously in suggesting what all the world sensed at the time: that Lindbergh's flight was not the mere physical adventure of a rash young 'flying fool' but rather a journey of the spirit, in which, as in the pattern of all progress, one brave man proved himself for all mankind as the paraclete of a new possibility."

Akira Kurosawa

JAPAN'S GENIUS FILM DIRECTOR

Lying in a pool of blood, Japanese film director Akira Kurosawa had just sliced his wrists and throat in utter despair. His film career, which witnessed an unprecedented string of highly successful financial and critically-acclaimed movies, suddenly slammed shut. His abrupt firing after two-weeks of filming 1970's *Tora! Tora! Tora!* and his first box-office failure in 1970's *Dodes'ka-den* had left Kurosawa sinking emotionally and psychologically.

Suicide in Japan has a long tradition and "is considered a natural, logical and permanently available response to experience and exhaustion of life's possibilities." For Kurosawa, it seemed to be the only avenue to take. Fortunately for us and the cinematic circles, his house maid came upon the bloody scene. He eventually healed and adopted the Japanese mantra of "You can fall down seven times in the same place, and if you stand up the eighth time you have won."

KUROSAWA INFLUENCE

To say Kurosawa's body of work is one of the most influential in America cinema is an understatement. Consider how George Lucas' 1977 *Star Wars* would have been written completely different if it weren't for Kurosawa. Actor Clint Eastwood and his starring roles in Sergio Leone's Spaghetti Westerns, including his 1967 classic *The Good, The Bad, And The Ugly,* may not have occurred without Kurosawa's groundbreaking films. It's possible today's films wouldn't contain as much graphic violence if the late 1960's New Hollywood young directors hadn't noticed Kurosawa's choreographed fighting sequences bordering on poetic bloodletting. And a who's who of copycats in Robert Altman, Francis Ford Coppola, Steven Spielberg, Martin Scorsese, and John Milius reflect Kurosawa's creativity on contemporary screens.

Lucas thought so highly of Kurosawa's 1958 *Hidden Forest* he patterned the characters of his *Star Wars* after the Japanese movie. Obi-Wan Kenobi possesses strong elements of General Makabe in *Forest* while Princess Leia morphed from the Japanese Princess Yuki. Queen Amidala's many disguises in 1999's *Star Wars: The Phantom Menace* copy Yuki's trick of dressing and acting like a handmaiden. Matashichi and Tahie, the farmers whose point of view unfolds *Forest's* narrative and who constantly bicker with one another, are similar to C-3PO and R2-D2 in their close, yet nipping friendship.

In Japan, the primary critique on Kurosawa's style while he was alive was the director foreswore the traditions of his country's cinematic unique aesthetics. In Kurosawa's defense, it was the American directors who copied his innovative style rather than vice versa. One time the imitation was so blatant Kurosawa took film director Sergio Leone to court for plagiarism when 1964's *Fistful of Dollars* was released. Kurosawa easily won his case since the court visibly saw as clear as day every scene in the Leone movie copied every scene in Kurosawa's 1961 *Yojimbo*.

Kurosawa is credited with producing the first modern action film. His 1954 *Seven Samurai* combined so many cinematic elements commonly seen in today's action films, including *Samurai's* American version, 1960's *The Magnificent Seven*, as well as 2001's *Ocean's 11*. Slow motion, which emphasizes prolonging the unfolding dramatics during action sequences, was first introduced by Kurosawa. Plot devices, such as the reluctant legendary fighter who is convinced to save a village populated by weaklings against savage invaders, are also unique in the writer/director's overall thematic structures.

KUROSAWA'S EARLY LIFE

Kurosawa was taught at an early age not to ignore life's uglier side. During Japan's 1923 Kuno Earthquake killing 10,000, Akira's older brother, Heigo, forced the future director to witness the carnage taking place and to remember such scenes.

It was Heigo who steered Akira into the movie business. Akira loved to paint on canvass while Heigo was obsessed with the cinema. Heigo's love of film extended to his employment as a "benshi," which, during the silent film era, were narrators giving commentary for both domestic and international movies. Hiego's passion for movies eventually rubbed off on his younger brother. Their close bond was broken when Hiego committed suicide from depression. Losing his brother and his only other sibling, a sister, early in his life influenced Akira's later view of life which was shaded in gloom and pessimism.

Kurosawa said with his brother's influence as well as viewing Abel Gance's 1923 silent *The Wheel*, featuring action shots of moving trains, convinced him he wanted to be involved in any capacity in the film industry.

"For me, film-making combines everything," explained Kurosawa, whose love of painting also remained with him through his dying days. "That's the reason I've made cinema my life's work. In films, painting and literature, theatre and music come together. But a film is still a film."

Kurosawa used his talent for painting later in his career when his eyesight began to fail as a way to describe the framing of a scene he wanted his cameraman to film. For the 1980 *Kagemusha,* a dress rehearsal for his 1985 classic *Ran,* Kurosawa devoted 10 years painting his storyboard panels to reflect each scene. The collection of these paintings accompanied his published screenplay on *Kagemusha* in book form, creating an impressive combination of a literature and artistic piece of work.

When Kurosawa first broke into Japan's film industry, he was hired as an assistant to the contract director. He reflected back on those days and claimed he learned more from the experience of assisting in the production of a film than if he had solely been a head director. In Japanese cinema during the country's pre-war days, assistants would perform pretty much every aspect associated with a film. Kurosawa learned how to interact with the actors, he assimilated all the knowledge that went into making costume designs, set construction and decorating, and he picked up editing skills during the post-production phase. Being an assistant director in those days was a stepping stone before being hired for a main director. Kurosawa lamented late in his life the industry doesn't afford the opportunity to today's directors to assimilate all the stages of film production fully as he did. Contemporary studios pigeonhole a talented person immediately into a director's role while the assistants remain as basically second-tier helpers with no chance of advancement.

"The role of a director encompasses the coaching of the actors, the cinematography, the sound recording, the art direction, the music, the editing and the dubbing and sound-mixing," Kurosawa detailed. "Although these can be thought of as separate occupations, I do not regard them as independent. I see them all melting together under the heading of direction.

"Unless you know every aspect and phase of the film-production process, you can't be a movie director. A movie director is like a front-line commanding officer. He needs a thorough knowledge of every branch of the service, and if he doesn't command each division, he cannot command the whole.

"A film director has to convince a great number of people to follow him and work with him. I often say, although I am certainly not a militarist, that if you compare the production unit to an army, the script is the battle flag and the director is the commander of the front line. From the moment production begins to the moment it ends, there is no telling what will happen. The director must be able to respond to any situation, and he must have the leadership ability to make the whole unit go along with his responses."

Surviving World War II by producing popular mainstream (some say propaganda) films during the war, Kurosawa understood "being an artist means not having to avert one's eyes."

PRE-PRODUCTION

KUROSAWA'S SCRIPTWRITING PROCESS

The commonality of the human condition was always a centerpiece in Kurosawa's themes whenever he embarked on a new project. "Human beings share the same common problems," he noted. "A film can only be understood if it depicts these properly. The characters in my films try to live honestly and make the most of the lives they've been given. I believe you must live honestly and develop your abilities to the full. People who do this are the real heroes."

Because Kurosawa devoted so much time and sweat equity toward each of his films, he made sure the effort would result in a worthy movie.

"When I start on a film I always have a number of ideas about my project," he remarked, "Then one of them begins to germinate, to sprout, and it is this which I take and work with. My films come from my need to say a particular thing at a particular time. The beginning of any film for me is this need to express something. It is to make it nurture and grow that I write my script- it is directing it that makes my tree blossom and bear fruit."

Kurosawa was always heavily involved in the writing process of his films. Teaming up with Shinobu Hashimoto and Hideo Oguni, Kurosawa labored on the script for *Seven Samurai* for a long 45 days. Japan's devastation in World War II, which ended ten years before the production of *Samurai,* caused a plague of sickness still commonplace when the trio was composing their script. The constant sitting began to take a toll on the scriptwriters' sedentary bodies and Kurosawa ended up in the hospital afflicted with roundworms.

But he saw the writing process well worth the pain since a film can only be as good as the paper containing the screenplay.

"With a good script, a good director can produce a masterpiece," said Kurosawa. "With the same script, a mediocre director can produce a passable film. But with a bad script even a good director can't possibly make a good film. For truly cinematic expression, the camera and the microphone must be able to cross both fire and water. The script must be something that has the power to do this."

Kurosawa was a huge admirer of William Shakespeare and in particular his play *Macbeth,* which eventually evolved into his 1957 critically-acclaimed movie *Throne of Blood*. He wanted to write a script based on the Japanese Middle Ages which paralleled the plot of Shakespeare's Scottish kingdom. Kurosawa saw strong thematic similarities between the two countries as described by the Elizabethan playwright. He had in his mind as early as the late 1940's to create such a picture, and was geared to produce one immediately after *Rashomon* premiered in 1950. But Orson Welles delayed Kurosawa's ambition when the American director released his version of the play in his 1948 *Macbeth*.

Shakespeare's play was ideally suited for Kurosawa's love for the Japanese classical drama-form known as *Noh*. The *Noh* dramatics of Japanese theater leans on supernatural aspects of plot twists and uses ghosts as characters and masks or heavy make-up applied on the actors' faces to emphasize a character's personality. The traditional Japanese *Noh* also spotlights the Buddhist doctrine of this earthly life being ever-changing and the mortality of the human race as accepted as fact. Kurosawa envisioned all these set-pieces when he adapted one of Shakespeare's most supernatural plays, including the spooky old lady as a spirit in the misty forest. The general Washizu, rejected for salvation based on his past horrendous acts, also lends atmosphere to the spiritual world in *Throne* and becomes a wandering ghost himself. Kurosawa had his musical composer, Masaru Sato, rely on the *Noh* spare instruments of the flute and drum to serve as the movie's soundtrack.

KUROSAWA WORKS WITH THE SOVIETS

In one of the most unusual collaborations in film history, the Russian film studio, Mosfilm, approached Kurosawa in the early 1970's and asked him to suggest any story the director would like to direct for the Soviet Union movie company. Kurosawa, who had read Russian explorer's Vladimir Arsenyev account on his capable assistant, Dersu Uzala, told the film studio it was always his desire to produce a version of Uzala's story. The director had nixed the project when he first became interested in Uzala back in the late 1930's since he knew the movie had to be filmed in Siberia, where the Arsenyev book's adventures took place. Wartime measures restricted Japanese international travel at the time.

The Russian studio was shocked Kurosawa had even read Arsenyev's account, never mind was familiar with the explorer's working relationship with his guide. Very few people outside the Soviet Union had known about Arsenyev's adventures. The studio enthusiastically green-lighted the production, giving a shot in the arm to the struggling film director who hadn't produced a big hit since 1957's *Throne*. The film was so artistically recognized by the members of the Academy of Motion Pictures the movie earned the 1975 Oscar for Best Foreign Film.

Even though the picture was an ordeal to film given Siberia's nasty weather, Kurosawa saw it as a good diversion away from the Japanese film industry.

"When the river he was born in and raised in [i.e., the Japanese film industry] becomes polluted, he can't climb back upstream to lay his eggs - he has trouble making his films," said Kurosawa, using watery metaphors. "One such salmon, seeing no other way, made a long journey to climb a Soviet river and give birth to some caviar. This is how my 1975 film 'Dersu Uzala' came about. Nor do I think this is such a bad thing. But the most natural thing for a Japanese salmon to do is to lay its eggs in a Japanese river."

PRODUCTION

WORKING WITH HIS ACTORS

At the height of his career, Kurosawa was labeled by the press as a tyrant. But several interviews with his actors and his working film crews paint a picture of a detached and aloof director on the set. The description "intense" is repeated within the context of these interviews to reflect the concentration Kurosawa possessed on the set while directing his movies.

Those whom were employed by Kurosawa recognized and accepted his focused personality. Like John Ford, he was comfortable working with the same people in a number of films he produced. During Kurosawa's peak years of directing, if an actor or a crew member was not hired for his next film, then it was obvious he was displeased with the earlier work and effort.

One of his favorite actors he used time and time again for 16 of his films was Toshiro Mifune. Kurosawa was introduced to the Japanese actor when he was casting 1948's *Drunken Angel*. He said of his initial impression directing this talented performer, "I am a person who is rarely impressed by actors, but in the case of Mifune, I was completely overwhelmed."

On rare occasions the two did butt heads. Making *Seven Samurai* was stressful for Kurosawa and the cast. Lead actor Mifune, who had previously worked with the film director in several other movies and had enjoyed the experience, did not particularly relish being a part of the production in "*Seven.*" Because of the intensity of the shoot, the actor had undergone so much stress under Kurosawa's incessant demands he threatened the director at gunpoint during one particularly dramatic episode on the set.

Kurosawa's routine in preparing his actors varied little from movie to movie.

"I begin rehearsals in the actors' dressing room," he said, describing the process similar to D.W. Griffith's, but in much greater detail than the early director. "First I have them repeat their lines, and gradually proceed to the movements. But this is done with costumes and makeup on from the beginning; then we repeat everything on the set. The thoroughness of the rehearsals makes the actual shooting every time very short. We don't rehearse just the actors, but every part of every scene - the camera movements, the lightning, everything."

As a director, Kurosawa was insistent his actors remain in character throughout the production, similar to the "method-acting" practices of today. He demanded the actors physically live on the set before and during filming, they address each other by their characters' names and wear the costumes and make-up they would appear in. His filming for the most part went smoothly because of these long rehearsal sessions.

Kurosawa's coaching of his actors is clearly evident by one of the highlights in 1953's *Ikira,* where Takashi Shimura sings *Song of the Gondola* on the swing. The director told him to "sing the song as if you are a stranger in a world where nobody believes you exist." Clearly the mournful tune sung by Shimura strikes at the heart of the most jaded viewer.

The script's meaning for *Rashomon* was confusing for the cast reading its pages. "What does it mean?" collectively asked the actors. Kurosawa said the story is a reflection of life. And life, as he told them, does not always present clear meanings.

"Human beings are unable to be honest with themselves about themselves," Kurosawa revealed about the characters in his films. "They cannot talk about themselves without embellishing."

MONEY PROBLEMS AFFECT KUROSAWA

Kurosawa's focus on acting was so acute he felt even his movies' settings could directly impact his actors. For the *Seven Samurai,* Toho Studios had a replica of a historically-accurate peasant village used in other films ready to serve as a backdrop. Kurosawa nixed the idea and had a complete village built at Tagata on the Izu Peninsula in Shizuoka. The director's reasoning was "the quality of the set influences the quality of the actors' performances. For this reason, I have the sets made exactly like the real thing. It restricts the shooting but encourages that feeling of authenticity."

The budget kept rising with each day during *Seven Samurai's* production because of Kurosawa's excessive exactness to detail. The studio was so concerned with the expenditures they decided to shut down the project--twice. Kurosawa's reaction: without saying a word, he simply went fishing. He knew the studio had sunk so much money into the film it wouldn't abandon the film. Both times, Kurosawa was correct. The studio executives came back and asked him to resume *Samurai's* production.

Kurosawa gradually appreciated budgetary actuaries when he was producing 1957's *Throne of Blood*. The plot called for the action to take place in a castle and Kurosawa originally thought building a cheap facade for the castle was all that was required. As the pre-production planning eventually proved, the scenes to be filmed made it obvious the studio would have to build sections of the interior castle and not just merely the outer walls. Enlisting the help of the United States Marines, stationed at a nearby American base in Japan, Kurosawa was able to minimize the expense of constructing the sets. The Marines' help resulted in *Throne's* budget coming in well under the projected costs since the director had to hire only a handful of carpenters to build the castle complex.

AN OBSESSION TO DETAILS

Kurosawa's obsession to detail was so excessive that during one scene he had a chest sitting among many pieces of furniture painted, stripped, and repainted several times before he was satisfied with the look. On another occasion, he insisted an existing stream running through his set flow in the opposite direction to improve the visual effect. In his brief reign as director of *Tora! Tora! Tora!* he required the actors playing the crew on a Japanese war ship dress in uniform throughout the production and salute him on the set as real sailors do to an admiral.

In another movie, the director was concerned about a particular house when he was filming a brief sequence from a train. He ordered the roof of the house be removed and replaced because he felt it was destroying his shot by being so unattractive. He also insisted, while directing historic period productions, his actors wear their costumes every day for a couple of months prior to the shoot so when it was time to film the outfits would look like they hadn't been just taken off the rack and put on for the first time.

Kurosawa's obsessiveness to his films opened new channels of creativity the cinema hadn't seen before. The innovative director popularized the use of multiple cameras to capture the action of a battle, adopting *Mr. Smith Goes To Washington* Frank Capra's method of using a number of camera set-ups to record one scene.

Kurosawa employed a number of cameras in *Seven Samurai* to capture the battle scenes raging throughout the village. Like recording a sporting event, the director didn't want to stop the flow of the combatants as they rode their horses and ran around killing one another. He positioned his cameras at different locations in the village to capture the entire battle. Using the emerging movie technology, Kurosawa's cameramen attached the newly-developed telephoto lenses to their cameras giving them the ability to rack tightly into the action and then zoom back out for wider shots, all within the focal point. The look created a revolutionary visual to cinema, one the film director continued to perfect for the remainder of his career. The long focal-length camera shots first introduced in his action films became a cinematic standard in most American Western shootout scenes.

Kurosawa also designed moving the camera on a dolly 180-degrees around his protagonists while filming. Kurosawa's directions to his cameraman to film directly into the sun, a long-standing taboo in Hollywood, illustrated such a shot can be used effectively in a movie's narrative. In *Rashomon,* he is also credited in popularizing the newly-invented light-weight 35mm camera as a "hand held" innovative way to film. The smaller cameras were especially effective in *Rashomon* where the characters are seen walking through the woods.

One pesky problem with filming in the forested location in *Rashomon* was the existence of thousands of slugs living above in the trees. On a number of occasions, the slugs dropped onto the actors' heads while the camera was cranking. To ward off the slugs, which caused numerous retakes, the actors and crew found a solution made up of salt to repeatedly smear themselves, a mixture the slugs avoided.

Since *Rashomon* was filmed in black and white, Kurosawa noticed during the rainy scenes at the Rashomon Gate, the raindrops were practically invisible. He huddled with his special effects crew and came up with the idea of mixing black ink with water in the container of the rain machine to produce a visible rain shower. The inky droplets are clearly shown on the Woodcutter's face just before the rain stops.

DIRECTING CAN'T BE THIS HARD, CAN IT?

Kurosawa had one of those moments he wished he could do over which impacted the career of one of his actresses. A love scene was scripted in *Samurai* between the characters Shino and Katsushiro. The director wanted to emphasize the special romantic moment reflected in the eyes of Shino, played by actress Keiko Tsushima. He called for creating a glittering glow in her eyes, and the only way he and his special effects crew could think of to get that look was to use angled mirrors set low on the ground and reflect the light narrowly on her eyes. Unfortunately, the scene required numerous retakes, and because of the laser-like reflection, Tsushima's eyes were overexposed to the light. She would suffer bad eyesight the rest of her life.

Another unfortunate moment occurred on the same production. The script called for the samurai and the villagers to burn down the bandits' hideout. Fire trucks were hired to put out the fire once Kurosawa was satisfied with the shot. But all the area firetrucks were fighting actual blazes several miles away during the scheduled day of the shoot. To bide its time while waiting for the trucks, the crew sprayed gasoline without the expert guidance of the firemen through several areas of the hideout to insure a good, hard burn when given the word "action."

At last the fire trucks arrived, the matches were lit and the camera rolled. However, the fire spread much faster than anticipated and flamed up considerably. A separate scene using the same fire backdrop was scheduled to be filmed next. With the flames creating such a firestorm, there was only one chance to record the following scene.

"Keep going," yelled Kurosawa off-camera as actor Yoshio Tsuchiya was attempting to save his character's wife inside the hideout (The actress wasn't really in the burning hut.). The roof collapsed as Tsuchiya got to the door and his windpipe was severely burned as a result of the inferno.

The fire had spread so fast the grass on the hillside above the village went up in flames. Kurosawa was in deep distress over the calamity engulfing his actors and his expensive movie set, but the cameras recorded all the pertinent scenes, which appear in the finished film.

The wild fire episode wasn't the only traumatic incident to befall the film director and his crew during the production of *Seven Samurai*. The final battle scene was originally planned to be filmed in the month of September, but because of shooting delays the sequence wasn't shot until February. A heavy snow storm descended on the village the day before the scheduled climatic filming. Since the other scenes didn't even contain a hint of snow, the crew was tasked with getting rid of the white stuff by spraying water on its surface. To compound matters, a rain machine was scheduled to create a torrential rainstorm to highlight the chaotic action of the battle scenes.

The village, with its dirt streets, turned out to be one muddy mess. Adding to the muck saturating the set, the ground became frozen with below freezing temperatures the previous night. The actors, wearing open-toed period sandals, were in utter agony as they scampered around the frigid surface with shards of ice sharp as razors cutting through their skin. Actor Toshiro Mifune said he had never been so cold in his life shooting the sequence. Kurosawa wasn't spared from the wet frozen turf. He was forced to stand in the frozen mud directing his actors. The ordeal was so injurious to the director he lost several toenails in the process.

POST-PRODUCTION

KUROSAWA'S EDITING SECRETS

Unique among film directors, Kurosawa's favorite part of producing a movie was editing. His obsessiveness on the film set led to an equally detailed fixation in the editing room. After a day's shooting and viewing the rushes, Kurosawa hunkered down for the evening in the editing suite. Kurosawa was heavily influenced by Soviet filmmaker Sergei M. Eisenstein, who introduced to the film world fast-paced editing and who, like the Japanese director, worked his editing magic on his own films.

Hiroshi Nezu, the production supervisor for Kurosawa's films, remarked, "He is most concerned with the flowing quality which a film must have. The Kurosawa film flows over the cut, as it were."

For *Seven Samurai's* multi-camera footage, Kurosawa during the end of the day went over each camera's processed film and edited the pieces seamlessly, discovering what gaps needed to be filmed in the battle sequence the next day.

Such "flowing quality" observed by Nezu incorporated Kurosawa's new editing techniques, including his novel usage of wipes, axial cuts and cutting on motion between sequences, editing techniques copied by later directors, including George Lucas in *Star Wars.*

So confident Kurosawa was in his editing skills he convinced a very reluctant actor Seiji Miyaguchi to take on the role of a samurai. The wary Miyaguchi said he had never touched a sword before, never mind appearing in a film where he had to display such expert skills. Kurosawa told the actor with his directorial camera angles and his ability to edit the swordplay footage, all he would need to do is learn some rudimentary sword skills.

Miyoguchi trusted the director and agreed. Right before filming his action sequence, Miyaguchi embarked on a two-day crash course on handling the heavy sword. When it came time for the actual filming, Miyaguchi muscles were so worn out from all the strenuous practice he could barely move his body, let alone pick up the sword--but he did once the camera rolled.

THE CHANGING JAPANESE MOVIE LANDSCAPE

Many credit Kurosawa in leading the "Golden Age of Japanese Cinema" during the 1950's when he was one of the premier directors producing his country's most highly regarded films. As the years progressed from that magical period, however, Kurosawa observed the country's new film producers and directors strayed from what made the 1950's so special in Japanese cinema.

"A film must be made with the heart, not the mind," Kurosawa philosophized. "I think today's young filmmakers have forgotten this and instead they make films through their calculations. That is why Japanese films no longer have an audience. In all honesty, films must be made to target the hearts. During the time of (film director Yasujiro) Ozu, my mentor, and also in my time, no filmmaker made films based on theory and calculation, and that was why Japan's cinema was capable of shaping its golden years. Young filmmakers use techniques to humiliate the audience. This is wrong. We must serve cinema and make a film that would stimulate the audience. Ultimately, the aim should be to make an artistic film. That's simple, isn't it?"

Kurosawa admitted he lived basically a mundane life if it weren't for his work and passion for film.

"I believe that what pertains only to myself is not interesting enough to record and leave behind me," Kurosawa candidly revealed. "More important is my conviction that if I were to write anything at all, it would turn out to be nothing but talk about movies. In other words, take 'myself', subtract 'movies', and the result is zero."

His dedication to making the perfect movie took up most of his life. His family claimed he would never say or think about anything other than his films. On the occasional days he was at home, Kurosawa was so concentrated in his work he would sit quietly by himself while his mind was conjuring up scenes for his next film. Kurosawa's married life simply wasn't geared for raising children, which he honestly admitted despite raising two of them. While directing 1985's *Ran,* his wife, Yoko Yaguchi, whom he was married to for 39 years, died. He suspended the filming for just one day to mourn her passing before he went back to direct on location.

Kurosawa worked as long as he was physically and mentally able, directing his 30th and final film in 1993 with *Madadayo* before passing away in 1998.

"Movie directors, or should I say people who create things, are very greedy and they can never be satisfied," Kurosawa reflected on his later years. " That's why they can keep on working. I've been able to work for so long because I think next time, I'll make something good."

TOP TEN AKIRA KUROSAWA MOVIES

#1--SEVEN SAMURAI (1954)

Likely the most imitated movie in all cinematic history. *Seven* is George Lucas' favorite film and it is easy to see why. A small group of Samurai are asked by terrorized villagers to protect them from a large band of marauders. The trials and tribulations of the training sessions set up for a wiz-bang attack on the villagers and their protectors. Film critic James Berardinelli said, "*Seven Samurai* is an unforgettable masterpiece -- the work of one of the world's greatest filmmakers at the height of his powers."

#2--RASHOMON (1950)

Human nature, where the ego clouds one's perspective, undergoes a series of events in the film that put Kurosawa on the cinematic map. Three separate people tell different accounts of a rape and murder in the woods. Ingenious camera placements and a universal narrative create a unique experience in movie viewing. The film kicked off the "Golden Age of Japanese Cinema." Time Magazine at the time when *Rashomon* was first released published this prediction of the film's influence, "*Rashomon* is a novel, stimulating movie going experience, and a sure sign that U.S. film importers will be looking hard at Japanese pictures from now on."

#3--IKIRU (TO LOVE) (1952)

A government bureaucrat is told he only has a short time to live. Finding a purpose in an otherwise meaningless life, Takashi Shimura, who plays Watanabe a city government worker, discovers and commences working on a noble deed. Wrote Roger Ebert, "Over the years I have seen *Ikiru* every five years or so, and each time it has moved me, and made me think. And the older I get, the less Watanabe seems like a pathetic old man, and the more he seems like every one of us."

#4--RAN (1985)

Kurosawa's big-budgeted color epic. The director said that while writing in the middle of scripting he realized the story was following the parallel lines of Shakespeare's *King Lear.* "In *Ran,* the horrors of life are transformed by art into beauty," wrote film reviewer Bob Graham. "It is finally so moving that the only appropriate response is silence."

#5--DERSU UZALA (1975)

Receiving the Academy Award for Best Foreign Film, this movie chronicles the guidance of a Siberian trapper leading a group of Russian explorers tracking through the wilds of Russia at the turn of the 19th-century. This was the movie that rejuvenated Kurosawa's creative drive after his attempted suicide. Soviet financing allowed him to make one of the more emotional yet historic pictures ever produced. "Every frame of *Dersu Uzala i*s simply beautiful to look at," wrote Brian Gibson. "Kurosawa's 140-minute masterpiece is a quietly captivating experience."

#6--THRONE OF BLOOD (1957)

An interesting variation on Shakespeare's *Macbeth* set in Japan about the same time as the original. This film comes as closest to the traditional *Noh* style of dramatic presentation as Kurosawa would ever produce. Literary critic Harold Bloom called *Throne* "the most successful film version of *Macbeth.*"

#7--THE HIDDEN FORTRESS (1958)

George Lucas loved this movie so much he adopted elements of *Fortress* and incorporated them into his pioneering film *Star Wars.* Film writer David Ehrenstein compared *Fortress* to D.W. Griffith's greatest works. "The battle on the steps (anticipating the climax of *Ran*) is as visually overwhelming as any of the similar scenes in Griffith's *Intolerance.* The use of composition in depth in the fortress scene is likewise as arresting as the best of Eisenstein or David Lean."

#8--STRAY DOG (1949)

Dog is considered Japan's first detective film, shot in a film noir style. The opening credits shows a panting dog underneath the title. When the film was reviewed by American censors before it could be screened in the United States, they thought the dog had been injured by Kurosawa's crew and were going to have the director change the opening. With the title symbolically depending on that opening shot, Kurosawa was incredulous. He remarked this was the only instance he wished Japan had not lost World War II.

#9--THE BAD SLEEP WELL (1960)

Kurosawa's nephew came up with the original idea of corporate greed in Japan. The director and several other writers reworked the script, which took the form of a variation of Shakespeare's *Hamlet*. Ed Park of Village Voice praised the film. "Opening with a bravura wedding sequence and ending with a sycophantic bow to a replaced telephone receiver, the film has its longueurs, but Mifune's buttoned-down avenger is a compelling portrait of righteous obsession foundering on unpredictable reality."

#10--KAGEMUSHA (1980)

Kurosawa considered this film as the prelude to his hit movie *Ran*. They share similar themes and this picture was nominated for the Academy Awards Best Foreign Film. George Lucas and Francis Ford Coppola convinced 20th Century Fox to make up the budgetary shortfall after Toho Studios was considering canceling the film because its production costs were running high. The two directors were rewarded by the high box office receipts this movie generated during its initial release.

Ingmar Bergman

THE SWEDISH GENIUS BEHIND "DEEP" MOVIES

Students examining their syllabus in Film School Studies 101 look in trepidation as they eye one session devoted to Swedish director Ingmar Bergman. Their vague knowledge on the director consists of a serious, tedious thinker whose bleak films are obsessed with death, dying and metaphysics.

Nothing could be further from the truth.

Certainly, Bergman steered film from pure entertainment to more intellectually challenging, philosophical "art" movies. But through all his cerebral posing of existential issues, Bergman knew how to deliver his universal messages while holding his audiences' attention.

"Bergman's first and foremost an entertainer," says his most ardent fan, Woody Allen. "So it's not like doing homework."

FAMOUS FILM DIRECTORS' FAVORITE DIRECTOR

Francis Ford Coppola cites Bergman as his favorite director. Polish director Krzysztof Kieslowski relates "He's the only director to have said as much about human nature as Dostoyevsky or Camus." Martin Scorsese added, "If you were a teenager in the '50's and '60's on your way toward becoming an adult, and you wanted to make films, I don't see how you couldn't be influenced by Bergman."

The "in" thing back then was, if you were a male teenager and wanted to impress the opposite sex, recite a Bergman quote and you had the ultimate pick-up line.

Bergman's international exposure during the late 1950's was perfect timing for him and the world as cinema was reaching for greater depth. He preceded "modern" European directors such as Michelangelo Antonioni, Frederico Fellini and Jean-Luc Godard by a mere whisker, but his impact on them was immense. In fact, film courses in universities were being established at the same time as the more popular Bergman movies were released, giving film professors something deeper to work with by analyzing his existential themes similar to those found in the greatest works of literature.

PERSONAL LIFE REFLECTED IN HIS FILMS

Bergman is one of a select few film directors who brought to the screen his personal story and childhood angsts. In 1982's *Fanny And Alexander,* Bergman reflected on his own upbringing when his Lutheran minister father, who later in life became a spiritual advisor to the King of Sweden, doled out punishment akin to medieval torture to his misbehaving children. The young Ingmar's confusion between what the love his father preached in his church and what took place behind private doors would dominate the director's narratives throughout his film career. Some of Bergman's most complex and popular movies examine God's place in the world and His effect on human souls. One may accurately state film work became Bergman's therapy.

Strong parallels abound between his 1955 *Smiles of a Summer Night* and Bergman's life at the time he made the film. Harriet Andersson, the maid in the film, was ending her relationship with Ingmar. Shortly before filming began, Bergman found a new lover in Bibi Andersson, who played a small role in *Smiles.* The movie, a mixed-romantic bedroom farce, contains a scene which takes place on a Stockholm stage where the two Anderssons appear in the same sequence, a charming reminder to today's viewer how Bergman's love life intersected with his professional one.

Viewing *Smiles,* Bergman's breakout film, there is very little visible evidence Bergman was going through some very difficult times when he was directing the picture. His personal finances were sinking him in a pile of debt. The production company behind *Smiles,* Svensk Filmindustri, told the director if his film didn't make any money at the box office, the studio would refuse to finance his next project. He was experiencing severe stomach pains, so much so his body shed 25 pounds filming *Smiles.* His affair with Harriet Andersson, co-starring in the film, was dissolving.

But because of the light-hearted theme in *Smiles,* his spirits were uplifted. Bergman said the production brought him out of a depression he claims would have resulted in suicide if he hadn't been involved in such a buoyant movie.

Happily, the film proved a success and made a profit. *Smiles* was so lucrative it assured Bergman's complete creative independence, unheard of in the film industry at the time. Because Bergman films had low budgets and the film company Svensk Filmindustri recognized the jewel the studio had on its hands, the director was able to produce personal topics of his own choosing.

PRE-PRODUCTION

SCRIPTWRITING A PANACEA FOR BERGMAN

The process of scriptwriting and directing his movies was therapeutic to Bergman throughout his movie career. Before making 1957's *The Seventh Seal,* the Swedish director had a terrible fear of death, putting a crimp on his creativity. Bergman was in Stockholm's Karolinska Hospital suffering from stomach problems when he began writing *The Seventh Seal.* Surrounded by people who were sick and occasionally dying, Bergman was seized with thoughts people normally avoid: death. As he delved deep into the theme of cessation while writing his script, Bergman found his fears, although not completely eradicated, were alleviated to the point he could think and talk about mortality after the movie was released.

In other films, such as *Wild Strawberries,* the director harkened back to his childhood with images of family gatherings which were brought to light in his memory bank.

"I'm deeply fixated on my childhood," said Bergman. "Some impressions are extremely vivid, light, smell, and all. There are moments when I can wander through my childhood's landscape, through rooms long ago, remember how they were furnished, where the pictures hung on the walls, the way the light fell. It's like a film, little scraps of a film, which I set running and which I can reconstruct to the last detail, except their smell."

Bergman related how the story structure of 1957's *Wild Strawberries* took hold. He was driving from Stockholm to Dalarna and happened to pass the town of Uppsala, where he was born and raised. He stopped by his grandmother's old house on the way. An idea popped into his head as he nostalgically thought of how it would be if he opened the door of his grandmother's house and inside would be all his relatives, including his parents, holding one of their frequent family gatherings.

"So it struck me - what if you could make a film about this," said Bergman, "that you just walk up in a realistic way and open a door, and then you walk into your childhood, and then you open another door and come back to reality, and then you make a turn around a street corner and arrive in some other period of your existence, and everything goes on, lives. That was actually the idea behind *Strawberries.*"

While writing the script for *Strawberries,* Bergman had in mind veteran Swedish actor Victor Sjostrom for his lead character, Professor Isak Borg. He developed *Strawberry's* Dr. Borg around Sjostrom's personality. During pre-production when he sat down with his casting team, Bergman couldn't envision anyone else playing the leading role than the 78-year-old actor. The director, however, was too nervous to call him because he had idolized the actor since his childhood. Bergman persuaded someone else involved in the production to contact Sjostrom. The aging actor, not feeling all that great, was reluctant to devote such a long period of time to the central character of the picture. But he agreed to meet Bergman to hear him out and review the script. Upon receiving the actor's offer, Bergman went to Sjostrom's apartment for a discussion on the movie and left him the script.

The following morning Bergman answered a call from the actor, who said he would do the movie, but under one condition: he wanted to be home by 5 p.m. to have a shot of whiskey exactly at that hour—and no later. Bergman agreed to the stipulation.

Strawberries turned out to be Sjostrom's final film, even though the actor lived three more years after the picture was released.

Another film to affect Bergman in a very personal way was 1961's *Through A Glass Darkly*. He selected the island of Faro as the setting for this four-character movie, a location where he eventually purchased a home. Bergman was so impressed with *Glass* he said, which was unusual for him, "the film is above reproach technically and dramatically."

Throughout his life Bergman was fascinated with the subject of death, and his 1968's *The Hour of the Wolf* addresses the time of evening when the body's resistance to death is at its weakest.

"The time between midnight and dawn when most people die, when sleep is deepest, when nightmares are most palatable," said Bergman on the premise of *Wolf* and its bewitching hour of 4 a.m. "It is the hour when the sleepless are pursued by their sharpest anxieties, when ghosts and demons hold sway. The hour of the wolf is also the hour when most children are born."

STAGE HIS FAVORITE MEDIUM

Bergman admitted the stage was his first preference over film as far as directing goes. "I would love to be carried out dead directing from the stage," Bergman reflected about his future death. In fact, when Bergman gave up feature filmmaking in 1984 he continued to direct plays until he was 85 in 2003.

As an author who wrote and directed a number of plays throughout his career, Bergman, during the early 1940's, gravitated towards film work simply because it paid the bills. When Bergman was a little boy, his grandmother used to sneak him into movie theaters partly because his strict father had forbade the young Ingmar to see any films.

Bergman remembered dipping his toes into making movies for the first time.

"I've had to learn everything about movies by myself," Bergman said. "For the theater, I studied with a wonderful old man in Goteborg, where I spent four years. He was a hard, difficult man, but he knew the theater- and I learned from him. For the movies, however, there was no one. Before the War (World War II), I was a schoolboy. Then, during the War, we got to see no foreign films at all. By the time it was over, I was working to support a wife and three children. Fortunately, I am by nature an autodidact, one who can teach himself- though it's an uncomfortable thing at times. Self-taught people sometimes cling too much to the technical side, the sure side, and place technical perfection too high."

Bergman said of the stage versus film, "The theater is like a faithful wife. The film is the great adventure -- the costly, exacting mistress."

After producing several movies Bergman began to appreciate film as something the stage could not duplicate.

"No form of art goes beyond ordinary consciousness as film does, straight to our emotions, deep into the twilight room of the soul." reflected Bergman. "To shoot a film is to organize an entire universe. Film as dream, film as music."

One of Bergman's most famous films, 1966's *Persona,* contains the spirit of August Strindberg's one act-play *The Stronger.* The Strindberg one-scene drama has two female characters, one who speaks, and the other who is silent, a storyline which parallels *Persona.* Bergman was in the Sophia Hospital in Stockholm with pneumonia and acute penicillin poisoning when he composed the first draft of the script for *Persona.*

PRODUCTION

COMFORTABLE WORKING WITH SAME CREW

Bergman was fortunate to work with a consistent technical film crew during his 50-plus movie career. Two-time Oscar winner cinematographer Sven Nykvist created the mood shots Bergman is famous for while a team of eighteen loyal technicians carried out Bergman's on-set demands. British director David Lean, known for his sprawling epic films, once asked Bergman how large was his film crew. "I always work with 18 friends," Bergman answered. "That's funny," reflected Lean, "I work with 150 enemies."

Unlike Alfred Hitchcock, who famously labeled actors "cattle," Bergman employed a company of Swedish actors and actresses he felt comfortable directing. The troupe was a collection of Swedish actors he could depend on to give reliably breathtaking performances. In the later part of his career, Bergman's scripts became sparer, and the director relied on his regulars to improvise their dialogue in each film. He became so familiar with some of his actresses that his romantic affairs with several of them produced at least one child (the child being with Liv Ullman, whom he fell in love with while making *Persona*) as well as caused the ruination of a few of his five marriages.

Another working colleague who edited a great portion of his films was editor Ulla Ryghe. During post-production of *Glass,* Bergman and Ryghe spent over two months editing the movie, working from nine in the morning until the wee hours of the evening, an unusually strenuous schedule for both.

NOVEL SHOTS TO THE MOVIES

Bergman brought numerous original images to the screen which are frequently imitated in today's cinema. His famous "Bergman composite two-shot" consisting of lighting each person in the same frame separately. The lingering close-up, first introduced shooting the reflective Victor Sjostrom at the conclusion of *Strawberries* ("My best close-up in all my films," remembers Bergman, who has been acknowledged as the master of close-ups.). And the "Persona" shot, consisting of one actress looking straight ahead into the camera while the other in profile is looking off frame to the side.

In the middle of filming *Persona*, Bergman, alongside cinematographer Sven Nykvist, thought the movie's medium shots were becoming uninteresting. They felt in order to get deep into a person's psyche, close-up shots were required to satisfy their goal. They framed *Persona*'s most intense sequences around a series of close-ups.

Bergman, who writes his own screenplays, had a view of his "scripts to serve as skeletons awaiting the flesh and sinew of images."

His directing philosophies evolved over a number of years.

"My professor told me when I started in the '40s that a director should listen and keep his mouth shut," he recalls. "Took me a long time to understand I talked too much. Now I know you should listen with your ears - and your heart."

One of the most iconic images in cinema is the final minutes of *The Seventh Seal,* showing a small group of characters who had just died from the plague dancing up a hillside with an unusual cloud formation in the background. Bergman was on location when he saw the exceptional clouds and wanted to show "Death" leading those who had just passed away joyously dancing up the incline. Most of the actors had called it quits for the day and had left for home. The director asked some production technicians breaking down the day's set as well as a few tourists who were visiting the area to dress themselves in the period outfits used in the film and had them prance up the slope. Totally unscripted, this improvisation was shot in only one take and is a breathtaking finale to a landmark film.

RELIGIOUS VIEWS

Bergman's personal philosophy on living changed throughout his life.

"My basic view of things is - not to have any basic view of things," he said. "From having been exceedingly dogmatic, my views on life have gradually dissolved. They don't exist any longer."

And that includes his views of the afterlife.

"When I was young, I was extremely scared of dying," he noted. "But now I think it a very, very wise arrangement. It's like a light that is extinguished. Not very much to make a fuss about."

In 1963's *Winter Light,* Bergman could readily identity with Tomas Ericsson, the pastor who questions God's existence after a member of his sparse congregation had committed suicide. The second film in what is considered Bergman's "spiritual" trilogy (*Through A Glass Darkly* and 1963's *The Silence* round out the other two films), all deal with God's existence on earth. *Winter* addresses the ending of *Glass* where the idea of love is proven to be evidence that God does indeed exist. But the pastor's dealing with the suicide in *Winter* leads him to wonder.

"I think I have made just one picture that I really like, and that is *Winter Light,*" said Bergman. "Everything is exactly as I wanted to have it, in every second of this picture."

As an agnostic who felt each person possesses a divine spirit within, Bergman, celebrating his sixtieth birthday, conversed with his and Ullman's five-year old daughter. Bergman asked what she would be doing on her sixtieth birthday. The little girl answered she'll have a big party. "Will I be there?" asked Bergman. The girl looked up at him and said, "'Well, you know, I'll leave the party and I'll walk down to the beach and there on the waves you will come dancing toward me'."

Such is the power of Bergman and his films.

TOP TEN INGMAR BERGMAN FILMS

#1--THE SEVENTH SEAL (1957)

In *Seal* Bergman popularizes his "silence of God" theme when a knight returns home from the Crusades and discovers Death is scheduled to take him away. To delay the inevitable, he challenges Death to a game of chess, allowing Bergman to explore how death and its theological relationship with a population in the Middle Ages afflicted with the plague are handled. This film solidified Bergman's reputation as the premier Scandinavian film director.

#2--WILD STRAWBERRIES (1957)

Vivid memories of the past allow an aging professor to reflect on his life and the people who have made such a huge impact on him. This was film director Stanley Kubrick's second favorite film of all-time. Writer Roger Scruton noted, "The camera stalks the unfolding story like a hunter, pausing to take aim at the present only to bring it into chafing proximity with the past. In *Wild Strawberries,* things, like people, are saturated with the psychic states of their observers, drawn into the drama by a camera which endows each detail with a consciousness of its own. The result is not whimsical or arbitrary, but on the contrary, entirely objective, turning to realities at every point where the camera might otherwise be tempted to escape from them. *Wild Strawberries* is one of many examples of true cinematic art."

#3--PERSONA (1966)

This is Bergman's most analyzed film in that there are so many themes (people's double nature, the losing of one's mind, as well as the identity people take for themselves), all of which are visually illustrated symbolically. Bosley Crowther of the New York Times described the film as a "lovely, moody film which, for all its intense emotionalism, makes some tough intellectual demands." The framing of Bibi Anderson and Liv Ullmann, one looking towards the camera and the other in profile, is a standard in today's cinema.

#4--SMILES OF A SUMMER'S NIGHT (1955)

Bergman's most accessible and humorous movie, produced early in his career. Critic Pauline Kael said, "Bergman found a high style within a set of boudoir farce conventions: in *Smiles of a Summer Night*, boudoir farce becomes lyric poetry."

#5--CRIES AND WHISPERS (1972)

When one of the sisters comes down with a terminal disease, the reunion with the two other sisters sparks past memories about the how they treated each other during their childhood, memories that bubble up in dramatic fashion. Reviewer James Berardinelli was especially effusive of Harriet Andersson's performance as the dying sister. Her role was "so powerful that we feel like intruders watching it. She screams, whimpers, begs, and cries. She craves death and fears it. Ego-free performances like this are few and far between these days, and almost never to be found in Hollywood."

#6--WINTER LIGHT (1963)

Bergman professed *Winter* as being his best film as far as he intended the movie to be. Variety felt the film would appeal to one segment of the population, while the other portion of potential viewers would be totally disinterested in the subject-matter. "An extremely moving and fascinating film for the religiously aware and a somewhat boring one for the religiously indifferent."

#7--THROUGH A GLASS DARKLY (1961)

Harriet Andersson plays a schizophrenic woman whose vacation on a remote island with her family is anything but pleasant. Her primary delusion is she has visions of God; but these images are of a spider rather than a beam of illuminating light. Roger Ebert placed the film in a proper perspective. "We're struck by Bergman's deep concern that humans see the world as through a glass, darkly, and are unable to perceive its meaning."

#8--HOUR OF THE WOLF (1968)

In Bergman's only horror film, an artist reveals to his wife he's experiencing nightmares about his past. His remembrances occur to him deep into the evening, at the 4 a.m. hour. The New York Times said *Hour* is "not one of Bergman's great films but it is unthinkable for anyone seriously interested in movies not to see it."

#9--FANNY AND ALEXANDER (F&A) (1982)

Loosely based on Bergman's childhood, this long (clocking in at three hours-plus, and that's the shorter version) and lush film was awarded four Oscars, including Best Foreign Film and Best Cinematography (Sven Nykvist). *F&A* was Bergman's last theatrical release, but he went on to direct several television productions. Said actor Matthew Macfadyen, who studied the movie in school: the film "featured just the most extraordinary acting I'd ever seen." As a student, the film was shown as "an example to follow – an example of people acting with each other. They all knew each other well in real life, the cast, and they rehearsed for a long time and shot it very quickly. The result is extraordinary."

#10--SUMMER WITH MONIKA (1953)

There was a time when everyone thought Sweden and its movies were the most sexually liberated in the world. One of the main reasons was Bergman's *Summer,* which contained several nude sequences of actress Harriet Andersson. The United States was introduced to this film in 1955 when Kroger Babb, known for his exploitation films, bought the rights to show *Summer* in America. He renamed it *Monika, the Story of a Bad Girl* and edited out most of the boring parts to pare the length down to 62 minutes from its 96-minute original length.

Walt Disney

THE GENIUS BEHIND ANIMATED FEATURE FILMS

Skeptical observers labeled it "Walt's Folly."

The owner of a small Hollywood film studio was spending years and over a million dollars in hard cash to create a cartoon featuring a young homeless woman taken in by seven short, adult mine workers.

Since inception, the project was taking a life of its own. Walt Disney Studios, the fledging animation outfit known for producing Mickey Mouse cartoons, was betting its entire finances on an old Brothers Grimm fairy tale. The studio's owner, Walt Disney, went on a hiring binge, employing scores of animators and establishing an in-house art school to remold their drawing skills to a higher sophisticated level of "cel animation" never seen before on the screen.

The story's framework was constantly fluid. Walt, ever the perfectionist, sometimes rejected months of his animators' labor to sharpen the plot's focus.

"I had spent eight months working on this soup sequence," recalled Disney animator Ward Kimball. "Walt calls me into his office and says 'I'm going to have to take out that soup sequence. The film has to go back to the witch.' It kinda hurt."

When the last frantic flurry of frenzy working on last-minute cels by the animators to meet the hard deadline set for the film's premier, and when Disney's last penny was spent, Walt and his brother Roy, who managed all the debt the studio was racking up, held their collective breath on December 21, 1937, at Carthay Circle Theater in Hollywood. As the movie's final credits rolled, the audience all rose in thunderous applause, marking a true milestone in film history.

Snow White And The Seven Dwarfs was the first United States cel animated feature film, and the cartoon-movie would revolutionize cinema. New York Times film reviewer Frank Nugent saw *Snow White* as important cinematically as D.W. Griffith's 1915 *The Birth of a Nation*. Russian film director Sergei Eisenstein, the master of edited montages, declared *Snow*

White the best film he'd ever seen. And Charlie Chaplin added the film "even surpassed our high expectations. In Dwarf Dopey, Disney has created one of the greatest comedians of all time."

Snow White directly influenced Orson Welles' *Citizen Kane* as well as Italian film director Federico Fellini. Woody Allen claimed *Snow White* was the first movie he had ever seen and his love for movies started right there. The 1937 film began a successful string of Disney animated feature films that have gone on to entertain generations of children--and adults--ever since.

Snow White up to this point in Disney's career as a Hollywood business owner was a huge, make-or-break gamble. No one had produced such a movie like this before, never mind a long "cartoon." While *Snow White* was being produced, observers in the movie industry said the concept would never be successful. As history has proven, *Snow White* became a block-buster sensation and has resulted in becoming one of the biggest money makers in Hollywood history.

As the first feature animated film in the United States, *Snow White* broke many technological barriers Walt was inventing on the fly. Looking back on the innovations created in the making of *Snow White,* Disney, although exhilarated with the process, wished he "could yank it back and do it all over again."

Creating *Snow White* was unprecedented for the scale of its production, requiring literally an army of talented employees to create the feature. Over two million "cels," or illustrated panels, were drawn with a palette of colors approaching 1,500 shades of paint. The industry's best animators were hired for the feature film with 32 highly-skilled artists and more than 100 assistants collaborating alongside them. Working in the next room were 167 "in-betweeners," 20 layout artists, 25 drawers painting backgrounds in watercolor, 65 animators devoted solely to the effects, and 158 female inkers and painters.

During the initial phase of *Snow White,* Disney wanted the movie's emphasis placed on the seven dwarfs. Each dwarf was a representation of real people Walt and the animators knew. Naming each one, with their individual personalities, was tougher than they thought when the idea was first proposed. Someone brought up the name "Dopey" as one of the dwarfs, a character who wasn't the sharpest person on the planet. A group of animators scoffed at the moniker since they felt the label was too contemporary (circa 1937) for an old German fairytale. Walt slept on the "Dopey" name and returned the next day to say it was perfect. To defend his argument, he claimed the term "dopey" appeared in a Shakespearean play. Knowing Walt was well read, the animators went along with Disney's statement and didn't question his vast knowledge. Yet, scouring through the body of the Shakespearean works, there's no evidence the word "dopey" appears in any of the playwright's dramas, comedies or sonnets.

Each dwarf has his own unique movements and body language. The animators were tasked to give each dwarf a distinctive strut and personality since no two people, even dwarfs, walk and behave the same way. In the "Heigh Ho" scene, the dwarfs' movements were especially challenging to the animators even though they were marching to the same song. Animator Shamus Culhane described the sequence as one of the most difficult drawing assignments in his career. Each character had to be mapped with a blue pencil and a ruler because the point of view of the "camera" required unusual angles and perspectives while the dwarfs were joyfully returning home from a long day on the job.

To compound the difficulty, when the film's animation was in its first stages of storyboarding, animator Frank Thomas had Dopey, who was always lagging behind, catch up to the other dwarfs by hopping. Walt loved the visual so much he wanted Dopey's hop to appear in all the other scenes where he was walking with the dwarfs. Once the animators heard that, they were highly upset. That extra few hops created a lot more work for them.

"I worked six months on that g..damn thing," bemoaned Culhane, "and it doesn't last a minute onscreen."

Painting the backgrounds in watercolor was a cheaper method of coloring than the gouache and oils used in more layered feature animated films. Disney relied on watercolors for his cartoon shorts. But in *Snow White,* as well as in *Dumbo,* watercolors were used extensively for the backgrounds, minimizing costs. The studio opted for the more expensive oils in 1940's *Pinocchio* and 1942's *Bambi,* and basically avoided watercolors until *Fantasia 2000.*

Disney was ingenious in motivating his animators to come up with novel ideas. He would offer a monetary reward of five dollars for anyone who could think of a sight gag that would make it into the film. This "Five Dollars a Gag" offer resulted in several hilarious scenes. One memorable antic belonged to animator Ward Kimball, who suggested a scene when the dwarfs come home and discover Snow White sleeping in one of their beds, their noses each pop up one at a time over the board at the foot of the bed.

With *Snow White,* the animated film became the all-time box office record holder for any movie released up to that point. *Snow White,* once it surpassed the previous mark, held on to the crown for exactly one year, only to be supplanted by mega-hit 1939's *Gone With The Wind.*

In addition to the box offices' cash registers accumulating piles of money at the end of each showing, *Snow White* was one of the first films to market the characters of the movie. Disney had the foresight to have the merchandise, such as dolls and figurines, of the dwarfs, Snow White, the Queen, and others who had appeared in the movie available in the stores by the time the film premiered.

Snow White earned Disney an honorary Oscar for his unique innovation for producing the animated feature film. His Academy Award was an unusual design with the traditional statuette on top of a base and seven miniature Oscars standing on a descending staircase. When Walt accepted the award during the ceremonies in an era before television where winners were given the latitude to take all the time they wanted at the podium, he went into great detail on his new film, *Pinocchio,* which was at the time in production. The monologue lasted 25 minutes and not one person in the audience was seen yawning.

Snow White was also released in European movie theaters before World War II. German associates to Adolf Hitler claimed *Snow White* was one of dictator's three favorite movies. The other two were 1933's *King Kong* and 1941's *Sun Valley Serenade.*

Disney retained his personal philosophy of constantly striving to improve upon the quality of his productions. Such forward thinking guaranteed the great success his and his company ultimately achieved. The outlook has kept the Walt Disney Company a dominant force in the entertainment industry right up to today.

"Around here we don't look backwards for very long," Disney said. "We keep moving forward, opening up new doors, and doing new things, because we're curious, and curiosity keeps leading us down new paths."

DISNEY'S EARLY CREATIONS

Walt Disney was fired from his first job as an animator for the Kansas City Star (writer Ernest Hemingway also worked at the newspaper a year before him in 1918) because management felt he "lacked imagination." This story is often cited as a reason for each individual to persevere, according to the Disney philosophy. "The way to get started is to quit talking and begin doing," was the mantra steering Disney toward his success.

Walt has given the screen a bevy of memorable characters. In one of his earliest creations, Oswald The Lucky Rabbit, Disney pioneered the cartoon brand by giving a human personality to this lagomorph Oswald, an element early cartoonists avoided when outlining their animated characters.

"I want the characters to be somebody," said Walt. "I don't want them just to be a drawing."

When Walt was unable to retain the copyrights to Oswald The Rabbit, he immediately turned to a mouse whom he named Mortimer, but latter changed to Mickey on his wife Lillian's suggestion. "I hope we never lose sight of one thing: that it was all started with a mouse," Walt famously said. Mickey Mouse starred in history's first talking cartoon, 1928's *Steamboat Willie*, catapulting Walt Disney Studios into a profit-making enterprise.

Disney's affinity towards animals and having the imagination to give them a personality similar to humans began early in his youth when he killed a small owl on purpose. He felt so guilt-ridden and regretful of the killing he vowed never to extinguish another animal's life again.

Disney developed an affinity toward animals and incorporated all sorts of wild and domesticated creatures into his films. The only animal he had a tough time placing into his movies was a cat. The reason for Walt's trepidation: "You can't tell them what to do."

One exception to the feline avoidance was Figaro, the pet kitten of Geppetto in *Pinocchio*. Ironically, Walt said Figaro was his all-time favorite character. When he saw the initial storyboards on *Pinocchio,* he instantly fell in love with Figaro and told his animators to put the kitten into the feature film as much as they could. Soon after *Pinocchio* was released, Disney released a cartoon with Minnie Mouse. In the short cartoon, Figaro replaced Miss Mouse's petite cocker spaniel, a peculiar typecast since kittens, once they grow up, eat mice.

"I don't make pictures just to make money," Walt laid out, "I make money to make more pictures." Walt made sure early in his career his cartoons reflected valuable life learned lessons he drew upon as a child, from young people taking on adult responsibilities in *Snow White,* to telling the truth and not following a bad crowd in *Pinocchio,* to turning a physical deformity into something positive in 1941's *Dumbo*.

In one of his more candid moments where he underestimated his films' positive messages, Disney said, "I sell corn, and I love corn."

DISNEY TRADEMARK INNOVATIONS

Because of all the money Disney was raking in with *Snow White,* he was able to build his new Disney Studios in Burbank, California. Having his very own complex allowed Disney and his animators to branch out and expand multiple creative ideas he and his team of animators were percolating. In Disney's feature films and shorts, Walt's trademark imprint was found everywhere. Even though his was the first animation studio to establish a "Story Department" to create plots and gags, Walt always injected his own ideas to enhance the films' visuals and narratives.

"The proper comedy for the screen is visual," Disney revealed. "Films try to get too many laughs out of the dialogue. We use pantomime, not wisecracks. Portrayal of human sensations by inanimate objects such as steam shovels and rocking-chairs never fail to provoke laughter. Human distress exemplified by animals is sure-fire. A bird that jumps after swallowing a grasshopper is a natural. Surprise is always provocative."

Walt conveyed his storylines to his animators in the most physical way. His physical gyrations detailing the movies' characters were legendary. His critical inspection of every animated cel sent shivers of anticipation through the hearts of those responsible for the drawings. Walt's insightful analysis elevated every Walt Disney Studio film light years ahead of any competing studio's animations.

Besides the breathtaking visuals presented in each new Disney feature film, Walt recognized to be successful his movies had to appeal to all generations, not just for kids. "We don't actually make films for children, but we make films that children can enjoy along with the parents," Disney said.

Walt's uncanny ability to foresee the future created many "firsts" in film, including the first three-strip Technicolor process onto the screen (*Silly Symphony Flowers And Trees* in 1932), the first stereophonic sound in theaters (*Fantasia* in 1940), and the first multi-plane camera, which gave a rich depth-of-field look to his scenes. The list of Disney's milestone achievements is almost endless. So monumental were Walt's accomplishments he holds the record for the most Academy Awards earning 29, as well as collecting four honorary Oscars.

HOW DISNEY CHARACTERS EVOLVED

Disney was attracted to the age-old legends and fables which came out of Europe through the centuries, stories he remembered from his childhood. Fourteen of the seventeen animated films produced during Disney's lifetime were drawn from those proverbial tales. *Snow White* was inspired by a venerable legendary German folktale adapted by the Brothers Grimm.

Disney was handed Italian children's author Carlo Collidi's *The Adventures of Pinocchio* by animator Norman Ferguson in 1937 when *Snow White* was in production. Walt had a few minutes to spare to read the book while sweating over *Snow White*. "Walt was busting his guts with enthusiasm," said Ferguson, remembering Disney's reaction upon reading the Pinocchio story. After the success of *Snow White,* Walt immediately assigned a team of creators to begin work on the Collidi story.

Disney's creative mind was always churning, morning, noon and night. "If you can dream it, you can do it," Walt said of his and universally everyone's imaginative mind.

For *Pinocchio,* Disney appointed animator supervisors to head teams for each of the film's characters. Ward Kimball was named to lead the team creating Jiminy Cricket. The assignment was Kimball's first position as supervisor and he didn't want to screw it up. Since Jiminy is a "cricket," Kimball's first design was to shape the character resembling the Gryllidae. When Walt saw the sketch, he thought the cricket was "too gross" and said he wanted Jiminy, one of *Pinocchio's* central figures, to appear adorable. Kimball went back to his drawing board and erased all of Jiminy's insect features. An admirer of the artwork of Johnnie Walker scotch whiskey, Kimball dressed Jiminy in the outfit the gentleman on the whiskey label was wearing. He also gave the cricket an oversized head and painted him green. Kimball felt after all his alterations Jiminy contained just a hint of resembling a cricket. Once Disney saw the new Jiminy, he loved it.

Years later, Kimball went on record saying how disappointed he was Jiminy lost all signs of being an insect solely to please Walt.

"The audience accepts him as a cricket because the other characters say he is," lamented Kimball

It wasn't for the lack of detail Kimball was disappointed in Jiminy. Artists applied 27 different colors to draw the cricket.

Pinocchio proved to be one of the most expensive films to make at the time of its release. Production costs tallied over $2.5 million, five times the projected budget of $500,000. One reason why the expenses escalated so high was Disney, seeing the lack of progress in *Pinocchio,* decided to suspend the work on it. He said the hiatus would allow his creative thinkers at the studio to give alternatives to the characters' appearances they were drawing such as Jiminy as well as to redirect the plot from the direction the story was headed toward.

FANTASIA'S FATE

Disney's most ambitious production his studio ever undertook was 1940's *Fantasia.* Walt had earlier released a series of short musical cartoons named *The Silly Symphonies,* but he wanted to elevate the sophistication of his cartoons by inserting classical music as an aural background to his animation.

Walt explained his ambition behind producing *Fantasia.* "In our ordinary stuff, our music is always under action, but on this ... we're supposed to be picturing this music—not the music fitting our story."

Using classical music was key to this action and Disney had hoped the general public would gain an appreciation toward what has been labeled as "high-brow music," the kind of pieces Walt said he personally would normally walk out whenever he heard the masters' work.

His studio was already busy developing a deluxe cartoon based on its most popular character, Mickey Mouse, when Walt ran into Leopold Stokowski, conductor for the Philadelphia Orchestra. Over dinner, Disney described to the renowned conductor the Mickey Mouse short cartoon his animators were working on at the time, named *The Sorcerer's Apprentice,* using a classical music score. Walt didn't tell Stokowski his animators were basing the cartoon on conductor Arturo Toscanini's effort. "I would like to conduct that music for you," Stokowski said enthusiastically. Walt was flabbergasted when the Philadelphia Orchestra leader offered his services.

Stokowski visited the Disney Studio shortly after he agreed to the project. His unannounced visit took Disney's animators by surprise. They were playing a 78-RPM record of Toscanini conducting his orchestra when they got word Stokowski was approaching. Like madmen, they ripped the album off the turntable just before the famed conductor walked into their office.

Originally Stokowski was willing to conduct the music for *The Sorcerer's Apprentice* for free. But as the costs mounted for producing the solitary Mickey Mouse short, piling up over $125,000 for expenses and counting, Disney felt one stand-alone cartoon would never bring in the kind of money to show a profit. So Walt expanded the musical cartoon concept to include besides *The Sorcerer's Apprentice* several more episodes to produce a full-length feature film. The projected movie would require more scoring. Stokowski agreed to an 18-month contract to oversee the entire music for *Fantasia.*

One idea Walt and Stokowski came up with was to have fragrances pump into the theater whenever certain segments of *Fantasia* were shown on the screen. They felt the aromas would enhance the film, creating another impression to address the viewers' senses. They selected gunpowder for *The Sorcerer's Apprentice,* jasmine for the *Waltz of the Flowers,* incense for *Ave Maria,* and so on. When they researched how to pipe in the smells, Disney realized there was no way a fragrance could fully clear the theater while the next one was scheduled to be blown in (this was before scratch and sniff boards.).

Once the project for *Fantasia* got rolling, Disney saw the movie's structure serving as the basis for re-releasing the film on an annual basis, with a couple of segments cut and new musical sequences inserted in their places. Walt's idea men storyboarded additional segments, including Richard Wagner's *Ride of the Valkyries* and Nikolai Rimsky-Korsakov's *Flight of the Bumblebee.*

Fantasia's disappointing box office receipts upon its release made Walt realize the film wasn't worth updating and he canceled further development on the project. Several decades later, well after Walt had passed away, these proposals were dredged up from the studio basement and re-introduced in *Fantasia 2000.*

Even though *Snow White* hired an army of employees to create Walt's first feature film, a far greater amount of Disney workers were involved in the making of *Fantasia.* Over five hundred animated characters appear in the 1940 movie. Walt's team numbered over one thousand artists and technicians laboring day and night to create the multi-layered picture.

With an eye toward color in *Snow White* and *Pinocchio*, Walt personally wrote down detailed instructions for the type of colors each episode should be used. But in *Fantasia,* Disney was hands off and gave his animators free reign on their color selection. The movie is noted for displaying more vivid colors than any other Disney animated feature film.

Disney animators employed humans to pattern several *Fantasia* characters and their movements. English film actor Nigel De Brulier was hired to trace the sorcerer's movements in the episode Mickey Mouse appears, *The Sorcerer's Apprentice.* The animators created an inside joke only they would know: they designed part of the sorcerer's character after their boss, Walt. The real name of the sorcerer is Yen Sid, "Disney" spelled backwards. And the sorcerer gives an occasional raised eyebrow. Walt displayed the same raised eyebrow-look whenever he was dissatisfied with the work of his animators.

For the demon Chernabog, actor Bela Lugosi (Dracula fame) was used to pose as the evil god for the *Night on Bald Mountain* segment. Lugosi labored several days at the Disney Studio where he was filmed doing demon-like poses. The animators would then plot his movements and animate them based on the Lugosi footage. Once Bill Tytla, the director of animation for the Chernabog character, saw the Lugosi film and the resulting rough sketches, he walked away disappointed. He spotted Wilfred Jackson, sequence director for *Fantasia* and thought his frame would be perfect for the demon. Jackson's movements were far superior to Lugosi's. The Chernabog seen on the screen is patterned after a Disney employee and not from the famous Hungarian-American actor who made Dracula the most feared creature on the screen at the time.

Two dancers' movements were filmed for use by the animators. Joyce Coles and Marge Champion's prancing served as choreography for the blossoms in *The Dance of the Reed Flutes* during *The Nutcracker Suite.*

Disney witnessed the depth and sophistication of *Fantasia* when the movie was fully completed. His said in his prediction: "*Fantasia* merely makes our other pictures look immature and suggests for the first time what the future of this medium may well turn out to be. What I see way off there is too nebulous to describe. But it looks big and glittering. That's what I like about this business, the certainty that there is something bigger and more exciting just around the bend - and the uncertainty of everything else."

DUMBO, THE SCALED-DOWN FEATURE FILM

Story designer Joe Grant and Dick Heemer expressed enthusiasm about a tale of a circus elephant who was badgered by members of a circus for the sole reason he had big ears. Disney thought the story was dumb, but the pair saw the potential in the big-top morality tale. The two composed several installments detailing the elephant's narrative and left one installment each morning on Disney's desk for him to read in his spare time. Walt was so hooked after reading several chapters he walked a beeline to the story department. "This is great! What happens next?" Walt queried the two. The story ended up being the feature-length movie *Dumbo*.

Grant and Heemer were the only two writers in the story department to develop the plot and characters for *Dumbo*. Employing just the two was not the way Walt did his normal story development on his previous films. He would usually get a crowd of writers to brainstorm for months before arriving at the final version of a movie. But in *Dumbo*, it was just the two story designers who brought this classic to fruition.

Pinocchio and *Fantasia* were initially a pair of busts at the box office for Disney. The two pictures were eating whatever profits Walt made on *Snow White*. When *Dumbo* was in the budgetary stage, Disney said the production would have to adhere to a tight expense sheet since the pennies were becoming scarce in his pockets.

Dumbo's supervising director Ben Sharpsteen was instructed by Walt that one way to save on the cash from hemorrhaging was to keep the production basic. Sharpseteen followed Disney's directions to a tee, guiding his animators to forego the lavish details created in the previous Disney features, especially eliminating the elaborate backgrounds.

When the picture was finished, the final tabulation for the cost of the production was $813,000, making *Dumbo* the least expensive of any Disney animated feature films. During the initial run, *Dumbo* became a great financial success for Disney, grossing over $2.5 million, much more than the *Pinocchio* and *Fantasia* films combined brought in during their original releases.

There exist numerous similarities between *Dumbo* and the Christmas classic Rudolph the Red Nosed Reindeer. Both concern young animals that are picked on simply because they have physical characteristics different from the others. Dumbo has really big ears while Rudolph has the illuminating bright red nose. In the final analysis, both end up becoming highly successful in their lives, which, not surprisingly, is attributive to their physical abnormalities.

Dumbo is the only movie in the Disney collection of feature films whose character the picture is named after but who never speaks. Dumbo is quite literally "dumb." And Walt always loved insider jokes to be subtly shown in the background. In *Dumbo,* seen visibly on the sign as the circus train leaves the grounds for the winter quarters is "WDP Circus." WDP stands for Walt Disney Productions.

REWORKING KIPLING'S THE JUNGLE BOOK

In the early 1960's as Disney Studios was cranking out both animated and live action feature films, many of these pictures were being skewered by movie critics and the paying public. When 1963's *The Sword In The Stone* gained little attention, Walt wanted to follow the mediocre film with a movie with higher standards. Bill Peet, a loyal story writer who had been with Disney for over twenty-five years, had suggested to his boss Rudyard Kipling's *The Jungle Book.* Walt green-lighted the project and for the next year Peet and his team composed the script and the accompanying storyboards. When Disney read the screenplay and viewed the artwork of the Kipling tale, he felt the overall atmosphere was too dark and overly dramatic. The writer and Disney argued about the project before Peet quit the studio in a huff.

Disney then assigned Larry Clemmons to head the *Jungle's* development. Walt's advice surprised Clemmons when he first was handed the assignment. Disney gave the Kipling book to him and said "The first thing I want you to do is not read it."

Because of his experiences with Peet, Walt decided to be heavily involved in both the story lines and its animated development.

Brian Epstein, the manager of the Beatles, the hottest band at the time, contacted Disney and asked if his band could be portrayed in *The Jungle Book* for some added publicity. Epstein was hoping the band's members would agree to be the voices of the characters drawn for the film. Walt was so enthusiastic about the offer he had his animators design a flock of lovable birds, called the Vultures, appearing in mop-top haircuts and speaking in Liverpool accents. As the animators were drawing feverishly, Epstein took his idea back to England. When John Lennon heard the proposal, with the band singing "That's What Friends Are For," he rejected his participation right on the spot. Lennon told Epstein Elvis Presley should play one of the characters instead.

Disney, upon hearing the rejection, then redirected the singing birds into a barbershop quartet and hired Chad of the British pop group Chad and Jeremy to sing the lead.

To record the voice of King Louie, jazz singer Louis Armstrong was originally planned to perform the duties. Once Walt viewed the storyboards, he felt there was no way an African-American could play an ape, even if he were a cartoon character, thinking the image would be far too racist. Listening to several prominent singers, the studio picked another jazz singer, Louis Prima, to take Armstrong's place. When *The Jungle Book* was released, there were howls of protests from cultural scholars who said King Louis had been vocalized by a black singer, feeding into an outrageously offensive racial stereotype which was vastly disturbing. Trouble with that argument was Louis Prima was of full Italian descent and spoke and sang in the film in his normal voice.

Walt wanted the ending to conclude with a girl from the "man village" enticing the movie's main character, Mowgli, to civilization. Animator Ollie Johnson thought the ending would be too clichéd as Disney designed it and argued his opinion. Johnson slowly changed his mind as he was animating the finale and eventually felt it was the perfect way to wrap up the film. The animator was glad the boss got his way.

1967's *The Jungle Book* was the last animated feature film Disney personally supervised. Walt passed away in December, 1966, before the premier of *Jungle.* When the studio showed a private screening right before *Jungle* was released to the general public, Walt's personal nurse, Hazel George, approached Johnson and tearfully brought up the final scene of the movie where Bagheera and Baloo saunter off into the sunset. Nurse George, who spent the last moments with Walt, said she felt the poignant ending was just how Walt went on his way up to heaven.

During the production of *Jungle,* the animation division of Disney Studios was on the brink of being dissolved because the high cost of making animated feature films as well as the public's lack of interest in the box office for a genre that was proving unprofitable. The studio, without the animators' main cheerleader, the late Walt Disney, told the division if *Jungle* performed as poorly as its last animated feature, *The Sword and the Stone*, the group would be folded. Joyfully for the many people who look forward to Disney's animated movies today, *Jungle* ended up making a ton of money for the studio. In fact, *Jungle* ranks as the seventh-highest grossing film in the 20th century in the United Kingdom.

When actor and president of the Academy of Motion Pictures Arts and Sciences Gregory Peck viewed *Jungle,* he felt Disney's personal final animated film was deserving of not only earning a Best Picture nomination but also should receive the Oscar for Best Picture. Peck's lobbying efforts failed to produce the results he wanted. The Academy finally came around to Peck's view when, 20 years later, its voters nominated a Disney feature animated film, 1991's *Beauty and the Beast,* for Best Picture.

THE IMPORTANCE OF SOUND

To accompany the dazzling array of images contained in a Disney animated feature, Walt attached extreme importance to the sounds and music of his movies. For the voice of the Old Witch in *Snow White,* the elderly hag who offers our heroine the poison apple, Disney animators had envisioned the transformed queen speaking in a raspy voice. Lucille La Verne was hired for the voice of the Wicked Queen. While she was recording the queen's dialogue, she overheard the animators say a hoarse-type of vocal chords would be needed for the "Old Hag." She interjected herself into the conversation and said, "I can do it." The animators were skeptical. She stepped out of the recording room, went to the women's restroom, and came back to speak, vocalizing in the perfect husky voice they were seeking. The animators asked La Verne what method she used to change her voice. She answered, "Oh, I just took my teeth out."

The voice of Snow White, Disney felt, should be unique. He never wanted Ms. White's distinctive voice to ever appear in another production, either in a cartoon or in a real life movie. When Adriana Caselottie was hired after she auditioned, Disney had her sign a very restrictive contract. The young Caselottie, a classically-trained singer, appeared to have quite a promising future, but she knew voicing Snow White was an once-in-a-lifetime opportunity. She accepted the restrictions, and besides having a very small part in 1939's *The Wizard of Oz,* she never voiced or sang in a movie after *Snow White.*

We take for granted today many films have soundtracks of their music released. Credit *Snow White* as the trailblazer in that department. All the music in Disney's previous cartoons was owned, in agreement, by the Bourne Company Music Publishers, known mostly for printing sheet music. There was little use for movie studios to hold the rights to their recorded music in those days since vinyl record sales were tiny and the sheet music business was barely profitable in itself--until *Snow White.* The film's songs became the rage once people saw the picture. Suddenly, Disney realized a nice profit could be made by putting out a record album consisting of all the songs in the movie. *Snow White* became the first movie soundtrack album released, but Disney had to pay the Bourne Company the rights to publish the studio's own music to use for the album. Years later, Walt was able to secure the copyrights to the music from all his films, all except *Snow White.*

In *Pinocchio,* Jiminy Cricket sings the Oscar-winning song for 1940, *When You Wish Upon A Star,* as the opening credits to the movie roll. The song, sung by Cliff Edwards, is also heard at the film's conclusion. The now familiar tune would eventually become the official song of The Walt Disney Company. The song is integrated in John Williams' musical score in 1977's *Close Encounters of the Third Kind's* ending scene on director Steven Spielberg's request.

DISNEY HABITS AND SUPERVISION

Even though Disney was the founder and head of one of America's largest entertainment business, he always hated to be referred to by his employees in the formal "Mr. Disney." Whenever someone called him "Mr. Disney" within the confines of his studio, he would reply, "Please, call me Walt. The only Mister at the Disney Studios is our lawyer, Mr. Lessing."

Walt's employees never showed a lack of respect in the Disney offices and hallways when dealing with him. He always wanted to see his workers grinding away when they were on the "clock." The animators had a secret code they whispered among each other whenever Walt was approaching. "Man is in the forest" was their secret code, attributed to the famous line in 1942's *Bambi.*

While her boys were growing up on a farmstead in the Midwest, Walt's mother cooked the simplest of meals. The basic diet remained with Walt throughout his life, even though he could afford caviar and filet mignon every day if he wanted to during his later years. He ordered hamburgers almost daily, supplemented with chili and beans. His preference to those plain foods even carried over whenever he traveled internationally. Disney's aides lugged a number of cans of chili stuffed in suitcases for his consumption. Despite staying in five star hotels, Disney had his staff instruct the most renowned chefs cooking in the hotel restaurants to heat up a can of chili for his dinner.

One habit Disney never allowed the public to see was him smoking. He was addicted to cigarettes, especially when he was working. Walt was what can be classified as a "chain smoker," lighting up one cigarette after he drew down his previous one. Such a lack of oxygen in his lungs created a wide range of behaviors, from cordial to angry. Disney smoked three packs a day and he preferred unfiltered cigarettes, the stronger the better. His favorite brands were Camels and Lucky Strikes.

The United States Surgeon General in 1964 released his office's report first connecting the use of tobacco to cancer. Diane Disney, Walt's daughter, read the highly-publicized report and purchased a carton of less harmful filtered cigarettes for her dad. She gained a promise he would smoke them instead of his stronger favorites. Walt thanked her for the gift. But before he put the first cigarette from her gift carton in his mouth, he tore off the filter.

"I promised her I'd use them, but I didn't tell her how I would use them," Walt said with a twinkle in his eye.

Disney developed a smoker's cough through the years. Whenever he was walking down the hallway to check up on his employees, the cough would be a dead giveaway to his staff signaling it was time to hit the animation boards. The cough and the Bambi line gave Disney the impression his employees were the hardest working stiffs in the world.

Disney died of lung cancer two years after the US Surgeon General issued his report.

Even though Walt's public persona was that of the avuncular type, there were occasions when his fangs came out in private.

One instance was when he was turning 35 years old. His close brother and business associate Roy thought it would be a great idea if his employees threw Walt a surprise birthday party. A couple of animators came up with the idea to spice up the celebration. On their own, they created a short cartoon of Mickey and Minnie Mouse consummating their relationship. When the cartoon was shown during the birthday party, the film instantaneously became the highlight of the office bash. Walt laughed at the cartoon, but inside he was seething. He asked in a playful manner who produced the short. The two animators, proud of their achievement, stepped forward to accept his praise. Walt simply said "You're fired" to the pair and abruptly turned around and walked out.

His employees loved working with Walt for the most part even though he was demanding of their creative juices. He was known to terminate several members of his employees through the years, as seen during his surprise birthday party, promoting him to say at one time, "You know, every once in a while I just fire everybody, then I hire them back in a couple of weeks," Disney joked. "That way they don't get too complacent. It keeps them on their toes."

Disney did sour on at least half of his employees, however, when, in the middle of making *Dumbo,* a large number of his animators walked out during a long and bitter strike. Walt took it personally and he considered the walk-out an affront for all the great generosity he had bestowed to his workers in the past. He was so bitter about those who went on strike he had his remaining loyal animators working on *Dumbo* draw some characters resembling those who went on strike as the clowns who "hit the big boss for a raise."

Walt prohibited his employees from wearing any facial hair, including mustaches, even though he personally sported one all his life. He wanted to sustain the "clean-cut image" he felt was so important for his company to maintain before the public. He made only two exceptions to the rule, Ub Iwerks, who helped create Mickey Mouse, and Bill Tytla, recognized as the best creative animator in the Disney fold. Both wore mustaches.

In the creation of *Snow White,* Walt was especially appreciative of his hardworking animators and other employees who had labored countless hours without receiving overtime compensation, which he couldn't afford to pay during the production. In a most unusual acknowledgement in a Hollywood movie for their efforts, Walt placed a statement in the opening of *Snow White's* credits: "My sincere appreciation to the members of my staff whose loyalty and creative endeavor made possible this production--Walt Disney."

DISNEY MOVIE PRESENTATION CHALLENGES

New York City's Radio City Music Hall was the setting for a number of Disney movie premiers. *Snow White* was the first. The management at the end of *Snow White's* run at the Music Hall was forced to replace all the seats' velvet upholstery in the theater. There was a noticeable stench after each showing of the sequence where Snow White is lost in the forest with scary monsters chasing her to the dwarfs' home. Management discovered the young children in the audience were wetting their pants because they were so frightened of the hair-raising scene.

An even creepier sequence keeping children up at night since its release is the *Fantasia* segment on the *Night on Bald Mountain,* the concluding episode of the feature film. When the public first saw the picture in 1940, parents flooded the Disney Studios with calls and letters complaining their children were completely terrified at the *Bald Mountain* segment. The increasing upswell of a large number of parents' grievances over the years became so overwhelming the segment was edited out of the VHS home version when the movie was first released in videotape format.

Since that initial video roll out, the Disney Studios restored the segment, with all its terror-filled images, into its original place.

The Hays Office, which oversaw the moral production code for Hollywood for decades, zeroed in on the *Pastoral Symphony* segment and placed its stamp of disapproval showing the female centaurs with their bare breasts exposed. The censors insisted those half human, half horse creatures cover their breasts. Disney instructed his animators draw garlands over the fronts of the female centaurs to hide the offending anterior flesh.

Fantasia opened in New York City's Broadway Theater. Because of the large expense of setting up the sound system for the movie's musical soundtrack, management was forced to charge a higher-than-normal cost for a ticket. Word soon got out how unique the movie was. Tickets, at least in New York City, became strong in demand. Extra telephone operators had to be hired to handle the avalanche of ticket requests. At the Broadway Theater, *Fantasia* ran for 57 straight weeks, a record breaker for a movie projecting at the venue.

RKO Pictures, the original distributor of *Fantasia,* didn't quite see New York City's success reflective of the rest of the country. RKO was hesitant to give the film a nation-wide distribution after learning the two-hour plus movie featured only classical music with no overall plot and very little dialogue. Walt decided to distribute the picture himself. Thirteen theaters nationwide were set up with an audio system called "Fantasound." The system required a series of oversized audio speakers strategically placed throughout the movie houses, creating for the viewers a feeling they were in the chambers of a live orchestra.

RKO later handled the distribution for the re-release of *Fantasia,* dispensing prints of the movie to hundreds of theaters but foregoing the elaborate sound system to play just mono audio. In addition, RKO tied *Fantasia* to another movie in a double bill, the 1942 western *Valley of the Sun.*

When first released worldwide, *Fantasia* bombed at the box office, partly because the war in Europe put an estimated forty-percent damper on its potential revenue. So popular were Disney films after *Fantasia,* theater owners chomped at the bit to get their hands on the movies when the Disney Studio re-released them. All except for *Fantasia.*

As 1969 rolled around a limited run of *Fantasia* was offered for those theater owners who had to guts to show the movie. Those owners who stepped forward were in for a surprise when they discovered a youthful audience flocking to the film's showings. Word got out the movie's images constantly filling the screen were similar to undergoing psychedelic drugs, sending college-age viewers scurrying to the theaters' seats. Disney redirected marketing *Fantasia's* re-release to be geared toward the drug culture's yearning for those colorful images.

Seeking to further to appeal to that demographic base, Disney released *Fantasia* to the home market in videotape form with high expectations. The film eventually broke all records for VHS sales.

RKO Pictures came down with another case of the nerves when Disney detailed his latest production, *Dumbo,* stating the movie lasted only 64 minutes. RKO executives couldn't see a major promotion built around such a short film. They offered three suggestions: to either cut *Dumbo* to a short-subject to front-end a major motion picture, lengthen the movie to at least 70 minutes, or release it as a Grade B picture, where RKO would distribute the picture to smaller movie theaters. Disney put his foot down and said no way, and RKO ultimately relented. In the final analysis, RKO was very happy Walt got his way so financially lucrative was *Dumbo.*

One of the most prestigious honors for anyone to receive back in the 1940s was to appear on the cover of Time Magazine. *Dumbo,* whose release was on October 31, 1941, was so popular when the picture hit the theaters, Time editors selected *Dumbo* to appear on one of its December covers. But the attack on Pearl Harbor on December 7, 1941, bumped the baby elephant off the front cover for good.

There exists a huge market for the drawings, or "cels," used in Disney films, especially for his earlier movies. The *Dumbo* cels are the rarest of the rare. In those days, once a scene from the animated movie was approved and incorporated into the picture, the cels were considered expendable. For office entertainment, Disney employees would use the cels like skateboards to slide down the hallways. Also, the animators loved the sound of the "pop" whenever they bent a cel containing grey paint, a color which happened to make the loudest sound. Since the entire movie's elephants were grey, there was a lot of popping going on around the office.

DISNEYLAND

Walt's earliest memories were from his father, Elias Disney, who, as a carpenter, told his sons about the incredible things he witnessed while he was constructing the 1893's Chicago World's Fair, which introduced America's first ferris wheel. Those memories stuck with Walt as well as his younger brother Roy as their entertainment movie empire grew increasingly richer by the year.

Walt's mind was always on par with the younger set. As a millionaire, he was always thinking about kids' toys. For example, he built an adult-size train set wrapping around his mansion in Holmby Hills, California. He loved being the train engineer, taking children and adult guests around his grounds and sounding the train's horn.

Walt became excited about amusement parks for families when he visited the second oldest entertainment park in the world, Tivoli Gardens in Copenhagen, Denmark, founded in 1843. Viewing the layout of the park as well as soaking in the utter joy of children being with their parents, Walt pondered the possibility of building an amusement park with his Disney brand attached to the park.

He assigned a designated Disney Studios team as well as gathered experts in the amusement parks field to design an entertainment center, which he labeled Disneyland. Living in Los Angeles and familiar with the mild year-round climate, Walt decided to locate his park in the Los Angeles vicinity. During the late 1940s, he gathered specialists in demographics to determine where the fastest growth of population within the next 10 years was going to occur in the region, where vast acreage surrounding the city consisted of farmland and undeveloped fields. The experts pinpointed the small community of Anaheim. Secretly, Disney bought over 160 acres of orange and walnut groves for what was then a bargain price and then set out to finalize the park's design on the drawing boards before embarking on constructing the massive park. As predicted, the population growth swept over the area, serving as a great support system for the soon-to-be popular park.

"I believe in the family unit," said Disney. "I believe in the family having fun together, enjoying things together, which is what Disneyland is."

To help promote the park nationwide, Walt turned to television in the early 1950s, an emerging alternative medium to cinema. He produced 1954's *Disneyland Show* and a year later *The Mickey Mouse Club*.

Disney first met the future CEO of McDonald's Ray Kroc while the two were training to be World War I ambulance drivers for the Red Cross. When the park was being built, Kroc contacted Disney and inquired about placing a McDonald's inside Disneyland. Walt saw the menu and prices for McDonald's and felt Kroc should raise the price of the fast-food restaurant's french fries from ten to fifteen cents. Kroc refused, feeling people wouldn't pay such a steep price for the fries. Walt was insistent that Kroc raise the price of his fries. Failing to come to an agreement over the pricing, both agreed to not move forward with the restaurant located in the park.

In 2013's *Saving Mr. Banks,* Tom Hanks as Walt escorts Emma Thompson, playing *Mary Poppins* author P.L. Travers, through Disneyland. Hanks looks up to see his dad Elias Disney's name emblazoned on one of the windows. The irony is Hanks, who has appeared in numerous Disney-produced films, including 1984's *Splash,* 1989's *Turner And Hooch*, and the voice of Woody in

1995's *Toy Story,* is a distant relative of Walt.

WALT NEVER FORGOT WHERE HE CAME FROM

Walt's adolescent work ethic and his Midwestern upbringing never left him despite the millions he made ever since Mickey Mouse was created. In the final years of his life he would have the Sherman brothers, composers of the *Mary Poppins* music, play his favorite song, *Feed The Birds,* in his office. Staring out the window, Walt would be preoccupied by his private thoughts during the song's playing. At the *Bird's* conclusion Walt was always tearful, a testimony of how, despite his enormous wealth and power, he had never forgotten the sentimentality every one of us has been blessed with and which was the secret to his success.

TOP TEN WALT DISNEY MOVIES DURING HIS CAREER

#1--SNOW WHITE AND THE SEVEN DWARFS (1937)

The granddaddy of all animated feature films, *Snow White* established more "firsts" in the animation field than any other movie in cinematic history. The movie received a rousing standing ovation from the audience witnessing history when it premiered in Hollywood. *Snow White* opened the door for more Disney feature animated films and established a genre that will exist as long as cinema remains alive. Even today, wrote critic John Flynn, "So perfect is the illusion, so tender the romance and fantasy, so emotional are certain portions when the acting of the characters strikes a depth comparable to the sincerity of human players, that the film approaches real greatness."

#2--PINOCCHIO (1940)

The movie that followed *Snow White* is no less an enjoyable and expertly-crafted animation from Disney. Only from Walt could a film have been produced that is as enjoyable to view as well as offers life-long moral lessons without all the overt righteousness most films on a similar vein contain. Frank Nugget of the New York Times wrote when *Pinocchio* was first released, "*Pinocchio* is here at last, is every bit as fine as we had prayed it would be—if not finer—and that it is as gay and clever and delightful a fantasy as any well-behaved youngster or jaded oldster could hope to see."

#3--DUMBO--1941

Addressing a universal problem where people with physical abnormalities can permanently be disturbed by those who are picking on them, *Dumbo* entertainingly examines the problem as well as offers a solution, rare for Hollywood movies. Clocking in at only 64 minutes, *Dumbo* was met with skepticism from theater owners who were leery about featuring such a short movie. But with lines running out the doors to see *Dumbo*, their frowns turned to smiles as the money poured through the box office window. Critic James Plath drew parallels between this film with a work of Ernest Hemingway's, commenting, "*Dumbo* was for Disney what *The Old Man and the Sea* was for Hemingway: a simple but powerful story that's brilliantly rendered and succeeds precisely because it is so simple, archetypal, and true."

#4--THE JUNGLE BOOK (1967)

Disney's last animated movie he personally had input. *Jungle* contains some of Disney's most catchy songs and character personalities of any film from his studio's rich treasures. This is the movie that saved the Disney Studios' animation department from extinction. Life Magazine labeled *Jungle* as Disney's best flick since *Dumbo*, while Time Magazine chimed in by saying, "The result is thoroughly delightful. The reasons for its success lie in Disney's own unfettered animal spirits, his ability to be childlike without being childish."

#5--FANTASIA (1940)

Walt's experimental film is an amazing visual tour de force, a feat that has never been equaled in cinematic history. Containing very little plot, the movie is broken down into segments, all accompanied by some of the finest music ever composed. The animation is breathtaking and the imagination of the Disney animators has never been better. LA Times, at the time of its release, said *Fantasia* was "caviar to the general, ambrosia and nectar for the intelligentsia." The critic felt the film was "courageous beyond belief." The New York Times ran a review reading in part "motion-picture history was made last night. *Fantasia* dumps conventional formulas overboard and reveals the scope of films for imaginative excursion. *Fantasia* is simply terrific."

#6--BAMBI (1942)

Bambi's reputation has increased over the years and is considered one of Disney's better films. Who can forget the chase scene where Bambi sees his mother shot dead? There are so many memorable moments filled with pathos that members of the viewing public could be seen visibly wiping away tears, emotionally distraught over what they witnessed in the cartoon. Jonathan Rosenbaum noted "This animated feature based on Felix Salten's book about the coming of age of a fawn and his various forest friends (including the beloved Thumper) does convey some of the primal emotional power of Disney's features during this period."

#7--ONE HUNDRED AND ONE DALMATIANS (1961)

The expense of producing animated feature films was increasingly making them almost cost prohibitive. *Dalmatians* was the first movie to use Xerox photography to assist in producing drawings cheaper and faster than the old hand-drawn method. The spotted dogs posed a particular problem during pre-production conversations, but the new technology allowed the process to be completed in half the normal time. The film had its certain charm, too, with Time Magazine praising *Dalmatians* as "the wittiest, most charming, least pretentious cartoon feature Walt Disney has ever made."

#8--LADY AND THE TRAMP (1955)

In another Disney first, *Lady* was the inaugural animated feature film to be made in the CinemaScope widescreen process. Class divisions spring up in canine land as a refined female American Cocker Spaniel living in the luxury of comfort suddenly has to share her confines with a male stray mutt. Film critic James Kendrick said of *Lady,* "In many ways it is closer to the man Walt Disney's view of the world than any of his preceding films, especially the way it is filtered largely through his sense of nostalgia for the Victorian era."

#9--CINDERELLA (1950)

Two years in the making, this endearing tale of a poor young woman, treated horribly by a strong-willed, jealous sister, only to get her just rewards from a handsome, rich prince, salvaged a struggling Disney studio at a time it really needed a cash cow to put their finances back in good order. Receiving three Academy Award nominations, including Best Song, *Bibbidi-Bobbidi-*

Boo, Cinderella still entertains young audiences today with its elevated hand drawings. The Chicago Tribune loved the film, saying "The film not only is handsome, with imaginative art and glowing colors to bedeck the old fairy tale, but it also is told in a gentle fashion, without the lurid villains which sometimes give little lots nightmares. It is enhanced by the sudden, piquant touches of humor and the music which appeal to old and young."

#10--PETER PAN (1953)

This is the final collaborated film for Disney's so-called "Nine Old Men," a group of animators who worked on Walt's animated feature films from *Snow White* on. The fairy *Tinker Bell* gets an expanded role in *Peter* while the mayhem accompanied by a robust musical score comes swift and furious. Time Magazine thought highly of Disney's version of *Peter Pan,* **saying the feature film was** "Ornamented with some bright and lilting tunes, it is a lively feature-length Technicolor excursion into a world that glows with an exhilarating charm and a gentle joyousness."

Federico Fellini

The outline of Italian film director Federico Fellini's next movie had been germinating in his mind for several years.

He had lined up a producer for financing the film as well as a contract. Sets were being erected and the crew and actors had already been hired. All that was needed was a script and a confident director to proceed.

But Fellini, just coming off what was arguably the most successful Italian film up to that time, 1960's *La Dolce Vita,* was having extreme self-doubts. He began writing a letter to his producer saying he was confused and he couldn't proceed on the production, when one of the grips came into his office and told him the crew wanted him to join in a party they were holding.

It was a toast the studio's electricians and grips were having, to recognize another "masterpiece" Fellini was about to direct. At that point he suddenly realized the crew had placed its entire faith in him.

"I listened to a fountain and the sound of the water, " Fellini recalls, "and tried to hear my inner voice. Then I heard the small voice of creativity within me. I knew. The story I would tell was a writer who doesn't know what he wants to write."

He went back to his office to tear up the letter to his producer.

Fellini changed the movie's "writer's block" theme to a "director's block," and what emerged is one of the most heralded films to emerge out of Europe in the past century, "8 1/2". The picture has spawned a slew of artistic "mental-block" films since, including *All That Jazz* and *Stardust Memories.* But it was Fellini's new approach to filmmaking and his creative genius at unfolding a story that was the most original film in the early 1960's, setting the stage for one of the most inventive and influential films to ever grace the silver screen.

When the film came out, everyone was scratching their heads upon the meaning of *8 1/2.* The ambiguous title is not really all that murky since Fellini had earlier directed six feature films and two short movies as well as co-directed 1950's *Variety Lights* with Alberto Lattuada up to the time he embarked on 1963's *8 1/2.* Add together all of Fellini's work and the sum becomes eight and one half. The picture, even judged from all the other movies he had produced or viewed in his lifetime, is one of Fellini's all-time favorites.

EARLY YEARS--ITALIAN NEO-REALISM PIONEER

As a news and radio reporter in World War II, Fellini was able to avoid the fighting in his homeland before hooking up as a scriptwriter for several Italian neorealistic films such as *Rome, Open City,* and *Paisan,* recognized classics which inspired the French and English New Wave films later in the 1950's.

Reflecting on his earlier life, the former journalist, now famous film director, admitted he would have been a totally unreliable reporter if he had stuck with a newspaper and magazine career.

"Anyone who lives, as I do, in a world of imagination must make an enormous and unnatural effect to be factual in the ordinary sense," Fellini related. "I confess I would be a terrible witness in court because of this--and a terrible journalist. I feel compelled to a story the way I see it and this is seldom the way it happened, in all its documentary detail."

He did revere his place in bringing the neorealistic genre to the forefront, an aesthetic influence so impactful on today's movie makers, a fact leading Fellini to wax philosophically, "You exist only in what you do."

SCRIPTWRITER

Early in his career, Fellini sharpened his writing skills by working for the Italian humor magazine *Marc' Aurelio* for nearly four years. His non-film background was similar to two other international film directors listed in this book where an earlier full-time professional job had nothing to do with film: Ingmar Bergman, who started in live theater and Akira Kurosawa, who began as a Japanese painting artist.

Writing scripts about his personal experiences, a perspective in his movies that continued throughout his career, Fellini's first films were met with apathy. But two straight Oscars for 1955's *La Strata,* the very first film to receive the Academy Award for Best Foreign Film, and 1957's *The Nights of Cabiria,* whose plot Bob Fosse adapted onto the Broadway stage as *Sweet Charity,* launched Fellini's international fame.

Fellini felt his scripts were always constantly in a state of flux, especially while filming. Unlike Alfred Hitchcock, who detailed every scene before landing on the set and who didn't deviate from his screenplays, Fellini felt his scripts were simply launching pads to begin his filming, deviating from his pages as the production progressed. The director/writer let the filming experience and the actors' personalities dictate the direction his pictures veered. In 1955's *The Swindler,* actor Broderick Crawford appeared on the set one day drunk. Instead of bemoaning the situation, Fellini reshaped the day's scenario to fit the Crawford character's' tipsiness into the story.

HIS EARLY YEARS AS A FILM DIRECTOR

Fellini wasn't always the well-known internationally-recognized director of the silver screen. The director had just been given the green light to produce *La Strada,* with his wife Giulietta Masina as the female lead. Before production began, Masina was acting in another movie with Anthony Quinn, an international star. She arranged a meeting between her husband and Quinn. At that late date shortly before filming, Fellini was still casting around for the perfect actor to play the strongman for the male lead. At first Quinn turned down this unknown director since he didn't know the quality of Fellini's previous films nor was he confident in the director's expertise behind the camera. Fellini knew right away Quinn was perfect for the role, and he harassed the actor for days to sign him.

Quinn was good friends with actress Ingrid Bergman and her Italian director husband, Roberto Rossellini. One night they had dinner together. The actor mentioned about this Fellini guy bugging him to play in his movie. Coincidentally, Rossellini had a print of Fellini's latest movie, 1953's comedy-drama *I Vitelloni.* After the actor watched it, Quinn realized what a genius director Masina's husband was, the one who had been pestering him for days. He immediately contacted Fellini and the rest is history.

When it came time to sign a contract to star in *La Strata,* Quinn opted, instead of receiving a salary for his role, to be paid a percentage of the movie's profits. Quinn's agent was livid when he heard his client's agreement to such terms, and he immediately changed the contract to get the actor's salary upfront and cancel the percentage stipulation. Later on, seeing how "*La Strada*" became a cash cow for Fellini and company, Quinn lamented his agent's decision, saying the change in the contract cost him several million dollars.

Quinn's agent wasn't the only one not to see the potential in *La Strada,* which was loosely based on D.W. Griffith's 1919 *Broken Blossoms.* Fellini first approached the financiers of his previous films to see if they would back the movie. The money men said they liked the script but didn't see any reason the picture would make any money. Other producers were put off by the fact Fellini assigned his wife, Giulietta, to play the lead female role, something they couldn't see working. But they were unable to persuade the director to look for a more marque actress.

Fellini was persistent, though, and started filming even before he received any financing for the movie. The production stopped shortly after filming because of the lack of funds as well as Masina spraining her ankle severely in an off-set accident. While his leading lady--and wife--was recuperating, Fellini, during the several weeks of the work suspension, was finally able to secure financing for the movie.

But the layoff created a problem for Quinn. He was set to play the title role in *Attila,* scheduled to be filmed in a nearby location where *La Strada* was being shot. When Fellini resumed filming again after his wife's recovery and the monies rolling in, Quinn said to himself he was committed to the Fellini project and prepared to do the almost impossible. Quinn would act for Fellini in the mornings while driving to the *Attila* location in the afternoons and evenings to shoot the Dino De Laurentiis-produced epic.

When he saw the release of both films, Quinn said, despite Fellini's much lower budget, he felt *La Strada* was a far superior movie. Pope Francis would concur, citing *La Strada* as his favorite film.

Masina's character, playing an unimpeachable clown who is deserted by Quinn, reflects Fellini's outlook on innocence. "Put yourself into life and never lose your openness, your childish enthusiasm throughout the journey that is life, and things will come your way," Fellini said, emphasizing his personal motto.

FELLINI'S STRIKING VISUALS

The films of Fellini rely on striking images as well as symbolic gestures and characterizations. For *La Strata,* the director revealed that each of the three main characters represented different worldly elements. Quinn, with his barely-civilized behavior, was earth; Masina, whose tears were overwhelming to audiences, was water; while Richard Basehart, playing the lighthearted Fool, was air.

As co-writer of *La Dolce Vita,* meaning "the sweet life" or "the good life," Fellini said he was inspired by the dresses resembling large flowers worn in Rome en vogue when he was writing the script. His original idea for the movie is visible in some of the overstated dresses seen throughout the movie. One particular sequence, the party at the castle, shows a pair of women's outlandish costumes on display.

Fellini possessed those rare traits where his imagination heavily influenced the aesthetics of his movies.

"The visionary is the only true realist," noted Fellini. "Our duty as storytellers is to bring people to the station. There, each person will choose his or her own train. But we must at least take them to the station, to a point of departure."

In *La Dolce Vita,* the iconic scene where Swedish bombshell Anita Ekberg and Marcello Mastroianni are seen romping in Rome's Trevi Fountain (shot in January, Mastroianni put on a wet suit under his clothes and drank vodka for antifreeze while brave Ekberg wore nothing under her skimpy dress) proved Fellini's visuals were way beyond anything cinema had seen before.

What is more startling in Fellini's work was Mastrioianni was able to deliver his lines, albeit few, flawlessly in the fountain scene while being completely drunk.

The director complained to his crew before filming at the fountain the water appeared to be really dirty. In a stroke of good luck, there was an employee from the Scandinavian Airlines System on the scene hearing Fellini's complaint. He called the airline's office at the Rome Airport and asked them for a supply of green ocean dye marker airlines have in stock for sea emergency landings. Fellini was at first skeptical, but was willing to experiment with the liquid. Sure enough, when the green fluid was poured into the water of the fountain, the dirty tinge disappeared. The SAS employee was hailed as the hero of the day by cast and crew, and especially by the director.

As evidenced by the fountain scene, Fellini used a combination of real structures and fabricated ones. Set designer Piero Gherardi had a field day mixing the two together, complementing the age-old buildings with modern artsy construction. The production was also filmed in real nightclubs, with Gherardi-designed embellishments assisting in the looks. The Bassano di Sutri Palace, which is located just north of Rome, served as a location for the famous party scenes, with some real-life Italian aristocrats asked to play the roles of servants, waiters, and guests.

Fellini's lasting influence once *La Dolce Vita* was released is enormous even today. "Paparazzi," the term describing a horde of news photographers getting candid shots of celebrities, was first coined in *Vita.* Fellini was inspired to name one of the characters in the movie, Marcello's photographer friend Paparazzo, from the Italian word for sparrow, "passero." The director felt the photographers surrounding the celebrities in a frenzy sort of way reminded him of a flock of sparrows. Some scratch their heads at Fellini's explanation, saying the word is a derivative of the Italian word "papataceo," which is a rather big and pesky mosquito. The co-writer of *La Dolce Vita,* Ennio Flaiano, said he came up with the name of the photographer from a 1901 travel book penned by George Gissing, whose character in the book was named Signor Paparazzo.

Inspiration comes in varying forms for Fellini. In 1965's *Juliet of the Spirits*, Fellini's first color film, the director claims he swallowed a LSD tablet while preparing to make this off-the-wall movie.

1973's *Amarcord* appears to have similarities to Fellini's upbringing, but the film director denies any resemblance shown on the screen to his childhood. He said it was purely a coincidence, like all his films. "All art is autobiographical," Fellini said, deflecting the parallels of his life and *Amarcord*. "The pearl is the oyster's autobiography."

FELLINI'S DIRECTING METHODS

Fellini always felt he had more in common with silent film directors than to his contemporaries. His method of directing was more Italian-style than Hollywood-style. As a common practice in most Italian films of that era, audio recorded on the set was mostly discarded in the editing room while the actors' would re-record their dialogue in the studio's narration booths. The audio recording was then dubbed onto the existing footage. Sergio Leone, the American film director famous for his spaghetti westerns, remembered growing up in Italy and seeing all the Italian movies dubbed. Leone would take that method to Hollywood and process most of his film projects patterned after the Italian model, remastering most of the audio during the post-production phase.

This practice allowed Fellini to talk to his actors while filming, to direct them spontaneously, emphasizing their physical movements. In fact, in every Fellini film his characters appear to dance rather than walk.

There exists footage of him directing his actors while the cameras were rolling. He's shown as being somewhat bombastic and occasionally short-tempered with his cast and crew. But eventually, Fellini always got on film what he wanted out of his actors.

Even though the script he brought on the set would eventually be different once he got into the editing room, Fellini, as well as his actors, claimed he wouldn't allow his cast to improvise their scenes while filming.

"It's absolutely impossible to improvise," he noted. "Making a movie is a mathematical operation. It is like sending a missile to the moon. It isn't improvised. It is too defined to be called improvisational, too mechanical. Art is a scientific operation, so I can say that what we usually call improvisation is in my case just having an ear and eye for things that sometimes occur during the time we are making the picture."

FELLINI'S METHODS OF EDITING

After filming, Fellini would always hunker down with his editing team to splice together all the shot footage. For *Nights of Cabiria,* Fellini worked with his editor Leo Catozzo. It was during the time editing *Nights* Catozzo came up with an editing splicer which made putting together film more efficient. The CIR self-perforating adhesive tape splicer, or simply knows as "The Catozzo," was so successful the editor patented the device, making him extremely wealthy. Catozzo also won an Academy Award in 1989 for advancing the technology of editing.

People who worked with the director said Fellini nailed down the details of the actors' dialogue and the direction for all his movies only in the editing room. Fellini would rewrite some of his characters' dialogue to express, he felt, a clearer meaning than what was originally filmed. This caused the changes of the spoken dialogue not quite synching with the actors' lips in the footage already shot.

Fellini entered the production of *8 ½* with the bare minimum of a written script. Filming took place while the laboratory for development and printing at Cinecitta Studios workers were on strike. The strike caused Fellini, who loved shaping a majority of his films on a regular basis by viewing each day's footage at night, to alter his shooting habit since he was unable to watch the "dailies" while shooting 8 1/2.

The ending of *8 ½* shows a bunch of eccentric people dancing around a spaceship in a field with the sun setting. Fellini's original intention for the film's conclusion was to show Marcello, who looking out the window is lost in thought, accompanied by his wife in a train bound for Rome. As the train is about to enter a tunnel, he looks up and sees all the characters who were in the movie smiling at him. The spaceship dancing sequence was intended solely for the trailer, but as Fellini was editing, he felt the trailer footage would be more appropriate for the ending than the train scene. After all, Fellini reminded himself of the note he had attached to the eyepiece of the camera while filming, summing up the movie's theme: "Remember, this is a comedy."

The ending also reflects one of Fellini's main philosophies of life. "There is no end," Fellini used to say. "There is no beginning. There is only the infinite passion of life."

Fellini also recognized the ups and downs of this joyous festival called life. "Happiness is simply a temporary condition that precedes unhappiness," explained the director. "Fortunately for us, it works the other way around as well. But it's all a part of the carnival, isn't it."

FELLINI'S LATER FILMS--FANTASY

Fellini was always a big fan of comic and humor publications. He admired comic book writer/artist Stan Lee and bought as many Marvel Comic books as he could get his hands on, especially those highlighting superheroes Spiderman and the Hulk. This love of comic books would continue throughout his life and may explain why his later films bordered on the surreal.

After reading C. G. Jung's book on dreams, Fellini's films from the mid-1960's took a turn towards fantasy. The switch in direction suited Fellini perfectly since he always felt his style was more similar to a painter than a literalist. *Juliet of the Spirits* and 1969's *Fellini's Satyricon* are definitive examples of how every frame of Fellini's touch could be framed and hung in any art museum.

"Our dreams are our real life," Fellini explained. "My fantasies and obsessions are not only my reality, but the stuff of which my films are made. Talking about dreams is like talking about movies, since the cinema uses the language of dreams; years can pass in a second and you can hop from one place to another. It's a language made of image. And in the real cinema, every object and every light means something as in a dream."

Satyricon, one of Fellini's most fantasy-driven films, features two homosexuals in the lead role. Critics were puzzled by the fact that for the first time in the director's illustrious career he hired foreign actors and not Italian performers to play such central roles. Fellini replied simply, "Because there are no Italian homosexuals."

Today's viewers are equally perplexed the movie has *Fellini* attached to the title *Satyricon.* The reason lies in the maneuverings of fellow Italian film director/writer Gian Luigi Polidoro, who first got wind Fellini was considering a movie based on ancient Roman writer Petronius' satire *Satyricon.* Polidoro registered the name *Satyricon* before Fellini thought about it and began production of his version earlier than Fellini did. Filing a court case to sue Polidoro for the use of the title was a futile effort for Fellini, so he changed his movie's title to *Fellini-Satyricon.* Not only did Polidoro get to keep the Petronius book's name, but he agreed to receive $1 million from United Artist, the distributors for Fellini's movie, to keep Polidoro from releasing his now-completed cheaper version until Fellini's picture was fully seen in the theaters.

THE TWILIGHT OF HIS CAREER

Throughout his illustrious career, Fellini was recognized by the Academy for his outstanding work. He gained four nominations in the Best Foreign Film category and he won Oscars for all four: *La Strada, The Nights of Cabiria,* 8½, and 1973's *Amarcord.* That achievement, unprecedented for foreign directors, was basically downplayed by Fellini. "In the myth of the cinema, Oscar is the supreme prize." he said.

But he also saw the artistry of film as superior to the all the other forms of art humans have created.

"I'm just a storyteller, and the cinema happens to be my medium," said Fellini. "I like it because it recreates life in movement, enlarges it, enhances it, distills it. For me, it's far closer to the miraculous creation of life than, say, a painting or music or even literature. It's not just an art form; it's actually a new form of life, with its own rhythms, cadences, perspectives and transparencies. It's my way of telling a story."

When Fellini received the Academy Awards Lifetime Achievement Oscar in April, 1993, he felt he had another 25 years of directing. "I would like, near the end of my life, in that period of coma so close to death, to have a dream vision which reveals to me the mysteries of the universe," said Fellini that summer. "And then to wake up well enough to make a film about it."

Fellini would never get his chance. A few weeks later, after celebrating his 50th wedding anniversary to Giulietta, in the autumn of 1993, Fellini, 73, would slip into a coma and never wake up. But his films shown on the screen today are as alive as the day he made them.

TOP TEN FEDERICO FELLINI FILMS

#1--8 1/2 (1963)

What began as a basically unprepared production and evolved throughout the filming process right down to the final edit, *8 ½* reflects the enormous talents Fellini possessed in showcasing life in a serious, yet lighthearted vein. We follow a fictitious Italian film director as he deals with his latest unfulfilled project in the middle of marital problems. The magic of the main lead, actor Marcello Mastroianni, along with Fellini's whimsical touch truly makes this film one of the greats in European, if not in the world's, cinematic history. Bosley Crowther of the New York Times, wrote the film was "a piece of entertainment that will really make you sit up straight and think, a movie endowed with the challenge of a fascinating intellectual game. If Mr. Fellini has not produced another masterpiece –another all-powerful exposure of Italy's ironic sweet life –he has made a stimulating contemplation of what might be called, with equal irony, a sweet guy."

#2--LA DOLCE VITA (1960)

We follow a shallow gossip magazine writer as he attempts to examine life's deeper meaning among the lame world of celebrity and celebrity-worshipping. The famous fountain scene is one of cinema's highlights and capsulizes the atmosphere constituting the facade of images inundating the media of yesteryear when this was produced--and it still pertains to today. This was Roger Ebert's second favorite film behind *Citizen Kane*. Rick Mele said of the movie, "Along with his later *8 ½*, *La Dolce Vita* is regarded as one of acclaimed Italian director Federico Fellini's best-loved and most influential films. The '60s-set tale of one man's struggle with the so-called 'sweet life'."

#3--*LA STRADA* (1954)

Fellini transferred all he had absorbed of the recently-ended Italian neorealism movement which he was a major part of, and made a sweeping statement on childhood innocence in the face of hard life reality. Quinn has never been crueler as a guardian of Giulietta. His treatment of her reflects an immoral behavior he finally realizes was wrong well after it was too late. An Italian movie critic wrote at the time, "Fellini attains a summit rarely reached by other film directors: style at the service of the artist's mythological universe. This example once more proves that the cinema has less need of technicians—there are too many already—than of creative intelligence. To create such a film, the author must have had not only a considerable gift for expression but also a deep understanding of certain spiritual problems."

#4--NIGHTS OF CABIRIA (1957)

Lots of people experience heartbreak at the termination of a love relationship, but hardly anyone can experience the enormous disappointment when Cabiria's bond with fiancé Oscar turns into yet another corrupt affair. The ending of Fellini's masterpiece will give even the most pessimistic viewer a reason to hope. Emanuel Levy praised the film, noting, "Fellini's masterpiece, which won the Foreign-Language Oscar, features Giulietta Masina in her most heart-breaking performances, playing a naive prostitute who endures an endless series of devastating misfortunes with her soul intact."

#5--AMARCORD (1973)

Although the director denied this being an autobiography of his childhood, there are paralleled similarities between the director and the boy's story in this film. Probably Fellini's funniest movie, *Amarcord* offers numerous set-pieces that'll have the viewer in stitches. The life of an adolescent has never been unfolded in the manner Fellini has shown here. Vincent Canby said of this Oscar-winner, "When Mr. Fellini is working in peak condition, as he is in '*Amarcord,*' he somehow brings out the best in us. We become more humane, less stuffy, more appreciative of the profound importance of attitudes that in other circumstances would seem merely eccentric if not lunatic."

#6--JULIET OF THE SPIRITS (1965)

Fellini's tribute to an aging, unhappy wife who has the courage to face new horizons in normal everyday living. Guilietta again plays a tragic-comedic character whose life is disintegrating, yet discovers new resources to enliven her experiences. Fellini's full use of color is reflected in his first color-produced film. Stephen Holden of the New York Times wrote, "Fellini went deliriously and brilliantly bananas with the color to create a rollicking through-the-looking-glass series of tableaus evoking a woman's troubled psyche."

#7--GINGER AND FRED (1986)

Aging dancers try to rejuvenate their talents by appearing on a television show. A parody on Ginger Rogers and Fred Astaire, this film is also noted for the legal wrangling of Fellini's studio, MGM, and his producer, who were taken to court by Ms. Rogers, who felt the Lanham Act would shield her from such a parody. The case, which the judge upheld for the film industry, resulted in the so-called "Rogers test' in subsequent lawsuits. TV Guide saw the film as "A warm and very human story about two people who share a little bit of love, interwoven with director Fellini's diatribe against the inanity of the modern television age."

#8--I VITELLONI (1953)

Rejuvenated Fellini's early career after stumbling in his previous film, 1952's *The White Sheik.* This comedic character study shows five young men who are experiencing pivotal moments in their lives. This is the movie that impressed actor Anthony Quinn to star in Fellini's *La Strada*. It also played a big influence in Martin Scorsese's *Mean Streets.* Michael Wilmington, who worked for the Chicago Tribune, said of this, "In Italy, it remains one of Fellini's most consistently loved movies. It should be in America as well... If you still remember that terrific drunk scene, Alberto Sordi's pre-*Some Like It Hot* drag tango or the way the little boy balances on the train track at the end, you should know that this picture plays as strongly now as it did in 1956 or whenever you first saw it. I know I had a ball watching *I Vitelloni*a gain.' It reminded me of the old gang."

#9--ROMA (1972)

If Fellini denied *Amarcord* having any biographical traces of his boyhood, he was not as dismissal of viewers thinking this movie depicted his impressions he gained while moving from the small town in the country to the bustling city of Rome when he was transitioning his life after high school. The film is a character study of all he had met in Rome. Roger Ebert wrote, "Fellini isn't just giving us a lot of flashy scenes, he's building a narrative that has a city for its protagonist instead of a single character."

#10--FELLINI--SATYRICON (1969)

Lushly photographed, Fellini's examination on ancient Rome shows the surreal side of the director as he gives his take on the culture that at the time had inflicted civilization's most dominate race. The New York Times labeled *Satyricon* as "the quintessential Fellini film, a travelogue through an unknown galaxy, a magnificently realized movie of his and our wildest dreams."

Stanley Kubrick

THE UNPARALLELED GENIUS

Young Stanley Kubrick experienced what has gone on in the corporate world for a thousand years: the inevitable clash between a young, relatively inexperienced yet incredibly talented perfectionist going against a well-known veteran whose work was recognized as the top in his profession.

Kirk Douglas, star and producer of the 1960 epic *Spartacus,* described Kubrick on his first day directing on the movie set as "wide eyed and pants hiked up looking like a kid of seventeen." Actually 30, Kubrick, a former Look Magazine photographer recently-turned-film director who made just two major motion pictures, was directing noted cinematographer Russell Metty, veteran cameraman for Orson Welles, Howard Hawks and Douglas Sirk, among others.

Metty, hired by the movie's original director, Anthony Mann, routinely took control of the set after directors issued instructions before disappearing into their trailers. He was stunned when Kubrick began looking through the camera and setting up shots. "This kid's going to tell me where to put the camera?" Metty said. "You've got to be kidding."

Things became so heated that when it was time to shoot a scene with Kirk Douglas and Tony Curtis, Kubrick looked over the set Metty had lit and noted, "I can't see the actors' faces." Metty, sitting in his chair, kicked a light on a tripod with wheels toward the actors and yelled, "There, is there enough light for you?"

Kubrick looked at it, looked back at Metty and replied, "Now there's too much light."

The studio chiefs forced Metty, threatening to quit, to work with Kubrick throughout the long production. To get paid his contract, Metty begrudgingly deferred to Kubrick whenever a disagreement arose. The cinematographer garnered an Oscar for his work on *Spartacus,* but the award was not lost on Kubrick. His experience on the set with Metty and actor Kirk Douglas was an eye-opener for the young director.

Much to his dismay, the director was handed a script he couldn't alter in any way. Kubrick felt the screenplay was chock full of dumb moralizing as well as failing to point out the hero's faults, as history books have detailed. The director's experience in *Spartacus* confirmed his opinion of what was wrong with Hollywood. He vowed never to work in the American motion picture industry again. Seeing the lack of authority he had as a director, he further promised himself to never relinquish full control over any of his future films. To fulfill his personal pact, Kubrick abruptly packed up and relocated to England where he began a body of groundbreaking pictures that proved unparalleled in the annals of cinema.

Kubrick's move to England solidified his immense influence in several movie categories. He introduced with stunning force the modern science-fiction movie in his 1968 film *2001: A Space Odyssey*. He elevated the sophistication level of horror movies in his 1980 *The Shining,* lent real-life authenticity in historical-period motion pictures in 1975's *Barry Lyndon,* and practically invented the screen's political satire brand in 1964's *Dr. Strangelove or: How I Stopped Worrying And Love The Bomb.* Kubrick's films frequently show the inhumanity of people's institutions and the impactful harm the establishment inflicts on the individual; in other words, how the dark side of the human species can dominate over pure innocence.

A PHOTOGRAPHIC GENIUS

"Nobody could shoot a better movie in history," said Steven Spielberg, who noted Kubrick's composition, lighting, framing, innovative dollying and tracking shots are unapproachable.

Spielberg's assessment on Kubrick's visual style is hardly surprising since Stanley was the rare director who combined his passion for both cinema as well as still photography. Kubrick, never much of a student in the Bronx, New York, school system, where his average was a lowly 67%, skipped school to see double-feature films. He developed a love for photography to compliment his joy playing chess and listening to jazz during his early teens. Needless to say, Kubrick was not a big fan of education in the classroom, recalling, "I never learned anything at all in school and didn't read a book for pleasure until I was 19 years old."

Submitting a photograph to Look Magazine of a vendor selling newspapers blazing the headlines on the death of President Franklin D. Roosevelt, Kubrick, a high schooler at 16, was encouraged by the national publication's purchase of his photo. His photo accompanied Look's article on FDR's passing. The connection with the magazine led Look to offer Kubrick part-time work, leading eventually to a full-time position. Upon his failure to get into any universities full time because of his low grades (he was allowed to attend a handful of classes at a local college), Kubrick's main focus became photography.

Kubrick made the transition from photography to film directing by independently producing his own short documentaries, beginning with a 16-minute portrayal of boxer Walter Cartier in his 1951 film *Day of the Fight.*

"To make a film entirely by yourself, which initially I did, you may not have to know very much about anything else, but you must know about photography," Kubrick reflected later in his career.

"One of the things that gave me the most confidence in trying to make a film was seeing all the lousy films that I saw," added Kubrick. "Because I sat there and thought, 'Well, I don't know a thing about movies, but I know I can make a film better than that.'"

Kubrick never completely surrendered his affection with photography. He and actor Peter Sellers, an equally passionate amateur photographer, compared each other's pictures they snapped on the movie set while working together on two films.

Kubrick's expertise in still photography was easily transferable over to motion pictures where he occasionally operated the movie camera. In filming the offensive of the military take-over on Burpleson Air Force Base in *Dr. Strangelove,* Kubrick was behind the lens of a hand-held camera, capturing the action documentary-style.

Kubrick's eye for framing established a pattern of filming well-balanced compositions in many of his scenes, a visual harmony illustrating each side optically containing equal weight. Balanced framing such as the hotel corridors shown in 1980's *The Shining* as well as its concluding chase in the maze is reflective of Kubrick's photographic aesthetics. This harmonizing of the two sides of the frame is seen in the computer room of the spaceship in *2001.* Such symmetry reflects the great amount of attention Kubrick spent on his visuals, pointing to both obvious and subtle symbolism in his plot and within the scenes of his movies.

LOVED THE CLOSE-UP

Kubrick was the opposite to director Billy Wilder's aversion in the use of the close-up. Wilder was a great admirer of Kubrick's films, claiming the director "never made a bad picture," and called the first half of 1987's *Full Metal Jacket* "the best picture I've ever seen." But Wilder didn't share Kubrick's love of the close-up. To heighten the intensity of his actors' emotions, Kubrick would call for the close-in when the scene carried an especially dramatic moment, positioning his camera tight on the actors' faces.

In a highly-charged scene in 1957's *Paths of Glory,* Kubrick shows a close-up of actor Ralph Meeker's face as he is about to hit his colleague Private Pierre

Arnaud.

Encompassing those numerous close-ups was the Kubrick-patented "The Glare." This shot consists of an actor angling his head downward slightly with his eyes peering upwards. The Glare calls for the actors to look directly into the camera, reflecting the disturbed mental breakdown churning through their characters' inner turmoil. The famous poster of 1971's *A Clockwork Orange* illustrating the iconic shot of Malcolm McDowell as Alex, and Jack Nicholson's close-up with the same posture in *The Shining,* reflect both characters' erosion of mental stability. Tom Cruise in 1999's *Eyes Wide Shut,* during the cab ride scene, adopts Kubrick's trademark position as his thoughts become increasingly paranoid, while Private Pyle's madness in *Jacket* is captured before the camera assuming the same posture.

To mask those inner anxieties, Kubrick's films ironically portray his leading characters on the screen to be relatively laid back and emotionally distant. Emphasizing such a seemingly relaxed attitude, Kubrick has most of his characters speak slowly. Their conversations with others contain pauses, sometimes lengthy in their hesitations. Unlike Orson Welles' common practice of his actors speaking over each other, Kubrick very rarely overlaps his dialogue passages.

KUBRICK'S SCRIPTWRITTING

The subjects Kubrick selected for his movies were for the most part based on previously-published novels and short stories. The director claimed he was attracted to certain plots simply because he found the stories so interesting. He also sought out story lines which had the protagonists devising a plan to tackle a particular situation, only to have those plans turn disastrous for them and others involved. "If it can be written, or thought, it can be filmed," Kubrick observed.

During the writing phase of his movies, he would compose the preliminary screenplay himself or bring aboard an experienced writer or a team of wordsmiths to shape his ideas based on his first drafts.

"A great story is kind of a miracle," Kubrick said on adapting other writers' stories onto the screen rather than invent the plots himself from scratch. "I've never written a story myself, which is probably why I have so much respect for it. I started out, before I became a film director, always thinking, you know, if I couldn't play on the Yankees I'd like to be a novelist. The people I first admired were not film directors but novelists. Like Conrad."

One writer Kubrick admired was Vladimir Nabokov, the author of the controversial novel *Lolita.* Kubrick contracted him to write the screenplay for the 1962 movie *Lolita.* The Russian departed from his novel to make the plot more palatable to the screen. Once filming began, no one had the guts to tell Nabokov only a portion of his script would eventually be incorporated into the movie. Nabokov's script proved to be excessively long, over 400 pages, and many of his passages could never pass the censors. Kubrick was able to arrange a special viewing of the picture shortly before *Lolita* had its premier and invited Nabokov to the screening. Although Nabokov said he enjoyed the film and complemented its director and actors, the writer was disappointed so the little of his material appeared in the final release. Prizing his own time, Nabokov said his biggest regret being involved in the project was knowing his effort was a complete waste of his time. His name does appear in the credits for his screenplay work. Not totally squandering all his precious time on a basically discarded script, Nabokov later published in book form his version of the script named *Lolita: A Screenplay.*

The only script Kubrick wrote completely by himself without any assistance from the pros was 1971's *A Clockwork Orange.* His *Clockwork* screenplay is strikingly similar to Anthony Burgess's 1962 novel of the same name. In fact, Kubrick's script was so close to the Burgess book the actors and the director would refer to the paperback book always laying around on the set when the script pages weren't readily available.

The Kubrick *Clockwork* script did depart from the novel's ending. In both the screenplay and the book, Alex, after his rehabilitation, reverts back to being violent. The book extends the Kubrick ending by having Alex undergo a catharsis realizing cruelty to others isn't in his gene pool. Burgess has him marrying and living a decent life ever after whereas Kubrick's work concludes with Alex harboring violent thoughts and exhibiting his sexual drive in front of an approving audience.

Kubrick spent months, sometimes years, extensively researching any potential project that interested him before embarking on the production. One subject he was totally obsessed with since his childhood was the life of French Emperor Napoleon Bonaparte. He had his staff canvass several bookstores to buy everything on the French leader in preparation for a projected film on the Bonaparte. They purchased over one hundred books, all of which he read. Studying for later project, *Dr. Strangelove,* Kubrick researched the subject of nuclear destruction by reading nearly 50 books.

In laying the groundwork on his Napoleon epic, Kubrick scouted several potential filming locations, selecting Romania for his central setting. One reason Romania was ideal for the director was its government agreed to commit 40,000 Army soldiers as well as 10,000 horse cavalry for the battle scenes.

The release of 1966's *War And Peace* as well as the financial box office bomb of 1970's *Waterloo* dissuaded movie studios from funding any further Napoleon epics. Kubrick was frustrated with the rejections coming his way but was still persistent enough to return to the project repeatedly.

As a substitute for the sprawling Napoleonic theme movie studios might finance, Kubrick looked to William Makepeace Thackeray's *Vanity Fair*, a novel set around the time Napoleon ruled France. But Kubrick gradually discovered he couldn't reasonably address the book's dense plot within a three-hour length. When he heard a television series was being shopped around based on *Vanity Fair,* Kubrick turned to another novel of Thackeray's, *The Memoirs of Barry Lyndon, Esq.*

For the making of *Barry Lyndon,* Kubrick had planned to shoot his exteriors as well as some interior scenes in Ireland. Word got out the director was filming actors dressed up as English soldiers in his upcoming movie. Once the Irish Republican Army heard of Kubrick's plans, the IRA placed the director on its hit list. Kubrick, getting wind of his inclusion on the IRA list, abruptly changed the location of his filming of *Barry Lyndon* to England.

The director's creative mind was constantly churning with ideas resulting in a number of proposed scripts Kubrick wrote but have remained to this day unpublished and unproduced as films. Those screenplays include a World War II adventure story about a band of German soldiers receiving a mission during the waning days of the war (co-written with Richard Adams), a church minister turned safecracker, and a profile of John Mosby, the leader of Mosby's Rangers, a Confederate guerrilla troop operating in Northern Virginia during the Civil War.

Kubrick was considered a workaholic when it came to his profession. During one stretch when the director was showing signs of exhaustion, his wife persuaded him to take a rare vacation to unwind. During the vacation, she spied her husband writing on blank notepads. She inquired what the heck he was writing. His answer was some ideas of a future film project popped into his head and he was writing them down before he would forget what they were all about.

In addition to his work intruding into his vacation, Kubrick was known to pick up the phone and call certain people a number of times during the day to discuss an idea that cropped up in his imagination. Sometimes those phone calls would ring in the early hours of the morning since Kubrick was a light sleeper and was able to snooze for only a few hours a night.

In his research for *Paths of Glory,* Kubrick and his team studied World War I and the European armies' strategies. Winston Churchill, prime minister of the United Kingdom during World War II and who participated in the earlier world war, described *Glory's* battle scenes as very accurate, especially how trench warfare was depicted. Despite the French government's condemnation of the movie when it was released, Churchill said the film replicated exactly how the upper echelons of the military's thinking operated in those days.

Kubrick felt actor Kirk Douglas would be perfect for the role of Colonel Dax, the officer in charge of a regiment of French soldiers who refused to go over the top of the trenches in an obvious suicidal charge. Douglas, upon reading the script, readily accepted the role but with reservations. "Stanley, I don't think this picture will ever make a nickel, but we have to make it."

The actor's prediction was spot-on about the box office receipts since *Glory* didn't make as much money as the producers had hoped despite the movie's positive reviews. One of the reasons was because of the film's somber ending Kubrick submitted to the studio a revised screenplay with a more upbeat ending since he felt the book's gloomy closure would be death at the box office. When he reflected upon his new ending several days later, he saw the novel's finale was far more appropriate. Humphrey Cobb, the novelist for *Glory,* reflected the funereal conclusion by drawing the title of his book from a line of Thomas Gray's 18th-century poem *Elegy Written in a Country Churchyard.* The line extracted read, "The paths of glory lead but to the grave."

Worried that reverting back to the darker ending would be poison to the studio funding the project, producer James Harris resubmitted Kubrick's script containing the pessimistic closing without notifying the studio of the changes made at the end. He felt no one in the studio would read the entire script, especially its concluding scene. His gut feelings were right--studio executives stamped their approval on the script without thoroughly digesting the full screenplay, confirming Harris' opinion.

Kubrick's works inject a healthy dose of dark humor, especially seen in *Dr. Strangelove.* Kubrick was attracted to Peter George's novel, *Red Alert,* and felt the plot would make an ideal thriller. The book's premise dealt with the possibility of a nuclear war unintentionally breaking out. Writing a first draft based on George's novel, the film director noticed his work was slowly shaping into an amusing script bordering on the absurd. Terry Southern, the veteran satirical writer, was brought on board to refine the screenplay. Both agreed to slant the script toward the farcical and made numerous alterations to the original book as well as changes in the names of the characters to Merkin Muffley, DeSadesky, and Kissoff.

Kubrick was always attracted to science fiction. His life's ambition was to produce "the proverbial good science-fiction movie." He admired sci-fi writer Arthur C. Clarke's works. When Kubrick approached Clarke with a proposal to co-write a script, the novelist suggested some previous works of his would make a good framework for the screenplay. The novelist asked Kubrick to look at his 1948 short story, *The Sentinel,* about a group of astronauts on the moon who discover an alien structure. Another offering was Clarke's short story, 1953's *Encounter In The Dawn,* where three astronauts travel to a distant planet and come upon alien life. Lastly, Clarke mentioned his 1953 novel, *Childhood's End,* which describes how friendly aliens spawn a golden age of life on Earth. Kubrick decided to combine all three of Clarke's works into his new movie.

Clarke and Kubrick agreed the director would write the script for *2001* with assistance from Clarke, while the sci-fi writer would parallel Kubrick's script with an accompanying novel by the same name. For their research, the two watched a number of science fiction movies. They were especially interested in producer George Pal's 1950's movies, most notably his 1955 *Conquest of Space*, giving Kubrick several ideas to insert into his storyline.

For the title, *2001: A Space Odyssey*, Kubrick dug deep into the ancient Greek classic *The Odyssey* by Homer. The Greek poet's title inspired him since "it occurred to us that for the Greeks the vast stretches of the sea must have had the same sort of mystery and remoteness that space has for our generation."

"*2001* would give a little insight into my metaphysical interests," Kubrick said working on the project." I'd be very surprised if the universe wasn't full of an intelligence of an order that to us would seem God-like. I find it very exciting to have a semi-logical belief that there's a great deal to the universe we don't understand, and that there is an intelligence of an incredible magnitude outside the Earth. It's something I've become more and more interested in. I find it a very exciting and satisfying hope."

The screenplay took 58 days to complete with revisions going back and forth between the two as they shaped both the script and the book. One scene Kubrick insisted on which Clarke was uneasy about was when the astronauts are discussing the problem of HAL inside the pod where the computer outside could read their lips through a porthole. After viewing the movie Clarke said he was glad Kubrick stuck to his guns inserting the scene. Clarke realized with the evolution of modern computers it would become only a matter of time before they would be programmed to read human lips, especially assisting deaf people in their ability to understand others speaking.

Once the script and the novel were completed, they decided the film would precede the book as Kubrick thought the *2001* publication of the novel could hurt his film at the box office.

PREPARATIONS KUBRICK MADE BEFORE FILMING A MOVIE

The working relationship between Douglas and Kubrick continued soon after *Glory* when Douglas took on the producer role for the Roman epic *Spartacus*. Douglas hired Kubrick after he fired the original director, Anthony Mann, who reportedly directed just the salt mine sequence seen in the beginning of the movie. Douglas didn't see eye to eye with Mann after spending a few days with him filming the scene. Douglas, acting in the lead role as Spartacus, thought Mann wasn't forceful enough to handle some of his actors, many of whom were big stars with strong personalities. He foresaw looming troubles with Mann's docile personality as well as the immensity of the production after he had seen him working on the set. Later on Douglas felt badly how he treated Mann and lobbied for the director to take the reins in 1965's *The Heroes of Telemark,* where the actor was in the lead role. Mann did not carry a grudge against the actor following his firing and tried to recruit Douglas for his 1964 epic, *The Fall of the Roman Empire.*

Douglas later regretted inviting Kubrick on board as their relationship deteriorated as the filming went on. Douglas vowed afterwards to never work with Kubrick ever again.

In the 2015 film *Trumbo* profiling screenwriter Dalton Trumbo, blacklisted from Hollywood in the 1950s because of his Communist leanings, Douglas offers the writer a chance to rewrite an earlier submitted draft on *Spartacus*. Trumbo agrees. During that time, credit couldn't go to those blacklisted despite their contributions to the film. As the *Spartacus* production was nearing completion, Douglas held a meeting with those involved in the film and asked who should receive the screenplay credits in the titles. Kubrick raised his hand and volunteered his name as the writer. Douglas was surprised a director would claim to be the screenwriter when he didn't compose the script. Douglas then made the monumental decision to credit Trumbo as the main scriptwriter, a decision that broke the invisible shield of a decade-old boycott of the Hollywood blacklisting.

As he was planning his shots before the actual production, Kubrick scheduled to film his scenes at a leisurely clip of just two camera set-ups per day. The studio thought at that pace Kubrick's shooting timetable would place the movie well over the projected release date. The studio executives demanded the director set up and shoot 32 scenes per day. Kubrick felt the studio's ambitious schedule bordered on madness. The two parties finally agreed to eight daily set-ups as a good compromise.

KUBRICK'S EYE IN PICKING ACTORS

Casting the role of the teenage girl Lolita for the 1962 film *Lolita,* Kubrick's first English independently-produced movie, was difficult in the extreme. The censors were looking very carefully at this film about an adult male's affair with a young teenager. Kubrick was cautioned the actress he selected couldn't look really, really young. Nearly 800 teenage girls auditioned for the lead, including Haley Mills, whose father John Mills was rumored to have nixed his daughter's participation. Disney Studios had Haley under contract and was also allegedly applying its veto power.

Kubrick was looking at the possibility of the young Joey Heatherton for Lolita. Her father, Ray Heatherton, anticipated the highly visible role would be deadly to her career, fearing she would always be typecast as a promiscuous sex kitten. He rejected the idea. Sue Lyon, 14,, partly because she had larger-than-normal breasts for her age, was chosen to play the 14-year-old. For the movie the character's age was increased a couple of years from the Nabokov's original book pegging Lolita's age at 12.

Kubrick treated the *Lolita* project with utmost care because of its sensitive, controversial nature. One scene Kubrick was especially cautious about was when James Mason, playing Professor Humbert Humbert, is staring at Lolita's picture next to the bed while making love to her mother, Shelly Winters. To soften the visual, Kubrick had the pair fully dressed lying on the bed while Lolita's picture is seen in the background.

Another example of Kubrick's sharp eye in spotting unknown movie talent was in canvassing actors for *Dr. Strangelove.* The director was scouting George C. Scott, considered for a role as General Buck Turgidson, performing in William Shakespeare's play, *The Merchant of Venice.* By chance he noticed in the same play the young actor James Earl Jones on the stage. Kubrick pegged Jones to portray a B-52 bombardier on the way to Russia to drop a nuke. *Dr. Strangelove* became Jones' film debut.

The War Room, located deep in the bowels of the Pentagon in *Dr. Strangelove,* contains a huge screen pinpointing the location of missile silos situated throughout the United States. Kubrick was amazed his technical advisors were able to establish each silo since their locations were top secret. When the advisors informed the director the placements were all fiction, Kubrick asked if they could glean from their contacts in the Defense Department where the safest place would be if there were an all-out nuclear holocaust. Upon consulting with government officials, they told Kubrick West Cork in Ireland was the place to be for nuclear survival. After the release of

Dr. Strangelove, where the film mentions this Irish location, a number of wealthy Europeans bought homes in the West Cork area, sending real estate prices skyrocketing.

KUBRICK'S INTEREST IN THE PARANORMAL

Kubrick was inspired by Stephen King's book *The Shining* to make a suspenseful film intended to raise the sophistication level of typical horror movies.

"I've always been interested in ESP and the paranormal," Kubrick revealed. "In addition to the scientific experiments which have been conducted suggesting that we are just short of conclusive proof of its existence, I'm sure we've all had the experience of opening a book at the exact page we're looking for, or thinking of a friend a moment before they ring on the telephone. But *The Shining* didn't originate from any particular desire to do a film about this. I thought it was one of the most ingenious and exciting stories of the genre I had read. It seemed to strike an extraordinary balance between the psychological and the supernatural in such a way as to lead you to think that the supernatural would eventually be explained by the psychological: 'Jack must be imagining these things because he's crazy.' This allowed you to suspend your doubt of the supernatural until you were so thoroughly into the story that you could accept it almost without noticing. The novel is by no means a serious literary work, but the plot is for the most part extremely well worked out, and for a film that is often all that really matters."

To get the cast for *The Shining* in the proper mood before filming, Kubrick made the actors watch a trio of films. Since David Lynch was one of Kubrick's favorite directors and his 1977 film *Eraserhead* one of his all-time favorites, Kubrick included the Lynch movie as well as 1968's *Rosemary's Baby* and 1973's *The Exorcist* as required viewing for Jack Nicholson, Shelley Duvall, and the rest of the cast.

"There's something inherently wrong with the human personality," Kubrick explained about his fascination with the horror genre. "There's an evil side to it. One of the things that horror stories can do is to show us the archetypes of the unconscious: we can see the dark side without having to confront it directly. Also, ghost stories appeal to our craving for immortality. If you can be afraid of a ghost, then you have to believe that a ghost may exist. And if a ghost exists, then oblivion might not be the end."

Kubrick's obsession with details included finding just the right exteriors and interiors for his sets. He sent his scouting crew far and wide to research the perfect locales for ideas in designing his sets. The Timberline Lodge in

Mount Hood, Oregon, served as the exterior backdrop for *The Shining*. The lodge's management, reading the script and seeing all the wiggy things going on in Room 217, asked Kubrick not to use the room number because no one in their right mind would ever stay in that room once the movie was released. Kubrick readily understood, switching the room to a number the lodge didn't have, number 237.

When fans of the movie enter the Timberline Lodge, they wonder why its interior doesn't appear as anything like the one in the film. That's because the director's scouting team took several photos of other grand lodges. From those photos the set designers went to work drawing up a composite of the best interior each lodge had to offer aesthetically. The Ahwanee Hotel, now the Majestic Yosemite Hotel in Yosemite, California, provided much of the movie's interiors, duplicated on a constructed sound stage of Elstree Studios in London, England. Roy Walker, supervisor for production design, copied the hanging chandeliers, fireplace and its mantle and windows based on the Yosemite hotel's interior. People checking into the Yosemite hotel ask the front desk personnel if this is "the Shining hotel." Walker also took photos from the Arizona Biltmore Hotel in Phoenix and patterned its striking red bathroom for the men's room seen in *The Shining*.

While Kubrick was personally scouting locations for his upcoming film, *Full Metal Jacket,* he borrowed his wife's new SUV. The director was chauffeuring cinematographer Douglas Milsome, the focus puller filling in for Kubrick's frequent Director of Photography John Alcott, who didn't feel up for the job, and technical advisor at the time, Lee Ermey. Kubrick spotted what he thought would be a great location to film a scene. Behind the wheel, Kubrick was so intense in describing the portion of the script where this particular location would fit, he ran off the road and crashed into a six-foot deep trench, causing his vehicle to roll on its side. Without missing a beat, Kubrick continued discussing the scene as he climbed out of his wife's car. The three walked around the potential shooting location after the accident and proceeded to walk straight home.

The studio and Kubrick ran ads throughout the United States requesting young wanna-be actors to mail videotapes of their acting abilities for roles in *Full Metal Jacket*. The studio's mailboxes were inundated with over 3,000 audition tapes. Kubrick personally scoured over eight hundred of them to find the right matches.

In preparation for *Jacket,* Kubrick read from the script one of his Marine recruits reporting to boot camp was described as chubby. Selecting actor Vincent D'Onofrio for the role, the director made him gain several pounds to fit the profile as Private Pyle. His instructions to the actor were "I want you to be big -- Lon Chaney big."

D'Onofrio took his assignment seriously, gaining 70 pounds before appearing on the set. He broke Robert De Niro's record weight-gain for a movie role. De Niro, playing boxer Jake La Motta in 1980's *Raging Bull,* gained a then-record 60 pounds to reflect La Motta's post-boxing lethargy. After filming was over, D'Onofrio, through an intensive physical training regiment, spent nine months to shed the poundage gained for *Jacket.*

THE IMPORTANCE OF BATHROOMS

One of the most bizarre trademarks of Kubrick in his movies is many of the pivotal twists in his plots take place in the bathroom. In *Paths of Glory,* Kirk Douglas, playing the lead Colonel Dax, makes his first appearance in a bathroom washing his face. Likewise, George C. Scott's character as a general in *Dr. Strangelove* is first seen in a bathroom. The lavatory is also the setting for the final scene in the same movie for Sterling Hayden as the deranged General Ripper. The sign, "Zero Gravity Toilet" is visibly seen on Discovery One in *2001,* providing the only joke Kubrick said he drew up for the otherwise serious movie. Astronaut David Bowman toward the ending of *2001* explores the bathroom in the alien home. In *Clockwork* Alex and his vicious gang break into a couple's house and savagely beat the owner and rape his wife, all the while Alex is bellowing *Singin' In The Rain.* Later on the owner of the house has generously taken Alex in, not knowing who he was until the gang leader starts belting out *Singin' In The Rain* in the bathtub.

Bathrooms as we know them today were nonexistent during the 1700s. But that didn't stop Kubrick from sneaking one in during a scene in *Barry* when Marisa Berenson, while taking a bath, has a despondent Ryan O'Neil tell her he's sorry for what he did, a crucial point in the film. *The Shining* contains two pivotal bathroom scenes: the first where Delbert Grady as a bathroom attendant converses with Jack in the lodge's rest room, and the second where Wendy hides in the bathroom while Jack is chopping the door down with his axe. For the memorable conclusion of the first half of *Jacket,* the shocking suicide scene takes place inside the barrack's bathroom.

KUBRICK'S UNUSUAL FILMING SCHEDULES

Even though people have an image of Kubrick laboring for decades over one project, in his early movie career he steadily churned out films at a rather fast clip. From 1953's *Fear And Desire* to 1975's *Barry Lyndon,* Kubrick average about one film every two years. It was during his later years he spent an inordinate amount of time in the preparation before shooting. *The Shining* took five years from conception to its final release, for *Jacket,* seven years, and for his last film, 1999's *Eyes Wide Shut,* it was twelve years before a version of it was completed.

Clockwork was an anomaly in the Kubrick cannon since his relatively quick turnaround from the beginning of filming to its release took a mere one year, warp-speed for the director's later years. This film marked the shortest production Kubrick ever clocked.

Clockwork was in sharp contrast to Kubrick's next movie, *Barry.* Kubrick was given a relatively large $11 million budget, considered one of the richer funded movies at the time. Filming alone took over 300 days and had two stoppages during the shoot. Its cast and crew were essentially tied down for two years before the filming was wrapped.

The Shining's actual filming days weren't quite as long as *Barry,* but they were lengthy by any movie-making measure. The studio booked the Elstree Studios in London, England, for 17 weeks to shoot the horror flick, but the filming took just shy of a year to complete. The unanticipated long shooting schedule delayed other productions waiting in the wings to use the movie studio, including Warren Beatty's 1981 *Reds,* and Steven Spielberg's 1981 *Raiders of the Lost Ark.*

One particularly difficult shoot to set up in the massive Elstree Studios stretched over a month to film was *The Shining.* The maze, appearing outside the lodge in the movie was really a life-sized hedged maze constructed inside the studio. The maze was so complex in its design crew members working inside the twisting paths frequently had to use their walkie-talkies to communicate with assistants up in the studio's girders to help them get out.

The filming of *Jacket* was so laboriously long one of its lead actors, Matthew Modine, had walked to the alter to get married, conceived a child with his wife, seen his child delivered, and celebrated the child's first birthday, all within the movie's shooting schedule. Every father has the strong desire to witness the birth of his child and Modine was no exception. When it came time for delivery, Kubrick refused to let the prospective dad go to the nearby hospital to comfort his laboring wife. Modine, not taking kindly to the director's disapproval, said he was so determined to attend the delivery he was planning to injure himself so he could be whisked to the same hospital as his wife. Kubrick, realizing how important it was for his actor to attend his baby's delivery, released him from the set.

PERFECTIONIST IN TOTAL CONTROL

When Kubrick moved overseas to England, he demanded--and received--complete control over his productions. Beginning with *Lolita* until his final movie, *Eyes Wide Shut*, Kubrick, ever meticulous and obsessed with the most minute details, micromanaged every production. In addition to giving input into his own scripts Kubrick was heavily involved in the film set designs and lighting. He would frame each shot behind the camera and worked lengthy hours alongside his editors during post-production. He produced only eight films during that period in England and every one is considered a classic.

He was so involved in the production of his movies he even provided the heavy breathing sound heard in the space suit when Astronaut Bowman is outside the spaceship in *2001*. Kubrick also made sure to show next to the spaceship's ejection mechanisms for its pods a set of replacement instructions for the explosive bolts after they were expended.

Just before the release of *2001*, Kubrick was obsessed with details most normal film directors tasked others to handle. The studio was planning to distribute the film as a "road-show release" to be screened first in only large cities. With the limited, big theater release, a preliminary overture, intermission and exit musical score was scheduled to be played. During the final days before *2001's* limited release, the studio cancelled the opening and closing music, retaining only the intermission. Kubrick learned of where the studio was inserting the intermission into the movie, but felt the break should be placed in a different part and let the studio know about his preference. Of course the studio said yes. He also selected the intermission music while audiences were grabbing snacks and going to the rest rooms. Kubrick even insisted all the theaters dim their lights exactly at one minute before the movie resumed playing the second half, not a second earlier nor a second later.

Theater owners were relieved Kubrick had only one other film after *2001* containing an intermission, and that movie was *Barry*.

When he completed the final cut of *Clockwork*, Kubrick demanded from the studio--and received the luxury--of coordinating the movie's entire advertising campaign. Such marketing campaigns include approving the designs of the films' posters and all the commercials and trailers to be shown in the theaters, on television, and heard through radio outlets.

The process of viewing the proposed movie posters for *The Shining* reflects Kubrick's obsessiveness to detail. He hired famed American art designer Saul Bass to draw up drafts of the posters for display. Bass and his team designed nearly 300 poster layouts before Kubrick was happy with the one eventually used to advertise *The Shining*.

Kubrick even had the control of each reel of film in every movie house showing *Clockwork*. The obsessive director was concerned the owners of the theaters, worried about certain violent scenes, would slice them out to appease some of their audience members' moral tastes. Kubrick's tasked his distributors to force these owners showing *Clockwork* to switch the reels once a week for authenticated, inspected reels to run the following week.

DIFFICULT TO WORK WITH

Although he denied being a perfectionist Kubrick was not easy to work for during his productions, according to multiple sources. Doug Trumbull, visual effects designer for *2001,* was ready to chuck his career because of Kubrick's unrelenting pressure.

"He was difficult, he was demanding," remembered Trumbull, who would continue his special effects craft in Hollywood years afterwards, including working with Steven Spielberg in his 1977 *Close Encounters of the Third Kind*. "His level of quality control was absolutely near perfection."

Kubrick was notoriously known for insisting on multiple takes from his actors. He felt his actors needed several repeat performances just to get used to being in front of the film crew, finding their camera marks, and getting into a "deeper place," as Nicole Kidman said of Kubrick's obsessiveness when she acted for him in *Eyes Wide Shut.*

Scatman Crothers, 69 years old, in his scene with boy-actor Daniel Lloyd discussing the shining, reportedly performed a world-record 148 takes before Kubrick was satisfied. During one of the later takes, Crothers became so frustrated with the amount of times he had to redo the scene he reportedly cried out, "What do you want, Mr. Kubrick?" In his next picture, 1980's *Bronco Billy,* Crothers broke down in tears after shooting his first scene with director Clint Eastwood. Known for his spare shooting, Eastwood said he was satisfied with the actor's one take.

The last scene in *Clockwork* shows Malcolm McDowell romping with a woman on the floor while an audience surrounding the two claps in approval. Kubrick demanded 74 takes before he felt the scene was correctly filmed.

During the same movie professional bodybuilder David Prowse was tasked with lifting Patrick Magee sitting in his wheelchair down a flight of stairs. Prowse heard about the enormous amount of takes Kubrick demanded from his cast and assessed lifting such a heavy load repeatedly down the stairs would literally kill him. He approached the director and said something that completely shocked the onlooking film crew. No one, besides Peter Sellers, ever told Kubrick to his face by asking if the director could minimize the amount of filming for this one scene. "You're not exactly known as 'one-take-Kubrick', are you?" Prowse begged.

Kubrick didn't appear stunned by Prowse's comments, laughing at the request and said he would try to ask as few repeats as possible. Remarkably for the demanding director, the scene of Prowse carrying Magee down the flight of stairs required only six takes. Despite the remarkably low number, the ultra-fit Prowse was barely able to stand up after the day's shoot, so exhausted was he lugging such a heavy load.

In *Barry,* to get that one shot to satisfy him, Kubrick called for over 100 takes for the scene where Ryan O'Neil walks up to Lady Honoria for the first time.

An interviewer once asked Kubrick why he needed so many takes for his scenes. "Because actors don't know their lines," he answered.

In one of his fewest amount of takes Kubrick requested was the scene in *The Shining* where blood streams through the closed doors of the elevator. Kubrick said the scene was a wrap after an astonishingly low three takes. But setting up the scene for each take required a long nine days from the crew. For the first two takes Kubrick complained the liquid "doesn't look like blood." The elevator scene is drenched with the color red, just as every shot in *The Shining*, whether obvious, like the elevator oozing blood, or more subtle.

Another marathon film-making scene was the one in *Jacket* where the American soldiers attempt to capture the building housing the Viet Cong sniper who had shot their friend Eightball. Kubrick filmed the scene over a 30-day stretch, a period where actor Dorian Harewood remembered the experience as "lying on the ground for a whole month."

The mop scene in the bathroom in *Jacket* between Joker and Cowboy took 62 takes to satisfy the director. Amazingly, later in the shoot, Cowboy's death scene, a complex one at that, consisted of only five takes.

EXPECTED PERFECTION EARLY IN HIS CAREER

Kubrick's on-set perfectionism was displayed early in his filmmaking career by his first days of shooting *Paths of Glory*. Kirk Douglas remembered the young Kubrick directing veteran actor Adolphe Menjou. "He made Menjou do the same scene 17 times. 'That was my best reading,' Menjou announced. 'I think we can break for lunch now.'"

Even though stomachs were gurgling because the lunch-hour was well past, Kubrick told the French actor he required another take. While the crew was resetting the scene, Menjou went ballistic on Kubrick, demeaning the director's parents as well as questioning his ability to handle the production and its crew. After Menjou's long and abusive rant, Kubrick, standing stone faced in front of the sputtering actor, calmly said, "All right, let's try the scene once more."

Menjou followed Kubrick's orders without another peep from him.

"Stanley instinctively knew what to do," Kirk Douglas said.

The realistic trench and battle scenes Winston Churchill had praised in *Glory* was quite a logistical undertaking to construct. The studio was able to secure a 5,000-square yard pasture outside Munich, Germany, by paying the farmer who owned the property the costs for the potential crops he couldn't grow for the season. The trenches and shell holes required 60 workers digging 24 hours a day for three weeks to recreate the 1916 muddy WW1 battlefield. Eight camera cranes were erected throughout the field to follow the fighting.

The technical director overseeing the accuracy of the period balked at Kubrick insisting the trenches where the soldiers were standing be six feet wide instead of the four-foot-wide trenches WW1 soldiers had constructed on the front lines. The director needed the extra two feet to film his planned fluid shots utilizing the dolly with the camera maneuvering throughout the trenches. The trenches seen in the picture are six-feet wide.

To play the French soldiers, over 600 off-duty Munich policemen were hired to wear the French uniforms. One of the extras, Richard Anderson, recalls, "The trench was gruesome. It just reeked, and then the weather was so lousy--it was cold, it was freezing and overcast and gray. We were all sick. We all had colds, we were all sick from the first week. We all looked awful, but it certainly added to the movie."

Those policemen, many whose fathers and grandfathers participated and died in WW1, had undergone three years of mandatory training in the military and weren't showing any signs of fright before and during the battle scenes. Kubrick had to remind them repeatedly they were performing as soldiers who were facing almost certain death with bombs exploding in the fields and German machine gunners firing at them. The extras, remembering their fathers or close relatives, became emotional when they were assigned their "dying zones," the places where they had to fall pretending to be hit. The policemen were given specific paths to follow and were told not deviate from their lines. They were warned to not pretend to be courageous by leaving their paths and leap from foxhole to foxhole. The reason: some of the foxholes contained explosives, and if those charges went off while the soldiers were in the holes, they would be severely burned.

Actor Timothy Carey, playing Pvt. Maurice Foley, had been irritating Kirk Douglas, who played his lawyer during the court martial scene, because of his erratic acting. Carey was one of the soldiers facing the military tribunal simply because he was "socially undesirable." Kubrick loved to give Douglas a humorous verbal jab once in awhile on the set. During the courtroom dialogue the director said to Carey, "Make this a good one, because Kirk doesn't like it."

Carey was becoming increasingly troublesome to Kubrick as the production wore on. At one point in the shoot, for publicity reasons to boast his visibility as an actor, Carey fabricated his own kidnapping. Kubrick and producer James Harris eventually fired him right before the concluding execution scene was to be filmed. The scene called for the three soldiers to be lined up before a firing squad, and because of Carey's dismissal, only two could distinctively be shown. A body double filled in for the Carey character when a wide shot was needed. Without seeing his face, the stand-in is also seen giving a confession to the priest right before the shots ring out.

Kubrick was directing the emotionally-packed "last meal" consisting of roast duck for the condemned French soldiers inside the prison in *Glory*. In the second take Carey, who was still employed, failed to repeat the way he tore tearing into duck from the previous take, which didn't match the continuity of the initial shot. The crew needed to obtain a new roasted duck to reshoot the scene. Kubrick, unhappy with the eating sequence, ended up shooting the scene 68 times before he was satisfied. And yes, the crew had to purchase and cook 68 ducks to serve to the actors.

In the same movie, shot in Germany, Kubrick, whose fuse was rather long, became very angry on the set one day. After repeated takes of one particular scene, film producer James Harris, well versed on German labor laws, approached the director to inform him, after an arduous 63 takes, that forcing employees to extend their working hours past the requisite amount was against the law. Kubrick went ballistic and insisted everyone stay until the scene was correct in his mind. After take 74, the director called the day a wrap.

SPARTACUS ADVENTURES

One of the most memorable scenes in *Spartacus* is when the Roman general, after the defeat of the slaves, asks among the survivors who is Spartacus. One after the other the defeated slaves rose up to claim, "I am Spartacus." Douglas, who thought up the scene and wrote it into the script, was proud of its emotional impact and asked Kubrick how he liked it. In front of the entire cast and the crew, Kubrick shot back he thought "it was a stupid idea." Douglas, upset, ripped into the director for what the actor felt was the director's misguided opinion.

On a side note, to really ramp up the cheering during that particular *Spartacus* scene, the production sound engineers recorded a Michigan State University crowd yelling out the name Spartacus during a break in the 1959 Spartans/Notre Dame football game, motivating Michigan State to win 19-0.

It was standard practice in the late 1950s and early 1960s for a lavish epic movie to be filmed in the region around Rome, Italy, for the backdrops as well as for the inexpensive labor, both in constructing the sets as well as for the extras appearing in front of the camera. Despite Kubrick's desire to follow the normal practice to make *Spartacus* in Italy, Universal Pictures president Edward Muhl wanted to buck the trend and produce the film in southern California to prove Hollywood studios could make an epic film domestically without breaking the bank. A compromise was made between the studio head and the director by filming most of the interior scenes in Hollywood and shooting the huge battle scenes overseas.

Spartacus is noteworthy for the accurate battle sequences between the Roman soldiers and the rebellious slaves. Kubrick arranged for the sprawling climatic battle to be shot outside of Madrid, Spain, on a grassy plain with undulating hills. Long before the use of computer generated imagery, Kubrick hired over eight thousand soldiers from the Spanish Army to dress up as Roman infantry. He directed the immense cast from the tippy-top of a high tower. That particular battle sequence required six weeks to shoot.

When filming on the ground the battle's aftermath, Kubrick was so precise in his dead body arrangements that in preparation for a moving tracking shot he assigned each extra an individual number and brief written instructions on where to lay and what position to assume before the cameras rolled by. A few of the scenes of the bloody battle and the post-battle slaughter had to be cut because several preview audiences as well as members of the Legion of Decency reflected their disgust at such carnage. Some of the techniques used in *Spartacus* parallel those shown in the Babylonian battle scenes of D.W. Griffith's 1916 *Intolerance*, where dwarfs with fake lower bodies were sliced in half and phony limbs on amputees were chopped off by combatants.

In the re-issuance of *Spartacus* seven years later, another 22 minutes were edited out, with the ending receiving special attention. In the original movie, Douglas is on the cross shirking in pain. Jean Simmons, playing Spartacus' wife, originally said at the base of the cross, "Oh, please die, my darling," which was cut in the later release. With all those edits, the viewer was left to think Spartacus had already died when she and Peter Ustinov drive away in his cart, something that didn't happen in the initial release.

Preparing for the final crucifixion scene, the crew took an inordinate amount of time to get Douglas positioned on the cross. After the morning hours ticked by, Douglas was finally up for his scene. However, just as the camera crew was about to film the scene the assistant director yelled out it was lunchtime. Everyone scampered to the canteen tent to eat, leaving the poor actor suspended for the duration of the break.

KUBRICK'S PERFECTION CONTINUES IN ENGLAND

A misunderstanding during the filming of *Lolita* caused a permanent rift between Kubrick and cinematographer Oswald Morris. One day Kubrick heard that photos extracted from the dailies' film footage had been published in a newspaper. The director confirmed the images in the paper and was highly upset with the person responsible for all the shot film during the production, cinematographer Morris. The veteran cameraman strongly denied the accusation, but Kubrick insisted Morris was responsible for those published photos. Much later it was discovered an assistant at the lab where the film was processed had been the culprit and had sold the prints to the newspaper. An icy relationship existed between Kubrick and Morris for the duration of the filming, and once the real offender was revealed, the director never retracted from his accusation. A bitter Morris promised himself he would never handle the camera duties again for Kubrick.

2001's cinematographer Geoffrey Unsworth, an award-winning director of photography, told Morris later he didn't gain any pleasure working with Kubrick either. Unsworth claimed the director suppressed any creative juices he brought to the set. The cinematographer witnessed a man who had the need to control everything and everybody. "Kubrick would give me the set-up and I would go in and light it," Unsworth lamented to Morris. Kubrick went so far as selecting the important pieces of furniture prominently displayed in the spaceships as well as selecting the type of fabric for the actors' clothes.

A most unique fashion in its day, the signature clothes worn by Alex in *Clockwork,* was designed partly by chance, reflecting Kubrick's desire to try something different. Actor Malcolm McDowell was a huge cricket fan and had brought a protective cup with him while he was being fitted for the costume for his character Alex. Kubrick, spotting the cup in the jockstrap while McDowell was dressing, noticed the actor was putting the strap under his pants. Just for grins, the director asked McDowell how would the jockstrap look outside his paints. The actor tried it and both agreed the positioning of the suspensor which no one normally wears on the outside would accentuate the weirdness of Alex's personality.

Kubrick was even concerned about the skin pallor of his actors and actresses. Marisa Berenson remembers the director telling her when she received the role of Lady Lyndon in *Barry* to stay out of the outdoor sun. He wanted to retain her pale skin without a hint of a tan. She also recalled how the director was unusually shy when he was near her. He gave her handwritten notes on the way the actress should say and do certain things when the cameras rolled.

The set for *Strangelove* contained an unusually upbeat atmosphere for a Kubrick production, continuing throughout the shoot. Even though Kubrick's normal attentiveness to each detail was evident, his crew immediately addressed his every command with thorough alacrity. Humorous situations, helped by Sellers' comedic lines, lifted the spirits of everyone on the set. The more difficult the shot, the louder the laughter was when the scene was considered a success.

Kubrick had instructed actor George C. Scott to ham it up playing General Turgidson in *Strangelove,* advice the actor accepted but didn't appreciate at the time of the shoot. In one particular scene, Scott is walking about the War Room and suddenly trips and hits the floor. He immediately springs up and continues talking, not making any mention of his fall. In the editing room, Kubrick felt Scott was ad-libbing, and since the shot was the best take in the scene, he left it in. Scott later said the fall was really an accident. The actor, upon viewing his performance in *Strangelove,* said even though he didn't appreciate his over-the-top performance at the time playing the general was one of his all-time favorite acting accomplishments in his career.

An actor who made a promise to himself never to work with Kubrick again was Slim Pickens, who was riding bronco as the nuke dropped from the B-52 bomber in *Strangelove.* For that scene alone where the actor rode the descending nuke bomb, the director called for over 100 takes. Kubrick contacted the actor for the role of Hallorann in *The Shining,* but Pickens said no way.

For *The Shining,* Kubrick shot an amazing total of 1.3 million feet of film for the 142-minute movie. The normal ratio is five- to ten-feet of shot film for one foot used in the final cut. For this movie, Kubrick printed—yes that's printed—102 feet of film for every foot seen in the released movie. In *2001,* he shot 200 times what the final film footage consists.

The evidence of multi-takes in *2001* is clearly seen by viewing the screens inside the Discovery One spaceship. Kubrick's team set up 16mm film loops running as rear-projections for the screen monitors. There were so many takes demanded by the director for the scenes with the monitors playing in the background, the film projecting in the monitors shows signs of extreme wear with visible scratches. This evidence is especially viewed in the pod monitors.

Nearly every scene in *2001* was filmed on an inside studio sound stage, with the exception of the "skull-smashing" sequence. The clip shows one of the apes discovering he can use an animal bone as a weapon. The sequence was filmed a short distance away from Shepperton Studios in a field on top of a platform. The camera was stationed below the platform to get an upward shot of the bones flying, including the famous toss of the bone the ape used as a weapon thrown up into the sky. Trouble was the filming had to stop whenever a jet flew into frame. And multi-take Kubrick was using so many animal skulls for the scene the crew nearly ran out of them.

The scene of the ape throwing the bone into the air then cutting to a command module in space is one of the most famous "jump cuts" in cinematic history. However, the vessel is not a spaceship everyone thinks it is but rather a nuclear container floating around earth. The bone weapon of the caveman transforms to the nuclear weapon of the twentieth century. In one of drafts of the screenplay Kubrick was working on, the conclusion of *2001* was to have the "star child" blowing up the nuke container as well as all the other nuclear weapons orbiting around the world. Kubrick soon realized the ending would be just like the ending of his last film, *Dr. Strangelove*. Instead, to conclude the film, Kubrick inserts the lingering picture of the baby in the womb hovering over earth.

Shooting in the open air for the caveman-busting-up-the-bones scene in *2001* reminded how much Kubrick missed filming outside the studio. In his next production, *Clockwork Orange*, Kubrick elected to shoot his movie almost exclusively on location, which, because of the project's limited budget, was far cheaper to film than on a studio set. His main source of lighting was with basic Lowell Light Kits, commonly used by film students to shoot low-end movies. Much of the film's lighting derived from the natural sunshine and its residual illumination.

Other corners Kubrick took to minimize the costs for *Clockwork* included placing the camera on a wheelchair to get several dolly shots as well as shooting with smaller, inexpensive handheld cameras. This is Kubrick's first film where he called for the movie industry's dreaded camera attachment, the zoom lens. For audio most of the actors wore state-of-the-art wireless microphones, unusual for its time since most audio was recorded by the more reliable boom mic. To audio loop the small amount of dialogue whose quality recorded on location contained some imperfections, Kubrick operated a standard Nagra tape recorder by himself to record McDowell and other actors during post-production.

Because of the limitations imposed by the checkbook, Kubrick wasn't as obsessive on getting perfection in every frame in *Clockwork*. Actor McDowell saw Kubrick in a different light than the reputation preceding him. He appreciated the director's attention to detail but the amount of takes needed for McDowell's scenes, with the exception of the movie's finale, was few since the director said the actor "got it right" from the get-go.

"If Kubrick hadn't been a film director he'd have been a General Chief of Staff of the US Forces," said McDowell. "No matter what it is -- even if it's a question of buying a shampoo it goes through him. He just likes total control."

McDowell's role as Alex was only his fourth movie and the actor began to develop what he considered a close friendship with the director during *Clockwork's* filming. Once the picture was released, however, Kubrick didn't give him any indication he wanted to keep in contact. McDowell said at the time he was pretty hurt by being snubbed by Kubrick. He later learned after several subsequent films the intimacy established between an actor and the director and other cast members is only fleeting, and his expectations of life-long friendships with working colleagues were short-lived after the productions' "wrap-up" parties.

McDowell did retain a friendship with Kubrick's wife, Christiane, and when he visited Kubrick's grave soon after the director's death, the actor had an emotional wailing over his burial site.

Nicholson, before making *The Shining,* heard about Kubrick's stickler for details while making his movies, but he never heard of any director requiring this: Kubrick demanded all his actors be available for his crew to set up the lighting, something stand-ins normally do. Because of this, the actors had to arrive at the studio much earlier than usual so they could sit or stand in for the lighting technicians before filming began.

Because he had such a fear of flying, Kubrick never journeyed to Vietnam, no less to the tropics, to film *Full Metal Jacket,* a movie about the Vietnam War. All the interiors were shot on the set of Pinewood Studios and inside the Bassingbourn Barracks, near Cambridge, England. To create an outdoor location resembling a Vietnam landscape, Kubrick hired set designer Anton First, mainly because he loved how First's work was portrayed in the 1984 film *The Company of Wolves.* For the battle scenes, which were supposed to duplicate the fight in Hue, Vietnam, Kubrick and his team were able to use the abandoned gasworks at Beckton, England. The set designers contoured the gasworks to make a believable Vietnam urban setting. To obscure the nearby London skyline, the team fired up billows of smoke throughout the set, especially seen in the mass grave sequence. Over two hundred palms were transported from Spain as well as thousands of cheaper tropical plastic plants from California. Kubrick, seeing the imitation plants, simply said, "I don't like it. Get rid of it."

Kubrick explained his attention to detail: "I do not always know what I want, but I do know what I don't want."

So realistic Kubrick insisted *Jacket* appear, he had his assistants round up a stash of MREs or Meals Ready-To-Eat rations just like the soldiers ate during the Vietnam War. He filmed the actors eating the contents of the packets while on patrol.

KUBRICK'S USE OF PSYCHOLOGY

Kubrick was well-read as well as being an ardent fan of psychology, the science of the mind and human behavior, a theme a few of his films were centered around. He felt an understanding of the human brain provided an insight into a majority of his characters. Kubrick, knowing actor Malcolm McDowell had a tremendous fear of reptiles, inserted into the script in *Clockwork* some scenes with him and a snake named Basil. He wanted McDowell's character Alex to appear more powerful with the slithering animal, but the director also wished to play a practical psychological joke on the young man.

The character Jack Nicholson plays in *The Shining* is psychotic as well as high-strung. To get him into an ugly mood, Kubrick restricted the actor's diet to only cheese sandwiches during a crucial two-week stretch. Kubrick knew Nicholson hated with a passion cheese sandwiches.

Kubrick's knowledge of psychology played a huge factor in shaping Shelly Duvall's character in *The Shining*. As the isolated, tormented wife Wendy, the actress showcased her vulnerability and terror as she realizes Jack, her husband, is gradually turning insane. To portray her heightened state of emotion, Kubrick played mind games with the actress on the set. Kubrick seemingly lost his temper repeatedly at her, claiming she was wasting everyone's time. The director made her feel abandoned, telling the actress everyone has "no sympathy at all" for her because she was creating most of the problems on the set. He would pick on her constantly in front of the crew, a tactic Duvall later reflected was to make her situation feel utterly hopeless.

After the movie was released, Kubrick praised Duvall's performance as well as her ability to act in a manner so few actresses could pull off. Duvall countered that playing Wendy was personally one of her best acting jobs on the screen but was also one of the hardest ordeals in acting she has ever experienced. The actress suffered from nervous exhaustion beginning in the middle of the production onward. The experience made her physically ill and resulted in losing some of her hair. Duvall cried so many times in so many takes she literally ran dry of tears and had to drink water constantly to hydrate herself. She knew Kubrick was trying to pry the best performance out of her and said looking back she wouldn't trade her experience with the director for anything. But, drawing a deep breath, she admitted she could never go through the ordeal again.

Nicholson wanted to be prepared for his scenes well before filming began. For one sequence, the so-called "Gold Room" scene where Jack converses with the lodge's bartender, he and actor Joe Turkel spent six weeks rehearsing their lines to make sure they were perfection once the two walked on the set.

Unfortunately for the two of them, Kubrick constantly changed the dialogue and action for the next day's shoot by banging out new lines and scenarios on his typewriter late into the evening. Those changes were printed and handed to the cast early the next morning. Nicholson eventually learned not to prep himself for the next day's shoot by reading the original script. He just waited for those newly-printed pages to arrive at dawn before he would rehearse his lines.

Physically for Nicholson, acting in *The Shining* with Kubrick's multiple takes was an exhaustive one. He was living with Anjelica Huston at the time of the shoot and she remembers him, after long hours at the studio, coming home and stumbling straight to the bedroom. He fell completely limp onto the bed and instantaneously fell fast asleep without hardly saying a word.

One of the highlights of *The Shining* is when Nicholson slices through the bathroom door in his attempts to get his wife and son who are trying to escape his clutches. The actor once volunteered as a fire marshal and was well practiced in the art of swinging an axe. To set up the scene, the props department, not knowing the actor's experience with an axe, constructed a door in the studio that looked sturdy but in reality was easy to chop apart. Kubrick required three days to get the take he needed and the props department ended up installing 60 "stronger" doors for Jack to tear through.

The ending of the axe sequence shows Nicholson thrusting his head through the hole of the bathroom door and announcing "Heeeeere's Johnny." Kubrick never heard the famous line said by Johnny Carson's sidekick Ed McMahon since the director lived in England and was unable to see Carson's *The Tonight Show*. Perplexed and not reading the line in the script, Kubrick was almost going to cut the line in the final release before someone convinced him of the phrase's importance.

Nicholson also experienced Kubrick's relentless demands the director dished out to everyone. The actor, though, didn't receive anywhere the wrath Duvall did. He later admitted he had a smooth relationship with the director on and off the set. But when it came time after the movie's release to acknowledge the accolades of *The Shining,* Duvall and Nicholson were somewhat dismayed the critics' and the viewers' opinions all spoke highly of Kubrick's talent in creating this vastly-acclaimed movie while the film's actors barely received any praise on their contributions to the film' success. Both individually spoke of their resentment toward not receiving much of the credit.

Kubrick films rarely employ children. Danny Lloyd, the seven-year-old boy in *The Shining,* playing the son of Jack and Shelly, was an exception. Lloyd performed his patented finger pointing spontaneously when he was auditioning for his role before Kubrick, a movement the director used in the movie. Kubrick, knowing this was Danny's first film, was careful not to expose him to the horrific elements in the movie. Danny thought he was acting in a domestic drama and not in a blood-soaked film. In the yelling scene between Jack and Wendy when Shelley carries her son out of the room, Kubrick didn't want Danny to be exposed to such verbal violence. He had Ms. Duvall carry a lookalike dummy instead. Years later Danny viewed a PG-rated version of the film. It wasn't until Lloyd was in his late teens he finally saw the released picture we all have come to admire and have nightmares about.

This perfectionism on the set failed to extend to Kubrick's dressing habits. Until the early 1970s, the director wore a suit and tie on the set while working with cast and crew. Kubrick had an epiphany moment when he decided to discard the suit and go to the film set with just casual work clothes. So obsessed was he with making movies, the director didn't like to take one second to decide what clothes to wear. He would have a closetful of indistinguishable pants and shirts he could scoop up and put on without thinking for one nano second. It was about the same time he decided to grow his hair and beard long, surrendering his clean-cut image.

CHESS-PLAYING EXPERT

To relieve the stress that comes with directing a full-blown movie Kubrick loved to play chess with as many members of his cast and crew who were willing to compete. It was reported he would win a vast majority of those contests. The director was considered a master-level player in the game. Before becoming a filmmaker, when Kubrick was a young man living in New York City he would often hustle for money against other so-called masters of chess in the local parks.

Filming *Dr. Strangelove* he challenged actor George C. Scott for a game of chess while on a break when the crew was setting up for the next shot. Scott, who considered himself quite a good player, was thoroughly outplayed by Kubrick, earning the actor's grudgingly respect. The games also kept the hyper-charged Scott in focus while on long breaks.

Another actor who was a decent chess player was Tony Burton, who was on the set for a brief role as the garage owner Larry Durkin in *The Shining*. He arrived at the studio with his chess set hoping someone would play a game or two with him while there was a break. Once Kubrick saw the chess board his eyes lit up and challenged Burton to a game. Since the day was getting late, the director released the cast while the crew set up for the next day's shoot. Burton and Kubrick remained after the crew left and played a series of games, resulting in only one loss for the director. Concluding the evening, Kubrick thanked the actor for the challenging games saying it had been awhile since someone had given him as good of a game as Burton had.

Kubrick's American roots also extended toward his love for the hard-hitting sport of football. He was so obsessed by the game that, in the era before satellite TV, he coerced his friends to tape several games and mail the cassettes to him for his viewing. His American tastes also gave him an appreciation for television sitcoms such as *Seinfeld, Roseanne* and *The Simpsons*.

When viewing Kubrick's films what are so striking are his unique, lush visuals. His images are so impactful his sequences can reveal a story without a bit of actors' dialogue. Kubrick was so visually-oriented, both in still photography and in motion pictures, he was constantly fascinated with simple 30-second television commercials. He was amazed an entire story could be told visually in such a short period of time.

"Observancy is a dying art," explained Kubrick on why his movies are so sublimely visual. "The feel of the experience is the important thing, not the ability to verbalize or analyze it."

Kubrick elaborated his position on the visual being superior to any other medium, especially the printed word.

"I think it is fairly obvious that the events and situations that are most meaningful to people are those in which they are actually involved- and I'm convinced that this sense of personal involvement derives in large part from visual perception," Kubrick explained. "I once saw a woman hit by a car, for example, or right after she had been hit, and she was lying in the middle of the road. I knew that at that moment I would have risked my life if necessary to help her... whereas if I had merely read about the accident or heard about it, it could not have meant too much. Of all the creative media I think that film is most nearly able to convey this sense of meaningfulness; to create an emotional involvement and a feeling of participation in the person seeing it."

IMPROVISING ON SET WITH ACTORS

Kubrick was known to be a stickler to the exact dialogue written in his scripts, similar to director Wilder and his personally composed screenplays. Kubrick frowned on an actor changing one word or adding additional dialogue. He gave two performers an exception, Peter Sellers and Lee Ermey. Sellers, who was in two Kubrick films, *Lolita* and *Dr. Strangelove*, added greatly to the director's scripts. In the prologue to *Lolita,* Sellers set the tone of the movie's dark comedy with his brilliant passages which weren't written in the script's original pages. For his role of Clare Quilty, an admirer of young Lolita, Sellers imitated the voice of Kubrick. One of the more memorable lines Sellers voiced in the opening scene which hit home to Kubrick was his reference to the director's previous effort, *Spartacus*. Mason asks the drunken Quilty "Are you Quilty?" Quilty responds, "No, I'm Spartacus. You come to free the slaves?"

The Seller's character of Quilty in *Lolita* wasn't quite as fully developed in the script as what appears in the final cut. As the production progressed, Kubrick decided to expand the Quilty role, disguising Sellers into several different characters to camouflage his stalking of Humbert and Lolita. Kubrick realized he had a good thing going with the spontaneous talents of Sellers, allowing the actor to improvise his lines. Because of Seller's quick thinking, the director wanted to capture Sellers' lines all at once as opposed to filming several takes by just one camera. Kubrick used up to three cameras to shoot Sellers' spontaneous dialogue. The actor felt his best take was his first one, but "multiple-take" Kubrick insisted Sellers repeat his scenes several times, feeling his execution sharpened with each successive shot.

Sellers' performance in *Lolita* was so endearing Kubrick hired him for the director's next film, *Dr. Strangelove*. The actor was signed to play three people, including the title character, Dr. Stangelove. Columbia Pictures witnessed the cash register ring at the box office showing *Lolita* and felt Sellers was the primary reason for the substantial increase in receipts. The studio signed the actor for an astronomical (at that time) $1 million, nearly 55% allocated for the *Dr. Strangelove* production. Kubrick, stunned by such an amount, said "I got three for the price of six."

But the expenditure proved well worth it. Sellers was nominated for Best Actor at the 37th Academy Awards, becoming the only actor nominated for playing three separate roles.

Seller's easiest character for him to play was British Officer Lionel Mandrake. During World War II, Sellers was in the British Royal Air Force and he simply mimicked his commanding officer to a tee.

In the same movie Sellers played the United States President, imitating presidential candidate Adlai Stevenson.

With the actor largely improvising the former Nazi Dr. Stangelove, which ironically had the least screen time of all his characters, the editing of the scene during his monologue detailing his plans for the future of the United States civilization was difficult. The actor's character, suffering from Alien hand syndrome, had his involuntary right hand at one point raise to a Nazi salute and at another point press against his neck in an attempt to strangle him. Such antics had the cast surrounding Sellers clearly suppressing its laughter. Kubrick and his team had to perform editing miracles by inserting close-ups and cutaway shots to avoid the smirking on the surrounding actors' faces.

The glove Sellers placed on his right hand was borrowed from Kubrick, who, as a micromanager, wore them to adjust the hot lights situated on the floor of the set. The glove created an image of an evil monster and added a sinister aspect to the Strangelove persona. Kubrick, unusual for him on the set, was in stitches laughing at Seller's antics throughout the filming.

Vietnam War veteran Lee Ermey was originally hired to serve as Kubrick's technical advisor for *Jacket*. Ermey personally viewed the auditions of numerous candidates for the role of Gunnery Sgt. Hartman, the Marine basic training drill instructor, and wasn't impressed by any of their deliveries. He asked the director if he could try out for the part, but Kubrick, who saw Ermey in an earlier film, wasn't too impressed by his acting abilities. He calmly turned down the offer. Ermey suddenly commanded Kubrick in a loud, Marine Corps voice, to stand at attention when he was spoken to. Reflectively, Kubrick did as he was told. After submitting an audition videotape, Emery was awarded the role.

Kubrick was so drawn by Emery's use and elocution of the English language the two collaborated to produce the basic frame-work of his dialogue. On the set the actor improvised about fifty percent of his lines. What was so miraculous for a Kubrick production, Ermey required just two to three takes for each of his scenes to satisfy the discriminating director. The only time where multiple takes were needed, 37 in all, was the Jelly Doughnut scene. Ermey's voice became raspy as each successive take was called for.

Early in the shoot, Ermey yells at Private Cowboy, demeaning him in front of the others by saying he looks like the kind of guy who enjoys sex with another guy "and not even have the gd common courtesy to give him a reach-around." "Cut," Kubrick told his cameraman. "What the hell is a reach-around?" Once Ermey explained to the director what the phrase meant, Kubrick, chuckling, called for a retake, asking the actor to say the line again, which is in the final version.

To achieve the spontaneity Kubrick was looking for in Ermey's interaction with the actors playing the recruits, Kubrick isolated the ex-Marine from the others until filming was ready to take place. He refused to have the Ermey and the privates interact with each other during breaks on the set.

In the middle of the movie's production, Ermey was driving his jeep when it slid off the road. The crash resulted in several broken ribs on Ermey's left side. He was unable to move his left arm for four and half months and some of the scenes shot during the recuperation period has Ermey's left arm pretty much stationary because of the pain he experienced when he moved the arm.

OTHER SPUR-OF-THE-MOMENT IDEAS

Since Kubrick had been mostly excluded from the scriptwriting process in *Spartacus,* he reluctantly allowed his main actors, Peter Ustinov, Charles Laughton, Laurence Olivier, and of course, actor/producer Kirk Douglas, to rewrite their roles the way they thought their characters would converse and act. Such latitude was rare for Kubrick and he remembered the actors' harsh demeanors on the set when it was time to edit the movie. Those extra scenes the actors added on their own ended up on the cutting-room floor, much to the actors' disappointment. Douglas predicted the previous director Anthony Mann would be unable to control those four stars' strong-personalities, and true to form the actors frequently butted heads with each other on the set, especially Laughton, whose arrogance rubbed everyone the wrong way. One day Laughton left the set in a huff because he didn't get his way and told Douglas he was going to sue him for shortening his role.

The reworking of the script by the actors did cause some paranoia for Kubrick on the set when the three actors, without Douglas on the scene, were seen visibly whispering among each other behind the back of the director. Sneaking up to them during one particular parlay, Kubrick discovered they were simply reading the script in lowered voices to each other.

Towards the end of *Clockwork's* production, Kubrick shot a scene where McDowell is eating in the hospital. The crew, including the director, was getting tired and bored with the scene. To liven up the atmosphere and to keep everyone attentive, McDowell began "popping" his mouth open for the food while he was being fed by a nurse. Kubrick liked the improvisation so much he kept the footage in the finished version.

Jack Nicholson came up with an idea Kubrick loved in *The Shining,* but the suggestion caused immense aggravation for the camera crew. The script called for a scene of "Jack not working." Nicholson, who loved tennis, thought up the scheme of throwing a tennis ball against the wall to show how Jack was passing his time. Kubrick carried the visual forward by having the camera film the ball bouncing off the wall and hitting the camera square on the front of its lens. Keeping the camera constantly rolling, he had his crew attempt the difficult shot again and again throughout the day. No success. Then, between setting up for the next scenes the following days, he had crew members try their luck again when, after more than a week of tossing the ball, someone nailed the shot.

A memorable sequence in *The Shining* is where Nicholson is tapping away on his typewriter while Duvall walks up and asks him a question. The actor remembered the times he was a writer and his girlfriend would interrupt him while he was concentrating on his work. He reminded himself on the set how he felt during his girlfriend's interruptions and allowed his anger to flow naturally, ad-libbing his dialogue along the way: "Or if you come in here and you DON'T hear me typing, if I'm in here that means I'm working!"

Kubrick's obsessiveness to details included in this scene pages of the typewritten "All work and no play makes Jack a dull boy" in all sorts of geometrical patterns when Shelley spies on Jack's work. The director had his secretary spend weeks typing up those pages and additional pages not seen in the movie.

Kubrick heard when people use a typewriter each individual key struck on paper sounds to the ear somewhat differently than the other keys. Taking the observation as truth, he recorded a typist banging out the exact words, "All work and no play makes Jack a dull boy," and dubbed in the audio sequence, even when Jack is typing off camera.

The scene where Jack discovers Shelley rummaging through his paperwork beside the typewriter drew special praise from director Steven Spielberg. Spielberg said most directors would have shown Shelley in shock at seeing the same sentences Jack was typing, then cutting to Jack appearing over her shoulder with a menacing look. Both she and the audience would be scared out of their seats startled at Jack's sudden discovery. But in the movie the camera sweeps from a pillar at a distance behind Shelley with Jack emerging and observing her discovery. This distant view, cites Spielberg, extends the viewer's suspense of Shelley's vulnerability. When Jack announces his presence, Shelley shutters and picks up a bat, further extending the suspense. The second point for Spielberg is the movie's real shocker, which, he said should be limited to one per picture (see Spielberg's section under "Jaws") is saved for Jack's startling appearance when Hallorann is murdered.

The baseball bat Shelley picks up once she's discovered at the typewriter has an interesting insignia on it. *The Shining* is based on a Stephen King novel and the Maine writer is a huge Boston Red Sox fan. On the Louisville Slugger bat is Carl Yastrzemski's signature, the Red Sox Baseball Hall of Fame outfielder.

There is the famous scene in *Clockwork* where Alex, leading a house invasion, is filmed beating the homeowner's wife. During four days of filming this scene, the cast and McDowell went through several variations of the wife beatings and rape, but nothing was clicking for the director. He suggested McDowell dance while he was administering blows to the wife. The movements were an improvement but Kubrick felt a little music sung by Alex would elevate the scene. He asked McDowell if he could sing and dance while hitting her. The actor, limited in his musical repertoire, sang the only tune he knew the entire lyrics to, *Singin' In The Rain*. Once the take was completed Kubrick said the beatings were perfect. When the day's filming wrapped up, he told his office assistant to secure the rights to the song, which turned out to cost $10,000.

Gene Kelly, who had made the song famous in his 1952 film of the same title, viewed how his enduring song was used in *Clockwork* and he was appalled. Several years later, McDowell approached Kelly at a party they both were attending. Kelly saw the actor, abruptly turned around and walked away without saying a word.

INTRODUCED NEW TECHNOLOGIES

Kubrick's genius at adapting new technologies to his films is legendary. Slit-scan photography, used in the Star Gate segment of *2001,* front-screen projection and video assisting in the same film, were all recent innovations embraced by Kubrick. Using a NASA high speed camera lens, a 50mm Zeiss lens with an adaptor usually attached to still cameras which possessed the largest aperture used in any movie up to that time, Kubrick filmed the interior natural lighting sequences in *Barry Lyndon* with the lens. Kubrick did fall back on some electrical lighting for *Barry* in certain scenes, but he largely depended on natural light during the interior sequences using just candlelight and sunlight. The director wanted to retain the movie's atmosphere in line with the 18th-century paintings produced in the time period of *Barry,* with special emphasis on the paintings of Thomas Gainsborough.

Despite filming with the largest aperture in the history of cinema for the candlelight scenes in *Barry,* the focal range of the lens was very limited and narrow. The actors in the frame couldn't move forward or backward since their images would be out of focus if they did. A constant vigil over the range of focus was required for those scenes, insuring no one was moving beyond their marks.

Adopting the newly-invented Steadicam for low angle shooting in *The Shining* revolutionized how the camera could be used in movies. The moving apparatus for the camera was only the fourth film where it was employed, the others being *Glory, Rocky,* and *Marathon Man,* all released in 1976. The way Kubrick used the Steadicam, such as following Danny riding his tricycle through the lodge's hallways as well as the race through the maze toward the end of the movie, demonstrated the Steadicam could be used in major sequences as opposed to brief clips as in those previous films. Early in the production, Garrett Brown, the inventor of the Steadicam, was invited on the set to demonstrate his invention to Kubrick, who was initially leery to use it. Brown proved the Steadicam's versatility by shooting several scenes for Kubrick before the director realized its potential.

"Stanley would be happy with eight tape recorders and one set of pants," said his wife Christiane on Kubrick's love for technology.

When planning for the *Dr. Strangelove* shoot, Kubrick realized the U.S. Department of Defense would not be happy participating in a film portraying its employees as bumbling bumpkins. Since the interior of a B-52 bomber was classified top secret, Kubrick's researchers were able to get a picture of the insides from only a British aviation publication. The movie's set designer based the cockpit and bomb container area on that one magazine photo. Since an actual B-52 was unattainable from the Air Force for the aerial scenes, the exterior of the bomber heading towards Russia was shot using a ten-foot model with matte images of the landscape moving in the background.

As Kubrick embarked on his *2001* adventure, he was puzzled about how to create the special effects he had in mind as the script took shape. He saw one of the highlighted films being shown during the 1964 New York World's Fair, *To the Moon and Beyond.* Seeking the technical expert behind the film's special effects, Kubrick learned it was Douglas Trumbull, whom the director promptly hired. Kubrick wanted to show Astronaut Bowman hurling through infinite space towards his encounter with the aliens. Trumbull, in what became known as the Star Gate segment, was familiar with a process John Whitney had first used in Saul Bass's opening credits for Alfred Hitchcock's 1958 *Vertigo.* Whitney had used a slit-scan photography effect, resulting in a crazy, kaleidoscopic series of images. Melding the scan effects with a traveling camera going past lit artwork with its shutter remaining open produced periods of lush, colorful streaking.

Those techniques were later used by Trumbull in what is considered one of the most popular openings in television history, the ABC "Movie of the Week."

In *2001*'s opening segment, a large black monolith intrigues the ape men who constantly hover around it. Originally, Kubrick and Clarke had envisioned a transparent screen, similar to a movie screen, showing the apes how tools and other implements work. But Clarke rejected the screen idea later on, saying the concept was "too naive."

The appearance of the apes with their furry features wasn't the first choice of Kubrick and his costume designers responsible for outfitting these primates. When viewers first saw *2001* most thought the apes were the real deal, highly-trained primates going through their trainers' lessons. But the apes are actually humans underneath the tight-fitting furry costumes, with the exception of two chimpanzees acting as the babies in the bunch. The director had Stuart Freeborn's design team make outfits more similar to early human beings but without the fur. Unfortunately, *The Dawn of Man* sequence took place before humanoids had any concept of clothing. Placing naked full-length male and female anatomies on the screen would have earned a Motion Picture Association of America "X" rating. Hence, the humanoids appear more like apes cloaked in hair than the ancestors of mankind. Selected to play these forerunners of humans were mimes and dancers specially selected for their skinny limbs and narrow hips so the hair could be applied on tightly, avoiding the appearance of those cheap baggy gorilla suits seen in Grade-B movies.

HAL 9000, the spaceship's computer, started out as a roving robot. But Clarke predicted the artificial intelligence robotic would look antiquated in future years and elected to show just the computer's big red light throughout the film.

One of the more challenging special effects in *2001* perplexing Kubrick and his gang of technicians was the floating pen sequence seen inside the space shuttle. There were numerous attempts to pull off this floating pen trick, but nothing seemed to work until, by sticking the pen with two-sided scotch tape onto a clear piece of glass, the team held the glass in front of the camera. The flight attendant who grabs the pen in mid-air is actually pulling the pen stuck with scotch tape from the glass.

Kubrick didn't particularly care for the blue screen techniques still being developed by the film industry to showcase his scenic wizardry in outer space. The director was resolute not to duplicate the shoddy efforts of previous science fiction films and wanted *2001*'s realism to pop from the screen. He had his technical crew place all the space models in front of backgrounds which were black. Once filmed, a team of British animators would hand paint, frame-by-frame, the traveling matte shots, laboriously eliminating imperfections seen in the background. After almost two years of blotting out these blemishes with black paint, most of the British animators enthusiastically signed on soon after the completion of *2001* to draw the Beatles' 1968 animated movie, *Yellow Submarine*. Working with color in the Beatle's movie lifted their spirits from the blackness they were constantly immersed in the previous months.

The second half of 1987's *Jacket* contained numerous combat battle scenes. His director of photography, Douglas Milsome, had experimented with several techniques to duplicate the chaotic war experience so familiar with fighting infantry. Milsome discovered a camera with its shutter thrown off-synch would portray a realistic combat appearance. Steven Spielberg would use the same technique while filming his 1998 movie *Saving Private Ryan.*

Another newly-emerging technology Kubrick had no part in inventing but had the luxury of using during the later years of his career was editing his films by a computer. *Jacket* was the first movie by Kubrick to cut his footage using the newly-developed computer editor, replacing the century-old technique of physically splicing film together.

Despite all the wiz-bang technology floating out there in the movie-making world, Kubrick's advice to aspiring film-makers possessing a desire to produce a movie but intimidated by all the complex bells and whistles was, "Perhaps it sounds ridiculous, but the best thing that young filmmakers should do is to get hold of a camera and some film and make a movie of any kind at all."

MICROMANAGING THE EDITING PROCESS

Kubrick was just as active after the conclusion of filming by editing his films alongside his assistants. There were times when he performed the first cut alone, as he did in *Clockwork,* which initially ran almost four hours in length before he realized he needed extra help in his edit suite to pare down the film. Kubrick was as obsessive in the editing room as he was filming on the set. Editing the final dueling sequence for *Barry,* the standoff between Barry and Lord Bullingdon inside the barn, took an incredible 42 days before Kubrick was satisfied with the gun fight.

Editing *Jacket,* one of his editors, Martin Hunter, was amazed how tirelessly Kubrick worked throughout the post-production phase. During one session the two had been editing for hours. Hunter was becoming exhausted working in the suite for that length of time. Kubrick, stretching and also showing signs of weariness, agreed with Hunter's suggestion they take a break. The director noticed he had just received from a film festival a print of *Dr. Strangelove* and suggested for the relaxation break the two should check the reels to make sure they hadn't been tampered.

Kubrick owned many cats and loved every single one of them. He felt he had neglected them while away filming on location. Kubrick gathered sixteen of them and brought the clowder to the editing room so he could make up for lost time.

So detailed-oriented Kubrick was with his work, he prepared his films scheduled for foreign markets by editing the actors' voices dubbed in the specific language of the countries the picture was to be screened. At the time, the practice was more popular than displaying sub-titles. Kubrick personally selected the actors providing the voices. In what is considered one of the poorest voice-overs in the history of cinema, Kubrick chose actors Joaquín Hinojosa and Verónica Forqué to voice the Spanish version of Jack and Wendy for *The Shining*.

The icy relationship between Kubrick and actor Kirk Douglas in making *Spartacus* is legendary. One of the toppers was the Douglas insisted on close-ups of himself during the crucifixion scene at the film's conclusion. In the editing room Kubrick had his editor remove all the actor's close-ups. When Douglas reviewed the rough copy of the movie, he was so upset at what the director did he took a folding chair and attacked Kubrick with it.

Previously planned and filmed episodes sometime hit the editing floor when it becomes apparent the sequences don't fit the overall thematic structure of the movie. Such was the case in *Dr. Strangelove*. A long table in the War Room depicting a buffet-like setting of food in the room can be seen throughout the movie. The original purpose for the large quantities of food, which included several custard pies, was a food fight would break out between the Americans and the Russians at the end of the movie. The director had filmed the scene of food flung all over the place with uproariously results. When Kubrick's editing team assembled most of the movie and arrived at the insertion of the food fight, the director rejected the footage because in his mind the sequence appeared too "Three Stoogerish" to conclude a commentary on nuclear war. The food fight footage was hidden from the public until its showing as originally scripted at London's National Film Theatre shortly after the death of Kubrick.

THE USE OF MUSIC

Kubrick always saw strong parallels between music and film and attached great importance to musical scores in his movies. "A film is - or should be - more like music than like fiction," Kubrick related. "It should be a progression of moods and feelings. The theme, what's behind the emotion, the meaning, all that comes later."

Kubrick slowly withdrew from hiring composers writing original musical scores to accompany his movies. He became attracted to using previously recorded works, such as Johann Strauss ll's *The Blue Danube* and Richard Strauss' *Thus Spake Zarathustra* in *2001* and Gioachino Rossini and Ludwig von Beethoven score in *Clockwork*. He also used certain recognizable tunes as ironic pieces, as seen when rapist Alex sings *Singin' In The Rain* in *Clockwork* and when Vera Lynn's popular *We'll Meet Again* is heard concluding *Dr. Strangelove* in the middle of nukes exploding. The theme song to the 1950s *The Mickey Mouse Club* is sung by the Marines at the finish of a vicious Vietnam War battle, contrasting the innocence of the people safely back in the United States to those soldiers who just fought in horrific combat in Southeast Asia.

Composer Alex North, who scored the soundtrack for *Spartacus,* was tasked to compose the original music for *2001*. But Kubrick, who was playing classical music while splicing the film together in the editing room, was enamored with the traditional compositions. North was nearly finished writing the first half of the movie when Kubrick said he could stop since in the second half he intended to use only sound effects.

At the New York City premier, North settled into his theater seat to enjoy his music for *2001* when he heard Strauss' *Zarathustra* open the movie. Disappointed none of his music he composed ever made it into the film, he was ever resilient, reusing his rejected *2001* score for three later films, including 1968's *The Shoes of the Fisherman* and 1981's *Dragonslayer.*

Not heard on the musical soundtrack but very much present in the minds of Woody Strode and Kirk Douglas was the concerto of Russian composure Sergei Prokofiev during the making of *Spartacus*. Kubrick was familiar with the composer's works and thought the classical track piped through the outdoor speakers would put the actors in the perfect mood when filming the scene of the two waiting for their gladiatorial fight in front of an intimate Roman audience. The director saw the expressions of the two in the finished film and claimed the music, although not heard in the final release, set the perfect visual he was looking for.

Kubrick used the same technique in *Barry* when he played certain selections of classical music right before filming a scene to get his actors in the proper mood. Director Sergio Leone adopted Kubrick's technique of playing on his sets the movie's already composed soundtrack music during his 1968 filming

of *Once Upon A Time In The West.*
"Music is one of the most effective ways of preparing an audience and reinforcing points that you wish to impose on it," Kubrick observed. "The correct use of music, and this includes the non-use of music, is one of the great weapons that the filmmaker has at his disposal."

KUBRICK'S LASTING INFLUENCE

The influence in Kubrick's films cannot be overstated. Upon the release of *Dr. Strangelove,* the United States government made several changes to its nuclear program. The government's Defense Department, aware accidental nuclear war could occur by the events depicted in the movie, ordered safeguards in place so such a catastrophic situation would be avoided at all costs. In reviewing the government's program, members of Congress corrected the situation where Captain Mandrake, in his attempts to contact the Pentagon from the West Coast airbase where the B-52's were ordered to Russia, was unable to make a long distance call from the base's only working line via a pay phone because he didn't have enough change. Other points in the movie were cited by Congressmen to the military generals about the communication informational flow that had to be directed to the responsible staff during such a crises.

In one of the first meetings Kubrick had with book writer Clarke about a possible outer-space movie soon after *Dr. Strangelove* was released, they both looked up at the evening skies. The two noticed an object which appeared like a satellite going through its normal course when suddenly it changed direction. Clarke said they should call the military to report an UFO sighting. Kubrick responded, "After *Dr. Strangelove*, the Air Force doesn't want to hear from me."

Kubrick disliked trying to explain the meaning of his films. He felt each of his pictures should be judged on its own merits and shouldn't be explained within the context of his whole body of work. His biggest fear was to repeat himself in any of his films.

One picture he had been asked frequently to explain was the meaning of *2001.* Nearly 250 viewers walked out of the movie's premier before the film ended, including actor Rock Hudson, who asked, "Will someone tell me what the hell this is about?" Co-scriptwriter Clarke said, "If you understand *2001* completely, we failed. We wanted to raise far more questions than we answered."

Kubrick concurred with Clarke's assessment on *2001* and in movies generally. "I would not think of quarreling with your interpretation nor offering any other, as I have found it always the best policy to allow the film to speak for itself. How could we possibly appreciate the Mona Lisa if Leonardo Da Vinci had written at the bottom of the canvas, 'The lady is smiling because she is hiding a secret from her lover'? This would shackle the viewer to reality, and I don't want this to happen to *2001*.'"

In a later interview, Kubrick went further than his Mona Lisa analogy. "One of the things that I always find extremely difficult, when a picture's finished, is when a writer or a film reviewer asks, 'Now, what is it that you were trying to say in that picture?' And without being thought too presumptuous for using this analogy, I like to remember what T.S. Eliot said to someone who had asked him - I believe it was about *The Waste Land* - what he meant by the poem. He replied, 'I meant what it said.' If I could have said it any differently, I would have."

The confusing ending episode in *2001* completely baffled early viewers. In conducting their research Kubrick and Clarke approached astronomer Carl Sagan and asked him about his thoughts on how to show extraterrestrial beings. Kubrick went into the interview with Sagan envisioning actors dressed as aliens like other outer space movies. Sagan rejected the idea, claiming although we think aliens traveling into our solar system are far advanced to our modern civilization, we assume they would appear as recognizable life forms. Nothing could be further from the truth. To do so would lend "at least an element of falseness" to the aesthetics of the movie, Sagan said. The astronomer recommended Kubrick suggest, rather than visually show, this controlling extraterrestrial intelligence. Kubrick absorbed Sagan's advice. In a printed interview, Kubrick defended *2001's* vague ending, describing aliens, evolving millions of years before earthlings, as progressing to "immortal machine entities" and then, millions of years later, into "beings of pure energy and spirit that showed limitless capabilities and ungraspable intelligence."

Being invited to attend the premier of *2001,* Sagan emerged from the theater with a smile on his face, "pleased to see that I had been of some help."

Because of the ambiguity of *2001,* the opening weeks were disappointing at the box office. The studio, MGM, was ready to yank the movie when theater owners reported they were experiencing an upsurge in attendance paying to see the film. The owners noticed the picture was especially appealing to young adults who were flocking to their movie houses. Asked why young patrons were so engaged in *2001,* some stone-faced viewers revealed the film's popularity attributed to the Star Gate episode, with all its wild hallucination images, intensified by the psychotropic drugs they were taking before the movie's showing.

To this day there are some who believe the Neil Armstrong/Buzz Aldrin walk on the moon in July 1968 was all a hoax. *2001* was released just before the pair walked on the moon. The movie's moonscape was so realistic believers in this conspiracy felt it would be so easy to televise the U.S. astronauts on the existing studio set. Their suspicions were compounded by the live telecast purportedly on the moon transmitting fuzzy black-and-white images of the first walk.

One of the most legendary aspects of *2001* emerging after the movie's release was discovered when people advanced the three letters of H-A-L over by one, IBM is clearly implicated. Clarke, who used the letters H-A-L as an acronym for Heuristic Algorithmic Computer, was surprised by the publicity and denied the name was intentional. However, the IBM logo is seen throughout *2001*, printed on Dave's spacesuit forearm control panel, visible on the monitors where the two astronauts view *The World Tonight,* and labeled on the computer panels as the spaceplane is docking with the space station.

Other product placements seen in the movie that have since become archaic, include *Bell System*, which is now the long-distant carrier *AT&T*, *RCA Whirlpool*, now just *Whirlpool*, and *Pan Am Airlines*, now defunct.

No one can deny the vision of both Kubrick and Clarke has portended future innovations. David Bowie was inspired by *2001*, composing his 1969 hit *Space Oddity*, which catapulted the rocker on the musical roadmap. The Apple I-Pad is seen years before its invention by the tablet used by astronauts Bowman and Poole to watch the BBC news while eating.

2001 is the only movie in Kubrick's impressive portfolio to ever get a sequel, 1984's *2010: The Year We Make Contact,* directed by Peter Hyams. Kubrick offered no input to the spin-off whatsoever.

The one movie Kubrick ultimately regretted making was *A Clockwork Orange.* The controversy surrounding the movie so affected the director he had his assistant take all the footage not used in the final cut, which was a lot, and destroy it. When he read about a viscous rape in Lancashire, England, soon after the movie's release of a young Dutch girl by a gang whose members were belting out *Singin' In The Rain*, as well as hearing about a child beaten severely by an older kid who donned Alex's signature costume, Kubrick determined to have the film pulled from all the theaters in the United Kingdom. To compound his awareness to all the antagonism surrounding *Clockwork,* Kubrick and his family were receiving death threats from anonymous people disgusted with its violent content. Kubrick contacted Warner Brothers Studio, owners of the rights to *Clockwork,* and agreed to the director's request to pull the film from the UK.

Once the movie was withdrawn by Kubrick and Warner Studios, videotape businesses in England were so swamped with inquiries about obtaining a VHS copy some rental establishments posted signs stating "No, we don't have *A Clockwork Orange*." For the remainder of Kubrick's life, people in the UK who wanted to view the movie had to buy the copy from other countries, most of them from French video stores.

The popular Scala Film Club in London showed *Clockwork* in 1993 without gaining Kubrick's permission to screen it. Kubrick asked Warner to sue the club, which the studio promptly did. The court's verdict found the club guilty, sending the organization into near bankruptcy, only to be resurrected several years later.

Actor McDowell also had qualms about his participation in *Clockwork*. He was so ashamed of the picture, given the copycat crimes attributed to the film and especially his character, he vowed never to play in a violent role or appear in any socially-reprehensible movie again. As time tapered the film's controversies, the actor has gained an appreciation toward *Clockwork,* now considered one of the most highly regarded movies of all time.

Clockwork was nominated for Best Picture during the 44th Academy Awards. The released film was rated "X," along with 1969's *Midnight Cowboy,* the winner of that year's best picture, the only other "X" rated film ever to be nominated in the category. Later in the year, Kubrick agreed to cut out about 30 seconds of some really graphic scenes to lower the movie's rating to "R."

Researching archival footage of Kubrick provides little footage, if any, of him discussing his films. Upon release of his movies, Kubrick, unlike other film directors who march onto the talk circuit espousing their work, refused to be interviewed. Only on rare occasions, as in his daughter's documentary on the making of *The Shining,* did he even want to be on the other side of the camera. Word was he was planning to change his practice avoiding interviews when *Eyes Wide Shut* was released, but he died shortly before the picture's premier.

So rare were Kubrick's public appearances it was easy for him to deny he was the famous director when some members of the press were so bold enough to come to his house seeking an interview. He would open the door and reply "Stanley Kubrick isn't home" when they asked if the director was available to talk. Reporters were so frustrated by Kubrick's reclusiveness they began to make up "Fake News," such as one story having him firing a gun at an encroaching fan on his property, and then firing again at close range because the wounded person was bleeding on his lawn.

His distain toward film critics was quite evident from his comments about their profession. "I find a lot of critics misunderstand my films; probably everybody's films. Very few of them spend enough time thinking about them. They look at the film once, they don't really remember what they saw, and they write the review in an hour. I mean, one spent more time on a book report in school."

Possessing such an obscure public persona was especially unusual since Kubrick's films were so highly regarded during his lifetime. Seven of his last nine films were nominated for the Academy Awards in the Best Picture category. Compounding the befuddlement on his seclusion is he was nominated four straight times for Best Director, beginning with 1964's *Strangelove* and concluding with 1975's *Barry Lyndon*.

He explained his lack of superstar status with the public at large, saying, "I've never achieved spectacular success with a film. My reputation has grown slowly. I suppose you could say that I'm a successful filmmaker - in that a number of people speak well of me. But none of my films have received unanimously positive reviews, and none have done blockbuster business."

Kubrick did win one Oscar, for special visual effects in *2001,* but the statuette was awarded on a technicality. He contributed to some of the innovative effects introduced in the film but he didn't supervise the team largely responsible for all the tricks filmed during the making of the picture. The controversy slowly bubbled over, and the Academy changed its rules in the following years to give the Oscar to the person(s) most responsible for the special effects.

Only one performance Oscar was awarded to an actor in any of a Kubrick film. Peter Ustinov won Best Supporting Actor for his role in *Spartacus,* while Peter Sellers was the only other actor to garner a nomination by the Academy in a Kubrick-directed picture.

Ironically, the one movie receiving the most Oscars he directed and one of his most financially-successful movies in his career was *Spartacus,* a film Kubrick had disowned and wanted the film to be excluded from his portfolio. The movie does have all the hallmarks of the Kubrick touch, but because he felt he didn't have total control over all aspects of the production, which he had in the remainder of his films, he claims this is the one picture he didn't want to be associated. Today *Spartacus* is critically acclaimed as one of the best historical epics ever produced.

"From the very beginning, all of my films have divided the critics," described Kubrick. "Some have thought them wonderful, and others have found very little good to say. But subsequent critical opinion has always resulted in a very remarkable shift to the favorable. In one instance, the same critic who originally rapped the film has several years later put it on an all-time best list. But of course, the lasting and ultimately most important reputation of a film is not based on reviews, but on what, if anything, people say about it over the years, and on how much affection for it they have."

As other film directors in this series, Kubrick received a feeling of fulfillment few in life ever achieve in their professions. He said of the film process, "Anyone who has ever been privileged to direct a film also knows that, although it can be like trying to write *War and Peace* in a bumper car in an amusement park, when you finally get it right, there are not many joys in life that can equal the feeling."

Kubrick was one of those rare people who would die doing what they loved. Four days after finishing the first cut of his last movie, *Eyes Wide Shut,* Kubrick passed away, leaving a body of work that will be memorialized for as long as we have motion pictures.

Final note: even though the custom of printing "The End" at the conclusion of the credits had long been out of vogue, Kubrick kept the tradition alive right to his final movie.

TOP TEN STANLEY KUBRICK FILMS

#1--*2001*: A SPACE ODYSSEY (1968)

In terms of cinematic history, this movie has had more impact on science fiction films as well as other forms of motion pictures than most. *2001* is the film most aptly describing the Kubrickian style of visuals in lieu of dialogue. The picture also has stirred the most interpretations of its meaning than any other film released. Film reviewer for the Los Angeles Times said of *2001,* "The picture that science fiction fans of every age and in every corner of the world have prayed (sometimes forlornly) that the industry might some day give them. It is an ultimate statement of the science fiction film, an awesome realization of the spatial future--it is a milestone, a landmark for a spacemark, in the art of film." Added the Boston Globe, "The world's most extraordinary film. Nothing like it has ever been shown in Boston before or, for that matter, anywhere. The film is as exciting as the discovery of a new dimension in life."

#2--THE SHINING (1980)

Even though Nicholson and Duvall didn't receive the credit they thought they deserved for *The Shining's* critical success, their performances make a huge contribution to one of the scariest horror movies ever made. There are so many iconic moments in the film everyone involved will be immortalized through the remainder of human civilization. With great acting, a great script and Kubrick's visual genius, nothing can come close to the perfection *The Shining* has contained within its credits. Film critic Peter Bracke, who specializes in horror movies, said of its reassessment after barbed with critical stings when first released, "Just as the ghostly apparitions of the film's fictional Overlook Hotel would play tricks on the mind of poor Jack Torrance, so too has the passage of time changed the perception of *The Shining* itself. Many of the same reviewers who lambasted the film for not being scary enough back in 1980 now rank it among the most effective horror films ever made, while audiences who hated the film back then now vividly recall being terrified by the experience. *The Shining* has somehow risen from the ashes of its own bad press to redefine itself not only as a seminal work of the genre, but perhaps the most stately, artful horror ever made."

#3--DR. STRANGELOVE: OR HOW I LEARNED TO STOP WORRYING AND LOVE THE BOMB (1964)

When the world's existence is hanging by a thread because of a potential of nuclear holocaust during the Cold War, leave it up to Kubrick to insert a strong dose of dark comedy to liven up an otherwise depressing topic. Peter Seller's three-character performance is one of the all-time best acting jobs on the cinematic screen. *Dr. Strangelove* is a whirlwind of activity and the final message of "just live with it" sets any nervous willy worried about nukes completely at ease. John Patterson of The Guardian wrote, "There had been nothing in comedy like *Dr. Strangelove* ever before. All the gods before whom the America of the stolid, paranoid 50s had genuflected – the Bomb, the Pentagon, the National Security State, the President himself, Texan masculinity and the alleged Commie menace of water-fluoridation – went into the wood-chipper and never got the same respect ever again."

#4--PATHS OF GLORY (1957)

This early effort by Kubrick displays a remarkable visual sense while showcasing his ability to take a heartbreaking tale and make it one of the most moving war movies ever produced. The unfairness of war, both physical and emotional, is on full display here as the human drama shown within a World War I backdrop is beyond belief. As one reviewer commented on the film, "*Paths of Glory* is a transcendentally humane war movie from Stanley

Kubrick, with impressive, protracted battle sequences and a knock-out ending."

#5--SPARTACUS (1960)

Even though Kubrick disavowed everything about this epic concerning the leader of an ancient Roman slave rebellion, there is no denying the director's footprint is all over the film. From the elaborate battle scenes to the intimate moments of passion, *Spartacus* is a rip-roaring, lushly photographed adventure that will emotionally touch the most jaded viewer. Against the best of advice because the script was written by a blacklisted figure, President John F. Kennedy boldly crossed the street to view this spectacular. Film reviewer Peter Bradshaw wrote, "The great-granddaddy of Ridley Scott's *Gladiator* hasn't lost any muscle tone after nearly half a century, and Kirk Douglas's direct, unpretentious performance as the great slave-rebel Spartacus is more engaging than ever."

#6--BARRY LYNDON (1975)

Be prepared to be transported back into the 1700s as Kubrick presents one of the most realistic, aesthetically visual look into that particular era put to the screen. The historic costumes, the subtle acting in the manner we all envision how the people back then spoke and dressed, as well as a good, moral story, highlight the director's ambition to make at least one Georgian period piece since his Napoleon proposal went nowhere. Jim Ridley of the Village Voice wrote "Stanley Kubrick's magisterial Thackeray adaptation now stands as one of his greatest and most savagely ironic films, not to mention one of the few period pieces on celluloid so transporting that it seems to predate the invention of camera."

#7--LOLITA (1962)

Controversial when the movie was first released and still repels some today, this film with its highly charged theme of an older man bedding down with a young teenage girl is tastefully brought to the screen by Kubrick's magical talents. Peter Sellers, this time taking on four roles, is adroit in his ability to insert several varying personalities within his frame. Mason's depression permeates throughout the film and young Sue Lyons, whose career peaked here, gives a bravado performance as the nymph who stole Mason's heart. John Fortgang said, "*Lolita*, with its acute mix of pathos and comedy, and

Mason's mellifluous delivery of Nabokov's sparkling lines, remains the definitive depiction of tragic transgression."

#8--FULL METAL JACKET (1987)

Jacket consists of really two separate movies: the first half is a look at a Marine Corps boot camp during the Vietnam War, and the second half deals with the actual combat. Viewers are still undecided what half is more superior but there is no doubt Kubrick's visual talent is on full display. Time Magazine called *Jacket* a "technical knockout" and loved "the dialogue's wild, desperate wit; the daring in choosing a desultory skirmish to make a point about war's pointlessness" with "the fine, large performances of almost every actor."

#9--CLOCKWORK ORANGE (1971)

This dystopian film, one of Kubrick's quickest turnarounds and lowest-budgeted, was the one the director and actor Malcom McDowell regretted making, let alone releasing, because of the copycat violent acts following its release. Amazingly the Academy gave *Clockwork* a Best Picture nomination. One can see how Kubrick, who was intensely interested in the field of psychology, was attracted to the theme of society's attempts to control the brain and the behavior of the criminal mind. The New York Times film critic said of *Clockwork,* "McDowell is splendid as tomorrow's child, but it is always Mr. Kubrick's picture, which is even technically more interesting than *2001.* Among other devices, Mr. Kubrick constantly uses what I assume to be a wide-angle lens to distort space relationships within scenes, so that the disconnection between lives, and between people and environment, becomes an actual, literal fact."

#10--THE KILLING (1956)

This classic film noir, starring Sterling Hayden and Coleen Gray, about a bank heist at a horse track, is grabbing and is an early indication of the talent Kubrick would display through the remainder of his film career. Mike Emery, film critic, praised the film. "Kubrick's camerawork was well on the way to finding the fluid style of his later work, and the sparse, low-budget circumstances give the film a raw, urgent sort of look. As good as the story and direction are, though, the true strength of *The Killing* lies in the characters and characterizations."

Woody Allen

THE COMEDIC GENIUS LOOKING FOR LIFE'S ANSWERS

There's an accepted wisdom people either like Woody Allen films or they don't. In his vast portfolio of over fifty self-made films, even his most devout admirers know of a clunker or two. But out of Allen's body of work, there exists a number of films that have affected millions of viewers, striking a personal, inner cord few filmmakers are able to produce.

What's remarkable about Allen, who began as a comic and has a flair for funny one-liners, is his films are an unparalleled examination of contemporary society as well as the bit of neurosis he carries inside of himself. In the scope of relationships and the human species' mortality, Allen's movies stand out in an era of mass-produced pictures catering to juvenile audiences of today.

"I think that Woody Allen asks these important questions about is there a God, is there not a God, is there life beyond the grave," says Father Robert Lauder, a theologian and film scholar. "This makes him unique among contemporary filmmakers. It also makes him unique in America cinema. These are key questions that he keeps hammering away at."

As he experiences the aging process, Allen has observed the way people consider the passage of time.

"It isn't just psychological, when you're getting closer to death that time passes faster," he noted. "I think something happens physiologically so that you experience time in a very different way. It's also scary, as you'll see when you get older. It doesn't get better. You don't mellow, you don't gain wisdom and insight. You start to experience joint pain."

But he's thankful we have "time" to sort things out, saying "Time is nature's way of keeping everything from happening at once."

Allen harbors a deep philosophy on death and dying and he even sees some positives in the eventual ending of us all.

"I'm not afraid of dying," Allen revealed. "I just don't want to be there when it happens. There are worse things in life than death. Have you ever spent an evening with an insurance salesman?"

"On the plus side," he said later, "death is one of the few things that can be done just as easily lying down."

Allen notes there is always something that can be more dreaded than one's eventual demise. "There are worse things than death. Many of them playing at a theater near you," Allen said.

"I once thought there was a good argument between whether it's worth it to make a film where you confront the human condition, or an escape film," Allen mentioned, thinking of some of the deep messages he tries to convey in his films. "You could argue that the Fred Astaire film is performing a greater service than the Bergman film, because Ingmar Bergman is dealing with a problem that you're never going to solve. Whereas in Fred Astaire, you walk in off the street, and for an hour and half they're popping champagne corks and making light banter and you get refreshed, like a lemonade."

WOODY'S EARLY DAYS

Allen was introduced to movies by his mother at the early age of three when he saw 1937's *Snow White and the Seven Dwarfs*. He said from that moment he was hooked on films. Movie theaters became the place he considers to be his second home.

The movie house Allen spent time viewing his favorite pictures as a child was the Kent Theatre in Brooklyn, New York, filmed inside for 1985's *The Purple Rose of Cairo*. Allen remembers paying 12 cents per picture and said the theater was "one of the great, meaningful places of my boyhood."

He saw movies as a great diversion as he was growing up and he still thinks of cinema the same way.

"I love films because it's much more pleasant to be obsessed over how the hero gets out of his predicament than it is over how I get out of mine." he said.

Since his Brooklyn, New York high school days in the early 1950's, Allen has been working almost every day of his life. He outpaced the salary of his father before 12th grade by writing one-line gags for New York Post's Earl Wilson, Guy Lombardo, and Sammy Kaye among others. Progressing to scripting television shows, including *The Ed Sullivan Show* and *The Tonight Show*, Allen gained a reputation in entertainment circles as a "half-genius," according to comedian Bob Hope.

From his earliest public appearances, Woody wears thick, black glasses, something he hasn't changed over the years.

"The two biggest myths about me are that I'm an intellectual, because I wear these glasses, and that I'm an artist because my films lose money." Allen said.

"Those two myths have been prevalent for many years."

"Basically I am a low-culture person," Allen said. "I prefer watching baseball with a beer."

Encouraged to take his comedy on stage, Allen, in a stomach-churning initial performance at New York City's The Blue Angel Club in 1960, emerged to become one of television's funniest stand-up comedians. It was a natural progression from comedy routines on stage to the cinema when his screenplay for *What's New Pussycat* was bought and produced in 1965.

A FULL CONTROL DIRECTOR

Allen felt his written work was mangled during the production of *Pussycat*, and like Stanley Kubrick, vowed to obtain full control of his films when given the opportunity. Beginning with 1969's *Take The Money And Run*, a film he wrote, acted, and directed, Allen produced uproariously funny, such as 1971's *Bananas* and 1973's *Sleeper*. His 1977 Academy Awards Best Picture *Annie Hall*, clocking in at 93 minutes, the second shortest Best Picture to 1955's 91-minute *Marty*, proved to be pivotal in Allen's work, sparking a layer of intellectual seriousness woven in his comedic themes.

"I can't imagine that the business should be run any other way than that the director has complete control of his films," Woody reflected. "My situation may be unique, but that doesn't speak well for the business--it shouldn't be unique, because the director is the one who has the vision and he's the one who should put that vision onto film."

"My relationship with Hollywood isn't love-hate, it's love-contempt," described Woody. "I've never had to suffer any of the indignities that one associates with the studio system. I've always been independent in New York by sheer good luck. But I have an affection for Hollywood because I've had so much pleasure from films that have come out of there. Not a whole lot of them, but a certain amount of them have been very meaningful to me."

PRE-PRODUCTION

WOODY'S SCRIPTING IDEAS

There exists a strong parallel between Allen's screenplays and the experiences in his own life beginning with his childhood. Some consider *Annie Hall* as one of his most personal films, especially when there are similarities in Woody's relationship with ex-flame Diane Keaton, who was 31 at the time she made the film to Woody's 41 years. Critics point out Keaton was born Diane

Hall and her childhood nickname is "Annie." Her character in the film is dressed in Keaton's very own outfits hanging in her closet. When the movie was released, the fashion world took notice of Keaton's clothing style and became for a brief time quite the rage.

In *Annie Hall,* Allen even uses the same jokes in the same setting he told years before becoming the world-famous film director. The jokes he tells in front of the University of Wisconsin audience and his gags on a 1968 *The Dick Cavett Show* appearance mirror those same in the movie.

He does take liberty in showing the type of house he was brought up in *Annie Hall.* Despite living near the city's subway tracks as a boy, Allen didn't actually reside in a house underneath a rollercoaster as shown in the movie. While driving around Coney Island scouting for locations, Allen discovered the Kensington Hotel situated under the Thunderbolt coaster to reflect his boyhood home in *Annie.* Both, incidentally, were torn down in 2000.

Other resemblances to the writer and his movies' characters he plays on the screen are that both suffer from a long litany of phobias, including germs, death, cancer, crowds, heights, dogs, sunshine, insects and spiders. The characters Allen portrays are totally afraid of hotel bathrooms, just as he is, as well as all are vegetarians like him.

"With my complexion I don't tan, I stroke," Allen said of his aversion in being outside in the sun. "It's true I had a lot of anxiety. I was afraid of the dark and suspicious of the light."

Allen features himself in most of his films as a writer. In *Sleeper*, for example, he plays a poet by the name of Luna. In *Annie Hall* Allen appears as Alvy Singer, a comedy writer. For 1979's *Manhattan* Allen's role is a TV writer. In his later films he plays writers who are somewhat famous in the entertainment field of cinema or television.

Early in his career Woody appeared in every movie he directed. Beginning with 1978's *Interiors*, he chose to remain behind the lens solely as a director. His second non-appearance in his pictures was seven years later in *The Purple Rose of Cairo.* He does make a Hitchcock-like cameo in this film, however; in the opening scene, he's the guy placing letters up on the marquee.

Allen has also patterned certain characters after people he's known through the years. One such person Allen and actor Alan Alda remembers working with and disliking because of his dictatorial personality was creator, writer, and producer of the hit TV series *M*A*S*H**, Larry Gelbart. In the 1989 movie *Crimes and Misdemeanors*, Lester, played by Alda, shows Gelbart as an overbearing bore. Woody wrote the lines for *Crimes* Gelbart usually said, including "Comedy is tragedy plus time," and "If it bends, it's funny; if it breaks, it isn't."

Alda felt differently when Gelbart passed away in 2009, claiming "Larry's genius for writing changed my life because I got to speak his lines - lines that were so good they'll be with us for a long, long time; but his other genius - his immense talent for being good company - is a light that's gone out and we're all sitting here in the dark."

Conversely, the women in his movies are more likely to be free-spirited. But arriving from small rural towns where most were brought up in, their naivety become apparent as they try to adapt living in larger, sophisticated urban centers.

One film going against the grain of small-town upbringing is 1986's *Hannah and Her Sisters,* where the sisters are raised in New York City. Allen was inspired to create a movie about female siblings rather than about brothers, figuring there were more layers of complexities for women than men. After re-reading Leo Tolstoy's Anna Karenina, he was inspired to emphasize the female point of view. "I thought I'd like to make a film called *Hannah and Her Sisters,*" Allen said. "Maybe that comes from childhood; my mother had seven sisters, and their children were female, so all I knew were aunts and female cousins."

Mia Farrow, playing Hannah, and her real mother, Maureen O'Sullivan (Jane in 1932's *Tarzan the Ape Man*) as Hannah's mom, are paired for the first and only time in the movie. When Farrow and O'Sullivan both read Woody's script after they committed to the film they were initially disappointed.

"It was the first time I criticized one of his scripts," remembered Farrow. "To me, the characters seemed self-indulgent and dissolute in predictable ways. The script was wordy, but it said nothing. Woody didn't disagree, and tried to switch over to an alternative idea, but pre-production was already in progress, and we had to proceed. It was my mother's stunned, chilled reaction to the script that enabled me to see how he had taken many of the personal circumstances and themes of our lives, and, it seemed, had distorted them into cartoonish characterizations. At the same time, he was my partner. I loved him. I could trust him with my life, and he was a writer, this is what writers do. All grist for the mill. Relatives have always grumbled. He had taken the ordinary stuff of our lives and lifted it into art. We were honored and outraged".

Mia's personality largely shaped the Hannah character while Woody was writing the script. He said the characteristic traits of Hannah were "a romanticized perception of Mia. She's very stable, she has eight children now, and she's able to run her career, and have good relationships with her sister and her mother. I'm very impressed with those qualities, and I thought if she had two unstable sisters, it would be interesting."

Several admirers of Allen's *Hannah and Her Sisters* script were so impressed by the quality of the writing they aggressively lobbied to get the jurors on the Pulitzer Prize Board to nominate his screenplay, which would have been a first for a movie script. But the Pulitzer committee rejected the offer.

As an avid reader of Fyodor Dostoevsky, the 19th-century Russian novelist, Allen adopted several of his themes and plot devices. *Crimes and Misdemeanors* is obviously gleaned from Dostoevsky's most popular book, *Crime and Punishment*. Other films influenced by the Russian writer include his 2005 *Match Point*, 2007 *Cassandra's Dream*, and 2015 *Irrational Man*.

COMPOSES WITH A TYPEWRITER

Allen has always worked at a feverish pace. He has been, without a doubt, one of the busiest directors in cinema. Woody writes, produces, directs, and sometimes acts in just about one film per year, a pace he's been on since 1969. Such an ambitious schedule makes it appear he breezily cranks out his screenplays with little thought and effort. Nothing can be further from the truth. While conceptualizing *Sleeper*, the only science fiction film he has ever produced, Allen consulted with one of the most renowned writers in the field, Isaac Asimov, to see if his ideas shown in the movie were feasible. He approached another writer in the field, Ben Bova, to make sure what he was writing could reasonably take place in the far future.

Allen's production of *Sleeper* stopped in its tracks two other planned Hollywood feature films based on the H.G. Wells' 1898 novel *When The Sleeper Awakes*: a big-budgeted movie from American International Studio, and another from famous producer George Pal, who was shopping the idea around.

Allen has drawers overflowing with scraps of paper containing plot outlines of film possibilities. Throughout his 50-year movie career, as soon as Allen finishes the editing of one movie he gets behind his Olympia portable typewriter his mother bought for him when he was 16 and pounds out his next script. He opts for the typewriter over a personal computer, which he has never owned. Allen does have an e-mail account, but don't expect to get much of a reply if sending him one since his assistants screen the e-mails he receives.

"I've never felt that if I waited five years between films, I'd make better ones," illuminated Allen. "I just make one when I feel like making it. And it comes out to be about one a year. Some of them come out good, and some of them come out less than good. Some of them may be very good and some may be very bad. But I have no interest in an overall plan for them or anything."

He also knows his constant habit of writing and directing activity keeps him satisfied with his life.

"I'm trying to figure out what it is I'm supposed to be doing to enjoy myself and unwind, having finished a project," Allen says. "I hold off for a day or two, go for a walk and very quickly I can't stand it. I get into writing another script again, which I love doing."

One of the more unusual inspirations Allen received was listening to George Gershwin's *Rhapsody in Blue*, a record he has in his album collection. Allen was so influenced by Gershwin's composition he based his movie *Manhattan* and the film's themes around the music. The film director claimed the idea "evolved from the music. I was listening to a record album of overtures from famous George Gershwin shows, and I thought 'This would be a beautiful thing to make a movie in black-and-white, you know, and make a romantic movie.'"

Allen loves the city he's called home all his life, New York City. In *Manhattan*, he said, "I presented a view of the city as I'd like it to be and as it can be today, if you take the trouble to walk on the right streets."

Allen had the proverbial writer's block when it came to writing *The Purple Rose of Cairo*.

"This was a film that I just locked myself in a room," recalled Allen. "I wrote it and halfway through it didn't go anywhere and I put it aside. I didn't know what to do. I toyed around with other ideas. Only when the idea hit me, a long time later, that the real actor comes to town and she has to choose between the screen actor and the real actor and she chooses the real actor and he dumps her, that was the time it became a real movie. Before that it wasn't. But the whole thing was manufactured."

Having trouble developing one particular screenplay, Allen went on an European vacation in the summer of 1988. While touring, he came upon an idea for another script. He felt his new story would meld perfectly with the unfinished one sitting back home. Throughout his travels in Europe he scribbled on various hotel stationary to draft his new script, which eventually became *Crimes and Misdemeanors*.

Allen claims people don't truly see themselves as they really are. His theme in *Crimes and Misdemeanors* is "about people who don't see. They don't see themselves as others see them. They don't see the right and wrong situations. And that was a strong metaphor in the movie."

A THINKING-MAN'S DIRECTOR

Allen is a prototype thinking man's writer, weaving several philosophical tracts throughout his movies. His films contain constant references to older classical films, especially the work of Swedish director Ingmar Bergman. Allen makes several references to Bergman, as in 1975's *Love And Death* where the ending parallels in a comic fashion Bergman's *The Seventh Seal*.

There are also elements of Bergman's 1982 *Fanny and Alexander* in Allen's *Hannah*. In both movies, large families get together for the holidays (Bergman--Christmas, Allen--Thanksgiving) for three consecutive years. Each gathering illustrates phases in the families' lives. The first holiday feast shows everyone content. The second year's gathering percolates the oncoming brewing of trouble, and the third season has those characters resolving their problems. In addition, the Bishop's ghost in *Alexander* in the closing scene is similar to Mickey's reflection seen behind Holly. And having Bergman's regular actor Max Von Sydow in *Hannah* solidifies the similarities. Von Sydow wasn't able to be in *Alexander* even though he wanted to, but his agent saw the actor's busy schedule and told Bergman his client wasn't available.

One other Bergman element Allen has adopted is hiring the Swedish director's former cinematographer Sven Nykvist for several of his productions. The collaboration began in 1989 *Crimes* and has continued on pictures such as 1988's *Another Woman*, 1989's *The New York Stories*, and 1998's *Celebrity*.

Allen has acknowledged his great admiration for Italian director Federico Fellini as well. The subliminal effect the two film directors have on Allen's body of work is palpable.

"The directors that have personal, emotional feelings for me are Bergman and Fellini, and I'm sure there has been some influence but never a direct one," Allen revealed. "I never set out to try and do anything like them. But, you know, when you listen to a jazz musician like Charlie Parker for years and you love it, then you start to play an instrument, you automatically play like that at first, then you branch off with your own things. The influence is there, it's in your blood."

Allen also has a love for old silent movies. He's always wanted to make a comedy resembling those silent classics. His original plan was to make *Sleeper* where people living in the future are banned from talking, a film essentially without dialogue. There are still many sequences in *Sleeper* where the dialogue is kept to a minimum.

Silent movies were filmed in black and white, something Allen avoided until he made *Manhattan*. He immediately loved the look of the black-and-white textures, and would revert back to the non-color film stock in 1980's *Stardust Memories, 1983's Zelig, 1984's Broadway Danny Rose*, and 1991's *Shadow and Fog*.

PRODUCTION

MOST ACTORS LOVE WORKING FOR ALLEN

Most stars have been eager to work with Allen because of his proven success in elevating their acting to Oscar-worthy levels, including Kate Blanchett, Diane Wiest (twice awarded), Michael Caine, and Diane Keaton. These actors and others credit Allen for their Oscar-winning performances. Some though have turned down his offers to be in his movies, either because of the low salaries, conflicting schedules, or his controversial past.

Allen loves to direct unknown and up-and-coming actors. In *Annie Hall*, Woody paired himself with screen rookie Sigourney Weaver, making her cinematic debut. She's his blind date towards the end of the film, appearing two years before her breakout role in *Alien*. Another obscure actor struggling with his career, despite previously appearing in seven feature films and three television series, was Jeff Goldblum, playing a party guest in *Annie* who "forgot his mantra."

Another actress who was making a name for herself at the time she appeared in an Allen film was Meryl Streep. Her role in *Manhattan* coincided with her acting in *Kramer vs. Kramer*, winner of 1979's Best Picture Academy Award as well as earning her first Oscar for Best Supporting Actress. Streep, during breaks in *Kramer* co-starring Dustin Hoffman, would run over to the *Manhattan* set to film her scenes with Woody.

Viggo Mortensen, a young actor whose career skyrocketed in the 1990s, was asked by Woody to play a small role during a Hollywood party scene in *Purple Rose*. Allen didn't give the fledgling actor any lines or instructions but asked him to make up a good joke when the cameras rolled. Mortensen felt he told a real funny one and saw out of the corner of his eye Allen laugh and seemingly enjoying the gag. When *Purple Rose* came out, he bragged to his family his appearance could be his launching pad toward a spectacular acting career. He took all his friends and family to see the movie. But during the big party scene, he wasn't in it. Allen had dropped Mortensen's line in the final edit, much to the actor's chagrin.

Actor Michael Keaton was one who would love to be in an Allen film, and he was actually in one--and then wasn't. While filming *Purple Rose*, Keaton was the lead actor for ten days. As good as Keaton was, Allen felt Keaton had too much "modernity" and didn't quite fit his period piece set in the 1930s. Jeff Daniels was then elevated to the male lead and Keaton was given his walking papers.

Some famous people have turned down offers to appear in a Woody Allen film. The scene in *Annie Hall* showing Woody and Diane Keaton waiting in line to see a movie, an egotistical college professor pontificates upon Marshall McLuhan's theory of the media. For this scene Allen originally wanted either directors Federico Fellini or Luis Bunuel to magically appear in frame to counter the blowhard's knowledge of them. They both politely declined when they were approached by Woody. He was able to hire McLuhan as the public figure who walks into frame.

DIRECTING STYLE

Unusual for a director on set, Allen offers his actors little in character background or the motivation for the people they portray.

"I love his direction style because he's a director who has confidence in his actors and who doesn't try to muscle them around the set," said Oscar winner Mira Sorvino. "He allows them to blossom and makes them take the responsibility for their performance. The thing is when you're with somebody who says it's all you now, go, it really puts the ball in your court."

"I'm very nice to all the actors, and I never raise my voice," observed Allen. "I give them a lot of freedom to work, to change my words, and they see in five minutes that I'm not a threat. That they're not gonna have to worry. They are not dealing with some kind of cult genius or some kind of formidable person. Or someone who's a temper tantrum person. You know, they see right away that this guy is going to be a pushover for me. And I am."

"My sets are boring," Allen admitted. "Nothing exciting ever happens, and I barely talk to the actors. Directing is a great loafer's job. Much less stressful than if I were running around delivering chicken sandwiches in a deli somewhere."

Even when he's acting in a scene, Woody allows his actors to release themselves in character. The lobster scene with Allen and Diane Keaton in *Annie Hall* was the first to be shot on the film's schedule. Despite their past relationship flaming out, the two former lovers were able to laugh hysterically as they chase a marine crustacean throughout the kitchen. The sequence set the pace for the remainder of the shoot where the two constantly had a tough time keeping straight faces, so breezily reflective the work environment Allen establishes throughout his shoots.

Allen gave Alan Alda total freedom to ad-lib his part in *Crimes*. Alda's only scene originally written in *Crimes* was the party scene in the opening with Daryl Hannah. While filming, the director chuckled as Alda began improvising his lines. He so much appreciated Alda's talent at spontaneously speaking on top of his head that Allen expanded the actor's role as Lester and loosely scripted his part as the shoot progressed.

Allen does have a habit when directing to withhold the completed script from all his actors, with the exception of his leads. He hands his actors with minor roles only the pages they are speaking or are being spoken to.

He admits he's not the perfectionist like some of the film directors he looks up to. He feels he doesn't come close to a Stanley Kubrick, who's known to command multiple takes that drive some actors to insanity.

"Kubrick was a great artist," Allen admitted. "I say this all the time and people think I'm being facetious. I'm not. Kubrick was a guy who obsessed over details and did 100 takes, and you know, I don't feel that way. If I'm shooting a film and it's 6 o'clock at night and I've got a take, and I think I might be able to get a better take if I stayed, but the Knicks tipoff is at 7:30, then that's it. The crews love working on my movies because they know they'll be home by 6."

Like Billy Wilder, who eschewed close-ups as much as possible, Allen also tries to avoid the standard intimate framing. He chooses to film his characters' dialogue using long stationary shots or medium-range camera placements.

From time to time Allen examines his career as a director and appreciates the wonderful things that came with the profession.

"Making films is a very nice way to make a living," he said. "You work with beautiful women, and charming men, who are amusing and gifted; you work with art directors and costume people, you travel places, and the money's good. It's a nice living."

NEW YORK LOCATION SETTINGS

One city which probably doesn't care for Allen is Piermont Village, New York, 15 miles north of New York City, where the exteriors for Purple Rose were filmed. *Purple Rose* is a period piece set in the 1930s. Piermont Village allowed Allen's film crew to alter the modern appearance of its downtown shopping area with the removal of storm windows, storefront realignments, and window displays for what was scheduled to be a ten-day shoot. The entire area was sealed off from normal shopping during the short period set for filming. But a blizzard rolled in and what was originally a brief stretch of inconvenience turned into a nearly one-month movie production episode. With their lifeblood shut off, local merchants experienced huge financial losses. After the crew had packed up and left, hired contractors were still working to normalize the town several months later.

Another film location disruptive to the hosts occurred in Mia Farrow's New York City apartment for the *Hannah and Her Sisters* shoot. Her children had to tip-toe around their "home," sidestepping the film crew and all the lights and wires around the rooms. Farrow's kids could be seen by the crew doing their homework, getting ready for bed, sitting down for breakfast, lunch and dinner. The children were also pressed into service in front of the camera, with Daisy Previn and Moses Farrow playing Hannah's son and daughter while Soon-Yi Previn and Fletcher Previn are seen as guests during the Thanksgiving scenes.

Michael Caine, who won an Oscar for Best Supporting Actor in *Hannah*, remembers Mia in the dining room feeding dinner to her kids when an assistant director stepped into the room and said she was needed in her living room for filming. Calmly, she sat down her fork and knife, got up out of her chair, walked to the next room and began acting the character of Hannah.

Once the movie hit the airwaves, Farrow recalls turning on her TV and by chance *Hannah* was on. The situation was surreal for her to see the room she was sitting in on the TV screen.

One of Allen's more famous long-shot scene was in *Manhattan* underneath the Brooklyn Bridge. Shot in the early hours of the morning, this scene required the lights on the bridge to remain on until the film crew was finished shooting. Cinematographer Gordon Willis had made sure the city would override the automatic controls for turning off the lights when the sun rose. He planned to signal to the city crew stationed at the bridge's electrical box when they had completed filming the scene. Unfortunately, just as the cameras were rolling and the sun began rising over the horizon, one side of the bridge's lights turned off. The outage didn't ruin the scene, though, since Allen was totally satisfied with that take for the final edit.

POST-PRODUCTION

EDITING CHORES

Once his films are shot, Allen enters the phase of production some directors see as reshaping their original vision. For Woody, editing is the realization he may not fulfill his intended goals.

"Editing is that moment when you give up every hope you have of making a great piece of art and you have to settle with what you have," Allen has said of the post-production process.

For *Sleeper,* Allen shot over 35 hours of footage. Condensing the movie down to a 90-minute film proved extremely difficult for Woody and his editing team. All the marketing campaigns and theater schedules were in place, yet the editors were still working on the final version as the movie's premier approached. It was a mere two days before the scheduled opening when Allen was satisfied enough with the film to release *Sleeper.*

Susan E. Morse became Allen's personal full-time film editor ever since the stressful editing of *Annie Hall.* She had been an editing assistant to Ralph Rosenblum when they were tasked to take 100,000 feet of printed footage and boil it down to roughly 90 minutes for *Annie Hall.* The initial edit, taking six weeks to cut, greatly discouraged Allen. Co-writer with Allen on *Annie Hall,* Marshall Brickman, said the first 25 minutes of the rough edit was "a disaster." But the process allowed Brickman and Allen to draw out the strengths and excise the weaknesses of their screenplay and shape the movie into a more watchable product. Susan Morse took over most of the final editing and insured herself a long working relationship with Woody on the heels of *Hall's* success.

Allen didn't struggle all that much editing the ending of *Purple Rose* even though the studio wanted him to change the conclusion. He refused. The ending, he said, was the main reason he produced the film in the first place. Allen mentioned in a later interview the finale worked because the ultimate message of *Purple Rose* is "life is ultimately disappointing."

"If my film makes one more person miserable, I'll feel I've done my job," he said sardonically.

He did listen to the studio financing *Hannah*, however, when it suggested the film would be improved with a more upbeat ending. He thought about the studio's reasoning and agreed his original downer of a conclusion was not as good as the alternative offered. Upon reflection soon after *Hannah's* release, he regretted modifying the ending. The director felt he had been too "nice" to create the happy ending, something he rectified a couple of years later in *Crimes.*

Following the screening of *Crimes*, Allen was highly suspicious of his film when several Hollywood film critics heaped praise on the picture.

"I know I must be doing something wrong if my film is being viewed in some Hollywood character's screening room and a group of people there are saying, 'It's his best film,' when many of the things I attack are what they stand for," said Allen.

Another post-production trait Allen has while scoring his films is most of his movies from *Sleeper* onward never have any original music accompanying his pictures. He either uses for his music the standards he and his New Orleans Jazz Band records or extracts musical pieces from his large personal album collection.

Allen is an expert at the clarinet which he plays along with his jazz band every Monday evening at Manhattan's Cafe Carlyle when he's healthy, not involved in a film production or during the summer and fall months, a routine he's kept up with for a number of years. His fans would love to interact with him during his public evening performances, but the Carlyle has imposed strict rules when he plays: the audience is forbidden to speak to Allen. If someone tries (he usually ignores them), that patron is automatically ejected from the premises.

WOODY'S FAMOUS RELATIONSHIPS

Allen has had some interesting romantic relationships throughout his life. His years-long affair with Diane Keaton had just ended when she appeared in her second Woody-directed film, *Sleeper*.

In a harbinger which eventually evolved into a future film idea, Allen had taken notice of 17-year-old high-schooler, Stacey Nelkin, an extra in *Annie Hall*. Her brief appearance was edited out, but Allen, 42, began seeing her and ended up having a two-year love affair with her. Inspired by Gershwin's music and his relationship with the young Stacey, Allen based *Manhattan's* main plot around an older man (him) having a relationship with a high school senior, played by Mariel Hemingway. Muriel was nominated for the Academy Award for Best Supporting Actress for her role as the adolescent Tracy.

In *Hannah*, Michael Caine is portrayed as the husband of Mia Farrow. The casting of Caine is somewhat interesting in that he was the one who introduced Allen and Farrow to each other 20 years before the film's production and remained friends with the two throughout the years. The two were in a personal relationship as early as the production of *Purple Rose*.

Allen's twelve-year relationship with Farrow, who appeared in thirteen of his films, caused Allen more negative press than he had ever imagined. The director never married Farrow but became a surrogate father to fourteen of her children, ten of them adopted. He was accused by Mia of molesting a daughter towards the end of their affair in 1992 after Allen had pressed to gain custody of four of her children. To compound matters, Allen began romantically seeing Soon-Yi, Farrow's then 20-year-old adopted daughter.

Stories abound with Frank Sinatra, former husband to Farrow, lending support to Mia during the custody battle and volunteered, if Mia gave him her approval, to hire someone to break Allen's legs.

A highly-publicized court case absolved Allen when a medical examiner and a judge ruled there was no evidence of abuse, yet the director was denied custody of any of Farrow's children. Allen subsequently married Soon-Yi in 1997 and the pair has two adopted children.

"My one regret in life is that I am not someone else," he said despondently.

ASSESSMENT ON ALLEN'S FILMS

It is remarkable in Woody's opinion that some of the work he envisions on the typewriter fail to translate perfectly on the screen. His most critically-acclaimed movie that won 1978's Academy Award Best Picture, *Annie Hall*, was somewhat of a disappointment to him. He doesn't think much of the picture as compared to other films in his body of work.

United Artists felt differently about *Annie Hall*. After seeing the great financial success of the movie, executives at United Artists told Allen's long-time producers, Charles Joffe and Jack Rollins, to relay to the director the studio's sentiments, "From now on, make whatever you want."

Besides an occasional mega-hit like *Annie Hall* and *Match Point*, Allen's films make a modest profit, but not on the blockbuster scale.

"For some reason I'm more appreciated in France than I am back home," Allen said, noting most of his films' revenues derive from Europe, especially France. "The subtitles must be incredibly good."

Besides A*nnie Hall,* another film he was more disappointed in was *Manhattan*. Claiming this was the worst movie he had ever directed, Allen told its distributor, United Artists, to please keep the picture on the shelf unseen. He offered to direct another movie for free if they did so. "I just thought to myself, 'At this point in my life, if this is the best I can do, they shouldn't give me money to make movies.'"

Manhattan turned out to be his second most financially profitable movie he's ever produced, cashing in more money than even *Annie Hall*, and was the sixth biggest box office draw in 1979. He still can't believe he "got away with it."

Allen claimed *Manhattan* is a mixture of his two previous films, *Annie Hall* and his Bermanesque *Interiors*.

The highly-regarded cinematographer Gordon Willis has a different take on *Manhattan* than its creator, claiming of all the movies he's worked on, this

Woody Allen picture is his all-time favorite. Willis worked alongside Allen through the years until 1986 when a scheduling conflict precluded him from filming *Hannah*. Carlo Di Palma stepped in as cinematographer and the two continued working together for over a decade.

On the other hand, Allen claimed *The Purple Rose of Cairo* was his most favorite film he's ever directed.

"It was the one which came closest to my original conception," said Allen. "The seduction of fantasy, as opposed to the pain of real life, is a theme that has appeared in my work time and time again. This was something I never realized. It was pointed out to me by critics and friends over a period of years."

The other films of Allen's where fantasy and real life clash include 1972's *Play It Again Sam*, *Stardust Memories*, and *Zelig*.

Allen noted "For me, success is, I'm in my bedroom at home and get an idea and I think it's a great idea and then I write it, and I look at the script and I say, 'My God, I've written a good script here'. And then I execute it. And if I execute the thing properly, then I feel great. If people come, it's a delightful bonus."

Allan cashed in on a couple of lucrative real estate transactions, which, he claims, has made more money for him personally than from all his pictures combined. A Fifth Avenue penthouse which he bought years ago for $600,000 and sold after owning it for a number of years profited Allen a cool $17 million, while a New York City townhouse he renovated sold for $7 million over his purchase price.

ALLEN STATUS AS A GREAT DIRECTOR

Director, writer, and actor Allen has been elevated to the top tier of international film directors, according to numerous polls, sharing company with Frederico Fellini, Ingmar Bergman, and Jean Luc-Godard as far as his intellectually and insightfully humorous films go.

Allen attended the Academy Awards only once and that was right after 9/11 when he encouraged film producers to support New York City and continue their production investment in the Big Apple. He has been nominated for more Academy of Motion Pictures' Best Screenplays than any other writer. Billy Wilder, who had 19 Oscar nominations for writing and directing combined, still doesn't come close to Woody's 24 nominations in the writing, and directing categories. Allen also holds the record for longevity by being the oldest Oscar winner for the Best Original Screenplay, when in 2012 he won the award for *Midnight in Paris* at 76 years old.

Allen was on a historic hot streak for his screenplays from 1977 to 1979. He earned three straight Academy Award nominations beginning with *Annie Hall* (winner), followed by 1978's *Interiors,* and 1979's *Manhattan*. The Academy gave him a respite for a few years until 1984's *Broadway Danny Rose* was nominated for its screenplay preceded by three more consecutive Oscar nominations for Allen's writing.

One of those was 1986's *Hannah and Her Sisters,* which received more Academy Award nominations than any other of his films, totaling seven. *Hannah* won three Oscars, including Michael Caine and Dianne Wiest for Best Supporting Actor and Actress, while Allen garnered an Academy statuette for Best Screenplay. Four other nominations, including Best Picture and Best Director, capped Woody's evening.

Even though most of his fans love seeing his movies over and over again, Allen has a habit of never revisiting his films once they have been released. "I think I would hate them," he said. Allen describes the process of creating and directing where he actually derives his real joy in cinema. "Most of the time I don't have much fun," Allen related. "The rest of the time I don't have any fun at all."

He did elaborate on why he hasn't watched any of his films after their theatrical premier.

"I never see a frame of anything I've done after I've done it," he admits. "I don't even remember what's in the films. And if I'm on the treadmill and I'm surfing the channels and suddenly *Manhattan* or some other picture comes on, I go right past it. If I saw *Manhattan* again, I would only see the worst. I would say, 'Oh, God, this is so embarrassing. I could have done this. I should have done that.' So I spare myself."

Ironically he takes special interest with the integrity of his past films. Allen has in his contract to never allow television networks or airlines to edit his movies to fit a certain time limitation or to excise a racy scene.

Allen also has a clause in all his contracts that the titles of his films cannot be changed once released, including outside the United States. He had taken this action after *Sleeper* was changed by the French Canadians showing the movie in their French-speaking provinces to *Woody and the Robots*.

Allen has had a tough time naming his own movies while they are in the writing stage. His original title for *Annie Hall* was *Anhedonia*, which means the incapacity to feel pleasure. The studio producing the film, United Artists, was totally against using the name even though its marketers tried to work the title into a proposed ad campaign, a mind-bending effort on the studio's part to define the phobia. The director toyed with other titles for the same movie, including *Me and My Goy, A Rollercoaster Named Desire,* and *It Had To Be A*

Jew. Three weeks from *Annie Hall's* premier, Allen settled on the name of the main female character for the picture's title.

"I do the movies just for myself like an institutionalized person who basket-weaves," admitted Allen. "Busy fingers are happy fingers. I don't care about the films. I don't care if they're flushed down the toilet after I die."

He knows his constant writing and directing activity keeps him satisfied with his life.

"I'm trying to figure out what it is I'm supposed to be doing to enjoy myself and unwind, having finished a project," Allen says. "I hold off for a day or two, go for a walk and very quickly I can't stand it. I get into writing another script again, which I love doing."

Allen foresees the day where there may be a possibility his directing career will come to an end, like most other very successful film directors who saw their value not appreciated anymore.

"If they said to me tomorrow, 'We're pulling the plug and we're not giving you any more money to make films,' that would not bother me in the slightest." he felt. "I mean, I'm happy to write for the theatre. And if they wouldn't back any of my plays, I'm happy to sit home and write prose. But as long as there are people willing to put up the vast sums of money needed to make films, I should take advantage of it. Because there will come a time when they won't."

Allen anticipates the day when he will eventually die. The film director's death wish is, "I have one last request. Don't use embalming fluid on me; I want to be stuffed with crab meat."

"I don't want to achieve immortality through my work. I want to achieve it by not dying," noted Woody

Allen said in 2005, "I'm kind of, secretly, in the back of my mind, counting on living a long time. My father lived to 100. My mother lived to 95, almost 96. If there is anything to heredity, I should be able to make films for another 17 years. You never know. A piano could drop on my head."

TOP 10 WOODY ALLEN FILMS

#1--ANNIE HALL (1977)

No one can argue with film critic Roger Ebert that *Annie Hall* is "just about everyone's favorite Woody Allen movie." The movie marked a critical turning point from Allen's previous pure-comedy films where the yucks outweighed his occasional philosophical tracts. Some lamented the pivot, but others have lauded the shift to the deeply intellectual and philosophical direction.

#2--THE PURPLE ROSE OF CAIRO (1985)

Woody Allen said he considers this one of his most successful films in terms of what he originally had in mind when writing its script to what was ultimately released to the general public. Anyone who loves cinema will instantly relate to Mia Farrow's character. Wrote Vincent Canby of the New York Times at the time," I'll go out on a limb: I can't believe the year will bring forth anything to equal The Purple Rose of Cairo. At 84 minutes, it's short but nearly every one of those minutes is blissful."

#3--SLEEPER (1973)

Considered by film critics as the best of his pre-*Annie Hall* comedies. This lightly entertaining look into the future contains elements of old fashion slapstick with farcical situations. Roger Ebert aptly described *Sleeper* as Allen "giving us moments in Sleeper that are as good as anything since the silent films of Buster Keaton."

#4--HANNAH AND HER SISTERS (1986)

Three sisters lead very interesting lives involving an extended family caught in dramatical situations which are farcical yet touching. Containing Bergmanesque elements as well as drawing parallels to the 1960 Italian classic *Rocco and His Brothers*, this Academy Awards Best Picture nominee, and the one that earned Oscars for Michael Caine and Dianne Wiest, was cited by the late Roger Ebert as "the best movie Woody Allen has ever made."

#5--CRIMES AND MISDEMEANORS (1989)

One of Allen's deeper films, the writer/director confronts our mortality with a great dose of humor that makes the unavoidable tolerable. "The chief strength of the movie is its courage in confronting grave and painful questions of the kind the American cinema has been doing its damnedest to avoid," wrote John Simon.

#6--MANHATTAN (1979)

The follow-up to *Annie Hall,* this picture is highly regarded as one of Allen's top films. The subject matter is somewhat creepy, however, knowing the storyline of an older TV writer played by Woody is having an affair with a young high schooler paralleled the director's real life. *Manhattan* is one of the most gorgeously black-and-white photographed movies of all-time. Jack Kroll of Newsweek wrote, "Allen's growth in every department is lovely to behold. He gets excellent performances from his cast. The increasing visual beauty of his films is part of their grace and sweetness, their balance between Allen's yearning romanticism and his tough eye for the fatuous and sentimental – a balance also expressed in his best screenplay yet."

#7--LOVE AND DEATH (1975)

If you want to get a glimpse on how cinema "auteur" film directors have inspired Allen over the years, this film clearly displays all the movies he has thought highly. Love and Death showcases the works of Bergman, Sergei Eisenstein, the Marx Brothers, and Charlie Chaplin with humorous clarity. He also pays homage to Leo Tolstoy and Fyodor Dostoyevsky to the themes and situations portrayed here. Woody had labeled this movie as the funniest he had made up to this point in his career.

#8--BLUE JASMINE (2013)

Cate Blanchett, in her Oscar Best Actress winning role as a socialite wife, whose husband (think of swindler Bernie Madoff) had killed himself in prison, finds herself living life as a "normal" person. Critic Mike LaSalle wrote, "Blanchett in Blue Jasmine is beyond brilliant, beyond analysis. This is jaw-dropping work, what we go to the movies hoping to see, and we do. Every few years."

#9--ZELIG (1983)

In this docucomedy, a comedy posing as a documentary, Allen pushes the boundaries of early 1980s cinematic computer technology to portray himself as a celebrity in the 1920s. "We are infinitely pliable," wrote Calum Marsh in his review of *Zelig*. "That's the thesis of *Zelig*, Allen's wisest film, which has much to say about the way a person can be bent and contorted in the name of acceptance. Its ostensibly wacky conceit is grounded in an emotional and psychological reality all too familiar to shrug off as farce. We'll go very far out of our way to avoid conflict. *Zelig* seizes on that weakness and forces us to recognize it."

#10--EVERYTHING YOU WANTED TO KNOW ABOUT SEX (BUT WERE AFRAID TO ASK) (1972)

The final skit where Woody is part of the sperm team ready to go into a new world is worth the high ranking Top Ten alone. Probably one of the most brilliant sketches Allen has ever written. Seven episodes make up this film and it poses in Episode One the question everyone to this day asks, "Are Transvestites Homosexuals?" Critic Christopher Null said this is a "minor classic and Woody Allen's most absurd film ever."

Martin Scorsese

THE GENIUS WHO REINVENTED CRIME MOVIES

The scene is a reoccurring image in Martin Scorsese films: a teenager looks outside his window at the hustle and bustle in the city streets and sidewalks. This motif opens his 1990 *Goodfellas* and is repeated by the boy in Scorsese's 2011 *Hugo* as he peers out the clock window.

The future film director, suffering from extreme asthma as a child, was restricted from mingling with other boys in the tough neighborhood of Little Italy in New York City.

"I didn't go out of the house very much," recalls Scorsese. "I looked out the window and could see kids running down the street playing with garbage pails."

The young Scorsese absorbed the stories of his father and the immediate neighboring thugs and the criminal elements thriving in the area. He would apply those tales with their colorful characters to serve as templates in his films later on, giving us an unforgettable portrayal of the blue-collar mobsters applying their trade in the boroughs of New York City, images which ultimately reshaped cinema's modern gangster films.

Like Woody Allen, his upbringing in New York City was unforgettable and instilled a love for the city he was raised. Scorsese, who hates to fly, still lives in New York City and is constantly busy even when he's not directing or editing in his production suite on West 57 Street in Manhattan.

"Every time I get on an airplane, I know I'm not really an atheist," admits Scorsese. "'Oh God, dear God,' I say the minute the plane takes off. 'I'm sorry for all my sins, please don't let this plane crash.' And I keep praying out loud until the plane lands."

LOVE FOR MOVIES

Fortunately for the young Scorsese, his home was surrounded by numerous movie theaters which in the 1950's showed a wide variety of films, including biblical spectaculars of Hollywood, Italian Neo-realism, French New Wave, popular comedies, westerns and dramas. Not being able to play outside, viewing movies was Scorsese's one main avenue of entertainment open to him.

"There's no way I can compare a movie of mine to the films that formed me," said Scorsese on the movies he had seen growing up serving as lifelong inspirations.

Scorsese loved the cinema so much that in 1956 on the day he graduated from Parochial school he spent the afternoon watching John Ford's *The Searchers*.

SCORSESE'S CATHOLICISM

Paradoxically, viewing his films loaded with all sorts of violence, it is hard to believe Scorsese's young ambitions were geared toward Catholic priesthood.

"When I was a teenager," says Scorsese, "I really thought that that was what I was going to do in life--be a priest."

As a Catholic growing up, Scorsese was an altar boy serving at the Old St. Patrick's Cathedral, where years later, Francis Ford Coppola used the church as a backdrop for the baptism scene in 1972's *The Godfather*. The church experience served him later in life as he incorporated into his scripts religious feelings conflicting his main protagonists in 1967's *Who's That Knocking at My Door* and his breakout 1973 film *Mean Streets*.

A fact especially striking in his movies coming from a director with a strong religious background is the amazingly large amount of profane words said by his characters. Two of his films have established records for the number of "F-bombs," with 1995's *Casino* setting the record only to be beaten by 2013's *The Wolf of Wall Street* clocking in at an astonishing 569 times.

In most cases, his films conclude with his main characters and their associates meeting a deadly end. During the course of his movies, though, Scorsese's unsavory characters spend most of their time lavishing themselves with dazzling lifestyles most conscientious viewers would envy. The director draws upon the constant irony portraying the glamorous joyrides experienced by these immoral thugs, a lifestyle normally denied to them if they led decent, honest-working lives.

"I'm a lapsed Catholic," remarked Scorsese. "But I am Roman Catholic - there's no way out."

Despite going to seminary school for a year before being kicked out for bad grades, Scorsese harbored an ambition to graduate from New York University and then study for priesthood. However, the movie bug infected him during his time at NYU and he went on to earn his Masters in Film at the university.

"As a film student in New York in the early 60s, I was fortunate to be exposed to foreign and American classics as well as B-movies," remembered

Scorsese. "I saw film as a learning process, a cross-cultural language that brought people together to share a common experience. I'm still a film student. If I'm not out making films, I'm watching them over and over, painfully aware of how much there is to learn. It would be a shame if future generations did not have the same chance."

While hired as a part-time instructor for NYU teaching the likes of Oliver Stone and Spike Lee, Scorsese produced a graduate film, *Who's Knocking at My Door?* drawing the attention of a few Hollywood movie producers. He was hired to direct a low-budget movie for producer Roger Corman, 1972's *Boxcar Bertha.*

One of the veteran film directors Scorsese knew at NYU was independent director John Cassavetes. When Cassavetes saw *Boxcar Bertha,* he hated it. Cassavetes contacted Scorsese and said "You've just spent a year of your life making a piece of crap." Cassavetes loved *Who's Knocking* and advised him he should stick to something he knew about. The young director reflected on the candid assessment and set off to compose a screenplay based on his personal experiences as a boy in New York City's Little Italy, which eventually emerged as *Mean Streets*.

MEAN STREETS

Film critic Roger Ebert said "In countless ways, right down to the detail of modern TV crime shows, *Mean Streets* is one of the source points of modern movies."

Mean Streets would serve as a template for Scorsese's crime films such as *Goodfellas* and *Casino* where common street criminals are spotlighted as contrasted to those seen in Coppola's *The Godfather,* where the top echelon of the mobster world is shown.

In his crime films one or more of his characters always emerge as unpredictable or possess no conscience. Their violence is directed both inside the gang they're members of as well as outside the syndicate. Actor Joe Pesci's portrayals in several gangster roles serve as a perfect example of these traits.

"I was so pleased when Warner Brothers bought it because they had all the best gangster films," recalled Scorsese on his first personal film, *Mean Streets,* being produced by Warner Brothers Studio.

FILMS ABOUT PEOPLE YOU DON'T WANT TO KNOW

A quick examination at Scorsese's filmography highlights a few biopics of some truly real life disturbed personalities. Film critic Joseph McBride remarked Scorsese "makes pictures about the kind of people you wouldn't want to know."

1975's *Taxi Driver,* loosely-based on Arthur Bremer, who tried to kill presidential candidate George Wallace; 1980's *Raging Bull* (Middleweight Champion boxer Jack LaMotta); and *The Wolf of Wall Street* (swindler Jordan Belfort) are among those shady characters who, in the Scorsese portrayals, continue their lives well after their mendacious careers have peaked. Scorsese, however, doesn't draw to any conclusions and allows viewers to make up their own minds on how these characters continue to live.

Besides crime movies, Scorsese's body of work covers a wide-range of categories, from musicals to historical period films. He's commonly known as the "gangster director" who appears to be fixated on the criminal world. But the illusions are deceptive. Out of more than 50 films he's directed, only five fit into the crime category. The five, *Mean Streets, Goodfellas, Casino,* 2002's *Gangs of New York,* and 2005's *The Departed,* deal with the mob. He has admittedly made some racy films with some undesirable characters, such as *The Wolf of Wall Street,* but he's also produced one family film, *Hugo,* a movie he wanted to make so his daughter would be able to watch at least one of his pictures before she grew up.

SCORSESE IN FRONT OF THE CAMERA

Scorsese has been seen acting in some of his movies. In one instance, the last thing Scorsese wanted to play was a deviate who is about to kill his cheating wife in *Taxi Driver.* But the director was forced to fill in for the original actor who was unable to act as the creep because he was so sick. In his opinion, no one else was qualified enough to play the character on such a short notice, so, even though he claims he's very uneasy acting before the camera, he stepped in front and acted the scene.

"A friend of mine sent me that line: 'All this filming isn't healthy' on a note when we were making *Raging Bull,"* remembers Scorsese. "I think it was one of the cinematographers who had just seen *Peeping Tom.* And there is no doubt that filmmaking is aggressive and it could be something that is not very healthy. When you make a film, there are times in your life when you're burning with a passion and it's very, very strong. It's almost like a pathology of cinema where you want to possess the people on film. You want to live through them. You want to possess their spirits, their souls, in a way. And ultimately you can't stop. It has to be done until you get to the bitter end. You're exhausted. In some cases friends might have died, in some cases they don't come back, in some cases they can't make another picture. The only thing to do is try to make another picture. It's got to be done again. Now, I don't mean to sound dramatic, a lot of great films are made that way. And we might not only be talking about cinema here. We could be talking about other things, too. I would think that it might apply to other art forms. But I must say, that with that passion and that power, there is pathology in wanting to live vicariously through the people."

DE NIRO IN SCORSESE'S FILMS

The stark realism in a Scorsese film is reflected in how he directs. Relying on a staple of regular actors such as Robert De Niro, Joe Pesci and Leonardo DiCaprio, Scorsese's philosophy on directing is "more than 90 percent of directing is getting the right casting."

The one actor Scorsese is mostly identified with is De Niro, who has collaborated with Scorsese eight times, starting in their first film together 1973's *Mean Streets.* Even in productions where De Niro isn't being considered, Scorsese runs by the actor for his advice every screenplay he is about to direct. In the Scorsese films De Niro has appeared, the pair seemingly understand one another without having much of a conversation about a particular scene.

"And even now I still know of nobody who can surprise me on the screen the way he does -- and did then," praised Scorsese on De Niro. "No actor comes to mind who can provide such power and excitement."

Of all the movies De Niro has been in under Scorsese's direction, 1982's *The King of Comedy* is, in the director's opinion, the actor's best performance.

"I've come to know De Niro fairly well down the years," admitted Scorsese. "He's a very compassionate man. He's basically a very good man and you can see that in him. So he can take on characters that are pretty disturbing and make them human because of that compassion. It's taken me years to figure it out. He has an ability to make audiences feel empathy for very difficult characters because there is something very decent in him."

Film critics acknowledge De Niro brings to the set an intensity unlike no other actor. In *Mean Streets,* he plays the unstable Johnny Boy. Whenever De Niro and Richard Romanus, playing a loan shark who looks to settle some debts Johnny Boy owes him, were in the same scenes the two actors would bicker constantly on the set, even out of character. The scene where Johnny Boy pulls a gun after Romanus lunges at him shows De Niro verbally ripping into him. "I kept shooting take after take of Bobby yelling these insults, while the crew was getting very upset," remembered Scorsese. "The animosity between them in that scene was real, and I played on it."

De Niro is a "method actor," where an actor absorbs his character by literally living like the person during the course of the movie's production. In preparation for *Taxi Driver,* De Niro spent one month fifteen hours a day driving a cab in New York City. Since he was playing a depressed ex-Marine in the film, he researched mental illness. Even though De Niro had just won the Academy Awards for Best Supporting Actor in 1974's *Godfather: Part Two* shortly before taking the wheel of a cab, the actor said he was recognized only once while driving the city streets.

In a more demanding role, playing prize fighter Jake LaMotta in *Raging Bull,* De Niro took his part to the extreme. Well before the cameras rolled, the actor dragged himself through numerous punishing physical training sessions getting into tip-top shape and learning how to box. He sparred with LaMotta and others in over one thousand rounds of boxing. He signed up for three boxing matches in Brooklyn and remarkably won two of them. LaMotta later said De Niro could have been an authentic boxing professional, even a contender for a title, if he taken up the sport earlier in life.

The weight De Niro gained making *Raging Bull* was one for the record books. The script called for a lean LaMotta while he was boxing in the ring. In the later portions of the film the ex-boxer was portrayed to being much heavier. The scenes where De Niro as LaMotta is a boxer take up a better part of the movie and were shot first. For the heavier scenes, De Niro, the consummate method actor, chose instead of applying special artificial body prosthetics and makeup, personally to gain 60 pounds to show the contrast between the fit boxer and the older slothful night-club entertainer. Filming ceased after the boxing phase for the next several months while De Niro stuffed his face. The actor took a trip to Europe and ate the biggest pasta dishes he could find. He would then fire down vanilla milkshakes right before sleeping at night. Once De Niro bulked up, filming resumed, but only on a limited time schedule and acting for a minimum number of takes since the access weight thoroughly exhausted the fat actor pretty quickly.

De Niro's weight gain was a record until Vincent D'Onofrio put on 70 extra pounds in preparation for his character of a U.S. Marine in 1987's *Full Metal Jacket* (see the Stanley Kubrick section).

In *Raging Bull,* De Niro and Joe Pesci are brothers who end up having a contentious sibling relationship. De Niro and Scorsese first saw struggling actor Pesci in a low-budget film produced a couple of years earlier and felt he would be perfect for Jake's brother. De Niro proposed the two live together to form a brotherly bond as well as train in the ring before the production began. Filming the sequence where De Niro orders Pesci to hit him, Pesci didn't pull back on his punches; he really did hit De Niro. In the sparring scene, De Niro actually broke some of Pesci's ribs, accidentally of course. The footage ended up being used showing Pesci groaning after a punch, followed by a quick cut of the two sparring from another camera angle. Since the movie's release the two have remained close friends.

When Scorsese read Paul Zimmerman's script titled *The King of Comedy* about a frustrated comedian who wants to quickly reach the big time, the director immediately bought the screenplay, seeing the story's understated ambiguity between reality and fantasy existing in people's minds.

"*The King of Comedy* is my coming to terms with disappointment, disappointment with the fact that the reality is different from the dream," pointed out Scorsese.

The director also saw the script as "just a one-line gag: You won't let me go on the show, so I'll kidnap you and you'll put me on the show."

When time came to cast the role of Jerry Langford, portrayed in the movie as a Johnny Carson-type hosting a late-night TV talk show, Scorsese focused on Jerry Lewis. De Niro was hesitant to agree on Scorsese's selection, and in fact wrote a letter to the director stating his negative opinion. De Niro remembered the days when Lewis was paired with Dean Martin as well as the type of goofy characters he played in films after the separation. He thought Lewis' past on-screen persona wouldn't fit the *King's* written character who had to emote distress and uneasiness in a subtle way. Once the movie came out and critics lauded Lewis' performance, De Niro had to admit he was wrong and Scorsese was right in selecting the comedian. De Niro had personally seen Lewis on the movie set act with restraint and had reigned in considerably his previously demonstrative on-screen personality.

De Niro was obsessed by details of the characters he was playing during the preparation of his role as Jimmy Conway in *Goodfellas*. The real-life Henry Hill, a central figure portrayed in the film, said the actor would call him several times a day and ask how Jimmy, Hill's associate, would do things, like how would he hold his cigarette, how would he walk, and how would he pour ketchup on his meals.

PRE-PRODUCTION

SCORSESE THE SCRIPTWRITER

Scorsese didn't write all the screenplays he has directed, but he has composed a few. He co-wrote *Mean Streets,* titling the rough script *Season of the Witch,* named after Donovan's 1966 song. Film critic Jay Cocks was a big fan of detective fiction writer Raymond Chandler and remembered the line "Down these mean streets a man must go." He suggested to Scorsese "mean streets" would be a great name for his new film. Initially Scorsese thought the title was a bit too showy and highbrow to portray what he was trying to convey in the movie. But as time went on he concurred the title *Mean Streets* was the perfect one.

Scorsese inserted memories of his upbringing into what critics label his most personal film, *Mean Streets.* In fact, he and his co-writer, Mardik Martin, were inspired by the events portrayed in the screenplay by driving around New York City's Little Italy and composed the script in Scorsese's car.

One of more obnoxious characters in *Mean Streets* is Johnny Boy, played by De Niro. Scorsese remembers his uncle on his father's side, Joe the Bug, who was constantly in trouble with the police. De Niro fell into the role when actor Harvey Keitel was hired for the project. Both read the screenplay. De Niro was offered to play any of the four roles in the script. Keitel convinced De Niro he would be perfect for the character Johnny Boy.

While *Taxi Driver* was in pre-production, Columbia Studios, a bit timid about the subject matter, gave Scorsese a limited budget of $1.8 million to produce the movie, a low figure in anybody's book. De Niro had agreed with everyone else, including actress Cybill Shepherd and screenplay writer Paul Schrader, in order to keep the budget within reason he would sign for a paltry $35,000 (Scorsese was paid $65,000 to direct). Soon after signing the contract, De Niro earned the Oscar for his *Godfather* role and was commanding $500,000 to act in other films. Such a salary would have broken the bank and left little remaining for expenses to make *Taxi.* Once De Niro heard of Scorsese's dilemma the actor said he would honor the original contract, much to the director's relief. The salaries for all the actors tabulated less than $200,000.

When *Mean Streets* is mentioned, viewers think the film was filmed totally in New York City. Yet Scorsese's budget precluded shooting the entire production in New York because the film crew, members of the Teamsters Union in the Big Apple, was charging so much more than those union members in Los Angeles. Because of the expense Scorsese spent only six days in New York filming mostly exteriors. The production was pretty much made on-the-run when they were shooting in New York since he hired non-union workers and had to avoid the Teamsters.

The majority of the *Taxi* shoot, 27 days, took place inside Los Angeles studios, including the pool hall sequence.

"When I went to Hollywood in the '70s, what I saw of the old Hollywood was dying away," remembers Scorsese.

"What does it take to be a filmmaker in Hollywood?" said Scorsese, recalling those days when he had to scurry for the almighty dollar to make a movie. "Even today I still wonder what it takes to be a professional or even an artist in Hollywood. How do you survive the constant tug of war between personal expression and commercial imperatives? What is the price you pay to work in Hollywood? Do you end up with a split personality? Do you make one movie for them, one for yourself?"

Scorsese and De Niro were attracted by the Paul Schrader *Taxi* script. His screenplay reflected the turmoil and isolation Schrader was experiencing at the time he composed the screenplay, having gone through a recent divorce and shortly afterward a break-up with his girlfriend. Staying at the ex-girlfriend's apartment when he was homeless and unemployed and she was away for several weeks, Schrader found the process of writing cathartic for him. He began writing about loneliness, but as the composition progressed he discovered he was actually addressing the "pathology of loneliness." His script follows cab driver Travis Bickle, who, as Schrader began to realize, is similar to people suffering from extreme loneliness subconsciously. They reject others in order to maintain that isolation. But the cycle is vicious because the primary reason they are tormented is because they are alone.

Scorsese picked up on the isolation theme while directing *Taxi* and placed the camera angles in one particularly poignant scene to emphasize Bickle's loneliness. De Niro, playing Bickle, is on the hallway phone next to his apartment asking Betsy (Cybill Shepherd) for another chance to date. Betsy felt he was a creep on their first date and discouraged any further contact. The pathos Bickle feels, almost too unbearable to witness, is seen when the camera dollies to the side and then pans down the long, empty hallway he's standing in. Scorsese said the sequence was the most important one in *Taxi*.

Scorsese plotted out the entire film's camera movements without Schrader's script suggestions, save for one, which appears right after the dramatic shoot-out toward the end of the movie. The script called for an overhead tracking shot showing the aftermath of the shooting, which Scorsese filmed exactly as Schrader called for.

What is also so unusual about the Schrader script is Hollywood studios commonly rework purchased scripts several times before being approved for filming. Schrader's original screenplay on *Taxi* is pretty much what the final movie turned out to be. Scorsese had his actors improvise the dialogue throughout filming, but the main script is largely followed.

Scorsese called *Taxi* after its release as "my feminist film because it takes macho to its logical conclusion. The better man is the man who can kill you.

This film shows that kind of thinking, shows the kinds of problems some men have, bouncing back and forth between on their perception of women as goddesses and whores."

SCORSESE'S DEEP DEPRESSION

After his 1977 musical *New York, New York* received bad reviews and lackluster box office receipts, Scorsese went into a deep depression. He developed a cocaine habit which eventually sent him into the hospital.

"There are two kinds of power you have to fight," said Scorsese on his personal difficulties brought upon himself. "The first is the money, and that's just our system. The other is the people close around you, knowing when to accept their criticism, knowing when to say no. I was never interested in the accumulation of money, you know. And I never had a mind for business. There have been serious issues with money over the years. I have a nice house now, in New York. But there have been major, major issues. In the mid-'80s it was pathetic, I mean, my father would help me out. I couldn't go out, I couldn't buy anything. But it's all my own doing."

Earlier, De Niro was acting in 1974's *The Godfather: Part Two* when he picked up a book by boxer Jake LaMotta titled *Raging Bull: My Story*. He thought it would be a great idea for a movie, especially for his friend Martin to direct. He approached Scorsese about the possibility while the director was making *Alice Doesn't Live Here Anymore*. No way, said Scorsese, citing his lack of interest in sports movies.

"Robert De Niro wanted to make this film," reflected Scorsese. "Not me. I don't understand anything about boxing. For me, it's like a physical game of chess."

Not to be discouraged, several years later De Niro brought the memoir again to Scorsese, who was lying in the hospital from the effects of cocaine addiction, and proposed the project. De Niro kept pressing the director after he was released from the hospital. Scorsese caved and ultimately produced what is regarded as one of the best sports movies of all time. The director said De Niro helped him break his drug habit and lifted him from the depths of his depression by getting him back on the movie set.

One of the producers interested in *Raging Bull* was appalled by the portrayal of LaMotta while reading the original script, describing the boxer as written as "a cockroach." Scorsese and De Niro traveled to Italy to rewrite the screenplay to cast some positive light on LaMotta's behavior and personality. The rewrite proved to be the winner, bringing on board several interested producers.

During pre-production of *Raging Bull,* Scorsese focused on the passage of LaMotta's book where the boxer wrote, "Now, sometimes, at night, when I think back, I feel like I'm looking at an old black and white movie of myself. Why it should be black and white I don't know, but it is." The director used that passage to justify filming the movie in black and white as a departure from the 1976 Academy Award Best Picture, *Rocky.* Scorsese also wanted to show the film took place in the late 1940s and 1950s when boxing was a mainstay of early television. After his experience in trying to get the final, bloody shootout in *Taxi* accepted by the studios, he decided because of all the blood flowing during the boxing match there was no way he could film the brutality in the ring conveyed in color. Pounds of Hershey's chocolate syrup were poured in place of real blood during the making of *Raging's* gory scenes since the liquid would be more visible in the black-and-white film than red coloring.

MAPPING OUT A MOVIE

Scorsese arrives on a film set with a prepared series of shots. "Planning is always the hardest part of the writing of a film--figuring out what shots you're going to use," said Scorsese. In the planning stages of *Raging Bull,* Scorsese eschewed the normal filming of a boxing match which position several cameras outside the rink. He chose instead to have the punching scenes filmed with just one camera, a "third fighter' he labeled the camera, in the ring. He spent months in meticulous planning the proposed shots of each fight and the positioning of the camera. In the final release, the fighting scenes consist of a mere 10 minutes.

The movie's narrative follows the disintegrating personal life of LaMotta as well as his diminishing skills as a boxer. To portray his decline between the ropes in the later scenes of his boxing career, Scorsese constructed a larger ring to reflect LaMotta's lack of dominance while fighting.

The highlight of the movie is the final fight between LaMotta and Sugar Ray Robinson showing the Bull getting his brains pounded when he's against the ropes. Scorsese had a difficult time plotting the sequences to this brutal battle. He remembered the shower scene in Alfred Hitchcock's *Psycho* where Janet Leigh gets knifed to death. He saw striking similarities between LaMotta's final bloody fight and the gruesome shower scene. Scorsese obtained Hitchcock's shot-list of the famous shower sequence and then based his *Raging* shots on the master of thrillers' filming selection.

Scorsese claims through his movies he discovers a little bit of himself. "Well, I think in my own work the subject matter usually deals with characters I know, aspects of myself, friends of mine - that sort of thing," he said. "And we try to work it out. By 'work it out' I mean almost like 'work it through your system.' Particularly, I think, on films like *Mean Streets* or *Taxi Driver* from Paul Schrader's script. And *Raging Bull,* especially. At the end of that film, Robert De Niro was fine, but me - I left Jake LaMotta's character more at peace with himself than I was with myself. And I was hoping to get to that moment that he was at the end of the film. That moment where he's looking at himself in the mirror. I was hoping to get there myself. But I hadn't made it. So it's a matter of living through the cinema I think."

Scorsese said after *Mean Streets* he would never make another gangster film. But years later he became hooked on Nicholas Pileggi's book *Wiseguy,* the true story of a New York City boy, Henry Hill, who gets caught up with the Mob and ends up ratting on its members. Spontaneously, he called the author and said, "I've been waiting for this book my entire life." Impressed by Scorsese's resume, Pileggi replied, "I've been waiting for this phone call my entire life."

Scorsese decided to work alongside the author to develop a screenplay. They initially wrote an outline separately on how they envisioned the movie. When it came time to compare notes, they saw their outlines were very similar. They then began writing a detailed script together, a laborious months-long process. The two produced twelve drafts before they felt they had developed a perfect screenplay. During the course of writing the numerous drafts, they picked sections of the book they thought would work visually for a movie. Discarding the chronological order of the book, Scorsese convinced Pileggi the narrative should begin in the middle and then retract before thrusting forward. By doing this Scorsese hoped "the impact after about an hour and a half would be terrific."

The blueprint for beginning *Raging, Casino* and *Wolf* in the middle or at the end of the plots is consistent with the opening of *Goodfellas,* where the narrative picks up in the story's midpoint.

There was trepidation in giving Joe Pesci the role of the real Tommy DeSimone, who was much larger and more muscular than the actor. But Henry Hill after seeing the movie said Pesci nailed the character, portraying him as being 99 percent accurate.

One of the more unusual casting selections in *Goodfellas* was how Scorsese chose the actor for the lead role Henry Hill. Ray Liotta, who eventually was awarded the part, auditioned several times over the course of a year but was left hanging by the director and the casting supervisor when he attended the Venice Film Festival. Scorsese, also attending the film festival, was surrounded by personal bodyguards because of the controversy surrounding his recently released film, 1988's *The Last Temptation of Christ*. Several people wanted to talk with the director, including Liotta, who spotted Scorsese out in public. There was a lot of pushing and shoving by both sides, except for Liotta, who stood calmly to the side hoping to get a word in to Scorsese. The director looked at all the chaos and saw the non plussed Liotta. Scorsese instantly recognized the actor and knew right there Liotta would get the role of Henry Hill, who in the script is a calming influence to his out-of-control mob associates.

Unusual for many directors, Scorsese films contain an inordinate amount of off-screen narration voiced by the main characters. In particular, *Mean Streets, Taxi, Goodfellas, Casino,* 1999's *Bringing Out The Dead, The Departed, Hugo,* and *Wolf* all contain heavy doses of voice-overs. Scorsese claims to have been inspired by the French New Wave director Francois Truffaut 1962 film *Jules and Jim's* use of the voice-over.

ANOTHER COLLABORATION WITH PILEGGI

Pileggi, while assisting on writing the script of *Goodfellas,* read the story of a skimming operation in a Las Vegas casino. Pileggi wanted to write a book based on the operation, but Scorsese convinced the writer that both should collaborate on the screenplay first and then Pileggi could write an accompanying novel.

Scorsese said of the script, "There's no plot at all. It's three hours, no plot. So you know this going in. There's a lot of action, a lot of story, but no plot."

Scorsese wanted to keep the story, whatever plot there was, somewhat fictional, even though *Casino* was based on an actual event. One example is the screenplay names the casino where the criminals operate in as The Tangiers. The actual scandal happened at the Stardust Resort and Casino, which, although unsaid in the film, is alluded to three times in the musical soundtrack. The song "Stardust" is heard during the Ace/Ginger wedding, and then when Remo is questioning Marino in the Nicky/Ginger relationship scene, and finally during the end credits.

In composing the screenplay for *Casino,* Pileggi and Scorsese consulted with recently-paroled convicts who had been arrested by the FBI for their crimes in Vegas casinos. The two found the parolees were extremely hesitant to reveal how they cheated the casinos out of millions. The parolees and the FBI special agents, however, were open about other aspects of the gambling underwood, details the writers included in their screenplay.

Scriptwriters for ultra-violent movies compose so-called "sacrificial" scenes which are inserted in the context of their screenplays. They write these over-the-top scenes so the MPAA ratings board will demand the studios cut them, threatening the dreaded "X" rating would be attached to the film if they don't. Writers consider these to be throwaway sequences, creating a diversion to other, slightly less violent ones but more significant to the storyline.

In *Casino,* one "sacrificial" sequence is the "head in the vise" scene. There was no way the MPAA would ever let the scene pass, thought Scorsese. But much to the director's surprise, the board had no objection to the sequence. Actually, the only country insisting the scene be cut before the movie could be shown was Sweden.

The sequence emphasizes the Joe Pesci character, Nicky Santoro, and his gang's brutality against anyone getting in their way. Scorsese based the vice-squeezing torture scene on a true incident where an enforcer, Tony Spilotro, wanted to get information from Billy McCarthy, who had helped kill a pair of brothers in Spilotro's associated mob. Spilotro wanted to know who assisted McCarthy in the killings, but the gangster refused to reveal any information. First Spilotro's gang physically punched and kicked McCarthy. No information was given. They then took an icepick and pierced his groin. Still no talking. Amazingly, they put McCarthy's head in a vice and tightened it so much his skull, cracking, narrowed to just five inches wide. McCarthy, able to talk, still didn't reveal the name. Another twist of the handle of the vice popped one of McCarthy's eyes out of his socket. Under such torture, McCarthy finally revealed his partner's name. In the end, McCarthy survived the process, only to be soaked with lighter fluid and set on fire.

"Billy McCarthy was the toughest guy I ever met," complemented Spilotro. Scorsese duplicated the tale with all its gory details in *Casino.*

PREPARING FOR HIS PRODUCTIONS

Scorsese's reputation for producing some of cinema's highest quality movies has almost everyone in Hollywood knocking on his door wanting to be involved in his upcoming projects. In the initial phase of selecting the cast for *Casino,* the director looked for someone to play Lester Diamond, Sharon Stone's pimp in the movie. Actor James Woods heard about the role and felt the role would be ideal for him. Woods got wind Scorsese was looking at his resume and the actor called the director's office, leaving a message on his answering machine, "Any time, any place, any part, any fee."

Sharon Stone was equally enthusiastic about the possibility of working with Scorsese as well as the actor she most admired, De Niro. She once revealed to her acting coach, "I want to be good enough to work with Robert De Niro."

To fulfill her wish, her agent arranged the actress to be auditioned for the lead female role opposite De Niro in *Casino*. But Scorsese had to cancel two scheduled auditions with her because of important meetings. Trying to arrange another scheduled parley with the actress, Scorsese's assistants were told by Stone's agent the actress wasn't available. The agent felt the director wanted to be polite in meeting with the actress but was going to decline her services. Scorsese found out about Stone's reluctance to set up a third appointment, but was persistent in wanting to meet with her knowing, along with Pesci's opinion on the veteran actress, she would be perfect for the character of Ginger.

Hot on the trail, Scorsese tracked down Stone dining in a restaurant with a friend and sat down with her to clear up the misunderstanding. She received the role. To prepare herself for the character of the prostitute-turned-wife of De Niro, Stone had to watch three films Scorsese assigned to her: 1967's *Valley of the Dolls*, 1948's *A Woman's Vengeance*, and the Carl Theodor Dreyer 1928 silent classic *The Passion of Joan of Arc*.

THE DEPARTED ADVENTURES

While *Casino* doesn't appear to have a plot, *The Departed*, based on the 2002 Hong Kong movie *Infernal Affairs* did. Scorsese described *The Departed* as he accepted the Best Director's award for the Oscars "the first movie I have ever done with a plot."

Reading *The Departed* script with an actual concrete storyline, Scorsese was hooked. He signed on to the production, not realizing the script was an adaptation of the earlier Hong Kong film. Once he found out, he chose not to view the original movie so he could apply his own visual ideas into the project.

The Departed was pegged by the studio to be a low-budget film like its forerunner *Infernal Affairs*. What attracted Scorsese to the script was, as a fan of James Cagney's 1949 *White Heat*, the plot showed strong parallels between the older Raoul Walsh-directed picture and the Asian version which had a policeman working undercover embedded in a criminal gang headed by a charismatic leader. The budget ballooned when one Hollywood star after the next signed on to the production. Ultimately financed at ninety million dollars, half of the budget was soaked up by the high salaries of the cast.

One prized actor the producers were eyeing was Jack Nicholson, who was offered the role of Frank Costello, loosely based on Boston's James "Whitey" Bulger. The actor really didn't want to commit to the movie and told Scorsese. The director, the screenwriter William Monahan, and actor Leonardo DiCaprio, all sat down with the reluctant actor to try to convince him to be involved in the film. The trio finally wore him down. Nicholson said later he wanted to play a villain after acting in a series of comedies; he saw the character Costello as the height of evil.

Nicholson wrote in his contract he could wear a New York Yankees baseball hat. The cap was a departure from the Red Sox hat his character Bulger constantly wore on his head. Nicholson disliked Boston so much because as an avid Los Angeles Lakers basketball fan, he hated the Boston Celtics, heated rivals at the time of the production.

Another high-priced actor hired was Mark Wahlberg, a Boston native. He was one of the very few actors in *The Departed* who didn't have to attend "accent" classes to speak "Bostonian." Scorsese said Wahlberg's speech was so thick the movie would need subtitles to translate his dialogue.

One of the last actors to be hired for *The Departed* was Martin Sheen. Once he was approached, the actor was excited to work on the project since he always wanted to do a film with Scorsese.

The screenplay was set in Boston. Scorsese had planned to film the movie in the Massachusetts capital, but because the tax advantages offered in New York State were set at fifteen percent, the producers were insistent the filming take place in New York City. Certain areas of the city, they felt, could stand in for Boston. Scorsese had no choice and shot the bulk of *The Departed* in New York while spending a few weeks in Boston filming in locales which couldn't be duplicated in the Big Apple. *The Departed* was such a financial success the Massachusetts legislature, disappointed in not obtaining the movie's entire production, passed a hefty twenty-five percent tax credit geared toward film production.

One shot filmed in downtown Boston was at Matt Damon's (Colin Sullivan) apartment. The scene shows the Massachusetts State House from the window of his apartment. Cinematographer Michael Ballhaus used a matte special effect of a still photograph taken from the roof of Suffolk University on Beacon Street for the studio shoot depicting Damon's apartment. Coincidentally, the script has Sullivan taking night classes at one of New England's best colleges, Suffolk University.

SCORSESE INSPIRED BY OTHER DIRECTORS

The details Scorsese places in his films reflect his immense knowledge of cinematic history. Scorsese is a big fan of Federico Fellini. He recalled the Italian director used a different voice-over reflective of his main character's thoughts in 1953's *I Vitelloni* than the character's real voice. Scorsese remembered how effective the separation of the two "voices" was in the

Fellini film. He scripted the opening of *Mean Streets* where the main character, Harvey Keitel, is in the Church thinking "You don't make up for your sins in Church; you do it on the street; the rest is BS and you know it." That's not Keitel's voice heard on the screen but the voice of Scorsese.

Scorsese showed homage to director Howard Hawks' early gangster film 1932 *Scarface* in *The Departed*. The signature symbol in *Scarface* is the letter "X." Scorsese placed the letter subtly throughout the film to mark the death or the anticipation of death of his characters. The "X" in *The Departed* is seen when Sergeant Dignam is with Costigan walking in the airport. The "X" is also shown by its formation with a light shimmering through the window when Sullivan is in his office with Costello. Finally, where Queenan falls and dies, the broken glass takes the formation of an "X."

In one scene in *The Departed,* DiCaprio is questioning Joseph Riccobene, the bank robber who is a drug addict and who tells him Costello is an FBI informant. In the robber's living room is a television set showing the 1935 John Ford movie *The Informer.* The parallels between the two films are uncanny, yet Scorsese purposely intended the Ford film to be shown in the background.

"THE KING OF THE TRACKING SHOT"

Scorsese also takes a considerable amount of time preparing for his trademark lengthy tracking shots, so distinctive in his films. Nicknamed the "King of the Tracking Shot," Scorsese acknowledges those tracking shots are one of the most difficult sequences to set up, but the payoff when it works is well worth the time. The location in one particular memorable tracking shot for *Goodfellas* occurs in the Copacabana night club, a restaurant Scorsese was very familiar having gone there on the night of his high school prom. People still talk about the tracking shot where Henry Hill and girlfriend Karen are followed from the restaurant's entrance, winding through the nightclub's hallways and kitchen before finishing off at a reserved table front and center. Scorsese called for seven takes before he was satisfied with the shot. Comic Henny Youngman, giving his shtick on the Copacabana stage during the filming, screwed up his lines during one of the takes.

The director was forced to design the long tracking shot because the restaurant's management refused to let the film crew set up all its equipment at the front entrance. Filming from the front inward would have allowed a much shorter walk to the pair's table than what Scorsese eventually had to plan from the back door. Instead of editing a quick cut from the couple opening the exterior door to the main dining area, the director decided to make a symbolic sequence containing the long, unbroken walking shot. Scorsese has described the sequence as visually illustrating Henry's promising future with the mob. "It's his seduction of the girlfriend Karen, and it's also the lifestyle seducing him," explained the director.

Scorsese credits friend Brian De Palma for giving him the idea of undertaking this arduous Steadicam shot when he saw the staircase tracking shot of the gun battle in De Palma's 1987's *The Untouchables.*

Scorsese loves using the Steadicam for most of those long tracking shots. Before 1975, the year the Steadicam was first invented, Scorsese used a handheld camera in 1973's *Mean Streets* to record his moving shots. He chose the less expensive handheld method to the industry standard of laying down tracks for the camera's dolly, a savings for Scorsese's meager budget. The hand-held camera used in *Mean Streets* recorded some of Scorsese's more famous tracking shots in the film, including the 70-second stretch where the camera tags along Johnny Boy when he's in Charlie's apartment. Another noted tracking shot in the same movie is the riveting sequence during the pool hall fight.

There's a scene showing Harvey Keitel in *Mean Street* totally drunk. To get his viewers into the mindset of Keitel's tipsy state, Scorsese instructed his crew to strap a camera onto the actor's body and told Keitel to rock back and forth. To accentuate the drunken feeling, the director slowed the speed inside the camera.

Taking a cue from Japanese film director Akira Kurosawa, who first used the technique in *Seven Samurai,* Scorsese uses slow motion to show the sheer magnitude of carnage taking place in his movies. Four films especially utilize this technique: *Mean Streets, Taxi, Raging Bull,* and *Wolf.*

"Cinema is a matter of what's in the frame and what's out," revealed Scorsese.

Money was no problem in Scorsese's later career. The planning stages of *Casino* was so precise that even the preparation phase addressed the style of apparel De Niro and Sharon Stone would wear during the course of the film, which called for an inordinate number of different clothes. The actor was given 70 distinctive suits, shirts and pants, while the actress wore 40 designed outfits. The entire budget for the clothes alone clocked in at $1 million and the entire cast was allowed to keep their apparel after the production. As the movie progresses, the colors of the actors' clothes become more outrageous as the characters and their situations become more chaotic.

Also reflective of Scorsese's attention to detail was the way even a minor character in *Casino* was lit. The director was so detailed in his script's notes he instructed the lighting crew to spotlight the Italian actor Pasquale Cajano in every scene he appeared. This special highlighting of Cajano, the major crime boss in the mid-west overseeing the Las Vegas casinos' corruption, is carried all the way through to the final scene where he is with other mob figures. Cajano is lit up like a Christmas tree while the lesser criminals are less so.

The preparation going into a movie has changed for Scorsese over the years. Prior to his marriage and being a father, Scorsese said "My whole life has been movies and religion. That's it. Nothing else."

Now his priorities have shifted.

"I'm in a different chapter of my life," said the director. "As time goes by and I grow older, I find that I need to just be quiet and think. There have been periods when I've locked myself away for days, but now it's different - I'm married and we have a daughter who is in my office the whole time."

PRODUCTION

DIRECTING ON THE SET

Scorsese's concentration on the set is so intense he demands total quiet while setting up his scenes. Actor Liam Neeson noted, "He requires absolute silence on set, like everybody has to stop work when he's giving a direction or explaining a scene. I mean everybody — the guy that's painting 400 yards away has to stop. If he hears one tiny sound it's shattered for him so he commands that respect. He commands that silence."

"It's hilarious, the problems that arise when you're on the set," stated the director. "It's really funny because you make a complete fool of yourself. I think I know how to use dissolves, the grammar of cinema. But there's only one place for the camera. That's the right place. Where is the right place? I don't know. You get there somehow."

Scorsese gives a portrayal of himself, much to the surprise of many.

"Because of the movies I make, people get nervous, because they think of me as difficult and angry," said the director. "I am difficult and angry, but they don't expect a sense of humor. And the only thing that gets me through is a sense of humor."

Before each production, Scorsese gets together with his actors and rehearses their scenes. During these rehearsals he gives them plenty of wiggle-room for their dialogue. Through these sessions the director, with the help of an assistant, selects the best lines which were ad-libbed by the actors and writes them into the amended script. From the updated screenplay the actors feed off the revisions on the set.

A good example is the *Goodfellas'* scene where De Niro and Pesci drop in on Scorsese's real mother, Catherine, after the pair murdered mobster Billy Bates. The director didn't tell his mother the script describes that the dead body of the mobster Pesci had just murdered is contained outside in the trunk of his car. Scorsese's script has Pesci, the son of Catherine in the movie, and company dropping in for dinner and his mother warmly welcoming them. During the filming, Pesci subtly asks her if he could borrow a large knife. The knife, unbeknownst to Scorsese's mother, is to be used to slice up the corpse. All the dialogue during the dinner scene is almost completely ad-libbed with Catherine's lines joyously delivered.

The "You think that's funny?" scene in *Goodfellas* allowed Pesci to use an episode when he was a youngster employed at a restaurant upsetting a gangster by laughing inadvertently at one of his jokes. The mobster didn't think Pesci's laughing was an appropriate response from the young food handler. Pesci told Scorsese the incident and the director thought it was a good idea even though the incident wasn't in the script. Scorsese and Pesci didn't tell Ray Liotta about what Pesci was planning to do, so Liotta's reaction is genuine.

The irony of Scorsese and Pileggi receiving an Academy Award nomination for Best Screenplay for co-writing *Goodfellas,* brimming with witty dialogue, is that many of the lines spoken by the actors are mostly improvised.

Of all the actors Scorsese feels most comfortable allowing to improvise his lines is De Niro. The actor's ad libbing produced one of cinema's most famous lines, "You talking to me," which De Niro, as Travis Bickle, says repeatedly preparing for his assassination of a politician in *Taxi.* The script describes the scene simply as Bickle looks in the mirror while he practices drawing his gun from the holster. Seemingly De Niro, who had learned his method acting from the famous Stella Adler and her Stella Adler School of Acting, recalled an exercise where the instructor had her students practice out loud varying interpretations of a simple phrase. One student adopted the phrase "You talkin' to me?" While the camera was rolling recording De Niro mimicking the phrase before the mirror, the actor repeated the line while Scorsese was under the camera silently cheering him on to keep the different interpretations going.

In another case of improvising on the set, Carthy Moriarty, who plays the future wife of Jake LaMotta in *Raging,* and De Niro are actually making up their lines, but within the script's parameters, during the scene when the two first meet at the chain-link fence.

For the scene where De Niro and Sandra Bernhard appear at the door of Jerry Lewis' house in *King of Comedy,* most of the dialogue was made up on the spot. It took five days to shoot the house sequence, from the initial lines of house servant Kim Chan summoning Jerry until the couple's final departure. To heighten Lewis' disgust at the two interlopers in his house, De Niro was saying off-camera anti-Semitic statements to Jerry as a way of getting the comedian angry at him. Bernhard, in her first major role and who had received no formal training in acting, also improvised many of her lines with De Niro during the home invasion.

So familiar De Niro and Pesci with ad-libbing their lines by the time *Casino* was produced, Scorsese told the two where their conversations would begin and end and have them make up their dialogue between the markers.

Veteran actor James Woods also got on the ad-lib train in his role as a pimp in *Casino*. Scorsese allowed Woods to improvise most of his lines. Woods' brilliance in his spontaneous dialogue is seen during the phone call when Stone (Ginger) tells him she got married. Woods told Scorsese in order to make the scene more effective he should be snorting cocaine with another prostitute while conversing with Ginger on the phone.

In *The Departed*, Scorsese gave Jack Nicholson the liberty to improvise many of his scenes. The ad-libbing was perfect for the character Nicholson was portraying, illustrating the gangster's unpredictability. One great example is when the actor and undercover cop DiCaprio are talking when Nicholson, off script, pulls out a gun on him.

ADVENTURES ON A SCORSESE SET

De Niro, an intense actor, always wanted to be well-rehearsed before arriving on the set. Jody Foster experienced firsthand De Niro's preparation for the scene in *Taxi* where he sits with young hooker Iris (Foster) at a local restaurant. To rehearse the scene, De Niro phoned Foster and asked if she wanted to get some coffee and sharpen their lines. She agreed. Once they got together, De Niro went over their scene repeatedly. Foster began to lose interest but the energetic De Niro convinced her to recite her lines one more time. And another and another.

Because of *Taxi's* limited budget, Scorsese wanted to schedule the filming as tightly as possible. New York City served as a backdrop to the film and the director lucked out in so many ways in establishing the movie's mood by showing the city as a dirty, sweltering urban mess. *Taxi* was shot in the summer when New York City was undergoing a heat wave. The stench of the city is accentuated by the voice-over of De Niro: "There's an atmosphere at night that's like a seeping kind of virus." The city was also in the middle of a garbage strike with refuse covering the streets and sidewalks. Recalled Scorsese, "Everywhere I aimed the camera, there were mounds of garbage."

The assassination attempt scene in *Taxi* was scheduled to be filmed near the middle of the production. The make-up artists tasked with De Niro's appearance had a problem on their hands: the script called for Bickle to shave his head into a Mohawk, with a band of hair growing in the middle while his sides were bald. De Niro had more scenes to shoot later in the production requiring a full head of hair. Dick Smith, the head make-up artist, came up with the idea of placing a strip of thick horse hair on top of a fake skin cap and gluing it onto the actor's head. The Museum of Moving Images in Queens, New York, displays the hairpiece De Niro wore for the scene.

Bickle attempts to shoot a United States Senator. The movie inspired John Hinckley, wanting to impress actress Jody Foster, to shoot at President Ronald Reagan on March 30, 1981. Coincidentally scheduled on that same March evening was the 53rd Academy Awards, where *Raging Bull* was up for several Oscars, including Scorsese for Best Director. Because of the shooting, the awards show was postponed until the following day. Much of the press attributed the Hinkley shooting to the events shown in *Taxi*. Attending the ceremonies, Scorsese was escorted to the auditorium by several FBI Special Agents acting as his bodyguards.

Working for Scorsese was initially frustrating for Jerry Lewis in *Comedy*. The actor sat around for the first three days of the production waiting to be called on the set. Lewis knew he was getting paid for all his sitting, but with his derriere becoming sore, Lewis reminded the director all he had to do is to tell him what days he would be needed on the set so he wouldn't have to sit around waiting.

Scorsese defends himself for such situations when directing a movie, jarring even his most well-laid plans off schedule.

"I can't take shooting any scene for granted," notes Scorsese. "I just can't. The moment I do that, I have no idea what I'm doing. 'Oh, that'll be easy, I'll do that in five minutes.' Believe me, that never happens."

During the production of *Goodfellas*, Scorsese wanted to be as accurate as possible to paint a picture of the life inside The Mob. He was able to gather several associates of the actual people who were portrayed in the movie. The accomplices gave the director and the actors advice on the lifestyles of those they knew, how they behaved, and how they dressed, and how they carried themselves.

In one particular distressing scene that went awry, Pesci kills "Spider," the character played by Michael Imperioli. While the actor was being fired at with blanks, the squib filled with red dye exploded as designed in his chest. At the same moment, Imperioli badly cut his hand while he was holding a glass. Some members of the crew quickly whisked the actor to the emergency room at a nearby hospital. The doctors saw Imperioli's bleeding chest and thought he was shot by a bullet. They began to treat the badly bleeding wound as life-threatening when the actor told them what they were really working on was just spilled red dye. His cut hand was the injury the doctors should be focusing on, the actor said. The medics left the room immediately to treat the more seriously wounded in the hospital, making Imperioli wait for three hours before a doctor came in to stitch his hand.

No film director could be as much of a perfectionist as Stanley Kubrick, but on one occasion making *The Departed,* Scorsese showed shades of Kubrick's perfectionism by filming a sequence taking place on the subway, on the Red Line in Boston, with Martin Sheen and Leonardo DiCaprio. To get the sequence to Scorsese's satisfaction, the film crew and small cast rode the train about one hundred times back and forth throughout the line's system.

Echoing Alfred Hitchcock's phobia with police, Scorsese, while making *The Departed,* hired a large group of state policemen to be on the set as extras. The director said he felt more comfortable with the friends of the real criminals serving as advisors standing by while filming than with the law enforcement officers. "I was worried that there were cops all around me and they were going to take me in," joked Scorsese.

One person who was comfortable around law enforcers was actor Matt Damon, who prepared for his role as a Massachusetts State policemen in *The Departed.* The actor spent time alongside the state police for several days. Damon first attended the training academy where he was taught law enforcement techniques such as how to pat down and handcuff suspects among other proper police procedures. Damon drove besides the officers on their daily routine patrols and participated on several police drug raids.

Scorsese still loves to interact with up-and-coming film students and young filmmakers learning the craft of movie-making. The director is a teacher at heart, pointing out to students the techniques he uses on the film set, including his use of a special lens, called the split focus diopler, to get a deep focus effect which requires less light than the older method. The diopler lens allows both the foreground and the background characters to be in sharp focus at the same time.

"At this point, I find that the excitement of a young student or filmmaker can get me excited again," rejoices Scorsese. "I like showing them things and seeing how their minds open up, seeing the way their response gets expressed in their own work."

POST-PRODUCTION

EDITING ADVENTURES

Of all the phases in putting together a film, Scorsese has said editing is his favorite.

To help with the editing of *Mean Streets,* Scorsese was offered a helping hand from up-and-coming director Brian De Palma to splice some of the film's scenes. By and large, though, Scorsese, who edited his own pictures in film school, cut almost the entire movie. Since the production was much larger than his school projects, he not only was assisted by De Palma but also from Sidney Levin, who had just finished editing 1972's Academy Award nominee for Best Picture *Sounder.* Scorsese wasn't a member of the Motion Pictures Editing Guild so Levin agreed to take credit in the titles for the editing chore.

A short while after De Palma was giving Scorsese some editing advice in *Mean Streets,* the producers who were enthusiastic about their upcoming project, *Taxi,* were considering assigning De Palma to direct it. Before De Palma could read the script, the producers saw *Mean Streets* in a private viewing and loved De Niro's acting. The producers were so carried away with De Niro they told Scorsese the project would be his if he could convince De Niro to play the lead. After seeing the results of *Taxi,* De Palma said he was sorry he didn't get the chance to direct the movie.

While working on *Taxi,* editor Marcia Lucas along with producer Julia Phillips laughed hysterically at the outtakes of the scene where Cybill Shepherd and De Niro are having coffee and pie together. Shepherd kept screwing up her lines and De Niro was visibly upset at her inability to remember her dialogue. Shepherd may have been discombobulated when De Niro asks the waitress for an apple pie topped with melted cheese. The unusual pie/cheese combination derives from the 1957 confessional of serial killer Ed Gein, who was just arrested for the murder of a hardware store owner. Gein said he would confess to the murder as well as additional ones if he got his apple pie with cheese.

Back in 1976 violence on the screen wasn't anywhere near as graphic as it is today. Columbia executives were leery about the dramatic bloody shoot-out at the end of *Taxi,* worried the picture would receive the dreaded "X-Rating" label if the scenes were left in. They wanted the gun fight cut.

Scorsese felt without the concluding killings the film would be a hollow mess since the entire narrative depended on the "heroism" of Travis Bickle, who throughout the movie said he wanted to clean up the cesspool in New York City. Scorsese showed just the shooting sequence to his friend, Steven

Spielberg, who said the killing scenes in the brothel was brilliantly shot and edited. To satisfy the studio's concern, Scorsese and cinematographer Michael Chapman came up with the idea to mute the color of the blood spurting all over the place. They desaturated the red color during the post-production. The studio felt the change would be acceptable to the ratings board even though the blood had taken a pink hue instead of the graphic red.

Mean Streets and *Taxi* are quintessential movies about New York City, but Scorsese has since produced only a handful of pictures about the city he loves.

"If I continue to make films about New York, they will probably be set in the past," said the director, alluding to 2002's *The Gangs of New York.* "The 'new' New York I don't know much about. It's not that I'm against contemporary film. I'm open to it in general, but I find the new colors of the city, the new Times Square, kind of shocking. I guess I'm stuck in a time warp."

ENHANCING HIS EDITING STYLE

Scorsese sometimes coordinates the edits of his sequences based on selections extracted from his personal collection of record albums. For *Mean Streets* securing musical copyrights for the songs he inserted in the film took up almost half of Scorsese's modest production budget. One of his favorite bands is The Rolling Stones, the group Scorsese featured in a concert documentary, 2008's *Shine A Light.* The Stones' music is heard regularly in Scorsese's films, most notably the song *Gimme Shelter,* played in *Goodfellas, Casino,* and *The Departed.* While editing, Scorsese has the tempo of the selected tunes dictate the length of the edited clips in his final versions.

During the production of *Raging Bull,* Scorsese set up an editing suite in his personal apartment. Each evening after shooting all day he would edit the sequences in his apartment.

When filming *The Departed* in Boston, Scorsese took the day's footage to nearby Emerson College to view the dailies.

Speaking in dramatic terms, Scorsese remembers the process of filming and especially editing *The Departed* as especially grueling.

"Moral Ground Zero," Scorsese nicknamed the film. "I call it, all the characters killed at the end, basically everyone, and there was no place to go, after that. You know, I hardly did any press for that film. I was tired of it. I felt it was maddening. I mean, I like the picture, but the process of making it, particularly in the post-production, was highly unpleasant. I don't care how much I'm being paid, it'll kill me. I'll die. Very simply."

Another reason for the director's stress in the production of *The Departed* was he and his editing team were running late in finishing editing the movie because of its complexity and were still frantically working on the film a week before its scheduled public premier.

Scorsese worked with new technology when he began editing *Casino* for the first time on a digital computer editing system.

In reviewing the shots in *Casino,* the director said of all the shots he is most proud of and his favorite in the film is the one of Sharon Stone throwing all the chips on the craps table over her head. The camera is positioned above the table, capturing all the elegance and chaotic action of her tosses.

Scorsese is one of the most knowledgeable working film directors on the history of cinema from its early beginnings. He's familiar with the milestone 1903 film *The Great Train Robbery,* directed by Edwin S. Porter, and its famous medium shot of a gunslinger directly firing his revolver into the camera. Scorsese duplicated the scene at the end of *Goodfellas* when Loitta, playing Henry Hill, is in the witness protection program and is seen outside the house retrieving a newspaper. Loitta envisions Pesci shooting his gun at him point blank in the same framing as the 1903 movie.

Scorsese is also familiar with the early French filmmaker Georges Melies, who is portrayed in *Hugo.*

"The cinema began with a passionate relationship between celluloid and the artists and craftsmen and technicians who handled it, manipulated it, and came to know it in the way a lover comes to know every inch of the body of the beloved," Scorsese said. "No matter where the cinema goes, we cannot afford to lose sight of the beginning."

"Each film is interlocked with so many other films," he added on the current movies. "You can't get away. Whatever you do now that you think is new was already done by 1913."

Unusual for current movies but a technique Scorsese first used in *Mean Streets* and continued using through *Raging Bull, Goodfellas, The Departed* and *Wolf,* is freeze-framing the action. This pausing effect was first used by D. W. Griffith in his 1909 film *A Corner In Wheat.*

Studios will sometimes release a "director's cut" to collect more revenue from lengthened versions of films which were shortened for release because of time limitations. Scorsese frowns upon the practice. He feels the released final cut is as best as the movie can be and there isn't any sense putting out a longer one just for the sake of some extra change.

AFTER THE RELEASE OF SCORSESE'S FILMS

In *Raging Bull,* the character of Jake LaMotta is portrayed on the screen at times as a raving maniac. It was revealed LaMotta throughout his life was partially deaf, hearing only about 30 percent in his right ear and 70 percent in his left. He was frustrated in understanding people's conversations, thinking they were talking about him. When he saw himself characterized as a raging lunatic on the screen, the boxer underwent a cathartic moment, finally recognizing he was really a horrible husband and individual. He met with his ex-wife Vicki LaMotta after the movie and asked, "Was I really like that?" Vicki replied "You were worse."

Scorsese reflected later that while he was in production of *The King of Comedy* he was "unsettled" by the biting edge and harsh satire portrayed in the film. Both he and De Niro were exhausted after making the picture and both didn't collaborate on another movie until seven years later in *Goodfellas.* Scorsese also found *Comedy's* production particularly grueling because he was overworked and hadn't fully recovered from both fatigue and pneumonia. The compact shooting schedule didn't help his condition either.

Goodfellas broke all the rules of restraint regarding excessive violence and the inordinate amount of profanity. When the studio first saw the initial screening of the film, its executives were worried their entire investment would be poured down the drain, so revolutionary was the film's content. When the moment arrived to preview the movie the audience gave it an overwhelming thumbs down, reaffirming the studio's worries. But Warner Brothers went ahead and released the film without many changes, and the results received strong, positive reviews, solidifying Scorsese as a frontline film director.

The Departed, the Academy Awards' Best Picture in 2005, is the only movie to ever receive that honor as a remake of a foreign film. Clocking in at two and a half hours, Scorsese's effort is fifty minutes longer than the Hong Kong version.

The four Oscars, including Best Screenplay and Best Film Editing, propelled *The Departed* to become the third highest money-making film in Scorsese's body of work

"It seems to me that any sensible person must see that violence does not change the world and if it does, then only temporarily," assessed Scorsese on the messages his movies on crime convey.

He was asked about what his legacy in cinema will be when all is said and done.

"I don't know if there is any," said Scorsese. "Maybe a part of me wants there to be, if I'm being brutally honest, but the reality is it's a different experience now, cinema. Young people perceive the world and information in a completely different way to when I was growing up. So what I did in the past, I don't know how they'll see that in the future and if it will mean anything to them. I hope the scripts for *Taxi Driver,* or *Mean Streets,* or *Raging Bull*, or any of these things, will have some resonance in the future for other people, if they see them at all. Things fall out of favor, out of fashion. I have no idea. All I can do is hope to get to make another one."

As for the future, Scorsese says he loves writing, producing, directing and editing movies.

"Basically, you make another movie, and another, and hopefully you feel good about every picture you make," Scorsese says honestly. "And you say, 'My name is on that. I did that. It's okay.' But don't get me wrong, I still get excited by it all. That, I hope, will never disappear."

TOP TEN MARTIN SCORSESE MOVIES

#1--GOODFELLAS (1990)

All Scorsese's skills that were sharpened making his previous movies all come to a pinnacle in *Goodfellas*. In this film the director redefined the underground criminal movie category. Each scene can stand alone as a true mirror to the gangster mentality dominating the nation's cities. Scorsese places a strong dose of dark humor forcing us to laugh at even the most grotesque situation. The New York Times praised the film, stating, "More than any earlier Scorsese film, *Goodfellas* is memorable for the ensemble nature of the performances. The movie has been beautifully cast from the leading roles to the bits. There is flash also in some of Mr. Scorsese's directorial choices, including freeze frames, fast cutting, and the occasional long tracking shot. None of it is superfluous"

#2--RAGING BULL (1980)

The definitive sports movie, in fact, probably the best boxing film ever released, and that's saying a lot on a sport that has been heaily covered by Hollywood. Scorsese took on the project as a personal "rehab" production and he didn't hold back. One of the best edited films ever, Thelma Schoonmaker, who received an Oscar for her work, performed magic, especially during the intense boxing action sequences. Jason Best wrote, "It's certainly bruising to watch, thanks both to the ferocity of its fight scenes and the violent misogyny of its protagonist. This is a film that doesn't pull any punches when it comes to portraying machismo."

#3--TAXI DRIVER (1976)

A movie can't get any darker which addresses mental problems afflicting a small minority of modern gun-wielding assassins. *Taxi Driver* records the inner thoughts and experiences of a loner who Scorsese turns from a zero-to-a-hero. One of De Niro's top five performances in his career as a disturbed cab driver who feeds off the dirty air of a corrupt city. Wrote Roger Ebert, "*Taxi Driver* is a hell, from the opening shot of a cab emerging from stygian clouds of steam to the climactic killing scene in which the camera finally looks straight down. Scorsese wanted to look away from Travis's rejection; we almost want to look away from his life. But he's there, all right, and he's suffering."

#4--CASINO (1995)

A lushly photographed examination about the underground crime forces manipulating the gambling casinos of Las Vegas. De Niro and Pesci team up to give a portrayal of two different criminal elements lurking in the legal gambling world. Sharon Stone plays the female glamour angle swept up in the corruption of the criminal workings of this business. Todd McCarthy of Variety said "Martin Scorsese's intimate epic about money, sex, and brute force is a grandly conceived study of what happens to goodfellas from the mean streets when they outstrip their wildest dreams and achieve the pinnacle of wealth and power."

#5--KING OF COMEDY (1982)

Dark humor mixes with popular culture comedy in this unusual film about the overwhelming celebrity worshipping so rampant in this country. De Niro gives what Scorsese claimed is his best performance for the director as a wanna-be comedian who doesn't want to dignify the immensely hard work of beginning a stand-up career on the ground floor in dingy, smoke-filled comedy clubs. Jason Bailey, in his positive critique of *Comedy,* said of the film, "The tone it establishes is challenging, because there are funny scenes and situations which could easily be played for laughs, but that black cloud of tension and danger hangs over all of them, and Scorsese won't give you that release."

#6--THE DEPARTED (2006)

This is the movie that finally earned Scorsese his Best Picture and his Best Director Oscars, updating an earlier Hong Kong film called *Infernal Affairs*. He gathers an all-star cast to assist him in telling a story of a state police plant inside a criminal organization. Trouble is there's an inside plant from the criminal organization within the state police. There were many who felt his Academy Awards Oscar was given more for Scorsese's body of previous work than this being his best effort. In his acceptance speech, the director acknowledged as much, saying when he accepted the Oscar, "I just want to say, too, that so many people over the years have been wishing this for me, strangers, you know. I go walking in the street people say something to me, I go in a doctor's office, I go in a...whatever...elevators, people are saying, 'You should win one, you should win one.' I go for an x-ray, 'You should win one.' And I'm saying, 'Thank you.' And then friends of mine over the years and friends who are here tonight are wishing this for me and my family. I thank you. This is for you."

#7--MEAN STREETS (1973)

This movie gains notoriety as to the basic foundation to Scorsese's highly-stylized films that followed. The picture is a series of vignettes showing the criminal world of New York City and introduces De Niro as the wacko who will inhabit some of Scorsese's later work. The director's trademark music of The Rolling Stones, the unbridled violence breaking out throughout the film, and the false-bonds broken in trying to make that extra buck, are all revealed in this hard-hitting picture. Roger Ebert may have overstated the weight given in *Mean Streets* in his positive review, but he had the crystal ball predicting where Scorsese would be heading after this effort, writing, "In countless ways, right down to the detail of modern TV crime shows, *Mean Streets'* is one of the source points of modern movies."

#8--HUGO (2011)

Scorsese's first picture in 3D. What is noteworthy is *Hugo* shows the director's appreciation to early movie-making. There aren't too many films recognizing one of the true pioneers in cinematic development, but whenever a picture portrays Georges Melies, one of cinema's first film directors, the appraisal of the work has to be appreciated. This is a PG-rated movie, a rarity for Scorsese, allowing a younger audience to witness the talents of this gifted director. Roger Ebert had high praise for *Hugo,* writing, "*Hugo* is unlike any other film Martin Scorsese has ever made, and yet possibly the closest to his heart: a big-budget, family epic in 3-D, and in some ways, a mirror of his own life. We feel a great artist has been given command of the tools and resources he needs to make a movie about—movies."

#9—THE GANGS OF NEW YORK (2002)

This historical time-period movie covering the years leading up to the Civil War and to the infamous 1863 conscription riots, *Gangs* was nominated in eleven categories for the Academy Awards, including Best Picture and Best Director. *Gangs'* release was delayed by over a year since the original premier was scheduled right after the September 11, 2001 terrorist attacks on New York City. The studio felt the excessive violence in the movie would upset audiences who were still dealing with the thousands of deaths that day. Andrew Sarris wrote, "The result reverberates on the screen with a deadly force and fury more intense than anything Mr. Scorsese has yet achieved on the meanest and most beloved streets he could imagine or recall."

#10--SHUTTER ISLAND (2010)

Few people mention this Scorsese's collaboration with DiCaprio parallels the German Impressionist movie, 1920 *Dr. Caligari,* one of the most studied movies in all of film schools. Both share the theme of a person who thinks he's normal but is in actuality insane living in a mental institution. And the two films illustrate the thin difference between reality and fantasy existing solely in one's mind. The Wall Street Journal suggests viewers watch this film more than once: "Requires multiple viewings to be fully realized as a work of art. Its process is more important than its story, its structure more important than the almost perfunctory plot twists it perpetrates. It's a thriller, a crime story and a tortured psychological parable about collective guilt."

Steven Spielberg

It was only his second feature movie directing and already the production was well over budget and taking twice the time scheduled to film. Delays were maddening: the weather was choppy, the mechanical shark wasn't working, sailboats were floating into frame.

For the 27-year-old Steven Spielberg, he was demanding perfection, yet the studio budget crunchers were astounded at the daily expenses being racked up.

"I thought my career as a filmmaker was over," reflected Spielberg years later on the movie derisively labeled "Flaws" by the production crew. "I heard rumors back in Hollywood that I would never work again because no one had ever taken a film 100 days over schedule. There were moments of solitude, sitting on the boat waiting for a shot, thinking, this can't be done. No one is ever going to see this picture, and I'm never going to work in this town again."

But the "dailies" Universal Studios executives saw convinced them something exceptional was taking place off the Martha's Vineyard shoreline. The production crew, though, was getting peevish by the day. Spielberg heard rumors several members were planning to "accidentally" drown him once the last scene, where the shark chumps down on an air canister and blows up, was shot. He preplanned the concluding scene with his cameramen using four cameras and secretly had a speedboat spirit him away to the local airport as soon as everything was ready for filming.

Richard Dreyfuss and Spielberg were on the same puddle jumper plane to Boston and the actor asked how it felt filming the final scene. "They're shooting it now," Spielberg answered. Dreyfuss, aware of all the director's tribulations that went into making the movie, laughed uncontrollably.

"It was the worst experience of my life," Spielberg said on directing the shark movie.

When *Jaws* was released to a wide audience in June 1975, the film drastically changed the way Hollywood and its business model would operate. *Jaws* became the first summer blockbuster film ever, setting a pattern for today's Hollywood business model which concentrates its resources on fewer releases and more expensive films.

The movie's summer impact is remarkable since *Jaws* was originally scheduled for a Christmas launch. But the movie's production, delayed by the mechanical sharks' troubles, was overextended, forcing the film to be released in what was then considered the summer doldrum months for movie theaters. The hot weather season was when everyone played outdoors and no one gave a bit of thought of going inside to watch movies. Only the drive-in movies were popular at that time of year because a lot of necking and illegal drinking could be done inside those dark, lined-up cars. Hollywood studios recognized this and released their absolute worst movies in their inventory during that period.

Universal Studios knew they had a winner on their hands after viewing Spielberg's finished movie. The studio allocated over $700,000 for an ad campaign placed on television, radio and newspapers, an unheard of amount in the industry. With the buzz Universal created in the weeks leading up to the release of *Jaws,* even the hardiest outdoor campers went in droves to the indoor theaters to see the shark movie. Box office records fell when *Jaws* finally exhausted its summer run, becoming the highest financially grossing movie ever released up to 1975, eventually settling in at over a then staggering $100 million.

SHARK CHANGES SPIELBERG'S LIFE

Spielberg's career also changed after the premier of *Jaws,* catapulting him to become one of cinema's most popular film directors and producers, not to mention becoming one of the movie industry's richest creative forces.

It was a quirk of fate Spielberg was offered the opportunity to direct *Jaws* in the first place. Dick Richards, a relatively new-comer in Hollywood, was given first crack at the project's directorial helm. Universal Pictures producers met Richards after he read the script and were dismayed when he kept calling the voracious shark described in the screenplay as a whale. Knowing they didn't want to release another Moby Dick flick, the producers went looking elsewhere for directors, eventually turning to the young Spielberg.

Universal was impressed by Spielberg's previous film, *Sugarland Express.* During the initial meeting with those same producers who had rejected Richards, Spielberg noticed the still-unpublished Peter Benchley novel the movie was going to be based on sitting on a table and snapped up the book. Upon reading it, Spielberg said he loathed its characters and was cheering for the shark to win.

THE FEEL-GOOD DIRECTOR

Spielberg has been frequently criticized on capitalizing on making feel-good films such as 1982's *E.T. The Extra-Terrestrial* and 1981's *Raiders of the Lost Ark*. Yet the versatile director hasn't shied away from mature works, including 1985's *The Color Purple*, 1993's *Schindler's List,* and 1998's *Saving Private Ryan.*

To fully understand Spielberg, one has to study a boy whose upbringing didn't place him in the most popular student category. Bouncing around from state to state during his childhood, Spielberg was a geeky kid whose Jewish heritage was a source of prejudice for those around him. With a passion for motion pictures, though, he was able to defuse such biases by asking those who were picking on him to act in his amateur films using his dad's Super 8 mm camera.

One indelible image during his childhood that remained with him throughout his life was when his father drove him out to the desert when living in Arizona to witness a meteor shower. In a number of Spielberg's films taking place at night, the director shows shooting stars in the evening sky, one most notably in *Jaws,* which was accidentally filmed and inserted in the final version.

At an early age, Spielberg says he was enthralled by the train wreck sequence in Cecil B. DeMille's 1952 Academy Awards Best Picture *The Greatest Show On Earth* while watching the movie with his father at a local theater. Accepting the Cecil B. DeMille award during 2008's 66th Annual Golden Globe Awards, Spielberg said, "I think my fate was probably sealed that day in 1952."

His parents' marriage broke up shortly after he graduated from high school. The marriage was not rock solid when the boy was growing up. Many of his films contain themes that have either an absent father or one parent evading responsibility to his or her family. These storylines can be seen in 1977's *Close Encounters of the Third Kind, E.T.: the Extra-Terrestrial,* and 2002's *Catch Me If You Can.*

In *Close,* Richard Dreyfuss plays a father who abruptly leaves his family so he can figure out what's going on at Devil's Tower. His equally-mystified counterpart, Melinda Dillon is a single mother raising her three-year-old boy, who is kidnapped by aliens. Spielberg, having his own children well after directing *Close,* said he would never have had Dreyfuss desert his family in his quest to find what has been haunting him if he had to make the movie after having kids.

"I think every film I make that puts characters in jeopardy is me purging my own fears, sadly only to re-engage with them shortly after the release of the picture," revealed Spielberg. "I'll never make enough films to purge them all."

FILM LIFE AS A COLLEGE DROP-OUT

After graduating from high school, Spielberg interned at Universal Studios for two summers while attending California State University, Long Beach. Getting into Long Beach was no guarantee for Spielberg. The University of Southern California's School of Cinematic Arts had rejected him earlier before he was accepted at Long Beach. Dropping out of college after two years to work full time at Universal, Spielberg later took correspondence courses to fulfill Long Beach University's requirements for a Bachelor's Degree in Film. But he failed to submit a 12-minute film required by seniors in order to graduate. The college's graduation board waived the short film requirement for the director in lieu of Spielberg's *Schindler's List*, a movie the board's members said would qualify him for the school's diploma. Spielberg showed up for his May 31, 2002, graduation at Long Beach wearing the graduate's cap and gown to receive his bachelor's degree, 35 years after first enrolling at the university. As the director stepped up to receive his diploma on stage, the school's band struck up the theme to *Indiana Jones*.

"I think most of my movies are personal movies," reflected Spielberg. "I think the most personal movie I've made is *Schindler's List*. I think the second-most personal movie I have ever made is *E.T. the Extra-Terrestrial*. I also find *The Color Purple* to be a personal film for me. So I've made a number of personal films. But I haven't made a movie yet that is actually a mirror neuron of my factual life and I don't think I ever will. My sister wrote a script about our lives and that might come around again some day, but I've always stayed away from anything that is too biographical."

An independently-produced short film, *Amblin'*, in 1968, opened the door to television employment at Universal Studios. At Universal Spielberg directed several TV episodes, including *Night Gallery,* featuring veteran actress Joan Crawford appearing in one show. As a gift after completing his first direction of a TV show, Spielberg gave Crawford a Pepsi bottle containing a single red rose. The early directing effort established a tight friendship between Spielberg and Crawford, lasting until her death in 1977. Detroit Free Press reporter Shirley Eder was an observer on the *Night Gallery* set and approached Crawford during a break. The actress told the reporter that instead of writing a story on her she should "interview that kid, because he's going to be the biggest director of all time!"

Hollywood took note when Spielberg directed a made-for-TV movie, 1971's *Duel,* about a driver who ticks off a truck driver, igniting a rousing chase through the countryside.

One Spielberg's favorite shots is his patented "seeing-objects-through-the-rearview-mirror" framing, first used in *Duel.* He's used the signature mirror shot in *E.T. the Extra-Terrestrial,* 1993's *Jurassic Park, Schindler's List,* and 2001's *A.I. Artificial Intelligence.*

Besides famously meeting John Ford, Spielberg also absorbed the lessons English film director David Lean gave him while the two viewed together Lean's 1962 Academy Award Best Picture winner *Lawrence of Arabia.* Throughout the screening, Lean gave Spielberg a running commentary of how he shot the movie. Spielberg said picking the mind of Lean was a memorable moment in his life, claiming the session and subsequent multiple viewings of *Lawrence* influences the look and movement of each film he has directed. It's no surprise he cites *Lawrence* as his all-time favorite movie.

PRE-PRODUCTION

TACKLING SERIOUS SUBJECTS

To prepare for every movie he's about to direct, Spielberg undertakes a bit of aesthetic homework. "Before I go off and direct a movie I always look at four films," Spielberg revealed. "They tend to be *Seven Samurai, Lawrence of Arabia, It's a Wonderful Life,* and *The Searchers.*"

Scouring for projects during the first half of his directing career, Spielberg often focused on plots involving either children being in danger or episodes within the plot showing the plight of children.

"I always like to think of the audience when I am directing," Spielberg remarked, pointing to one of the reasons his career has been so successful. "Because I am the audience."

Spielberg is attracted to stories involving ordinary, middle-class people whom eventually stumble on things like aliens (*Close Encounters, E.T.*), prehistoric creatures (*Jurassic Park*), and historic artifacts (*Raiders*) among other discoveries the main protagonists stumble upon, setting the narrative in motion.

The first phase of Spielberg's film career was devoted to either space-themed films or adventure and light-hearted storylines. When he tackled the serious 1985's *The Color Purple,* the director later noted the sober   nature of this production allowed him to turn to a number of other resolute themes such as

1987's *Empire of the Sun* and 1994's *Schindler's List.*

"The older I get, the more I look at movies as a moving miracle," Spielberg reflected. "Audiences are harder to please if you're just giving them special effects, but they're easy to please if it's a good story. The audience is also the toughest critic - a good story that exists in your world may not be the first choice for an audience. So I just do the best I can."

Spielberg is heavily involved from the beginning in formulating the scripts of his movies. He's written two screenplays by himself, 1982's *Poltergeist* and *A.I. Artificial Intelligence.* He rewrites many of the screenplays from other collaborating writers before he embarks on the movie set.

One of his more unusual requests for directing a movie came from musician/movie producer Quincy Jones, who was handling some of the assignments for bringing Alice Walker's book *The Color Purple* onto the screen. He approached Spielberg to direct *Color.* Spielberg initially refused to be the director for the film set in the Deep South during the Depression since he felt he knew nothing about the region and the culture of the African-American community during the 1930's. He told Jones he felt a black director who could relate to the people in the story would be far more effective and appropriate to direct Walker's sensitive story.

"No, I want you to do it," argued Jones, "and besides, did you have to be an alien to direct *E.T.*?"

Spielberg was worn down by Jones' convincing persistence in logic and signed on to direct *Purple.*

Michael Crichton wrote a screenplay on his experiences as a physician in a hospital which caught the eye of Spielberg. While the pair was developing a projected movie on *ER, or Emergency Room,* Crichton had published a book about dinosaurs named *Jurassic Park.* Crichton's agents knew their client's book was a goldmine, and they began shopping the book around to several movie studios. The author was dismayed by his agents' lobbying since he felt Spielberg was the best person to direct his novel. The agents visited Warner Brothers Studio, who saw its director Tim Burton and his magic touch the perfect match, while Columbia Pictures thought director Richard Donner would give the story an extra pizzazz. Crichton had the foresight when signing the contract with his agents to give him the ultimate power to select the studio interested in securing the rights to his book. Universal stepped in and made an offer Crichton and his agents couldn't refuse. Spielberg's affiliation with the studio insured Crichton's first choice was going to direct the movie.

Once he got the dinosaur assignment, Spielberg set *ER* aside. Crichton was given the job of writing the film's screenplay. But as Spielberg does on all his movie projects, he hired other writers to collaborate on the script, with David

Keopp writing the final version. After *Jurassic* was finished, Spielberg and Crichton decided to go forward and produce a made-for-TV movie on the former doctor's hospital experience, which became the pilot for the long-running TV series *ER*.

Even though Spielberg makes a ton of cash from all his successful producing efforts, his passion is still working behind the camera on the movie set. "I'd rather direct than produce," Spielberg admitted. "Any day. And twice on Sunday."

LOVE FOR OUTER SPACE

Ever since his father instilled in him a love for looking at the stars that inspired him to make a high school science-fiction film, *Firelight,* Spielberg always had an interest in alien life from other solar systems. As his movie career took off after *Jaws,* he long harbored a wish to do a documentary or a low-budgeted film on believers who embrace the possibilities of the existence of UFOs. The idea eventually morphed into a large-budgeted full length project labeled *Close Encounters of the Third Kind.*

For the *Close Encounters* screenplay, Spielberg enlisted Paul Schrader, writer for Martin Scorsese's scripts, including *Taxi Driver* and *Raging Bull.* Schrader typed the first draft, but Spielberg didn't particularly care for his work. The director then hired other writers to redraft the Schrader script. Spielberg still wasn't satisfied and decided to incorporate the elements he liked in all the rejected screenplays to form the final version.

As the scripts were being developed and submitted, Spielberg was meeting with illustrator George Jensen to lay down the visual groundwork on his ambitious movie. They spent a good part of a year drawing and pouring over thousands of sketches which would eventually play a crucial role in the look of *Close Encounters.* Included in the early pre-production stage were the outlines to seven major sequences as well as the details of the final 24 minutes.

"The one ingredient I bring to all of my films is the ability to listen to anybody who has a good idea on the production," revealed Spielberg on his "teamwork" approach to making movies. "I'm very collaborative with actors, with my writers, with my editor, my cinematographer, with Johnny Williams, who does all of my scores. And I just think from a very young age my parents taught me probably the most valuable lesson of my life - sometimes it's better not to talk, but to listen."

"When you listen, you learn, you absorb like a sponge - and your life becomes so much better than when you are just trying to be listened to all the time," added Spielberg.

SPIELBERG'S LOOK AT THE PAST

Spielberg got the idea of *Raiders of the Lost Ark* from fellow director and friend George Lucas when the two were vacationing together in Hawaii after Lucas learned that his 1977 *Star Wars* was an enormous financial success after its initial release. The two were on the beach building a sand castle when Spielberg revealed it was always his life ambition to make a James Bond flick. Meanwhile, Lucas, who four years earlier had developed an outline about an archaeologist who stumbles upon the Biblical Ark of the Covenant, described his story as well as the concept adopting elements of those 1930s serial movies they both grew up watching. Spielberg was intrigued by the idea. Once the two returned to the mainland they approached screenwriter Lawrence Kasdan to develop the script.

Lucas had tentatively named his archaeologist protagonist Indiana Smith. Mulling over the leading character's name, Spielberg wasn't quite convinced Indiana Smith would flow easily off the tongue. What other common name would be fitting after "Indiana?" Spielberg asked himself. After pondering a few days, the name Jones popped into his mind. He eventually persuaded Lucas the name Indiana Jones had that panache lyrical sound audiences would grow to love.

Strangely, the *Raiders'* project was a tough sell for the two very successful film directors in approaching Hollywood studios for funding. Every studio they met with refused to support the picture, except for Paramount. Even then it took a lot of arm twisting from Spielberg and Lucas to get the studio to eventually support the project.

The evolution of the script for *E.T.* had an interesting beginning. Taking advantage of the downtime while the film crew changed sets on the Tunisia location for *Raiders,* Spielberg and Harrison Ford's then-wife Melissa Mathison began working on a screenplay based on a story Spielberg had in mind when he was filming the ending of *Close Encounters.* The finale of *Close Encounters* shows several small aliens walking out of the spaceship to greet the human volunteers willing to travel to the faraway planet. The director pondered the possibility that one of the aliens became stranded on earth during his visit here and was unable to get back to his planet.

Film studios have a standard industry practice of maximizing their profits by selling product placements to corporations that are seen in their movies, creating subliminal advertising for unsuspecting viewers. For the scene where Elliott sprinkles bits of candy on the ground to attract E.T., the studio approached Mars, Inc. to sell the company on the idea of using its M&Ms as the lure. Mars company heads saw drawings of E.T. and nixed the idea, thinking the alien was so homely anything associated with the film would scare children from eating its candy. The Hershey Company was then offered the product placement, which the Pennsylvania corporation happily signed on. Following the success of *E.T.* and the lovable alien creature, packages of Reese's Pieces flew off the shelves.

TURNING SERIOUS

Spielberg had been interested in being involved in a film based on a book on Oskar Schindler for several years, although he tried to pass the project on to other directors fearing he couldn't do the subject justice. He approached Martin Scorsese to direct the picture, but the New York Italian said a Jewish director would do a far better job than he could. Spielberg took his advice and approached Roman Polanski. The exiled director, who personally endured seeing his father taken to the very Krakow concentration camp depicted in *Schindler's List* and who himself escaped the Nazi clutches, said the story was too close to him to even consider. Director Billy Wilder late in his career wanted to make the film on Schindler as his swan song, but it was reported he was the one to convince Spielberg to take on the assignment.

Wilder offered any help he could give Spielberg, having lost his mother and relatives in the Holocaust. Spielberg took up Wilder's offer and his contribution to the first draft of the script is noteworthy.

Listening to Wilder's advice after directing 1991's *Hook,* Spielberg decided he would tackle the Holocaust-themed film. MCA studio head Sid Sheinberg encouraged Spielberg to direct the World War II-based movie, but under one condition: he had to make *Jurassic Park* first. "He knew that once I had directed *Schindler* I wouldn't be able to do *Jurassic Park*," reflected Spielberg.

His *Schindler* location scouting team gained permission to use the interior of the existing concentration camp, Auschwitz, for filming. The director declined since he didn't want to disrespect the thousands of victims who died in the camp. He was able to use the grounds next to the camp where he had his crew construct a facsimile of Auschwitz.

Schindler's was budgeted to be relatively expensive despite being filmed in black and white. The picture became the costliest black-and-white movie in history, surpassing 1962's *The Longest Day,* a World War II epic about D-Day.

SPIELBERG'S UNIQUE LOOK

A Spielberg film has its own unique look which is imitated but never improved upon. His mania for visuals borders on obsessive. Screenwriter Bob Gale recalled one visit to Spielberg's house, "There was a TV in just about every room, and there was always a television on. He'd have a conversation, and out of the corner of his eye he'd be watching TV and see something and get excited about it. He'd make a note, 'Find out the name of this actor or who directed this commercial.' He was always thinking about what he was seeing and filing it away."

"My movies are all different," describes Spielberg. "I've tried to make every movie as if it was made by a different director, because I'm very conscious of not wanting to impose a consistent style on subject matter that is not necessarily suited to that style. So I try to re-invent my own eye every time I tackle a new subject. But it's hard, because everybody has a style. You can't help it. It just comes off you like pollen. I mean, if you're a bee, you're a bee, but at the same time I try very hard to work a little out of the box every time I make a choice. And I had to go back to a box that I had helped invent in the 1980s to accomplish the task of bringing *Indiana Jones* back to life in the 21st century. We went right back to the blazing Technicolor style of the first three installments. For *Munich*, I certainly tried to bring an early-70s Hollywood style, a cinéma-vérité style, with zoom-lenses, and a lot of the tools that were used to make movies in the 70s, one of my favorites being 1973's *The Day of the Jackal,* the Fred Zinnemann film. But I didn't want to update *Indiana Jones* to the 1950s beyond hair, makeup, costumes and cars. I wanted it to look very similar to the first three pictures."

Spielberg very rarely conducts auditions for his leading roles. Whenever he decides to work with actors for the first time, Spielberg is familiar with their past performances. To cast the heroine opposite Harrison Ford in *Raiders,* Spielberg was impressed by little-known actress Karen Allen's appearance in 1978's *Animal House* and chose her to play Marion Ravenwood, a former lover of Indiana Jones.

For the occasional auditions he does conduct, mostly for children's parts where the resumes of young actors are spare, Spielberg is able to spot gems in the middle of a crowded field. Spielberg was looking for a 10-year-old boy to play the central role in *E.T.* when Henry Thomas stepped up and gave a performance securing his role as Elliott. To prepare for his lines which required him to emote a sentimental sadness, Thomas thought of his dog who had recently died. Once he was finished, Spielberg, teary-eyed, got up and said Thomas had the role. There was no need for him to look any further, he noted.

When casting for the abused wife in *Purple,* Spielberg was looking for a fresh face. Stand-up comedian Whoopi Goldberg was invited to audition for the part. She created a skit to find commonality with the director and portrayed a weed-smoking E.T. being arrested in Oakland, California for possession of pot. Not only was Spielberg howling, but producer Quincy Jones and singer Michael Jackson, also in attendance, found her highly talented. Whoopi was awarded the role, her first appearance in feature films.

Another fresh face Spielberg brought onto the big screen for *Purple* was talk show host Oprah Winfrey. She was always fighting a battle with her ballast and was attending a weight loss clinic when she received the call she was going to be cast as Sofia, who in the book carried a wide girth. When it was discovered she was in a "fat reducing farm," Winfrey got the orders to leave immediately.

In a first in Oscar history, Goldberg and Winfrey, both making their film debuts in *Purple,* were nominated for their acting in the same picture.

When Spielberg conducts auditions, he has a specific character's trait in mind for each role. He was recording casting tests to find a young actress to play a little girl in the group confronted by dinosaurs, a role that required the girl to scream uncontrollably. Eleven-year-old Ariana Richard's was asked by the director he "wanted to see how she could show fear," Richards recalled, "I heard later on that Steven had watched a few girls on tape that day, and I was the only one who ended up waking his sleeping wife off the couch, and she came running through the hallway to see if the kids were all right."

Spielberg had in mind actor Ralph Fiennes to play the German commander for the Krakow concentration camp in *Schindler's List* because he had what Spielberg called an "evil sexuality." To prepare for the rather husky Nazi commandant role, Fiennes drank gallons of Guinness to gain 28 pounds. The actor looked so much like the real Nazi Amon Goeth that when Mila Pfefferberg, a survivor of the concentration camp and was serving as a consultant for Spielberg, saw Fiennes she shook so uncontrollably she almost fainted. His appearance brought back vivid memories to her of the Nazi commandant.

For the role of Private Ryan, Spielberg was scouting for an unknown face, an actor with the All-American look who was relatively unfamiliar to the viewing public. Visiting his friend Robin Williams on the set of 1997's *Good Will Hunting,* Spielberg saw Matt Damon act and thought the obscure performer would fit the bill. But before *Private Ryan* was released, Damon walked on to the spotlight when he was honored for an Academy Award Best Actor nomination, thrusting the young actor into instant stardom.

Spielberg wanted Damon, who played Private Ryan, as a tagalong who appears late in the movie and has little interaction with the other soldiers under Tom Hanks' command fetching him. The director scheduled a boot camp for the actors playing the infantry soldiers, with the exception of Damon, to serve as a bonding experience prior to filming. The punishing physical training session was so excruciating to the actors they elected to quit, save for one. The lone holdout was Hanks, who seemingly enjoyed the sessions. Since Hanks was the senior actor who played the commanding officer in the film, his opinion carried the most weight. The training for the entire group continued as planned.

One of the requirements besides dynamic acting Spielberg requires of his actors is their ability to stare, especially to focus on something happening out of the frame.

SPIELBERG PAYS HOMAGE TO PAST DIRECTORS

Making films is a team effort. Even the most talented and successful film directors attribute a large part of their success on the collaborative efforts of their cast and crew who make magic following the words "Lights, camera, action."

"I get that same queasy, nervous, thrilling feeling every time I go to work," describes Spielberg on his production days and career. "That's never worn off since I was 12 years-old with my dad's 8-millimeter movie camera. The thrill hasn't changed at all. In fact, as I've gotten older, it's actually increased, because now I appreciate the collaboration. When I was a kid, there was no collaboration, it's you with a camera bossing your friends around. But as an adult, filmmaking is all about appreciating the talents of the people you surround yourself with and knowing you could never have made any of these films by yourself. My job was constantly to keep a movie family going. I'm blessed with the same thing that John Ford and Howard Hawks and Alfred Hitchcock were blessed with, a mini-industry very similar to the one from the golden era of Hollywood, where it was the same people making movies with you each and every time. And it makes life so much more enjoyable when you get to go home to your family and go to work with your other family. "

Spielberg is credited with the famous "Jaws Shot," showing actor Roy Schieder sitting on the beach observing the swimmers before spotting a boy being attacked by a shark. But the director adapted a sequence in Alfred Hitchcock's 1958 *Vertigo* where James Stewart gets dizzy climbing up the church steeple's stairs. Spielberg simply reversed the "forward zoom/reverse tracking" Hitchcock used (as well as Francois Truffaut's 1966 *Fahrenheit*

451 in the hallway scene) to accentuate Schieder's distress.

As an admirer of Hitchcock, Spielberg copied another scene in Hitch's 1959 *North by Northwest* where Cary Grant grabs Eva Marie Saint's arm as she's hanging onto the cliff's edge on Mount Rushmore. Spielberg juxtaposed the scene on Devil's Tower, located a scant 90 miles from Mt. Rushmore, where Melinda Dillon grabs Dreyfuss' hand while he's dangling on the cliff's edge just prior to viewing the landing site of the UFOs.

Raiders was based on those 1930s serial movies where the hero always wins, gets his girl, and never loses his hat. The good guys always wore hats in those days. Two reasons why the hat stays on the actors in those old serials: 1. For continuity since the hero gets in a number of fist fights, and if his hat fell off his head, the continuity of editing between two angles would be difficult. 2. A hero would never be without his hat on his head since it was in poor taste for any man of substance to be without one. As an inside joke, Indiana Jones does lose his hat in *Raiders* once as well as one time in each of the three sequels.

Spielberg stuck to the 1930s serial picture aesthetics, saying, "I made it as a B-movie. I didn't see the film as anything more than a better made version of the Republic serials."

LIGHTING ON SET

Spielberg loves to illuminate objects during night scenes by having his actors turn on their flashlights and attempt to discover the objects they are looking for in a foggy, misty or dusty atmosphere, creating an extra layer of suspense. This can be seen in *Jaws*, *Jurassic Park* and its sequel as well as in *E.T. the Extra-Terrestrial*. This reoccurring atmospheric is symbolic of his characters attempting to find themselves in an otherwise dark world.

"I've had darkness in all the films, in *E.T. the Extra-Terrestrial, Jaws,*" relates Spielberg. "There are moments in *Raiders of the Lost Ark* that are brutally dark. I just don't think people have stopped to study. They may not have stopped to think when they assume that I suddenly developed a dark side because of *Schindler's List*. When critics carp about my dark side, I always wonder, 'Well, did they really look in the shadows?'"

The combat scenes in *Private Ryan* are claimed by veterans who fought in World War II to be the most realistic they've witnessed on the big screen. To achieve that authentic look, cinematographer Janusz Kaminski set the cameras' shutters to ninety degrees. Such a maneuver resulted in an unusually jarring set of images which didn't make the combat scenes appear simply staged.

Spielberg spends his leisure time watching golf on TV as well as playing for hours video games, where he subliminally gathers much of his pacing for his action thrillers.

PRODUCTION

AT WORK ON THE FILM SET

Spielberg's preparation in scripting and planning before embarking onto a film set is reflected in his final releases. He possesses an incredible knowledge of films and TV that serves Spielberg well when he's directing actors. For certain dramatic scenes, Spielberg refers to past movie performances to describe the emotions he would like to elicit from his talent. Novice actress Whoopi Goldberg remembers his motivational advice in one scene in *The Color Purple.*

"We had a lingo because he's a movie fanatic like me," Goldberg said. "When I had a terribly wrenching scene with Danny Glover, he'd say, 'OK, it's *Gaslight* (the 1944 Ingrid Bergman film) time,' and I'd crack up."

Another rookie actress, Oprah Winfrey, was initially terrified and intimidated by Spielberg. He admits he was a "little frustrated" at first with Winfrey's inexperience, but his respect for her acting ability grew, so much so the director expanded her role as filming progressed.

Spielberg likes tension between the actors on the movie set when they're portrayed as adversaries in the script. In *Jaws* he had the ideal quarreling couple in Robert Shaw and Richard Dreyfuss. The former despised the latter in real life. Their friction is translated onto the screen when the two are basically at each other's throats.

Shaw had just come off his role as a buffoonish villain in 1973's Academy Awards Best Picture *The Sting* when Universal Pictures' producers financing *Jaws* suggested to Spielberg he should take a long, serious look at the actor to play professional shark hunter Quint. Spielberg was sold on Shaw despite experiencing some interesting episodes with the actor later in the production.

It didn't help Shaw loved his sauce, the 80% proof kind. "He was a perfect gentleman whenever he was sober," recalled Scheider. "But all he needed was one drink and then he turned into a competitive son-of-a-bitch."

At one point filming *Jaws*, Shaw was swilling between takes. He then began having drinker's remorse and said to no one in particular, "I wish I could quit drinking." Dreyfuss, taking Shaw's comments literally, suddenly clutched the drink out of his hands and threw the glass into the sea.

To make *Jaws* as accurate as possible, numerous props were staged to create authenticity. One prop is the beer Shaw is downing on the *Orca*. The beer is the local brew every Red Sox fan is familiar with, Narragansett. This popular Rhode Island beer had its jingle, "Hi neighbor, have a Gansett."

One of the highlights in *Jaws* is Shaw's monologue on the sinking of World War II's USS Indianapolis, the ship whose crew largely got chewed up by sharks in the Pacific Ocean. Shaw's character was on the vessel and experienced the horrors of the sharks feasting on the struggling sailors. The script called for the three who are chasing the great white shark drinking in the evening while undergoing "male bonding" on the boat. Shaw thought he would do what method actors do and drink the real pooch while saying his long monologue about the USS Indianapolis disaster. However, he began forgetting and stepping on his lines as he was becoming more inebriated, producing nothing worthwhile in the film canister after numerous takes. Feeling badly about wasting everyone's time, Shaw called up Spielberg well after the day's shoot was over and told him not to scrap the scene; he was convinced he could do his speech the next day. Spielberg cautiously approved and Shaw during the next day's session promptly nailed the monologue in just one take.

Quint's speech about his experience on the USS Indianapolis foreshadows his final demise in *Jaws*. The script and the Benchley book described Shaw's character going by way of Captain Ahab in Herman Melville's *Moby Dick,* with a harpoon rope tied around his leg and pulling him under as the shark submerges. Quint escaped the Indianapolis shark fest, so Spielberg felt the ending should drip with heavy irony by showing the shark applying its massive bite to the struggling Shaw just as the men on the USS Indianapolis had experienced.

In all the shots when the trio are chasing after the shark, Spielberg paid close attention never to show the land or any boats nearby even though the *Orca* was being filmed just a few hundred yards offshore. His crew motored after private boats floating into frame and told those manning the vessels to skedaddle. Spielberg's reasoning to all these laborious details was he didn't want the viewers to think the three shark hunters could just head back to the island's safe harbor instead of being isolated with the attacking shark deep in the waters of the Atlantic Ocean.

During the final third section of the film, all the footage was entirely filmed on the *Orca*. The rollicking waves also made the actors seasick on board as well as the cameraman who hand held the camera instead of planting it on a tripod. After seeing the movie's budget balloon, Spielberg called *Jaws* the most costly hand held movie ever produced.

Directing *Jaws* was a monumental ordeal for its director, who wanted perfection in every shot he filmed. Spielberg asked for 75 takes before he was satisfied with the sequence showing the *Orca* sinking temporarily trapping Scheider. The actor was dubious the rescue crew would be able to extract him in time in case the boat fully sank. He hid several axes throughout the cabin as life insurance in case the crew couldn't reach him in time so he could hack his way out.

Spielberg later reflected he was too much of a perfectionist on the set of *Jaws*. His inexperience producing a high-end motion picture caused him to stick to his guns when he insisted on creating a life-sized shark to be filmed at Martha's Vineyard where the book was set.

"I could have shot the movie in the tank or even in a protected lake somewhere, but it would not have looked the same," he said. "I was naive about the ocean, basically. I was pretty naive about mother nature and the hubris of a filmmaker who thinks he can conquer the elements was foolhardy, but I was too young to know. I was being foolhardy when I demanded that we shoot the film in the Atlantic Ocean and not in a North Hollywood tank."

For the residents and businesses on Martha's Vineyard, they were initially excited a major Hollywood studio would be using their island as its stage for the first time in its history. As the disruptions and delays mounted, the constant restrictions the production imposed on their lives began to wear down the natives' patience. However, who can't enjoy a summer on the Vineyard? The actors and crew certainly didn't, including Richard Dreyfuss, who's only noted domestic movie role before *Jaws* was in George Lucas's 1973 film *American Graffiti*. His stock as an actor was rising, though, and the production's long delays frustrated his ambitions to move on. "What am I doing here?" he joked to Spielberg. "I should be walking into Sardi's to applause and acclaim."

The original shooting was scheduled for 55 days, but because of the delays the production crew didn't wrap up until Day 159. In Spielberg's defense, his scheduled 12-hour filming days were condensed to only an average of four hours because of bad weather and those darned sharks' malfunctions (See Spielberg New Technology Section).

During the filming of *Jaws*, the studio set up a portable editing suite at Martha's Vineyard so editor Verna Fields could view and perform rudimentary edits from the daily footage Spielberg's cameramen shot. Because of the scarcity of footage with all the delays, Spielberg detailed, "we would shoot five scenes in a good day, three in an average day, and none in a bad day."

FROM THE OCEAN TO THE SKIES

After the experience with *Jaws* filming on the water, Spielberg vowed, "My next picture will be on dry land. There won't even be a bathroom scene." Sure enough, his next film, *Close Encounters,* is set in suburbia and in the western mountains. But the film did include a couple of bathroom scenes.

After leaving New England, he felt nothing could compare to the difficulties the director encountered in shooting *Jaws.* But he found out the Martha's Vineyard experience was peanuts compared to his encounters with *Close.* Spielberg admitted the UFO production was "twice as bad, and twice as expensive, as well."

Spielberg was able to cast in *Close Encounters* one of France's most illustrious and influential film directors during that country's "New Wave" era, Francois Truffaut. He agreed to play a French government scientist who heads the United States investigation into UFOs. Working efficiently directing his own modestly-budgeted films, Truffaut was becoming weary of the long shooting days Spielberg had scheduled. Compounding his frustration was the full plate of films he wanted to direct back home but couldn't because of the time he had to invest in *Close Encounters.* He was in disbelief that one helicopter sequence, budgeted for $250,000, was more than enough money for him to make a full-length feature film back home.

Spielberg was proud of the enormous set containing the landing strip for the alien's mothership. He escorted the French director through the set, thumping his chest about his crew's proud construction achievement. Truffaut, who was familiar with less expansive sets since his movies dealt with a handful of human, intimate relationships, wasn't quite as excitable as the young American.

Then Spielberg took Truffaut to another film set his crew was arranging where Jillian is in a hotel room watching TV and sees the Devil's Tower. Truffaut's eyes bulged out as he walked to the center of the room, elevated both his arms and said with a smile, "Now, THIS is a set!"

Despite acting in just two of his own movies, Truffaut came away with a deeper appreciation on the acting methods employed in the States. "Several times during the shooting Steven made me come out of myself," said Truffaut. "Thanks to that, I discovered a real pleasure as an actor."

He also came away being impressed by Spielberg's seemingly calm demeanor and jocular attitude when the pressure appeared to be smothering. "In the face of overwhelming hardships and innumerable complications that would, I suspect, have discouraged most directors, Steven Spielberg's perseverance and fortitude were simply amazing," Truffaut remarked.

DIRECTING CHILDREN

Unlike Hitchcock, who didn't like children and almost never employed them on the set, Spielberg takes the opposite tack. Actor Cary Guffey as Barry in *Close Encounters* was only three years old and his acting experience was zero coming into the production. Spielberg had to arrange a series of tricks to get the cute boy to react to certain events occurring in the movie. For one scene, Spielberg stood behind the camera holding a toy car behind him. When the camera began to roll, Spielberg took the toy car and held it up. Cary, looking at the camera and Spielberg, said the scripted word "toy." This is the scene where the boy looks out the window of the house and sees the illuminated UFOs.

In a later sequence, Cary has to show surprise when the aliens appear. To get the reaction needed, Spielberg, with two large containers next to the camera, had one of his crew dress up as a clown and another one as a gorilla and had them step into separate boxes before the boy arrived on the set. As the word "action" was said, the clown first popped out and Cary let out a delightful laugh. Then the guy in the gorilla suit emerged from his box. Cary's face is one of puzzlement, almost frightful. Then Spielberg cues the man in the gorilla suit to take off his mask. Cary smiles as he recognizes the man behind the mask.

In the final scene, when Cary is let off the mother ship, the script calls for him to be tearful. Spielberg asked him to pretend how he would feel if all his friends left him forever. It worked. The boy would be known as "one-take Cary" for the number of takes it took to get him to say and react to his lines.

Spielberg selected little girls between the ages of eight and twelve years old who lived locally in the Mobile, Alabama area to play the short aliens emerging from the mothership toward the end of the film. He thought their walk and movements would be more agile and similar to aliens than boys.

Spielberg also directed six-year-old Drew Barrymore for her role as the little sister of Elliot in *E.T.* While on the set one day, she kept forgetting her lines. Spielberg became frustrated at her constant brain freezes and started ripping into her. She cried like no other six-year-older could. Then someone told the director that, despite an extremely high fever, she felt she had to be at the studio to act her part. Spielberg, feeling tremendous guilt, came up to her, knelt down and gave her a big, warm hug, saying he was sorry several times while she was sobbing on his shoulder. He wrote a note and dispatched her home, telling her not to come back until she felt better.

CLOSE ENCOUNTERS SECRECY

Just as the arrival of the aliens in *Close Encounters* was shrouded in secrecy in the movie, the actual production was also under the strictest security. Spielberg felt he and the studios had invested so much into this film the idea could easily be copied and produced as a cheap, low-budget movie. For the final "third encounter," filming was done at the former Brookley Air Force Base in Mobile, Alabama. The base made the location an ideal place to secure the perimeter for everyone who entered. Trouble was the security was so tight that one day Spielberg had forgotten his ID card to get him in and he was turned back at the entrance by the security guards who didn't know who he was.

While he was in the middle of filming *Close Encounters,* Spielberg wasn't exactly clear in his own mind about the details of the appearance of the mothership. He told his special effects team only the spaceship would be huge, bulky and having no lights illuminating from the outside. Spielberg filmed the image in mind as he shot the scene of the crowd looking up as the spaceship descended, throwing a dark shadow over the onlookers.

He was hit by a lightbulb moment later after the Mobile shoot was finished when he was in India directing some additional footage for *Close.* He spotted an oil refinery dominating the horizon with its numerous lights shining on a web of pipes and other projections. Spielberg was so impressed at the complex he felt the mothership should look similar to the ornate, yet functionally sprawling refinery.

Not quite knowing the appearance of the UFOs before shooting was a common problem throughout the filming of *Close Encounters* where the director, cast, and crew had to react to the flying saucers which didn't exist on the movie stage. The special effects team added the spaceships well after filming was completed, creating some tense moments between the director and the actors listening to his commands. This was a complete departure from his nightmares while filming *Jaws* with all the mechanical malfunctions of the sharks, but at least the director could physically touch those sputtering swimming machines. Here, there was nothing to put his finger on, the process being so new and challenging to him.

Special effects supervisor Douglas Trumbull, who worked with Stanley Kubrick on *2001,* basically called the shots as to how the scenes should be set up and was grateful to Spielberg for placing all his trust in him and his technicians. "I'll never be able to thank him enough for having the confidence and the patience to see it through time and not panic," Trumbull said. "There was enormous pressure on the production all the time from the studio to keep moving on."

When it came to choosing his director of photography, Spielberg selected Vilmos Zsigmond, considered one of the top ten cinematographers in the industry. Zsigmond, who had previously filmed *McCabe and Mrs. Miller* and *Deliverance,* had previously worked with Spielberg on *The Sugerland Express.* Once briefed on the project, Zsigmond realized the scope of *Close Encounters* was much more immense than his previous effort with the director. Viewing the UFO landing set in the hanger at Mobile, Alabama, he estimated it would take at least one day for the lighting crew to pre-light the huge set, something the director hadn't scheduled. Producer Julia Phillips, busy with her abacus calculating the rising costs of the production, said the delay wasn't budgeted. But Spielberg and Trumbull saw the value of the strong lighting on the set because it would make matching his post-production work with matted UFOs much easier.

Phillips had a vendetta against Zsigmond as the days in Mobile dragged on. After two months into the production she lobbied studio executives to fire the cinematographer. They agreed and phone calls were made to other highly-regarded cinematographers whose schedules were open. The studio told them they were going to replace Zsigmond. The cinematographers all knew Zsigmond and his work and they admitted if he was unable to manage the filming, then no one could.

Zsigmond also noticed a difference in Spielberg while working alongside the director. The cinematographer found him to be more confident but less willing to talk about alternatives to camera placements and other production facets, a contrast to when he worked with him on *Sugarland*. He said "*Close Encounters* had the smell of a great movie. We fell into sand traps not because anybody made mistakes but because we were making things that had never been done before."

Producer Phillips wasn't the only one Spielberg had to battle to get the extra funding needed to complete the movie. Columbia Pictures executives also were reluctant to gush open the cash register for the director. For all the complexity of details on the technical and aesthetic aspects of the production, Spielberg was frustrated having to spend so much time on lobbying for more money. On one occasion where the script called for the control room windows at the Devil's Tower pad to shatter because of the immense sound coming from the mother spaceship, the cost to film such an effect was projected to run several thousand dollars, a figure the studio refused to spend. Spielberg reached into his own wallet to shell out the money, knowing the scene was that important.

RAIDERS' ADVENTURES

The memorable opening scene in *Raiders* showing a boulder rolling down the cave while Harrison Ford is barely out in front of it running for his life, had to be filmed twice, calling for five cameras positioned in different areas of the set. When Ford scampers out of the mouth of the cave, he stumbled in one of the takes. Because the fall looks so real, Spielberg selected the shot for the final cut.

Tunisia, the setting for part of *Raiders,* is a dry, hot, desert-like country posing difficulties for cast and crew filming outside in the blazing heat. Remembering how 54-year-old director David Lean operated in similar conditions for a long fourteen months while filming Spielberg's favorite movie, *Lawrence of Arabia,* Spielberg and Lucas, who was assisting the director, thought they could bear the conditions for the scheduled six-week shoot. As the physical stress mounted, however, Spielberg was able to shorten the filming in Tunisia to four-and-a-half weeks, shaving 12 days off to escape the brutal heat.

One of the more challenging scenes to film in *Raiders* was when Ford and Allen are trapped in the "Well of Souls," with hundreds of slithering snakes. The scene was shot in EMI Studios in England, the first of many trips Spielberg would take to the United Kingdom to produce his movies.

"I have made almost as many films in England as I have in America," said United States citizen Spielberg. "I will come back to England again and again."

To gather all those snakes for the *Raiders'* scene, crew members had to find truckloads of snakes within London and Southern England pet stores. The snakes they purchased were species found in all parts of the world and weren't indigenous to one particular area. Despite the crew's best efforts, once all the snakes were positioned on the studio floor, there were gaps. To fill in those spaces, several black hoses were sliced into the lengths of a standard snake to make the hoses look like serpents.

When Ford is first dropped into the large well, a cobra flares his flanks and spits at him. To film the effect safely, a glass was positioned between the actor and the killer snake. For the cobra to flare out, a toy rabbit was shown just behind the camera so the cobra reacted with pure venom, which it actually spits onto the glass. This cobra was so poisonous it killed a large python while the cameras were being set up.

The script called for close ups of Allen walking among the snakes in the well. The actress was absolutely terrified by snakes as well as her body double, who refused to tip toe through the slithering reptiles. Spielberg looked around for volunteers to stand in for Allen's legs and a snake handler came forward. The director looked at his legs and said as long as he shaved them and wore Allen's dress he would do.

THE BUSY YEAR OF 1981

To show a connection between a humanoid who was 10-years-old and a space alien, Spielberg had the psychological foresight to film most of *E.T.* eye level at Elliott's height. He also used his sentimental advantage of recognizing how children will attach themselves over a period of time to a living, breathing thing, no matter what the species. The director, looking for the huge, teary-eyed payoff at the end of the movie, designed the shooting schedule to parallel the plot chronologically from the beginning to the heart-tugging finale. The filming sequence produced the effect Spielberg was looking for in his childhood actors when E.T. climbs onto his spaceship to return back "home." Those tears from the actors, including the adults, are authentic.

1981 was a very busy year for Spielberg. Universal Studios had a contract with him precluding the director from being involved in any other movie while *E.T* was in production. But he spent an inordinate amount of time immersed in another of his projects, *Poltergeist,* which *Texas Chainsaw Massacre* director Tobe Hooper was tabbed to direct. Spielberg was heavily involved in the preproduction preparation of the script and scene layout of *Poltergeist.* Reportedly he went over to the nearby studio set where the production of *Poltergeist* was being filmed during breaks from directing *E.T.* to offer guidance to Hooper. The correlation between *E.T.* and *Poltergeist* is striking in that the happy outcome of the former is a fulfillment of suburban dreams, while the latter movie shows the nightmares surrounding suburban living.

DIRECTING DINOSAURS

While directing *Purple,* Spielberg's wife, Amy Irving, was pregnant. The director was setting up the scene showing Celie giving birth when coincidentally he received a call from Amy saying she was heading to the hospital to deliver. Spielberg informed his assistant director to handle the filming of the birth for *Purple* while he was attending his wife's own personal labors. As ever a detailed cinephile, he recorded his new baby, Max, crying and used his new son's bawling for Celie's own baby during the delivery in the movie.

To embark on the ambitious *Jurassic Park,* Spielberg planned to launch the multi-week shoot by first using the robotic animatronic Triceratops the special effects team, headed by Stan Winston, had constructed. This is the scene where the dinosaur is lying on the ground with breathing problems. Winston agreed with Spielberg the scene would make a good launching point for the cast to ease into their roles with dinosaurs. The tougher stuff, they saw, would come later. The director had a nostalgic sentimentality for this particular breed of dinosaur since as a boy his parents gave him a Triceratops for his first toy.

In *Jurassic Park,* Spielberg planned to have the fierce T-Rex appear for the first time in the movie by the frightened "tourists" sitting in their vans with the park's electrical grid shut off. He wanted the viewers in the theaters to experience for themselves the approaching danger of the menacing beast first-hand. The effects team was stumped on how to introduce the earth-shaking T-Rex who is unseen in the distance but whose advancing presence is felt by the stranded visitors. Spielberg recalled boosting the stereo in his car and seeing his side mirror vibrating to the sound of the bass. He thought showing a similar effect would be visually effective. The director didn't want to use the van mirror but thought having a cup water sitting in the van with oscillating rings would do the trick. Michael Lantieri, the mastermind behind numerous challenges such as this, was baffled, but didn't let on that his head was aching thinking of a solution. Days clicked by until the night before the scheduled scene was to be shot, Lanieri dragged out his guitar, placed a glass of water on top of it and strummed one of the strings. His eyes saw the glass vibrate, with the rings of the water rippling perfectly as Spielberg envisioned it. Lantieri spent the next day placing guitar strings underneath the van's dashboard and plucked the strings to simulate the T-Rex's approach shaking the ground.

To convey the ear-piercing roar of the T-Rex in certain scenes, Spielberg would take his megaphone and imitate the thunderous yell on the set. Spielberg's fake roar made the actors howl in laughter during several takes.

"After a scary movie about the world almost ending, we can walk into the sunlight and say, 'Wow, everything's still here. I'm OK!'" reflected Spielberg. "We like to tease ourselves. Human beings have a need to get close to the edge and, when filmmakers or writers can take them to the edge, it feels like a dream where you're falling, but you wake up just before you hit the ground."

For the wrap-up party after the last night of the *Jurassic* filming, Spielberg made a toast after everyone's glass had been filled to the brim with champagne, rattling off impressive statistics such as the movie taking two years of meticulous planning and four months of actual shooting. He added proudly that the original filming schedule as planned had been only twelve days longer than the actual shoot, and that was because a fierce typhoon ripping through the Hawaiian Islands had interrupted filming. The production was within its budget--a vast improvement over his first blockbuster, *Jaws*.

MORE SERIOUS DIRECTING ASSIGNMENTS

There are some instances where levity is needed on and off the set, especially when the cast and crew are immersed with the Holocaust every single day. Spielberg noticed his people on the set for *Schindler's* were getting very depressed as filming progressed. To lift the atmosphere, Spielberg phoned his good friend comedian Robin Williams and asked him if he could record some comedy routines to be played over the film location's loudspeakers. Williams did and his jokes lightened up those on the set. Some of the skits Williams recorded ended up being used in Disney's 1992 *Aladdin* where Williams provided the voice for the Genie.

Spielberg also unwound by watching episodes of *Seinfeld* every night after spending grim days directing *Schindler*.

Storyboarding, consisting of rough hand drawn sketches of scenes the director refers to on the movie set, is a regular aid Spielberg uses in his pictures. Unusual for Spielberg, according to actor Liam Neeson, *Schindler's List* was the first feature film the director claimed he didn't bother to storyboard.

Spielberg was aware of the Jewish tradition of placing small stones on the graves of people held in high esteem by visitors at cemeteries. In the midst of the *Schindler* production, Spielberg came up with the idea of attaching an epilogue to the movie where the real-life survivors saved by Schindler's heroic efforts would visit Oskar's grave at Mount Zion Catholic Cemetery in Jerusalem. It was a challenge to contact and fly several of the survivors, but the ending is noteworthy for its enduring emotional impact.

Private Ryan steps right out of the gate with one of the most epic battle sequences in cinematic history, the Allied landing on D-Day during World War II. The four-week filming on the Wexford County beach of Curroclue in southern Ireland involved over 1,000 paid extras as well as the Irish Army Reserves contributing 2,500 of its members. Originally, the film was scheduled to have been shot in England, but the British Ministry of Defense declined to offer the thousands of soldiers needed for the production. Spielberg received the offer from the Irish government to volunteer their troops, so the director moved his operation to the Emerald Isle. About thirty amputees were selected to wear prosthetic limbs. When a blank explosion occurs nearby their fake limbs rip apart from them, showing their arms or legs severed, a trick used by D.W. Griffith in his 1916 *Intolerance*.

The filming of the D-Day scenes first began on the water, then moved onto the water's edge the following days, progressing each day up to and over the sand dunes to the German bunkers. The entire D-Day sequence cost over $11 million alone to produce.

The director is also known to suddenly come up with an idea on the set which, in the final analysis, improves both the camera angles and the flow of the plot, similar to the directing style of his idol, John Ford. Spielberg developed this habit of veering away from his preconceived plans of positioning his cameras and sequential shots in his early movie, *Jaws*. This practice at improvising on the spur-of-the-moment was necessitated in his early movie because of technical problems with the unreliability of his mechanical sharks. Like Ford, Spielberg is a big proponent of "cutting-in-camera" where he envisions the sequence of shots which will appear on the screen and attempts to shoot them chronologically.

"I think 'cutting-in-the-camera' is the greatest lesson that any director can learn about filmmaking, because when you don't get it, you don't get it, and there's no way to go back and get it," described Spielberg's and John Ford's technique of sequential filming.

PERMITTING FREE-FLOWING DIALOGUE

Spielberg is also one of those directors who allows his actors to ad-lib their lines, but within reason. One of the most famous quotes in cinema, "You're gonna need a bigger boat," was improvised by Roy Scheider when he informed Shaw of his ship's liability after seeing the shark for the first time up close in *Jaws*.

In another ad-libbed scene making the final cut was in *Close Encounters*. Dreyfuss is dishing a pile of mashed potatoes on his plate while at the dinner table with his family. His daughter, completely unscripted, says, "There's a dead fly in my potatoes." The other members of the family were able to suppress their laughter and the scene was left intact.

The unforgettable scene in *Raiders* where Harrison Ford takes out his gun in a confrontation with an attacking swordsman who shows off his talent by whipping a large sword around was not in the script. Ford and several other members of the film crew had come down with food poisoning right before the scheduled scene in Tunisia. Spielberg, who always travels with cases of canned Spaghetti-O's, didn't get sick since he didn't eat the local food. Originally scripted were the two combatants involved in a physical punching match before Ford wins out. But after several attempts to get the fight right, the sickly Ford was unable to look convincing. The actor offered an alternative to Spielberg. "Why don't I just shoot the sucker," Ford said. Spielberg approved the suggestion and the results are on the screen.

In another scene, during a love tryst between Ford and Karen Allen aboard a ship, the actor decided to ad-lib what has become one of *Raiders'* more signature lines, "It's not the years, honey, it's the mileage."

For a pivotal scene in *Purple,* Whoopi Goldberg is in a conversation with Oprah Winfrey during the dinner episode. Spielberg wasn't quite satisfied with the earlier takes because of the awkward dialogue written in the script. He asked Winfrey, a rookie in front of the movie camera, to in her own words recapture the feeling of seeing Goldberg (Celie) shopping in the store while she was with Miss Millie. Goldberg, who made a living at comedy improvisation on the stage, went along with the impromptu. After a successful take, Goldberg got up from her chair and hugged Winfrey, telling her she is now a bonafide actress.

In *Private Ryan,* Tom Hanks has a scene talking to his soldiers where he goes on and on about what he does back home. The actor thought about the speech and realized his character would never discuss himself in such great detail. He relayed his feelings to Spielberg, who immediately concurred. Thus Hanks' biographical revelation is considerably abbreviated but more honest to his character's personality.

Those who work on several productions with Spielberg know when he gets upset he'll use his go-to swear word, "Rats!"

DIRECTING IN VIRGINIA

Spielberg is no stranger to the Virginia area. Numerous films, including 2002's *Minority Report,* were shot in Washington D.C. as well as on the state's Middle Peninsula near Gloucester. His 2005 *War of the Worlds* used the Shenandoah Valley for a battle sequence and in 2012 he spent considerable time in Richmond and Petersburg making *Lincoln. Schindler's List,* premiered in Washington, D.C.'s Holocaust Museum, where he gave $3 million to the museum.

SPIELBERG'S USE OF NEW TECHNOLOGY

Numerous books have been published about how the mechanical shark used in *Jaws* caused all sorts of consternation for the cast and crew throughout the production. Examining the shark models, Spielberg was initially proud of the accomplishments of his special effects crew before the shark was introduced to the salt water. The director took three of his friends, Martin Scorsese, George Lucas, and *Jaws* scriptwriter John Milius to the room where the shark sat during the testing phase. Ever curious, Lucas wanted to check out the inside mechanics to see how the shark worked and he stuck his head into the contraption's mouth. Spielberg and Milius decided to play a joke on Lucas, taking one of the controls operating the shark's mouth and clamped down on Lucas' head. They then moved the controls to open the mouth--and nothing happened. Lucas' head was stuck in the shark's mouth and he couldn't get out. After some maneuvering, the shark's mouth finally opened and a shocked Lucas was glad to find his head still attached to his body. They all bolted out of the special effects building, thinking they had busted the mechanics. Little did Spielberg know in a few short days that shark would cause more nightmares than the four could ever imagine.

The primary reason the mechanical shark isn't fully seen until toward the end of the movie is the saltwater did a number on its movable parts and electronics. The effects crew had never placed the shark into saline water and tested it before arriving at Martha's Vineyard for filming. Once in the ocean, the shark immediately sank to the bottom. A team of scuba divers on hand had to swim down to retrieve the limp fake shark. Thus began the ordeal of the effects crew in its attempt to keep the shark afloat and working. (Actually there were two mechanical sharks, one to turn left and the other to turn right.) And when shark did appear above the surface, it looked anything but terrifying.

"I had no choice but to figure out how to tell the story without the shark" recalled Spielberg, who had to think of shots needed on the spot to cover the scenes where the shark was supposed to appear but was unable because of malfunctions.

"It's what we don't see which is truly frightening," added Spielberg, echoing Hitchcock's philosophy.

Another bad break was when the *Orca* began sinking after an unscheduled accident ripped a hole in the hull. The actors' safety was paramount in Spielberg's mind when he yelled into his bullhorn for the nearby boats to rescue the three actors. The audio technician on board the *Orca* yelled back, "Screw the actors, save the sound department." The rescuers responded by getting everyone off the decks.

The film in the camera shooting the scenes on the sinking boat went under water before a crew member grabbed it. The crucial scene just filmed was encased in the leaky watery, salty canister. The cameraman had a lightbulb moment, realizing the solution used to develop film is saline, the same chemistry makeup as the sea. They flew the canister to New York City where the film lab successfully developed the precious celluloid.

Spielberg prides himself as one of the elite film directors who loves to incorporate the latest technology. Sometimes his ideas are way ahead of what the technical industry has to offer. He hired Trumbull to supervise the highly-visual *Close Encounters*. In the mid-1970s computer generated imagery (CGI) was in its infancy, and even though Spielberg was able to conduct a few tests on the appearances of spaceships by way of computer he found the results not too believable.

Spielberg is a huge fan of Merian Cooper's 1933 classic *King Kong*. Once he read Crichton's book *Jurassic Park* he knew he had to direct the adaptation. Spielberg even inserts a line said by actor Ian Malcolm, "What have they got in there? King Kong?" Taking Universal Studio's *King Kong Encounter* ride, Spielberg was impressed by the texture of the beast on display. He sat down with the initial designers of *Jurassic* and asked them to transfer Universal's aesthetic appearance to the dinosaur, with the smoothness and muscle tone similar to King Kong's.

Making a movie about dinosaurs posed a myriad of problems for Spielberg, a film about a modern day zoo hosting prehistoric giants. He hired a team of Hollywood's best special effects professionals in the industry, each with their own specialties and each foaming at the mouth to work with Spielberg. Dennis Muren, who created the breathtaking computer images in 1991's *Terminator 2*, was confident he could showcase the movie's entire line-up of dinosaurs on his advanced computer-generated equipment. Spielberg wasn't sold on Muren's idea, thinking the old-fashion "go-motion" used from the mid-1920's silent era would be the main component for the dinosaurs special effects in the movie. As a video gamer, Spielberg's felt Muren's computer effects would be similar to the cartoon characters he was so used to playing with in his Nintendo games. The director assigned Phil Tippett to head a team of go-motion special effects artists to handle the dinosaurs.

Muren was confident in the sophistication of the emerging computer technology capabilities. His team created a clip of what the computer was capable of creating. Muren revealed the results by showing the director the scene where the Gallimimus herd is seen traipsing around a field along with a T-Rex in the frame chasing the smaller dinosaurs. Spielberg and Tippett viewed the result. Both were astonished by the effects. Tippett somberly predicted "I think we're extinct" on his go-motion effects. Spielberg loved Tippett's lamentation so much he had actor Jeff Goldblum echo his exact words in the movie to Sam Neill while at the Visitor's Center.

Not all was lost for Tippett and his team. His go-motion effects were used when Muren saw a need to duplicate the motion of the dinosaurs to input into his computer. Placing motion sensors on Tippett's constructed miniature dinosaurs, the computer technicians were able to track each movement of the dinosaurs, replicating the exact flow of these creatures as they moved throughout the park.

When Muren and his crew proved themselves experts at creating realistic dinosaur images, Spielberg reconfigured the ending of *Jurassic.* Instead of originally showing the pesky Raptors being killed by the T-Rex skeleton hanging in the Visitor's Center after they chased the humans around the building, the director decided shortly before the filming was scheduled to end to have the ferocious T-Rex make one more appearance. He drew up the plans for the last day's shoot to have the actors pretend the T-Rex was in the Visitor's Center fighting the Raptors without the dinosaurs actually being in the room. The computer imagery would be added well after filming was finished.

When people think of *Jurassic Park* they think the film is loaded from beginning to end with dinosaur footage. But the movie has only 15 minutes of the beasts. Stan Winston's team of animatronics, or robotic dinosaurs, provides nine minutes of the footage while Muren's computer generated imagery fills out the remaining six minutes. CGI is used to show the entire dinosaurs' bodies while those scenes showing parts of the dinosaurs consist of the robotic construction.

"I'm as guilty as anyone, because I helped to herald the digital era with *Jurassic Park,*" said Spielberg, partly saddened by Hollywood's now dependence on computer special effects. "But the danger is that it can be abused to the point where nothing is eye-popping any more. The difference between making *Jaws* thirty-one years ago and (2005) *War of the Worlds* is that today, anything I can imagine, I can realize on film. Then, when my mechanical shark was being repaired and I had to shoot something, I had to make the water scary. I relied on the audience's imagination, aided by where I put the camera. Today, it would be a digital shark. It would cost a hell of a lot more, but never break down. As a result, I probably would have used it four times as much, which would have made the film four times less scary. *Jaws* is scary because of what you don't see, not because of what you do. We need to bring the audience back into partnership with storytelling."

Spielberg thought he came up with a great idea for filming the D-Day scenes in *Private Ryan* to reflect how the battle really looked like in the eyes of the soldiers attacking the Germans on the beach. He devised small mechanical drills affixed to the film cameras. When the explosion occurred nearby, the operator could turn on the drill to jiggle the camera. When he presented what he thought was his great invention to his cinematographer, he was gently reminded there was a lens called the shaker lens that did exactly what the director was looking for. Spielberg's hopes of getting into the Inventor's Hall of Fame were quickly dashed.

Spielberg did operate one of the several cameras filming the Omaha Beach scenes and some of the footage he shot eventually made the final edit.

POST-PRODUCTION

USING MUSIC TO EDIT

Spielberg is one of those directors like Stanley Kubrick who has temporary music, usually from other movie soundtracks, accompany the preliminary cuts of his films. Music composers usually score films once the movie is at or near completion.

Composer John Williams had first worked with Spielberg on his early film, *Sugarland Express,* and was hired to write the music for *Jaws.* Spielberg heard the two-note ostinato playing every time the shark was approaching his victim. The director said, "That's funny, John, really; but what did you really have in mind for the theme?" Spielberg admitted afterwards without that score *Jaws* would have been not been nearly as successful of a film.

"I've never used John Williams to tell people how to feel," said Spielberg. "I use John Williams to enhance my vision and my thoughts emotionally from scene to scene. He'll signal when the shark is coming, which are the most famous single notes next to Beethoven's Fifth. In telling a story, I will use every tool in my arsenal. I will do anything in my power to communicate the best story as I know how."

In *Close Encounters,* Williams ran by Spielberg hundreds of different musical note variations he composed to denote the aliens attempt to communicate with the earthlings. They both settled on the now widely-recognized five-note string. In the same film, what is opposite in how composers work in post-production, Williams scored the final scenes of the film before it was edited. Then editor Michael Kahn and Spielberg sat down and matched the footage shot to the music, giving those closing sequences a lyrical atmospheric ambiance.

Spielberg did a similar thing with Williams for *E.T. 's* ending. Williams was scratching his head after he made several attempts to score the music, trying to harmonize what Kahn and the director had edited. The ever pliable Spielberg allowed Williams to create his own composition and the editors would cut the film based on the musical score. Williams did and Kahn re-edited the film to Williams' orchestrated melody.

The unconventional method in *E.T.* gave Williams the opportunity to create a memorable composition, earning him the 1982 Academy Award for Best Original Score. The music was so popular Williams, with the Los Angeles Philharmonic Orchestra, gave a sold-out performance in 2013 at the Hollywood Bowl, conducting the soundtrack with the last reel of *E.T.* playing on the bowl's giant screen.

Williams has scored all of Spielberg's full-length movies up to 2015's *Bridge of Spies*, which had its music written by Thomas Newman because of Williams' health issues. *The Color Purple's* music was composed by musician/producer Quincy Jones.

After seeing the first cuts of *Jurassic,* Williams was so moved by viewing the rough version of the movie he wanted to compose "pieces that would convey a sense of awe and fascination, given it dealt with the overwhelming happiness and excitement that would emerge from seeing live dinosaurs."

Working on *Schindler's List,* Williams was shown the rough cut of the movie before he was ready to score the musical soundtrack. The composer was so emotionally wracked after viewing the film he told Spielberg he needed to take a walk. Reflecting on the picture, Williams returned and informed Spielberg what he saw required a far more talented composer than he was. Spielberg's retort, referring to the past classical musical geniuses, "I know, but they're all dead."

"If I weren't a director, I would want to be a film composer," said Spielberg, admiring Williams' talent at writing music.

HARDSHIPS IN THE EDITING SUITE

The editing process does have its challenges for Spielberg. In fact, the editing of *Close Encounters* was so complex, Spielberg to this day claims he has experienced nothing more difficult in his career than putting together the film's final 24 minutes. Just as the studio considered the filming of the picture to be a top-secret priority, Spielberg carried out the covert operation into the editing phase where he set up an editing suite in a Marina del Rey rented apartment instead of a studio suite, with 24-7 guarded security.

The difficulties in editing *Close Encounters* were stressful enough. But when it came time to edit *Jurassic Park,* the emotional toll was telling on Spielberg. The reason: the director was in Poland filming *Schindler's List* while at the same time he was assisting on editing the dinosaur movie at nights and on his weekends. He had set up a post-production suite for *Jurassic* nearby where he was filming the Holocaust movie. Spielberg was in communication with his editor Kahn and ILM, the digital effects company handling the dinosaur computer images, four times a week via a video link. Universal rented at $1.5 million per week two Polish television station's satellite channels--one for the visuals and the other for the audio. The setup showed Spielberg the special effects clips the experts back in Hollywood were working on.

The two movies couldn't have been more different. Spielberg days spent dealing with the horrific subject-matter in *Schindler's* contrasted with the maneuvering of digital dinosaurs. Dealing with questions from the Hollywood special effects technicians appeared to Spielberg trivial compared to the dark themes of the Holocaust he had to tackle during the day. He took at least an hour after leaving the Poland film set to prepare himself emotionally ready to face the dinosaurs. The director's interest in *Jurassic* began to diminish as time went on. He called it "a bipolar experience, with every ounce of intuition on *Schindler's List,* and every ounce of craft on *Jurassic Park.*"

Judging from Spielberg's schedule, as witnessed at how he juggled *Jurassic's* editing with *Schindler's* directing, shows he is a constant whirlwind of activity with his producing, directing, writing, and being a father to his children, all at the same time.

"I don't drink coffee," revealed Spielberg. "I've never had a cup of coffee in my entire life. That's something you probably don't know about me. I've hated the taste since I was a kid."

Universities offering paleontology courses and majors in the field were fortunate after *Jurassic Park* gained worldwide popularity. A record number of students, inspired by the dinosaurs and the characters who studied these large beasts, enrolled in record numbers in colleges offering the courses.

During the initial preview of *Jaws,* Spielberg noticed the audience screamed when the shark made its first appearance out of the water when Scheider is chumming in the back deck of *Orca*. Spielberg thought of a way to create "one more scare" scene that would send viewers jumping out of their seats. He revisited the night sequence where Dreyfuss is diving around Ben Gardner's sunken boat.

The studio, after 159 days financing the lengthy shooting schedule, was hesitant to spend another dime on additional filming. Spielberg decided to pay the extra expenses himself to film the extra scare scene. Editor Verna Fields had a back-yard swimming pool the director felt would be perfect to shoot the scene under Ben Gardner's boat. To recreate the ocean water, he poured a gallon of milk to make it murky while a body double suited up in Dreyfuss' scuba gear to fill in for the actor.

Spielberg, who was eventually reimbursed by the studio for his costs, recreated the bottom of the sunken boat, with the dead fisherman's head suddenly appearing out of the hull's gaping hole, scaring the surprised diver out of the water.

Spielberg had his wish fulfilled when the next preview audience jumped when the newly-shot scene was inserted. But when the shark first emerges out of the water later on in the movie while Scheider is chumming, the big "scare's" reaction from the audience was only half as frightful and loud as in the first preview. The viewers had already been shocked with the initial sudden "dead head appearance," Spielberg noticed, while by the time the second "big scare moment" arrived, they were on their guard, diminishing the pivotal clip's effect. The process taught him a lesson, which Spielberg later admitted: a picture can only contain one dramatic scary scene and that scene better be pivotal to the movie.

Jaws won the Academy Award for Best Editing, with Verna Fields, who had earlier edited George Lucas' *American Graffiti* among other movies, receiving the Oscar. Her work is often cited as one of the primary reasons why *Jaws* has become a classic, much to the chagrin of the then 28-year-old director. Although she was promoted by Universal Studios to an executive consultant position, Fields would never edit another Spielberg film. He opted to work with Michael Kahn, the editor for his next film, *Close Encounters*, who would continue to edit a great majority of Spielberg films for the next 30 years. Ms. Fields would pass away in 1982 when Spielberg had produced three additional films up to her death.

AFTER THE RELEASES OF SPIELBERG'S FILMS

In one of the most unusual coincidences of all time, Spielberg's UFO film *Close Encounters* was launched at the same time his good friend George Lucas premiered his space-themed movie, *Star Wars*. In another strange twist, Lucas' flick outperformed Spielberg's previous effort, *Jaws,* to become the new record box office champion.

French director Truffaut, as mentioned above, had a non-directorial acting role in *Close Encounters*. Truffaut's influential mentor, French director Jean Renoir, was so impressed by the movie he compared *Close Encounters* to the works of author Jules Verne and pioneer film director Georges Melies, who produced cinema's first science-fiction picture, 1902's *A Trip To The Moon*.

Close Encounters is cited as one of the most frequently shown movies on the silver screen in the history of cinema where it is viewed every night at the Devil's Tower KOA Campground.

President Ronald Reagan and his wife Nancy came from Hollywood backgrounds and their love for movies is legendary. The two invited Spielberg in the summer of 1982 to give a personal showing of *E.T.* at the White House, which he gladly did. The D.C. showing was the beginning of the longest theatrical run in the 1980s of a movie, projected over a year in many of the nation's movie houses.

Normally Spielberg's career is as non-controversial as any top-tiered director. However, when he was named director for *Purple,* the minority community was up in arms. The group felt a white director at the helm was a slap in the face toward talented African-American directors who had more honest emotional connections to the story. The black populace was even more furious with the results of the 58th Academy Awards, when, out of eleven nominations including Best Picture (but not Best Director), *Purple* received ZERO Oscars.

Alice Walker, the writer of the novel *Purple* was based on, was allowed to view the footage shot each day on location and in the studio. She was not impressed by the movie until she saw the final cut in a private showing. She couldn't believe how let down she was, in particular the opening scene where she thought it resembled too much of an Oscar and Hammerstein-type opening as seen in 1955's *Oklahoma.* Her opinion was supported by her hesitation in the selection of Spielberg as the director despite her seeing *E.T.* The author predicted before Spielberg shot *Purple* his treatment of the alien was similar to how he would treat "a person of color."

The skeptical Walker, however, changed her mind when she attended the premiere of *Purple.* The spirited audience, heaping glowing approval of the finished movie, convinced Walker that, although the narrative departed from her book, the movie hit the right notes to the themes contained in her novel.

Later in his career, Spielberg inked lucrative deals to direct and/or produce movies, making him the richest film director in cinematic history. By gaining a percentage of *Jurassic Park's* film receipts and other residuals, Spielberg realized a hefty $250 million for his efforts directing the picture, by far making the movie his most successful one in terms of profit.

For all the money he could have collected for directing *Schindler's,* Spielberg refused to accept one dime in royalties and other ancillary funds from the movie, saying to do so would be collecting "blood money." He instead donated all the money he would have made on the film to the Shoah Foundation, an organization preserving the records and testimonies of genocide survivors, including the Holocaust.

In another sign of generosity from the profits he made in *Private Ryan,* Spielberg donated money to the National D-day Memorial in Bedford, Virginia. The funding was contributed to build the Arnold M. Spielberg

Theater on the grounds of the memorial in memory of his father, who was a communications chief of a B-25 air squadron in India flying several combat missions during World War II.

The director didn't want to hold back on the excessive gore portrayed in *Private Ryan* since he wanted to depict war as it actually was, humans killing humans. Spielberg felt going into the production the graphic nature of the film would preclude it from becoming a commercial success. The project had been a passion of his to recognize the sacrifices his father and millions of other made during WWII, so he really didn't care about making any money. To the surprise of the director, *Private Ryan* turned out to be financially very successful in the theaters.

As an international marque director able to get his movies distributed globally, Spielberg has run into some problems concerning the different cultures constituting his overseas viewership. Malaysia banned *Private Ryan* when Spielberg refused to make a number of cuts the southeastern Asian country demanded in the finished film. In India, its Censor Board nixed showing *Private Ryan* because what they considered excessive violence. In order to show the film in this highly lucrative market, the board insisted Spielberg make a number of cuts to pare down on the movie's blood and gore. The director refused and withdrew the film from being shown in the country. India's Home Minister, having read the rave reviews of the war film, was able to view the movie. Moved by the picture, he made a phone call to the board and told them to revoke its insistence to any cuts. The board bowed graciously to his commands and *Private Ryan* turned out to be a big hit in the country.

Like most film directors included in this book, Spielberg rejects any opportunity to provide commentary in what is a common industry practice of offering director's remarks for their movies' DVD special releases.

SPIELBERG'S LATER YEARS

Past social security age, Spielberg continues to pump out movies at a prestigious pace at the time of this book's printing.

"Once a month the sky falls on my head, I come to and I see another movie I want to make," describes Spielberg on the reason why he's still inspired to make his next picture. "I dream for a living.

"The most expensive habit in the world is celluloid, not heroin, and I need a fix every two years," added Spielberg.

As all past influential geniuses, none wanted to retire from the set. Spielberg seems to be no exception.

"It boggles my mind how much I feel is left on my plate," revealed Spielberg.

"There are things on the other side of the supper table stewing in pots that I'm not really even aware of. I would retire if I didn't feel that way." As financially successful his films continue to be and as entertaining and impactful as they are, a Spielberg picture will always be a highly anticipated event from Hollywood's most imaginative director.

TOP TEN STEVEN SPIELBERG MOVIES

#1--JAWS (1975)

Purely for historical purposes alone, *Jaws* ranks in the pantheon of Hollywood's great movies. *Jaws* created the summertime blockbuster films, catapulted the thriller genre to new heights, and jump-started Spielberg's career to where it is today. There are so many "firsts" for *Jaws,* such as first nationally released film in thousands of theaters on the same day, first film to roll out a national advertising campaign, first to create a national hysteria for a phobia (going into the ocean); the list goes on and on. Cinema would never be the same again and despite three sequels attempting to capitalize on the *Jaws* phenomenon (none directed by Spielberg), nothing can approach the original.

#2--E.T. THE EXTRA TERRESTRIAL (1982)

Spielberg's admittedly second most personal movie, *E.T.* is one of those rare movies that hits the emotional chord throughout the age spectrum. Derek Malcolm of The Guardian wrote, "*E.T.* is a superlative piece of popular cinema, a dream of childhood, brilliantly orchestrated to involve not only children but anyone able to remember being one." Winning four Academy Awards, including John Williams' memorable score, *E.T.* did not earn Spielberg the Best Director Oscar, going instead to *Gandhi* director Richard Attenborough, who noted "I was certain that not only would *E.T.* win, but that it should win. It was inventive, powerful, wonderful. I make more mundane movies."

#3--SAVING PRIVATE RYAN (1998)

The first 20 minutes of the Americans landing at Omaha Beach during D-Day alone should make this World War II movie one of the best war films ever produced. Spielberg, however, relying on a perfect script, portrays the cruelty of battle as well as the philosophical dimensions surrounding the

inhumanity of military engagements with adroit expertise. The ending
anchors the sacrifices of millions of young Americans have paid towards the
preservation of the United States in this war as well as all previous and
subsequent wars.

#4--SCHINDLER'S LIST (1994)

Spielberg finally earned his Best Director Oscar as well as directed his first
Academy Award Best Film in this portrayal of one man's quest to save as
many Jews as he possibly could from the clutches of a brutal Nazi machine
intent on eliminating an entire religious race. British critic John Gross wrote,
"Spielberg shows a firm moral and emotional grasp of his material. The film
is an outstanding achievement." The movie ranks up there as being one of the
most personal films Spielberg has ever made. The depressing nature of the
subject-matter didn't get in his way of producing a powerful Holocaust-
themed movie, one of the most impactful ones in cinematic history.

#5--RAIDERS OF THE LOST ARK (1981)

Having fun while updating the aesthetics of 1930s serial adventure movies,
Spielberg pole-vaulted over that popular genre by producing one of the most
exciting and visually enticing movies for the ages. Observed critic Bruce
Williamson, "There's more excitement in the first ten minutes of Raiders than
any movie I have seen all year. By the time the explosive misadventures end,
any movie-goer worth his salt ought to be exhausted." The film is like being
on a roller coaster, with the thrills cascading from one episode to the next,
from one country to the next. Never would adventure movies be the same
again.

#6--JURASSIC PARK (1993)

For those who love computer graphics imagery in their movies, you can
thank Spielberg for producing this groundbreaking film which popularized
the use of CGI in cinema. The characters may be flat and dull but their
counterpart dinosaurs steal the show with breathtaking force. Read one
review, "*Jurassic Park* is a spectacle of special effects and life-like
animatronics, with some of Spielberg's best sequences of sustained awe and
sheer terror since *Jaws*." Film historian Tom Shone saw *Jurassic* as a
milestone in cinema. "In its way, *Jurassic Park* heralded a revolution in
movies as profound as the coming of sound in 1927."

#7--THE COLOR PURPLE (1985)

Spielberg proved he could tackle serious themes in his first effort in pure drama. Despite the many qualms from numerous circles about him directing such a sensitive project, the director proved his talents were more than able to produce a critically-acclaimed film. *The Color Purple* earned eleven Academy Award nominations, but alas, the Academy's voting block failed to award one Oscar for the film, tying 1977's *The Turning Point* as receiving as many nominations without gaining one golden statuette. Roger Ebert later said, "I can see its flaws more easily than when I named it the best film of 1985, but I can also understand why it moved me so deeply, and why the greatness of some films depends not on their perfection or logic, but on their heart."

#8--CLOSE ENCOUNTERS OF THE THIRD KIND (1977)

Close Encounters is another one of those milestone films Spielberg has produced in his long career, this time testing the limits of the special effects experts before computer-assisted imagery was fully developed. The movie made science fiction once again a proven genre for theater owners as subsequent films depicting space travel became money-making machines after *Close Encounters*. Nominated for eight Oscars, *Close* and cinematographer Vilmos Zsigmond's immense contributions for the film's stunning photography earned him the Academy Award win in that category.

#9--WAR HORSE (2011)

Remembering the unsung heroes of brutal World War I, Spielberg offers a moving tribute to the hundreds of thousands of horses who died in the Allied effort to hold off the German invasion to dominate Europe. Veteran film critic Rex Reed cited "*War Horse* is a don't-miss Spielberg classic that reaches true perfection. It's as good as movies can get, and one of the greatest triumphs of this or any other year."

#10--MUNICH (2005)

Probably his most controversial film, *Munich* describes a covert operation of the Israelis sending a squad of agents to track down the terrorists who kidnapped and killed the country's athletes during the 1972 Munich Olympics. Ian Nathan wrote "*Munich* is Steven Spielberg's most difficult film.

It arrives already inflamed by controversy. This is Spielberg operating at his peak — an exceptionally made, provocative and vital film for our times." The Israel government condemned the movie as pure fiction and numerous Zionist organizations called for the film's boycott. But Spielberg brings this thriller into a political stratosphere that is to be appreciated.

READING LIST

Chapter 1—D.W. Griffith

D.W. Griffith: The Years at Biography. Henderson, Robert. Farrar Straus & Giroux (January 1970)

D.W. Griffith and the Origins of American Narrative Film: The Early Years At Biograph. Gunning, Tom. University of Illinois Press (September 1, 1993)

D.W. Griffith: An American Life. Schickel, Richard. Limelight Editions (July 1, 2004)

Chapter 2—Charlie Chaplin

Chaplin: His Life And Art. Robinson, David. McGraw-Hill; 1st edition (1985)

Charlie Chaplin and His Times. Lynn, Kenneth. Simon & Schuster (March 3, 1997)

Charlie Chaplin: A Brief Life. Ackroyd, Peter. Nan A. Talese; 1st edition (October 28, 2014)

Chapter 3—John Ford

John Ford: The Man and His Films. Gallagher, Tag. University of California Press (April 20, 1988)

Print the Legend: The Life and Times of John Ford. Eyman, Scott. Simon & Schuster (March 31, 2015)

Wayne and Ford: The Films, the Friendship, and the Forging of an American

Hero. Schoenberger, Nancy. Nan A. Talese (October 24, 2017)

Chapter 4—Frank Capra

Frank Capra: Castastrophe of Success. McBride, Joseph. Simon & Schuster (April 15, 1992)

American Vision: The Films of Frank Capra. Carney, Raymond. Cambridge University Press (October 31, 1986)

The Films of Frank Capra. Scherle, Victor. Citadel (July 1, 1977)

Chapter 5—Orson Welles

Citizen Welles: A Biography of Orson Welles. Brady, Frank. NY Creative Publishing (August 21, 2015)

Orson Welles: A Biography. Leaming, Barbara. Limelight Editions (July 1, 2004)

Orson Welles, The Road to Xanadu. Callow, Simon. Penguin Books; Reprint edition (February 1, 1997)

Chapter 6—Alfred Hitchcock

Alfred Hitchcock. Ackroyd, Peter. Anchor (September 19, 2017)

Alfred Hitchcock: A Life in Darkness and Light. McGilligan, Patrick. It Books (September 14, 2004)

Alfred Hitchcock's Moviemaking Master Class: Learning about Film from the Master of Suspense. Moral, Tony Lee. Michael Wiese Productions (May 1, 2013)

Chapter 7—Billy Wilder

On Sunset Boulevard: The Life and Times of Billy Wilder. Sikov, Ed. Hyperion (November 17, 1999)

Billy Wilder. Dick, Bernard. Da Capo Press (August 21, 1996)

Some Like It Wilder: The Life and Controversial Films of Billy Wilder. Phillips, Gene. University Press of Kentucky (December 22, 2009)

Chapter 8—Akira Kurosawa

The Films of Akira Kurosawa. Richie, Donald. University of California Press (January 20, 1999)

The Warrior's Camera. Prince, Stephen. Princeton University Press (October 25, 1999)

Akira Kurosawa. Wild, Peter. Reaktion Books (November 15, 2014)

Chapter 9—Ingmar Bergman

Ingmar Bergman, Cinematic Philosopher: Reflections on His Creativity. Singer, Irving. The MIT Press (September 18, 2009)

Ingmar Bergman: The Life and Films of the Last Great European Director. Macnab, Geoffrey. I.B.Tauris (July 15, 2009)

Ingmar Bergman's Face to Face. Tapper, Michael. Wallflower Press (October 3, 2017)

Chapter 10—Walt Disney

Walt Disney: The Triumph of the American Imagination. Gabler, Neil. Vintage (October 9, 2007)

Walt Disney: An American Original. Thomas, Bob. Disney Editions (May 1, 1994)

How to Be Like Walt: Capturing the Disney Magic Every Day of Your Life. Williams, Pat and Denney, Jim. HCI (August 1, 2004)

Chapter 11—Federico Fellini

Federico Fellini. Wiegand, Chris. TASCHEN (April 15, 2013)

Federico Fellini: The Films. Kezich, Tullio. Rizzoli (March 2, 2010)

Federico Fellini. Tornabuoni, Lietta. Rizzoli (July 15, 1995)

Chapter 12—Stanley Kubrick

Stanley Kubrick, Director: A Visual Analysis. Ruchti, Ulrich. W. W. Norton & Company (September 17, 2000)

Stanley Kubrick: A Biography. Lobrutto, Vincent. Da Capo Press (May 7, 1999)

Stanley Kubrick: New Perspectives. Black Dog Publishing (July 7, 2015)

Chapter 13—Woody Allen

Start to Finish: Woody Allen and the Art of Moviemaking. Lax, Eric. Knopf (October 3, 2017)

Woody: The Biography. Evanier, David. St. Martin's Press (November 3, 2015)

Woody Allen: A Retrospective. Shone, Tom. Abrams (October 20, 2015)

Chapter 14—Martin Scorsese

Martin Scorsese: A Retrospective. Shone, Tom. Harry N. Abrams (October 7, 2014)

Martin Scorsese: A Biography. LoBrutto, Vincent. Praeger (November 30, 2007)

The Philosophy of Martin Scorsese. Conrad, Mark, Ph.D. University Press of Kentucky (June 8, 2009)

Chapter 15—Steven Spielberg

Steven Spielberg: A Biography. McBride, Joseph. University Press of Mississippi (January 4, 2011)

Shoot Like Spielberg: The Visual Secrets of Action, Wonder and Emotional Adventure. Kenworthy, Christopher. Michael Wiese Productions (November 1, 2015)

The Cinema of Steven Spielberg: Empire of Light. Morris, Nigel. Wallflower Press (February 13, 2007)

Printed in Great Britain
by Amazon